PSYCHOLOGICAL PERSPECTIVES ON MUSICAL EXPERIENCES AND SKILLS

Psychological Perspectives on Musical Experiences and Skills

Research in the Western Balkans and Western Europe

Edited by
Blanka Bogunović, Renee Timmers, and Sanela Nikolić

https://www.openbookpublishers.com

©2024 Blanka Bogunović; Renee Timmers; Sanela Nikolić (eds). Copyright of individual chapters are maintained by the chapter author(s).

This work is licensed under an Attribution-NonCommercial 4.0 International (CC BY-NC 4.0). This license allows you to share, copy, distribute and transmit the text; to adapt the text for non-commercial purposes of the text providing attribution is made to the author (but not in any way that suggests that they endorse you or your use of the work). Attribution should include the following information:

Blanka Bogunović; Renee Timmers; Sanela Nikolić (eds), *Psychological Perspectives on Musical Experiences and Skills: Research in the Western Balkans and Western Europe*. Cambridge, UK: Open Book Publishers, 2024, https://doi.org/10.11647/OBP.0389

Further details about CC BY-NC licenses are available at https://creativecommons.org/licenses/by-nc/4.0/

Copyright and permissions for the reuse of many of the images included in this publication may differ from the above. This information is provided in the captions and in the list of illustrations.

All external links were active at the time of publication unless otherwise stated and have been archived via the Internet Archive Wayback Machine at https://archive.org/web

Updated digital material and resources associated with this volume are available at https://www.openbookpublishers.com/product/0389#resources

Every effort has been made to identify and contact copyright holders and any omission or error will be corrected if notification is made to the publisher.

ISBN Paperback: 978-1-80511-218-1
ISBN Hardback: 978-1-80511-219-8
ISBN Digital (PDF): 978-1-80511-220-4
ISBN Digital eBook (EPUB): 978-1-80511-221-1
ISBN HTML: 978-1-80511-223-5

DOI: 10.11647/OBP.0389

Cover image: Psychology & Music illustration/logo by Stefan Ignjatović, CC0 1.0
Cover design: Jeevanjot Kaur Nagpa

Dedicated to

Ksenija Radoš
*for her pioneering work in founding the
Psychology of Music in the Western Balkans*

Richard Parncutt
*for his enthusiasm in spreading the
European spirit of unity in diversity*

Contents

Acknowledgments	xi
Notes on Editors	xiii
Notes on Contributors	xv
List of Figures	xxiii
List of Tables	xxv
List of Statistical Abbreviations and Symbols	xxvii
1. Introduction: Music Psychology Research in the Western Balkans and Western Europe *Blanka Bogunović, Renee Timmers, and Sanela Nikolić*	1
PART I: AESTHETIC AND EMOTIONAL EXPERIENCES OF MUSIC	**25**
2. The Role of Affective Dimensions in the Aesthetic Experience of Music *Dragan Janković and Maja Mađarev*	27
3. Aesthetic Experiences of Contemporary Music from the Perspectives of a Composer, a Performer, and a Musicologist *Sanela Nikolić and Ivana Miladinović Prica*	47
4. Aesthetic Emotions in Music: Theory, Measurements, and Cross-cultural Comparison *Renee Timmers, Scott Bannister, and Thomas M. Lennie*	73

PART II: MUSIC LISTENING IN CONTEXT   97

5. Sound Experience and Imagination at Early School Age:
   An Opportunity for Unleashing Children's Creative Potential   99
   Mirsada Zećo, Marina Videnović, and Lejla Silajdžić

6. Adolescent Musical Preferences
   and their Relationship with Schwartz's Basic Values   123
   Ivana Stepanović Ilić, Marina Videnović, Zora Krnjaić, and Ksenija Krstić

7. How Professional Musicians Can Better Connect to Audiences
   for Live Classical Music: Assessing Theory And Practice
   in the Light of the COVID-19 Crisis   143
   John Sloboda

PART III: MUSIC COGNITION
IN PERFORMANCE AND PRACTICE   163

8. Influences of Physical and Imagined Others
   in Music Students' Experiences of Practice and Performance   165
   Andrea Schiavio, Henrique Meissner, and Renee Timmers

9. 4E Music Cognition in Theory and Practice   189
   Andrea Schiavio and Dylan van der Schyff

10. Memorisation of Twentieth-Century Piano Music:
    A Longitudinal Case Study   211
    Valnea Žauhar, Dunja Crnjanski, and Igor Bajšanski

11. Memory for Music:
    Research and Practice for Performers   231
    Jane Ginsborg

PART IV: PSYCHOLOGY OF MUSICIANS—FROM MOTIVATION AND PERSONALITY TO ADDRESSING CHALLENGES AND ANXIETY — 253

12. Motivation and Personality as Factors of Musical Accomplishments: A Developmental and Cultural Perspective — 255
Blanka Bogunović

13. The Lived Experience of Radical Acceleration in the Biographical Narratives of Exceptionally Gifted Adult Musicians — 281
Olja Jovanović, Ana Altaras Dimitrijević, Dejana Mutavdžin, and Blanka Bogunović

14. The Personality of Music Students with Diverse Vocal and Instrumental Skills — 305
Ana Butković

15. Theoretical and Practical Challenges in Dealing with Music Performance Anxiety — 323
Katarina Habe and Michele Biasutti

16. How do European and Western Balkans Conservatoires Help Music Students with their Health and Well-being? — 351
Raluca Matei and Jane Ginsborg

17. Conclusion: Progressing the State of the Art of Music Psychology — 371
Renee Timmers, Blanka Bogunović, and Sanela Nikolić

Index — 387

Acknowledgments

This book is dedicated to two colleagues whose work, in different ways, enabled this volume—to Ksenija Radoš for dedicated, pioneering work in founding the psychology of music in the Western Balkans region, specifically Serbia, and to Richard Parncutt for his enthusiasm in spreading the European spirit of unity in diversity and efforts in promoting interdisciplinary and international music psychology research.

A particular expression of gratitude belongs to Renee Timmers, who was open and curious enough to respond to the idea of this project and join the team with two Western Balkans co-editors. She committed herself to embedding the ESCOM equality, diversity, and inclusion policy into this volume, and therefore, she made a difference by increasing the visibility of Western Balkans authors to a broader readership. In our joint endeavours, she had a significant input through constructive and efficient teamwork, professionalism, and support that strengthened this book, for which we co-editors are immensely grateful.

The book would not be possible without contributors from the Western Balkans and Western Europe, both senior and junior researchers, psychologists, and musicians, who willingly joined this unique project, for their enthusiasm, energy, and patience in making this volume worthwhile. We offer each of them our heartfelt thanks for agreeing to be a part of it. We are delighted and proud that John Sloboda chose to celebrate 50 years of his continuous publishing with us, by contributing his approximate 200th academic publication to this volume. His first academic paper was published in 1974 in the journal *Psychology of Music*,[1] which the publisher recently made open access. A valuable contribution was made by our dear colleagues who helped

---

1 https://journals.sagepub.com/doi/10.1177/030573567422001

in gathering data about music psychology development in the Western Balkans region—Ana Butković, Snježana Dobrota, Katarina Habe, Ina Reić Ercegovac, Sabina Vidulin, Valnea Žauhar and Sanja Kiš Žuvela.

We are particularly thankful to our reviewers for their valuable comments and suggestions in both rounds of reviews, which contributed to the quality of the manuscript. Our sincere thanks go to Scott Bannister, Ana Butković, Jane Ginsborg, Zora Krnjaić, Henrique Meissner, Ivana Miladinović Prica, Ivana Stepanović Ilić, Valnea Žauhar; and external reviewers, Bojana Bodroža, Michael Bonshor, Ioanna Filippidi, Alexandra Lamont, Slavica Maksić, Ljiljana Lazarević, Nicola Pennill, Nikola Petrović, Michelle Phillips, Stephanie Pitts, Hannah Rodger, Makiko Sadakata, Nataša Simić, and Marc Thompson. We express gratitude to two anonymous reviewers of Open Book Publishers for their keen comments and suggestions for improvement.

We are warmly appreciative to Rose Bell for her precise and dedicated English proofreading and understanding for deadline extensions. We thank our students for their devoted assistance in editing references and statistics, namely to Dejana Mutavdžin and Katarina Stekić, as well as to Stefan Ignjatović for designing the cover image and figures. The book was made possible by funding to support Open Book Publishers from the University of Sheffield, United Kingdom. We are grateful for financial support from the European Society for the Cognitive Sciences of Music and the Ministry of Education, Science and Technological Development of Serbia, which helped realise the conference leading up to this book, and finally, to Open Book Publishers for the open access publication of this volume.

Last but certainly not least, we owe a debt of gratitude to our loving family members—to Darija, Erwin, Jan, Lidewij, Milena, Miloš, and Natalija.

Notes on Editors

Blanka Bogunović holds a PhD in psychology and a BA in music performance (Flute). She is affiliated as a Full Professor of Psychology and Education Science at the Faculty of Music, University of Arts in Belgrade and is a guest lecturer at the Department of Psychology, University of Belgrade and Music Academy, University of Sarajevo. Her research interests are the motivation and personality of the musically gifted; specialist music education; music performance skills and expertise; and creative processes in making music. She is (co)author of five books and many articles and chapters related to her research interests. She is an ESCOM EC member-at-Large, ESCOM representative for Serbia, originator of the PAM-IE Conference, and co-founder and coordinator of the Regional Network Psychology and Music (RNPaM).

Renee Timmers is a Professor of Psychology of Music at the University of Sheffield. Her research concerns the expressive performance of music; music, emotion, and health; and multimodal and embodied experiences of music. She has co-edited two volumes published by Oxford University Press (*Expressiveness in Music Performance*; *Together in Music*) and two by Routledge (*Routledge Companion to Music Cognition*; *Sound Teaching*). She directs the research centre 'Music Mind Machine' in Sheffield and is past President of ESCOM.

Sanela Nikolić has a PhD in Theory of Arts and Media and a BA in Musicology, and is affiliated as an Associate Professor of Applied Aesthetics at the Faculty of Music, University of Arts in Belgrade, Serbia, where she teaches courses at all levels of study and coordinates Applied Research of Music (PRIMA) MA study program. She is the Managing Editor of the *AM Journal of Art and Media Studies* and was the International Association for Aesthetics Delegate-at-Large (2019–22). She is the author of two books. Her fields of interest include avant-garde art schools and practices; applied aesthetics as a critical history of the humanities; interdisciplinarity and transdisciplinarity in the humanities; and digital humanities. She is a Regional Network Psychology and Music (RNPaM) member.

Notes on Contributors

Ana Altaras Dimitrijević, PhD is a Full Professor at the Department of Psychology, University of Belgrade. Her teaching and research cover topics from educational and differential psychology, with a special focus on giftedness, emotional intelligence, and cognitive assessment. From 2010 onwards she has repeatedly served as an expert consultant in state-initiated projects on gifted education and has supported the implementation of individualised instruction for gifted students in Serbian schools.

Igor Bajšanski is a Full Professor at the Department of Psychology, Faculty of Humanities and Social Sciences, University of Rijeka. He holds a PhD in psychology from the Faculty of Humanities and Social Sciences, University of Zagreb. He teaches courses in cognitive psychology and psychology of learning. His research interests are metacognition, psychology of learning, and cognitive psychology.

Scott Bannister is currently a Postdoctoral Research Fellow at the University of Leeds and holds a PhD in Music from Durham University. Scott's central research interests are music and emotion; social and embodied cognition of music listening; music listening and hearing aid technology; psychophysiological responses; psychoacoustics; and neuroscience.

Michele Biasutti, PhD is a Full Professor of Experimental Pedagogy at the University of Padova. He deeply understands European Commission policies, methodologies, and working methods through his involvement in EC-founded programmes, projects, and institutions. He is a member of the editorial board of several journals and has published articles in high impact factor journals. He has been the director of international conferences and the author of seven books and about 280 articles, chapters, and conference proceedings papers.

Ana Butković obtained her BA degrees in flute and psychology, then her MA and PhD in psychology at the University of Zagreb, where she currently works as an Associate Professor at the Department of Psychology. She teaches mandatory and elective courses in the field of differential psychology. She participated in establishing the Regional Network Psychology and Music (RNPaM). She has published scientific papers on different topics, such as behaviour genetics, personality, intelligence, and the psychology of music.

Dunja Crnjanski is a pianist, piano teacher, and performer. Her main interests are contemporary music, free improvisation, and performing arts. She holds an MA in piano performance (Academy of Arts, Novi Sad) and has a specialisation degree in chamber music with a focus on contemporary repertoire (Faculty of Music, University of Arts in Belgrade). As a piano teacher and accompanist, she works at the secondary music school Isidor Bajić (Novi Sad). She is a member of Per.Art performing arts collective and is active in its 'Art and Inclusion' programme.

Jane Ginsborg has BA degrees in both music and psychology, and a PhD in psychology. She is Associate Director of Research at the Royal Northern College of Music, Manchester (from 2009), was President of ESCOM (2012–15), and is Editor-in-Chief of *Musicae Scientiae* (from 2019). Her publications include *Performing Music Research: Methods in Music Education, Psychology, and Performance Science* (Oxford University Press, 2021), and many articles and chapters on topics relating to expert music performance and musicians' well-being.

Katarina Habe, PhD works as an Assistant Professor of Psychology at the Academy of Music, University of Ljubljana. Because of her musical and psychological professional background, she successfully integrates the analytical and intuitive holistic approach in her research work on the psychology of music. Her research interests include the effects of music on people's overall well-being, both that of musicians and of the general population and individuals with special needs. She participated in establishing the Regional Network Psychology and Music (RNPaM).

Dragan Janković is an Assistant Professor at the Department of Psychology, Faculty of Philosophy, University of Belgrade. He received his PhD in psychology from the University of Belgrade in 2015. He teaches several BA, MA, and PhD courses in developmental psychology, psychology of emotions, and psychology of art. His research focuses mainly on affective processing, multisensory perception, developmental psychology, and empirical aesthetics, with a special interest in visual arts and music. He is a Regional Network Psychology and Music (RNPaM) member.

Olja Jovanović, PhD, is an Assistant Professor at the University of Belgrade, where she teaches courses in educational psychology. Her research and publications focus on the role of education systems in the educational and life trajectories of children and youth requiring additional support. Engaging in diverse contexts and settings has granted her extensive experience in educational research, particularly concerning the implications of this research for social and educational practices.

Zora Krnjaić, PhD is a Senior Research Associate and Head of the Institute of Psychology, Faculty of Philosophy, University of Belgrade. Her expertise in developmental psychology includes giftedness and expert thinking, everyday life and youth development in specific socio-cultural contexts, and youth policy. She has brought her scientific expertise into drawing up national strategies, policies and guidelines as well as projects and programmes intended to support the development of young people, especially gifted and vulnerable groups. She participated as coordinator of the Working Thematic Group for the Development of the First National Youth Strategy. She has taken part in over thirty research projects and programmes and published monographs and numerous papers in scientific journals. She is a European Council for High Abilities Correspondent for Serbia and, since 2008, and a Head of the Commission of Young Talents Fund of the Republic of Serbia.

Ksenija Krstić, PhD is an Associate Professor at the Department of Psychology, Faculty of Philosophy, University of Belgrade. Her field of interest includes socio-emotional development; attachment and close relationships; early childhood development; parenting; early childhood intervention; and adolescent development in specific sociocultural contexts. She has participated in more than fifteen national and international projects. She is a member of the International Society for Cultural-Historical Activity Research, the European Association for Research on Learning and Instruction, and the European Association for Developmental Psychology.

Thomas M. Lennie, PhD is an Assistant Professor of Psychology within the Department of Philosophy and Psychology at the American University in Bulgaria. His primary focus lies in the cognitive mechanisms of music-induced emotional episodes. He was awarded his PhD in Music Cognition from Durham University (UK) in 2023, fully funded by the Northern Bridge Doctoral Training Programme. His recent contributions to the field assess the role of goal-directed appraisal mechanisms in shaping musical affect across diverse contexts (Lennie & Eerola, 2022). He is currently in the process of establishing the first music psychology lab in Bulgaria, promoting research into music psychology in the Balkans.

Maja Mađarev graduated from the Department of Psychology, Faculty of Philosophy, University of Belgrade. She is a Research Assistant at the Laboratory of Experimental Psychology, Faculty of Philosophy, University of Belgrade, and a Teaching Assistant in Developmental Psychology and Psychology of Art courses. Her main fields of interest are psychological aesthetics and affective processing.

Raluca Matei is currently Postdoctoral Research Fellow in Performing Arts and Health at the Peabody Institute of the Johns Hopkins University, USA. She has a BA in both music and psychology, an MSc in health psychology, and a PhD in psychology from the Royal Northern College of Music, Manchester, with a focus on musicians' health and well-being from an interdisciplinary, real-world perspective. She also studied with Maxim Vengerov at the Menuhin Academy in Switzerland. Raluca is currently interested in training critical thinking as part of the conservatoire curriculum and in questioning current assumptions in classical music.

Henrique Meissner is a Course Leader for Practice-Based Research at the Prince Claus Conservatoire and a Senior Researcher at the Hanze

University of Applied Sciences in Groningen. Henrique studied recorder at the Utrecht Conservatoire and obtained her PhD in Music Psychology in Education at the University of Sheffield. Henrique is co-editor of *Sound Teaching: A Research-Informed Approach to Inspiring Confidence, Skill, and Enjoyment in Music Performance* (Routledge, 2022). Her research interests include instrumental music learning and teaching; expressiveness; and socially engaged artistic research in music.

Ivana Miladinović Prica, PhD is a musicologist and an Assistant Professor at the Faculty of Music of the University of Arts in Belgrade. She is also the board secretary of the bilingual journal *New Sound International Journal of Music*. Her current research focuses on the neo-avant garde and experimental practices in American, European, and Serbian contemporary music.

Dejana Mutavdžin is a PhD psychology candidate at the Faculty of Philosophy, University of Belgrade, where she has completed her BA and MA studies. She is affiliated as a Teaching Assistant of Psychology at the Faculty of Music, University of Arts in Belgrade. Her research interest is the relationship between different types of abilities, emotional intelligence, giftedness in non-academic domains, and opportunities for their acknowledgement in the educational process. She is a Regional Network Psychology and Music (RNPaM) member.

Andrea Schiavio is a Lecturer in Music Education at the University of York. He received his PhD from the University of Sheffield (2014), studying musical skill acquisition and development through the lens of embodied cognitive science. After his doctoral studies, he continued this research as a postdoctoral fellow in the USA (Ohio State University), Turkey (Bosphorus University), and Austria (KUG). From 2017 to 2022 he was based at the Centre of Systematic Musicology of the University of Graz, funded by the Austrian Science Fund (FWF). Andrea is the President of ESCOM.

Dylan van der Schyff is a Senior Lecturer in Music at the Melbourne Conservatorium of Music, University of Melbourne, where he coordinates the honours and graduate programmes in Jazz and Improvisation. He is an improvising percussionist and a researcher in interdisciplinary musicology. He received his PhD from Simon Fraser

University (Vancouver) and holds MA degrees in the humanities (Simon Fraser University) and music psychology (University of Sheffield). His postdoctoral work was hosted by the Faculty of Music at the University of Oxford.

Lejla Silajdžić, PhD in psychology, works at the Faculty of Education Science in Sarajevo as an Associate Professor, teaching various psychology courses for students who want to be preschool and elementary school teachers. She has additional education in mental health care, inclusion, systems therapy, and innovations in education. Her special areas of research and interests are developmental and educational psychology.

John Sloboda OBE FBA is Emeritus Professor at the Guildhall School of Music & Drama, where he was the founding director of the Institute for Social Impact Research in the Performing Arts. He is also Emeritus Professor at Keele and was a staff member of the School of Psychology at Keele University (1974–2008). He is a past President of ESCOM. His books include *Handbook of Music and Emotion* (co-edited with Patrik Juslin) and *Exploring the Musical Mind*, both published by Oxford University Press.

Ivana Stepanović Ilić, PhD is an Associate Professor of Developmental Psychology at the Department of Psychology, Faculty of Philosophy, University of Belgrade. Her areas of research include cognitive development in adolescence; socialisation and everyday life of youth; schooling and dropouts on all education levels. Ivana has participated in twenty-five research projects and published more than thirty papers in international and national scientific journals. She is a member of the International Society for Cultural-Historical Activity Research and the European Association for Developmental Psychology.

Marina Videnović, PhD is a researcher at the Institute of Psychology, a research unit at the Faculty of Philosophy, University of Belgrade. Her interests include adolescent socialisation during school and spare time. She combines qualitative and quantitative methodology for data-driven insights. She makes efforts to incorporate scientific research data in evidence-based policy advice. She is the chief editor of *Psihološka Istraživanja* [Psychological Research], a national journal in Serbia.

Mirsada Zećo is an Assistant Professor at the Department of Primary and Preschool Education and Rehabilitation at the Faculty of Educational Sciences, University of Sarajevo. As a musician, lecturer, and theoretician, she has been researching new streams in musical pedagogy, sound therapy, Himalayan sound bowls, planetary gongs, and other similar sound instruments. She is a member of the Musicological Society of Bosnia and Hercegovina and the Regional Network Psychology and Music (RNPaM).

Valnea Žauhar is an Assistant Professor at the Department of Psychology, Faculty of Humanities and Social Sciences, University of Rijeka. She holds an MA and PhD in Psychology from the Faculty of Humanities and Social Sciences in Rijeka. She teaches courses in experimental and cognitive psychology and the psychology of music. Her research interests are music cognition, metacognition, and higher cognitive processes. She participated in establishing the Regional Network Psychology and Music (RNPaM).

List of Figures

2.1	Regression plot between observed values (ratings of aesthetic experience) versus predicted values (aesthetic experience predicted by the model)	p. 35
2.2	Regression plots between observed values (ratings of aesthetic experience) versus predicted values (aesthetic experience predicted by the model) for music experts and non-experts	p. 38
2.3	Valence, Arousal and Cognitive evaluation (VACe) model of the aesthetic experience of music	p. 40
3.1	Performer's presentation of 'finding the right feeling' for the musical piece through combining parts of Savić's original and parts of Soler's score (the names of the two composers are indicated in red colour)	p. 58
3.2	Overview of research outcomes	p. 62
4.1	Aesthetic emotions arise from the interaction between individuals, groups and musical characteristics in particular social contexts. The moment-to-moment developments and affordances of music are particularly relevant for aesthetic listening experiences	p. 86
5.1	Photograph of the workshop setting. The faces of the participants are blurred to preserve their privacy. Photo from the private collection of the first author	p. 106
5.2	Percentage of the responses at each point of the Howard continuum of imagination	p. 111
8.1	Coding scheme	p. 170
10.1	(a) Session 3 (early) and (b) Session 16 (late)	p. 218
12.1	Integrative pattern of music achievements factors in early specialist music education. Figure translated and adapted from Bogunović (2010, p. 290).	p. 264
12.2	Integrative pattern of music achievements factors at adolescent age. Figure translated and adapted from Bogunović (2010, p. 294)	p. 268
13.1	Filip's life path	p. 303

List of Tables

5.1	Content of the workshops	p. 108
5.2	Examples of the children's answers	p. 113
6.1	Musical preferences: Structure matrix	p. 129
6.2	Canonical solution for Values and Musical preferences: The structure coefficients	p. 131
6.3	Results regarding the relation between musical preferences and values	p. 132
8.1	Overview of the participants	p. 168
10.1	Description of learning periods and practice sessions	p. 216
10.2	Results of multiple regression analyses for four learning periods	p. 220
13.1	Characteristics of participants	p. 286
13.2	Overview of the two life chapters and themes	p. 288
14.1	Descriptive statistics for four instrumental groups and results of ANOVA	p. 312
14.2	Descriptive statistics for six instrumental groups and results of ANOVA	p. 313
15.1	Summary of the studies on MPA conducted in the Western Balkan region	p. 329
16.1	Theoretical assumptions and models informing course design	p. 358
16.2	Course topics	p. 361
16.3	Respondents' assessment of students' perception of various aspects of health risks behaviour	p. 363

List of Statistical Abbreviations and Symbols[1]

ANOVA	analysis of variance
b	unstandardized beta (regression)
CFA	confirmatory factor analysis
d	d value (Cohen's d)
D	D value (Kolmogorov-Smirnov test)
df	degrees of freedom
E	expected value (chi-square test)
EFA	exploratory factor analysis
F	F statistics (Fisher's F; Welch's F; Levene's F)
M	mean
MANOVA	multivariate analysis of variance
N	sample size (full size)
n	sample size (sub-sample)
NS	non-significant
p	p value; probability of agreement (Cohen's kappa)
PCA	principal component analysis
r	r value (Pearson's product-moment correlation coefficient; effect size)
R	R value (regression)
R^2	R^2 value (regression)
SD	standard deviation
SE	standard error
SPSS	Statistical Package for the Social Sciences
t	t value (t-test)
U	U value (Mann Whitney U-test)

---

[1] Williamon, A., Ginsborg, J., Perkins, R., & Waddell, G. (2021). *Performing music research: Methods in music education, psychology, and performance science.* Oxford University Press. https://global.oup.com/academic/product/performing-music-research-9780198714545?cc=nl&lang=en&

Var	variance (sample variance)
α	alpha (probability of a Type I error; Cronbach's alpha)
β	beta (probability of a Type II error; standardized beta
Δ	delta (change; regression)
Ε	epsilon (error; regression)
η^2	eta-squared (ANOVA)
ηp^2	partial eta-squared (ANOVA)
χ^2	chi-squared (Box's test; chi-square test; Friedman's ANOVA)
<	less than
>	greater than

1. Introduction: Music Psychology Research in the Western Balkans and Western Europe

Blanka Bogunović, Renee Timmers, and Sanela Nikolić

The psychology of music is a flourishing field of research that uses interdisciplinary methods to investigate music perception, cognition, emotion, and performance in everyday and expert musical situations. It is a broad research area in the range of questions and topics that it addresses and the research methods that it employs. Ultimately however, these aspects are interlinked in aiming to understand what it is that makes musical encounters meaningful, accessible, individualised but also united. This volume addresses some of that breadth of thinking and understanding of the psychology of music. In its coverage, it is not unlike other review volumes on the psychology of music in addressing key themes related to popular topics such as musical learning and skills, emotions in musical experience, and aesthetic appreciation of music. It is, however, distinct in giving centre stage to research that is often overlooked due to geopolitical and linguistic reasons, in this case research that has been conducted in the Western Balkans.

The great majority of books published in the field of psychology and music come from Western Europe, the United States, and Australia, presenting comprehensive themes and works by prominent authors. These geographical areas tend to be over-represented, and work in other regions is relatively neglected. Studies by authors from the Western Balkans are scarcely presented in chapters of comprehensive books primarily because the research activities from this region are on the edge of international scholarly attention. Such restriction of attention has the danger of marginalising alternative perspectives offered by less dominant research cultures, reducing diversity of perspectives, debate and richness of understanding, a theme that is further discussed in the concluding chapter of this book (see Chapter 17 in this volume).

This book confronts this problem and aims to promote research from the Western Balkans, addressing the urgent issue of rebalancing the unevenness in scholarly dissemination that is influenced by language and associated regional privileges. The book presents work from both regions—the Western Balkans and Western Europe—in order to reflect the positionality of the research and to make complementary ties visible. As such, the book contributes to the understanding of cross-cultural perspectives on the psychology of music by presenting current research developments from two localities that both have strong research traditions in the psychology of music but have had limited systematic exchange. Further, this conception introduces the reciprocal interaction between researchers from two areas with diverse scholarly, academic, and music practice developments and backgrounds. It enables synergies of perspectives and promotes collaboration between the two regions. It encourages authors from the Western Balkans and advances the development of the psychology of music in the region by increasing the visibility and viability of research and possibilities for its application.

This book was conceived following a successful international conference on the psychology of music in Belgrade, Serbia, that hosted a large number of presentations by Western Balkan authors alongside authors from Europe more widely and authors from further afield. It made us realise that the psychology of music is in fact growing also in the Western Balkans, and that this research has overlapping themes with general trends in this research area, but also has some distinct interests and specialisms that offer a rich background in investigation, which is often being missed in the broader international literature. With this book we provide an enhanced platform, with the hope this research will find its justified place in the discipline and that its findings and implications will be employed to inform and increase understanding and thinking in this area and steer future directions.

Background of the book

The idea for this book originated after a chain of events, starting with the challenge issued by John Sloboda at the occasion of the 25th anniversary of the European Society for the Cognitive Sciences of Music (ESCOM, n.d.), who called for broader participation in publishing and ESCOM membership, particularly from those European countries with initial low participation rates (Sloboda & Ginsborg, 2018). The call was responded to by Richard Parncutt (ESCOM president 2015–2018) and Renee Timmers (ESCOM president 2018–2021), who launched the ESCOM Regional Development Initiative (Parncutt & Timmers, 2017) intending to promote the psychology of music across Europe, and to connect pockets of expertise bringing visibility to regional research activity.

In 2018, Blanka Bogunović became ESCOM regional representative for Serbia and set out to organise a local conference. She joined forces with Sanela Nikolić to create a dynamic network of academic, research and applied music and psychology institutions that provided the quintessence of interdisciplinarity—involving the Faculty of Music, University of Arts in Belgrade (the main organiser), the Institute of Psychology, the Faculty of Philosophy, the University of Belgrade and the Music Psychology Section of the Serbian Psychological Society. This led to two international conferences on *Psychology of Music—Interdisciplinary Encounters* (PAM-IE Belgrade 2019, n.d. and PAM-IE Belgrade 2022, n.d., chair Blanka Bogunović), bringing together regional, European, and inter-continental researchers and practitioners from 22 countries. Representatives of ESCOM gave support and added value through their presence and keynotes, thus promoting the event. This included John Sloboda, Renee Timmers (then ESCOM president), Jane Ginsborg, and Richard Parncutt, at the first conference, and at the second conference Andrea Schiavio (ESCOM president 2021–2024), David Dolan, Alexandra Lamont, and Heiner Gembris. The vivid response and rising interest in the Western Balkans region for the psychology of music and PAM-IE conferences resulted in the establishment of the Regional Network Psychology and Music (RNPaM, n.d.) foundation in 2020, which now gathers colleagues and students from the countries of former Yugoslavia, with a broad interdisciplinary background. In its three years of existence, the enthusiasm of the members brought forth several joint projects, conference presentations, and publishing. One of the joint projects is this book. The Western Balkans authors are members of the RNPaM. The international authors are ESCOM representatives who presented at the conferences.

At the same time, this book connects to the legacy of the beginnings of ESCOM, namely publishing books after conferences (e.g., Deliège & Sloboda, 1996, 2004; Deliège & Wiggins, 2006) to spread knowledge and promote music psychology research; and to share a vision of 'combining approaches from the arts and humanities, as well as sciences' (Sloboda & Ginsborg, 2018, p.17). The ideas of the ESCOM founders evolved over 25 years, spreading geographically through semi-virtual conferences, including countries from four continents (ESCOM-ICMPC 2018, 4 hubs, chair Richard Parncutt) and later, a fully virtual joint conference which provided an interdisciplinary and intercultural platform jointly organised across 8 hubs (ESCOM-ICMPC 2021, chair Renee Timmers). This fruitful seed was also planted in the Western Balkans region. Before we explain the main outline of the book, we will briefly sketch its broader context: the research that has been developing and expanding in the Western Balkans that researchers in music psychology should note.

History of the psychology of music in the Western Balkans

Therefore, we now direct our attention to the development of the psychology of music in the Western Balkans region to outline the beginnings and expansion of the discipline, since that is not well known. The Western Balkans region here refers to the countries of Southeast Europe that were previously part of former Yugoslavia—Bosnia and Herzegovina, Croatia, Montenegro, North Macedonia, Serbia, and Slovenia (Mazover, 2002). They have their shared past, but since the 1990s have evolved independently, including in terms of research on the psychology of music. Before 1990, there was a high level of mutual knowledge exchange and information sharing between these countries, as they were, since 1945, the equal parts of one state, the Socialist Federal Republic of Yugoslavia, founded after the Second World War. The idea to build a socialist society, in part through the empowerment of cultural and educational life, induced new education and child development policies. Schools were thus envisioned in the public space as the origin of social modernization, and they engaged numerous experts in the fields of psychology, pedagogy, film, art, literature, and music (Petrović Todosijević, 2018). Hence, psychology and pedagogy courses were gradually, from the 1950s, broadly integrated into the music higher education institutions (MHEIs), which were always a part of universities.

Research and publishing in the psychology of music at MHEIs has been accelerating since the 1970s due to the dedicated work and charismatic endeavours of a few scholars, particularly in Serbia and Croatia. After 2000, educational and research pursuits included psychology and music in various university departments, with a strong jump in academic growth after 2005, which was based on the input of the previous generation, especially by Ksenija Radoš, whose work was well known in all former Yugoslavian countries. The second reason was certainly the European-wide development of the psychology of music since the 1980s, especially in the United Kingdom, where the work of John Sloboda laid the path for new generations and new developments, which served as exemplary. Psychology of music and related courses became more often part of curricula, either as obligatory or elective courses, in various regional universities in the Western Balkans, which continue to serve as nuclei for its continuous growth. The MHEIs, in general, still have obligatory psychology and pedagogy courses, considering these domains as necessary for the individual development and well-being of young musicians and for their future work as music pedagogues. This educational policy is present in all Western Balkans countries and serves as a valuable remnant of 'old times.' The ongoing practice of employing psychologists in specialist music schools in Serbia also strengthens the link between academic music psychology and its relevant application in the education of musicians, contributing to further development of the discipline.

Nevertheless. continuous growth of the discipline in the area of the WB, the academic positions of psychology researchers and teachers in MHEIs and/or psychology departments are scattered and limited to one or two individuals per institution, mainly lacking systematic support and enhancement. Hence, the discipline's development is tailored to individual researchers' interests, educational and professional backgrounds, and endeavours, fuelled by personal dedication and devotion. Therefore, music psychology's advancement lies in the hands of academics, researchers, and practitioners, stemming from music, social and humanistic disciplines, as well as natural sciences, including psychologists, musicologists, music theorists, music pedagogues, music performers, psychiatrists, acousticians, computer scientists among others. Recently, valuable horizontal interdisciplinary networking between authors within the region has been increasing, and collaboration with European authors has also intensified in recent years.

Within this general trend, we shall briefly present in alphabetical order the developmental paths of the psychology of music in each country through pedagogical, research and applied perspectives.

Bosnia and Herzegovina

Here, interest in the psychology of music has existed since 2009 when an academic course was established at the Sarajevo Music Academy, University of Sarajevo, with Blanka Bogunović as a guest lecturer from the University of Arts in Belgrade. Before that, there was sustained inclusion of psychological knowledge in music education courses through the work of Selma Ferović (e.g., 2002, 2004).

Croatia

Since the foundation of the Music Academy in Zagreb in 1921, general psychology and educational psychology have been taught to musicians. In 1972–1980, at the Institute for Systematic Musicology, the development of tests for musical abilities was realised by Marijan Koletić and Milo Cipra, with Pavel Rojko and Stanislav Tuksar as collaborators. Later on, Pavel Rojko published the book *Testiranje u muzici* [Testing in music] (1981) and *Psihološke osnove intoncije i ritma* [Psychological foundations of intonation and rhythm] (1982/2012). The academic course Psychology of Music was founded in 2005 for music pedagogy and musicology modules, taught by Pavel Rojko and Nikša Gligo. It is worth mentioning that since 1974, music therapy courses have been intermittently integrated into curricula due to the pioneering efforts of a psychiatrist, music therapist and musician, Darko Breitenfeld (e.g., Breitenfeld & Majsec Vrbanić, 2011). At present the music therapy course is delivered by Daniel Crnković (2020). Since 2015 further developments of the discipline in the Music Academy was taken over by Sanja Kiš Žuvela, whose principal research interests are the analysis of 20th- and 21st-century music, music perception and cognition, music and language, cognitive linguistics, and issues of contemporary musical terminology (e.g., Kiš Žuvela, 2013; Kiš Žuvela & Ostroški Anić, 2019). Since 2021, more courses have been integrated, including those that refer to applications to performing and educational practice, led by Helena Dukić (2022) and Brigita Vilč (2019).

After 2000, psychology of music expanded to be included in several universities' psychology and music education departments nationwide. Interest in music psychology intensified at the Department of Psychology, Faculty of Philosophy, University of Zagreb, thanks to the work of Ana Butković and the introduction of the Psychology of Music course in 2010. Butković and her colleagues are interested in personality and music preferences (Butković et al., 2011), personality traits of musicians in diverse genres and instrumental groups (e.g., Butković & Rančić Dopuđ, 2017), and professional issues of music performers related to personality (e.g., Butković et al., 2022; Butković et al., 2015). A course in the psychology of music was also founded at the Catholic University of Croatia in 2013, now led by Blaženka Bačlija Sušić (e.g., Bačlija Sušić & Brebrić, 2022).

At the Department of Psychology, University of Split, a Psychology of Music course was founded in 2021 by Ina Reić Ercegovac and Snježana Dobrota. This interdisciplinary team shares a research interest in music preferences and their functions in emotion regulation, relatedness to personality traits, music styles, and music education implications (e.g., Dobrota & Reić Ercegovac, 2015, 2016, 2017). The research interests of these two very active authors were sparked in 2009, and later on included a collaboration with a Slovenian author (Habe et al., 2018). Selected topics of music psychology have been taught at the Teacher Education Faculty, University of Split, since 2005 as part of courses in music education.

At the Academy of Music, Jurij Dobrota University in Pula, the Music Psychology course was founded in 2006 in the Music Education Department. The first lecturer was Pavel Rojko (from the Music Academy Zagreb), then Snježana Dobrota (from the University of Split), and at the moment Valnea Žauhar (from the University of Rijeka). The interdisciplinary research collaboration is lively at this institution, involving psychologists, music theorists, music pedagogues, and teachers from music schools. The energising institutional support comes from Sabina Vidulin, who started several projects encompassing colleagues from several institutions in Croatia, Bosnia and Herzegovina, and Serbia. The main research topics are the cognitive and emotional aspects of music listening in the music-pedagogical context (e.g., Vidulin et al., 2020; Vidulin et al., 2022).

At the Department of Psychology, the University of Rijeka, music psychology research is developed by Valnea Žauhar in collaboration with piano teachers, music theory researchers, and active performers. The main research topics cover performance skills such as memorising and mastering technical demands (e.g., Žauhar et al., 2020).

Recent activities initiated by Croatian colleagues include the special issue of the national journal *Psihologijske teme* [Psychological Topics] on the psychology of music (Butković & Žauhar, 2023) covering empirical and theoretical contributions encompassing regional and authors afield. It is also worth mentioning that the third PAM-IE 2024 conference will take place in Croatia (PAM-IE Zagreb 2024, n.d., chairs Sanja Kiš Žuvela and Ana Butković).

Montenegro

An interest in psychological themes in music is still in its infancy in higher education institution in Montenegro. Still, some research has taken place in the Music Academy in Cetinje, University of Montenegro, due to the successful collaborative work of Jelena Martinović Bogojević and Branka Rotar Pance (University of Ljubljana) (2022) when the role of musical creativity in primary school education was investigated. The practice of joint music education research had already begun during collaborations between authors from Croatia, Montenegro, and Serbia (Vidulin et al., 2015).

North Macedonia

Some sporadic research was conducted by Zoran Mihajlovski, at the Ss. Cyril and Methodius University of Skopje. This resulted in new insights concerning personality differences among instrumental groups (2013), personality attributes of musicians through a developmental perspective (2017) and comparisons with non-musicians (2016).

Serbia

The psychology of music originated in Serbia in the 1970s and has been developing ever since, especially in Belgrade. It has a tradition of almost 50 years. The psychology of music in Serbia is strongly interdisciplinary, involving psychologists, musicians, music pedagogues and colleagues from humanistic disciplines. Through persistent development, the psychology of music has grown into a discipline that holds a small but strong position in the frame of psychology in Serbia.

At the Faculty of Music, University of Arts in Belgrade, the general pedagogy and psychology courses became a part of the education of musicians in the 1950s. They evolved in the 1970s with the work of Ksenija Radoš, when the encounters between psychology and music became more intense. The pioneering research and academic endeavours of Radoš (1975, 1983/1997) took place in parallel at the Department of Psychology and Institute of Psychology, Faculty of Philosophy, University of Belgrade and the Faculty of Music, University of Arts in Belgrade. She was interested in exploring the development and identification of cognitive aspects of musical abilities in children, their relation to intellectual abilities, and the measurement of musical abilities. As the culmination of these research activities, Radoš wrote the monograph *Psihologija muzike* [Psychology of music] in 1996. In this way, the psychology of music was established as a scientific discipline in Serbia. The Serbian Psychological Society awarded the book the National Prize for its contribution to psychology in 1996.

At the end of the 1990s, psychology of music was actively developed in a number of ways. In 1996, the Psychology of Music Section was founded within the Serbian Psychological Society, aiming to support activities in the field of the applied psychology of music and to bring together psychologists and musicians and the research and practice of music education. After 27 active years, it encompasses 30 members, mostly psychologists employed in specialist music schools from the whole of Serbia. For a short period (2000–2003), the Music Psychology Counseling Unit was operating within the same Society with a goal to stimulate and support the musical development of gifted students. Concerning academic development, in 1999, the Psychology of Music was established as a course at the Faculty of Music, and in 2014 at the Department of Psychology, Faculty of Philosophy, by Radoš. Since 2008 and 2014 respectively, both courses have been led by Blanka Bogunović.

At the Faculty of Music, the Pedagogical Forum of Performing Arts was founded by Vera Milanković (e.g., 2003) in 1998. The interdisciplinary research of music pedagogues and psychologists, from Serbia and the region (after 2010) was continuously presented in regular forum meetings. Later, the interest in binding pedagogy and psychology was continued by Milena Petrović (e.g., Petrović et al., 2017; Petrović & Golubović, 2018), covering themes such as absolute pitch, synesthesia, multimodality, zoomusicology, and singing.

The psychology of music started flourishing after 2006 at the Faculty of Music, University of Arts in Belgrade, due to the supportive academic environment that gave Blanka Bogunović the opportunity to develop the discipline further by enlarging the number of courses related to the psychology of music, and to intensify the interdisciplinary research in the field involving colleagues and PhD students (e.g., Bogunović, 2019, 2020, 2021; Bogunović & Vujović, 2012; Marković & Bogunović, 2015; Mirović & Bogunović, 2013; Mutavdžin et al., 2021; Popović Mlađenović et al., 2014; Živanović et al., 2018). Since 2014, Bogunović has been leading the Psychology of Music course at the Department of Psychology, University of Belgrade, where the interdisciplinary setting was created by the joint participation of music and psychology, PhD and DocArtes students, and where a fruitful collaborative exchange is taking place. Bogunović's research interests cover motivation, the personality of the musically gifted, music education, students' mental health, musical skills and achievements, the professional perspective, creative cognition in making music, and interdisciplinary research. In 2008 she wrote *Muzički talenat i uspešnost* [Music talent and successfulness] (2008/2010), which was awarded the 2009 National Prize for the scientific contribution to psychology by the Serbian Psychological Society. Twice, in 1996 and 2009, the highest national award for psychology was given to authors—Ksenija Radoš and Blanka Bogunović—from a relatively small field of the psychology of music, which demonstrated the recognition and appreciation of colleagues for their pioneering work and set high expectations for those leading the discipline.

International recognition came in 2018 when Bogunović was nominated to be the ESCOM regional representative for Serbia. The two PAM-IE Belgrade 2019 (Bogunović & Nikolić, 2019) and 2022 (Bogunović et al., 2023) conferences embodied the idea of creating a strong network of music and psychology institutions in Serbia and intertwining them with those from the Western Balkans region. As a result, the Regional Network Psychology and Music (RNPaM) was founded.

Another place in Serbia where the psychology of music was carefully nurtured was the Department of Psychology, University of Niš, where a group of enthusiasts led by Vladimir Nešić was developing the social psychology of music (e.g., Nešić, 2003) and experimental research on the aesthetic of music (e.g., Stankov et al., 2020). In 2013, at the University of Niš, the Center for Cognitive Sciences was founded by Mihailo Antović in the Department of English, where successful interdisciplinary work with strong international recognition is taking place (e.g., Antović, 2021; Antović et al., 2020). The main research themes include music, language, meaning, and cognition, and his work was crowned by a recent book on musical meaning (Antović, 2022).

Slovenia

In Slovenia, the first traces of interest in music psychology came into view rather early and were related to music education issues (Cvetko, 1938). Later on, there was more specific interest in music abilities (Pesek, 1997), with the intention of gaining more insight into relevant psychological aspects of music education. This was developed by the work of Barbara Smolej Fritz (2006), who expanded insights in psychological processes related to self-regulated learning. Innovative research was led at the University of Maribor by Norbert Jaušovec, following up on the 'Mozart effect', testing the effects of music exposure on brain activity during cognitive tasks, e.g., its effect on the learning process (e.g., Jaušovec et al., 2006) or visual brain activity (Jaušovec & Habe, 2004). Psychology of Music as a course was founded at the Department of Musicology,

University of Ljubljana, in 2009 by Leon Stefanija (2009) and Gregor Pompe (2005).

The systematic research and academic development of the psychology of music started with Katarina Habe, who established the discipline, first at the University of Maribor in 2009 and later at the Academy of Music, University of Ljubljana, in 2017 with courses referring to the applicative value of music psychological knowledge to musicians. Her research interests include performance anxiety and music's effects on cognitive functioning, in addition to the well-being and motivation of music students (e.g., Habe, et al., 2019; Habe et al., 2021).

Book preview

This book will only showcase a fraction of such a rich history of music psychology research in the Western Balkans. It includes many of the topics central to the research of the authors from this region and includes contributions from almost all of the leading institutes active in this area. We are happy and proud to present a book that involves contributions from 19 authors from the Western Balkans, complemented by collaborations with or contributions from 10 authors from Western Europe. All of the chapters offer contributions that are unique to this book.

We present research investigating musical experiences and performance skills from psychological perspectives, which are relevant to musicians, music educators and psychologists, both students and professionals, and should also be of interest to a broader readership. We highlight specific research approaches that have shaped the disciplinary profile of the psychology of music in the Western Balkans. The book also offers complementary research of the prominent Western Europe psychology of music discourse, which enables comparison, discussion, and synthesis across approaches within the two regions. We offer insights into a range of areas, but without the intention of giving a comprehensive overview as a handbook or companion would. Instead, chapters that provide context and review an area of research are alternated with chapters that present particular research studies. In this way, bird's-eye perspectives and detailed findings and methodologies are both presented.

The book includes 15 chapters and is structured in four parts. The first two relate to listening experiences, while the second two address music performance. These topics have been central to research in the Western Balkans region and also feature strongly in international research. The book is framed by this introductory chapter, where the aims, background, and purpose of the book are explained, and a concluding chapter. This final chapter reflects on how regional research traditions shape research questions and perspectives, and on the need to promote more systematic dialogue and exchange across geographical regions. To further integrate this critical reflection, many of the chapter authors explore the situatedness of their research, discussing its embedding in particular traditions or the possibilities and limitations of cross-cultural generalisation.

Part 1 presents three chapters that develop perspectives and insights on aesthetic emotions, from both the Western Balkans and Western Europe. Chapter 2, by Dragan Janković and Maja Mađarev, investigates the aesthetic experiences of listeners in two experimental studies, aiming to test whether aesthetic experiences of music may originate from a few basic mechanisms of affective processing, related to affective valence (pleasantness), affective arousal, and cognitive evaluation (e.g., represented by familiarity). This is tested by analysing direct responses to the music and associated meanings. The chapter concludes with an outline of a dimensional model of aesthetic appreciation. Chapter 3, by Sanela Nikolić and Ivana Miladinović Prica, presents a qualitative study of aesthetic experiences of contemporary music from the perspectives of a composer, performer, and musicologist, comparing their responses and developing insights into the relationships between music-related theoretical and practical knowledge and aesthetic experience. Data were analysed using Interpretative Phenomenological Analysis, assuming that classical music knowledge is reflected in the participants' communication of their emotional and cognitive processes and aesthetic responses. Chapter 4, by Renee Timmers, Scott Bannister and Thomas M. Lennie, reviews research on aesthetic emotions in music, taking into account theories, measurements, and cross-cultural comparisons. It summarises assumptions, methods, and debates, raising awareness of the context and socio-musical function in which aesthetic emotions in music listening and appreciation take place, in order to search for a novel, integrative approach to aesthetic emotions.

Part 2 examines psychological aspects of music listening in context. In three chapters, it explores subjective experiences while listening to music in different groups and contexts, moving from fostering creative imagination in early childhood education, to relationships between music and values in adolescents, to the perspective of adult audiences. Music educators and psychologists jointly carried out the innovative study presented in Chapter 5 by Mirsada Zećo, Marina Videnović, and Lejla Silajdžić in a primary school setting, which showcases the regional research networks of authors from the Western Balkans. It describes an inclusive approach to facilitating children's musical development, creativity, and imagination using unconventional vibrational, percussive instruments (gongs, Himalayan singing bowls, and Koshi Chimes) in early music education, fostering attentive listening and sound awareness in children. The following research study, Chapter 6, by Ivana Stepanović Ilić, Marina Videnović, Zora Krnjaić, and Ksenija Krstić, investigates music preferences in Serbian adolescents and how they relate to the values adolescents hold, using Schwartz's basic values. These are compared with music preferences and previously observed relationships with values in other socio-cultural settings. The final chapter in this section, Chapter 7, by John Sloboda, presents a review of the fruitful research projects that aimed to increase understanding of how artists and promoters can respond to audience needs through practical but theoretically grounded adjustments to the concert experience. It explores how more of what audiences seek can be added to live classical events through principled programme design, content, and presentation innovations. Special attention is given to reflections on the experiences, challenges, and opportunities faced by musicians giving concerts during the COVID-19 restrictions of 2020.

Part 3 explores Music cognition in performance and practice, and consists of four chapters, mainly from Western European authors. Chapter 8, by Andrea Schiavio, Henrique Meissner, and Renee Timmers, investigates how the social is implied in individual contexts and the individual is experienced in social contexts using a qualitative research approach. The study compares participants' reports on the felt experiences of others who may be imagined or physically present during individual and group practice or performance. Chapter 9, by Andrea Schiavio and Dylan van der Schyff, discusses perspectives offered by the orientation known as '4E cognition' (embodied, embedded, extended, enactive) on understanding of music cognition in a range of musical domains considering perception, (remote) learning, performance, and musical development. The next two chapters have memorisation as a common theme. Chapter 10, by Valnea Žauhar, Dunja Crnjanski, and Igor Bajšanski, presents findings of a new, longitudinal case study of the memorisation of a piece of contemporary music by a Croatian composer. The effects of the formal musical structure and technical complexity on the amount of practice undertaken by a pianist are investigated. The final chapter in this section, Chapter 11 by Jane Ginsborg, gives an overview of the history of research on the memorisation of Western classical music; a review of the early pedagogical literature on the topic; empirical research on musicians' memorising strategies; and a summary of the author's research on performance from memory using the longitudinal case study approach.

Part 4 is entitled Psychology of musicians: From motivation and personality to addressing challenges and anxiety, and it consists of five chapters. In this part, studies from the Western Balkans are highlighted to evaluate cultural perspectives and variations. The contributions mostly stem from the three-stage educational system for the musically gifted, typical for the Western Balkans, offering crucial insights into music psychology research concerning psychological, social, professional and educational precursors of musical achievement. At the same time, demands for practical applications are made that will foster the development of talent, instructions for enhancing the development of skills, strategies to overcome difficulties and contributions to musicians' health and well-being.

The first chapter of this part, Chapter 12, by Blanka Bogunović, opens up questions about the joint contribution made by motivation and personality in achieving musical excellence, pointing out their core role in subsequent developmental stages of music learning and performance accomplishments, covering a wide age span from 6 to 22 years. This study includes a cross-cultural perspective comparing the results from the Western Balkans with international studies. The long-term implications of the educational trajectory of musically gifted child prodigies are the focus of the qualitative research study reported in the next chapter, Chapter 13, by Olja Jovanović, Ana Altaras Dimitrijević, Dejana Mutavdžin, and Blanka Bogunović. The authors explore the lived experience of acceleration in music education from the perspective of four adult musicians from Serbia, considering psychological impacts on their musical development in adolescence and subsequent professional careers, as well as the role of socio-cultural contexts. In Chapter 14 by Ana Butković a quantitative research study that examined personality differences in a sample of music students with diverse vocal and instrumental orientations is presented, aiming to investigate whether personality traits are conceptually related to variation in job activity and choice across instrumental groups of music students. The final two chapters examine approaches to support musicians in coping with the challenges of an intensive career in music performance. Firstly, in Chapter 15 by Katarina Habe and Michele Biasutti, an overview of relevant contemporary models of music performance anxiety (MPA) is offered, complemented by a summary and discussion of the outcomes of research studies regarding MPA in the Western Balkans. This chapter emphasises the approach of reconsidering MPA as pre-performance excitement that can contribute to an optimal flow state during performance. The final study, Chapter 16, by Raluca Matei and Jane Ginsborg, directly compares approaches to promoting and sustaining the health and well-being of young musicians in music higher education institutions. The study captures and compares health education courses in music conservatoires in Southeast Europe and the Western Balkans, and discusses the implications of their approaches for future developments.

Conclusion

The unique presentation of research from the Western Balkans interleaved with research from Western Europe is of relevance and interest to scholars in music and psychology, including as an example of a way to address issues of inequality and the lack of diversity of research discourse in the major published literature. It reminds us that research is conducted in a particular context and tradition, supported by geo-political and linguistic structures that may benefit or disadvantage that research to varying degrees. This book will serve both the purpose of developing insights into the psychology of music, and that of advancing the visibility and recognition of the research tradition and activity in the Western Balkans. In the concluding chapter of the book, we will reflect more fully on the situatedness of research insights as we consider parallels in the approaches and findings of research developed in the Western Balkans and Western Europe, as well as some of the differences in emphasis and research directions, practices and insights, which are associated with developments in different specialisms, and differences in pedagogical approaches, cultural situatedness and the flourishing of skills and interdisciplinarity.

Through promoting the psychology of music knowledge and its applications, this book can foster the practice of music performance, music education, and psychological support in music schools throughout countries of the Western Balkans and internationally. It contributes to our understanding of the psychology of music by presenting new research and reflecting on developments in knowledge and understanding, including the situatedness of research within geographically shaped music practices and research traditions. The focus on authors from the Western Balkans helps to establish confidence and aspiration in this region whilst attracting a broad readership within the Western Balkans and beyond, showcasing the relevance of the psychology of music and its international links.

References

Antović, M. (2021). Multilevel grounded semantics across cognitive modalities: Music, vision, poetry. *Language and Literature: International Journal of Stylistics, 30*(2), 147–173. https://doi.org/10.1177/0963947021999182

Antović, M. (2022). *Multilevel grounding. A theory of musical meaning.* Routledge.

Antović, M., Mitić, J., & Benecasa, N. (2020). Conceptual rather than perceptual: Cross-modal binding of pitch sequencing is based on an underlying schematic structure. *Psychology of Music, 48*(1), 84–104. https://doi.org/10.1177/0305735618785242

Bačlija Sušić, B., & Brebrić, V. (2022). Encouraging and assessing preschool children's musical creativity. *Early Years. An International Research Journal.* Advance online publication. https://doi.org/10.1080/09575146.2022.2139356

Bogunović, B. (2010). *Muzički talenat i uspešnost* [Music talent and successfulness] (2nd ed.). Fakultet muzičke umetnosti i Institut za pedagoška istraživanja.

Bogunović, B. (2019). Creative cognition in composing music. *New Sound, 53*(1), 89–117. https://doi.org/10.5937/newso1901089B

Bogunović, B. (2020). Cognition in composing contemporary art music. In G. Grujić (ed.), *International Conference Vlado S. Milošević, ethnomusicologist, composer and pedagogue. Tradition as inspiration* (pp. 7–23). Akademija umjetnosti Univerziteta u Banjoj Luci.

Bogunović, B. (2021). Parental contribution to motivation and practice at the beginning years of instrumental tuition for the musically gifted. In S. Vidulin (ed.), *Music pedagogy in the context of present and future changes 7. Multidisciplinary crossroads: Researches in music education* (pp. 419–436). University of Jurja Dobrile in Pula.

Bogunović, B., & Nikolić, S. (eds). (2020). *Proceedings of PAM-IE Belgrade 2019*. Faculty of Music, University of Arts in Belgrade. https://www.fmu.bg.ac.rs/wp-content/uploads/2020/12/psychology-and-music-proceedings-sa-koricama-1.pdf

Bogunović, B., & Vujović, I. (2012). Metacognitive strategies in learning sight-singing. *Psihološka istraživanja, 15*(2), 115–133. https://doi.org/10.5937/PsIstra1202115B

Bogunović, B., Nikolić, S., & Mutavdžin, D. (eds). (2023). *Proceedings of the PAM-IE Belgrade 2022*. Faculty of Music, University of Arts in Belgrade. https://www.fmu.bg.ac.rs/wp-content/uploads/2023/08/zbornik-pam-ie-belgrade-2002_za-sajt_sa-koricama.pdf

Breitenfeld, D., & Majsec Vrbanić, V. (2011). *Muzikoterapija: Pomozimo si glazbom* [Music therapy: Let's help each other with music]. Music Play.

Butković, A., & Žauhar, V. (2023). Guest editors' note. *Psihologijske teme, 32*(1). https://pt.ffri.hr/pt/issue/view/888

Butković, A., & Rančić Dopuđ, D. (2017). Personality traits and alcohol consumption of classical and heavy metal musicians. *Psychology of Music, 45*(2), 246–256. https://doi.org/10.1177/0305735616659128

Butković, A., Ullén, F., & Mosing, M. (2015). Personality related traits as predictors of music practice: Underlying environmental and genetic influences. *Personality and Individual Differences, 74*, 133–138. https://doi.org/10.1016/j.paid.2014.10.006

Butković, A., Vukasović, T., & Bratko, D. (eds). (2011). *Ličnost i glazbene preferencije: XX Ljetna psihologijska škola* [Personality and music preferences: 20th Summer school of psychology]. FF Press.

Butković, A., Vukojević, N., & Carević, S. (2022). Music performance anxiety and perfectionism in Croatian musicians. *Psychology of Music, 50*(1), 100–110. https://doi.org/10.1177/0305735620978692

Crnković, D. (ed.). (2020). *Muzikoterapija. Umjetnost glazbe kroz umjeće lečenja* [Music therapy. The art of music through the art of healing]. Naklada Slap.

Cvetko, D. (1938). *Problem občega muzikalnega vzgajanja ter izobraževanja* [The problem of general musical upbringing and education] [Unpublished doctoral dissertation]. University of Ljubljana. https://www.dlib.si/details/URN:NBN:SI:DOC-SR7TVJ33

Deliège, I., & Sloboda, J.A. (eds). (1996). *Musical beginnings: Origins and development of musical competence.* Oxford University Press. https://doi.org/10.1093/acprof:oso/9780198523321.001.0001

Deliège, I., & Sloboda, J.A. (eds). (2004). *Perception and cognition of music* (2nd ed.). Psychology Press. https://doi.org/10.4324/9780203344262

Deliège, I., & Wiggins, G.A. (eds). (2006). *Musical creativity: Multidisciplinary research in theory and practice.* Psychology Press. https://doi.org/10.4324/9780203088111

Dobrota, S., & Reić Ercegovac, I. (2015). The relationship between music preferences of different mode and tempo and personality traits–Implications for music pedagogy. *Music Education Research, 17*(2), 234–247. https://doi.org/10.1080/14613808.2014.933790

Dobrota, S., & Reić Ercegovac, I. (2016). *Zašto volimo ono što slušamo: Glazbeno pedagoški i psihologijski aspekti glazbenih preferencija* [Why we like what we listen to: Music pedagogical and psychological aspects of musical preferences]. Filozofski fakultet Sveučilišta u Splitu.

Dobrota, S., & Reić Ercegovac, I. (2017). Music preferences with regard to music education, informal influences and familiarity of music. *British Journal of Music Education, 34*(1), 41–55. https://doi.org/10.1017/S0265051716000358

Dukić, H. (2022). In search of a story: Guided imagery and music therapy. In M.B. Küssner, L. Taruffi, & G.A. Floridou (eds), *Music and mental imagery* (pp. 200–216). Routledge. https://doi.org/10.4324/9780429330070

European Society for the Cognitive Sciences of Music (ESCOM). (n.d.). *About ESCOM.* https://www.escomsociety.org/

Ferović, S. (2002). Muzičke i tehničke aktivnosti u funkciji psihomotorne stimulacije [Musical and technical activities in function of psychomotor stimulation]. *Muzika, 6*(2), 21–28.

Ferović, S. (2004). Muzika u porodičnom životu u funkciji prevencije i muzikoterapije [Music in family life in function of prevention and music therapy]. *Muzika, 8*(1), 21–28.

Habe, K., Biasutti, M., & Kajtna, T. (2019). Flow and satisfaction with life in elite musicians and top athletes. *Frontiers in Psychology, 10*, Article 698. https://doi.org/10.3389/fpsyg.2019.00698

Habe, K., Biasutti, M., & Kajtna, T. (2021). Wellbeing and flow in sports and music students during the COVID-19 pandemic. *Thinking Skills and Creativity, 39*, Article 100798. https://doi.org/10.1016/j.tsc.2021.100798

Habe, K., Dobrota, S., & Reić Ercegovac, I. (2018). The structure of musical preferences of youth: A cross-cultural perspective. *Musicological Annual, 54*(1), 141–156. https://doi.org/10.4312/mz.54.1.141-156

Jaušovec, N., & Habe, K. (2004). The influence of auditory background stimulation (Mozart's sonata K. 448) on visual brain activity. *International Journal of Psychophysiology, 51*(3), 261–271. https://doi.org/10.1016/S0167-8760(03)00227-7

Jaušovec, N., Jaušovec, K., & Gerlič, I. (2006). The influence of Mozart's music on brain activity in the process of learning. *Clinical Neurophysiology, 117*(12), 2703–2714. https://doi.org/10.1016/j.clinph.2006.08.010

Kiš Žuvela, S. (2013). Between sound, word and image: Some ideas for an interdisciplinary teaching approach in music theory. In S. Vidulin Orbanić (ed.), *Interdisciplinary approach to music: Research, practice and education. Proceedings from the Third international symposium of music pedagogues* (pp. 427–438). Sveučilište Jurja Dobrile u Puli.

Kiš Žuvela, S., & Ostroški Anić, A. (2019). The embodied and the cultural in the conceptualisation of pitch space in Croatian. *Jezikoslovlje, 20*(2), 199–219. https://doi.org/10.29162/jez.2019.7

Marković, M., & Bogunović, B. (2015). 'Krojenje' in Serbian chant: Application of cognitive structural models of improvisation. *New Sound, 45*(1), 29–44. https://doi.org/10.5937/newso1545029M

Martinović Bogojević, J., & Rotar Pance, B. (2022). Musical creativity in the teaching practice in Montenegrin and Slovenian primary schools. *British Journal of Music Education, 39*(2), 169–182. https://doi.org/10.1017/S0265051722000018

Mazover, M. (2002). *The Balkans: A short history*. Weidenfeld and Nicolson History.

Mihajlovski, Z. (2013). Personality, intelligence and musical instrument. *Croatian Journal of Education, 15*(1), 155–172. https://doi.org/10.15516/cje.v15i0.606

Mihajlovski, Z. (2016). Musicians as a distinctive personality structure – Yes or no? *Croatian Journal of Education, 18*(2), 125–143. https://doi.org/10.15516/cje.v18i0.2113

Mihajovski, Z. (2017). Musical temperament from a developmental perspective. *Croatian Journal of Education, 19*(3), 98–115. https://doi.org/10.15516/cje.v19i0.2708

Milanković, V., Petrović, M., & Petrović, J. (2003). Tone constellation: A personal spatial scale presentation. Searching for an alternative approach to teaching music theory. In R. Kopiez, A. C. Lehmann, I. Wolther, & C. Wolf (eds),

Proceedings of the 5th Triennial ESCOM conference (pp. 413–415). Institute for Research in Music Education.

Mirović, T., & Bogunović, B. (2013). Muzičko obrazovanje i mentalno zdravlje studenata muzike [Music education and mental health of music students]. *Zbornik Instituta za pedagoška istraživanja, 45*(2), 445–463. https://doi.org/10.2298/ZIPI1302445M

Mutavdžin, D., Stančić, M., & Bogunović, B. (2021). To be connected: Supporting self-regulated learning in higher music education before and during the pandemic. *Psihološka istraživanja, 24*(2), 277–301. https://doi.org/10.5937/PSISTRA24-32702

Nešić, V. (2003). *Muzika, čovek, društvo. Socialno-psihološki pristup* [Music, man, society. Social-psychological approach]. Filozofski fakultet, Univerzitet u Nišu.

Parncutt, R., & Timmers, R. (2017, December 14). *ESCOM Regional development initiative*. https://www.escomsociety.org/_files/ugd/772b99_3ca4015bc0dc4d838e7949fd7c7c5878.pdf

Pesek, A. (1997). *Otroci v svetu glasbe: Izbrana poglavja iz glasbene psihologije in pedagogike* [Children in the world of music: Selected chapters of music psychology and pedagogy]. Mladinska knjiga.

Petrović, M., Ačić, G., & Milanković, V. (2017). Musicians' free associations on the given music concepts. *Glazbenopedagoški zbornik, 26*, 49–63.

Petrović, M., & Golubović, M. (2018). The use of metaphorical musical terminology for verbal description of music. *Rasprave: Časopis Instituta za hrvatski jezik i jezikoslovlje, 44*(2), 627–641. https://doi.org/10.31724/rihjj.44.2.20

Petrović Todosijević, S. (2018). *Reforma osnovnoškolskog sistema u Srbiji 1944–1959* [Elementary school system reform in Serbia 1944–1959]. Institut za noviju srpsku istoriju.

Pompe, G. (2005). *Povednost glasbenega toka in postmodernizem* [The expressiveness of the musical flow and postmodernism] [Unpublished doctoral dissertation]. University of Ljubljana, Faculty of Arts.

Popović Mlađenović, T., Bogunović, B., & Perković, I. (2014). *Interdisciplinary approach to music: Listening, performing, composing*. Faculty of Music, University of Arts in Belgrade.

Psychology and Music—Interdisciplinary Encounters, Belgrade, 2019 (2019). *Conference Call*. PAM-IE Belgrade. https://psychologyandmusicconference2019.wordpress.com/conference-call/

Psychology and Music—Interdisciplinary Encounters, Belgrade, 2022 (2022). *Conference Call*. PAM-IE Belgrade. https://psychologyandmusicconference.wordpress.com/conference-call/

Psychology and Music—Interdisciplinary Encounters, Zagreb, 2024. Conference Call. PAM-IE Zagreb. http://www.muza.unizg.hr/psymu2024/conference-call/

Radoš Mirković, K. (1983/1997). *Psihologija muzickih sposobnosti* [Psychology of musical abilities] (2nd ed.). Zavod za udžbenike i nastavna sredstva.

Radoš, K. (1975). Merenje muzičke sposobnosti [Measuring music ability]. *Psihologija, 8*(1–2), 81–93.

Radoš, K. (1996/2010). *Psihologija muzike* [Psychology of Music] (2nd ed.). Zavod za udžbenike i nastavna sredstva.

Regional Network Psychology and Music (RNPaM). (n.d.). *Home*. https://regionalnetworkpsychologyandmusiceng.wordpress.com/friends/

Rojko, P. (1981). *Testiranje u muzici* [Testing in music]. Muzikološki zavod Muzičke akademije u Zagrebu.

Rojko, P. (1982/2012). *Psihološke osnove intonacije i ritma* [Psychological foundations of intonation and rhythm] (2nd revised digital ed.). Muzička Akademija Sveučilišta u Zagrebu. https://dokumen.tips/documents/psiholoske-osnove-intonacije-i-ritma.html?page=4

Sloboda, J.A., & Ginsborg, J. (2018). 25 years of ESCOM: Achievements and challenges. *Musicae Scientiae, 22*(2), 147–160. https://doi.org/10.1177/1029864918764574

Smolej Fritz, B. (2006). *Motivacijski, kognitivni in metakognitivni vidiki samoregulativnega učenja pri nauku o glasbi* [Motivational, cognitive and metacognitive aspects of self-regulated learning in music education] [Unpublished doctoral dissertation]. Music Academy in Ljubljana.

Stankov, M., Milićević, N., & Jovančević, A. (2020). Effect of music on subjective experience of dance performances. In B. Bogunović & S. Nikolić (eds), *Proceedings of PAM-IE Belgrade 2019* (pp. 150–154). Faculty of Music, University of Arts in Belgrade. https://www.fmu.bg.ac.rs/wp-content/uploads/2020/12/psychology-and-music-proceedings-sa-koricama-1.pdf

Stefanija, L. (2009). Convolutions of musical meaning: A sociopsychological note on listening to music. *Musicological Annual, 45*(2), 55–76. https://doi.org/10.4312/mz.45.2.55-76

Vidulin, S., Martinović Bogojević, J., & Đurđanović, M.M. (2015). Importance, structure and outcomes of the music program in the primary school: The experience of Croatia, Montenegro and Serbia. *International Journal of Cognitive Research in Science, Engineering and Education, 3*(1), 67–80. https://doi.org/10.23947/2334-8496-2015-3-1-67-79

Vidulin, S., Plavišić, M., & Žauhar, V. (2020). *Cognitive-emotional listening to music at school*. Juraj Dobrila University, Academy of Music in Pula and Faculty of Philosophy in Rijeka.

Vidulin, S., Žauhar, V., & Plavšić, M. (2022). Experiences during listening to music in school. *Music Education Research, 24*(4), 512–529. https://doi.org/10.1080/14613808.2022.2098262

Vilč, B., Šečić, A., Kirac, I., Herman, I., Kraljević, N., & Brnić, S. (2019). Guided imagery and music in the preoperative period and during radiotherapy at University hospital for tumors. *Libri Oncologici: Croatian Journal of Oncology, 47*(2–3), 78–83. https://doi.org/10.20471/LO.2019.47.02-03.15

Žauhar, V., Matić, A., Dražul, A., & Bajšanski, I. (2020). Memorising the contemporary piano piece of music: The effects of the formal structure, pianist's segmentation, and technical difficulties. In B. Bogunović & S. Nikolić (eds), *Proceedings of PAM-IE Belgrade 2019* (pp. 69–77). Faculty of Music, University of Arts in Belgrade. https://www.fmu.bg.ac.rs/wp-content/uploads/2020/12/psychology-and-music-proceedings-sa-koricama-1.pdf

Živanović, M., Marković, M.V., & Bogunović, B. (2018). Structure of subjective experience of classical music. *Psihologija, 51*(4), 397–411. https://doi.org/10.2298/PSI170116009Z

PART I

AESTHETIC AND EMOTIONAL EXPERIENCES OF MUSIC

2. The Role of Affective Dimensions in the Aesthetic Experience of Music

Dragan Janković and Maja Mađarev

Introduction

Affective and aesthetic experiences are ubiquitous aspects of our experience of music. When we listen to music, we can effortlessly tell whether we like it or not or how it makes us feel. However, questions as to why we like or dislike some music, and what role emotions play in our aesthetic experiences, still have ambiguous answers. Although aesthetic experiences are common in everyday life, we still do not have a comprehensive theory that explains what psychologically constitutes such experiences. In the present chapter, we will offer a model based on dimensional theories of emotion, with special interest paid to the question of how our aesthetic experiences, although they may involve a great number of complex cognitive and emotional responses, can be related to a few basic mechanisms of affective processing.

Approaches to aesthetic experiences can generally be divided into two broad groups. In the first, aesthetic experiences are considered normal, everyday psychological experiences. Theories that are typical representatives of this approach suggest that our aesthetic experiences are only a special instance of the psychology of perception, cognition, motivation, or emotion (Silvia, 2012). In this approach, the intensity of aesthetic experiences in studies is mainly represented with some continuous dimension, such as: how much people like or dislike a certain stimulus, how much they evaluate it as beautiful or ugly, or how attractive or unattractive they find it. Of the many proposed measures, various factorial, psycholinguistic, and neuropsychological studies found the assessment of stimuli on the ugly–beautiful scale to be the most representative measure of our aesthetic experience, both for music (Istók et al., 2009) and for the visual domain (e.g., Augustin et al., 2012). The second approach includes theories where aesthetic experience is mostly understood as an idealised, exceptional experience, that sometimes occurs as a reaction to stimuli of special importance, most often to works of art. In this context, aesthetic experience can be viewed as an exceptional state of mind that is qualitatively different from everyday mental states (e.g., Marković, 2012).

Building on the strong connection between emotions and aesthetic experience, we believe that the psychology of emotion is the right place for studying the nature and origin of our aesthetic reactions, even though there are questions about whether music induces true emotions in listeners (e.g., Konečni, 2008). For example, Vladimir Konečni (2005) suggests that instrumental music cannot directly induce genuine emotions in listeners, and that when such emotions are induced they result only indirectly, by means of extramusical associations (e.g., in memory), rather than directly from auditory inputs. Other authors suggest that music does induce emotion in the listeners and that emotion is a central component for creating, learning, and interpreting music (e.g., Juslin & Sloboda, 2010; Juslin & Västfjäll, 2008). Most researchers today believe that music can induce emotions and the focus of discussion has shifted to the nature of these emotions.

One of the fundamental questions addressed in the psychology of music is whether the emotions we experience in relation to music differ from those we experience in everyday life (Juslin & Sloboda, 2010). These are usually termed aesthetic emotions and everyday emotions, respectively. According to one perspective, artworks mainly evoke the same emotions we experience in everyday life, such as happiness, sadness, pleasure, or surprise. According to another perspective, the emotions evoked by artworks are specifically referred to as aesthetic emotions, often without implying that these emotions are of a special kind. Recent studies on music and emotion, have frequently used the term aesthetic emotions in a more restricted sense, suggesting that music evokes unique or music-specific emotions (e.g., Scherer & Zentner, 2008). For a more detailed review of aesthetic emotions, see Chapter 4 in this volume. Here we use models of everyday emotions and explore how these may need to be extended to account for aesthetic experiences.

The structure of affective experiences of music

A final distinction to introduce is that between 'discrete' and 'dimensional' theories of emotion. Although a large number of different theories and models of emotion have been proposed by authors to date, these are two of the most influential. Discrete theories of emotions suggest the existence of a limited number of discrete categories, i.e., basic emotions (e.g., fear, anger, happiness, sadness) that are independent, irreducible to each other, accompanied by qualitatively different subjective experiences, with distinctive facial expressions, and having a special neurophysiological basis (e.g., Ekman, 1992). However, recent studies in affective science have questioned the reliability of evidence to support the main assumptions of this approach (e.g., Barrett & Wager, 2006).

On the other hand, dimensional models of emotion suggest that a large number of different affective experiences are actually based on a smaller number of underlying dimensions or neurophysiological systems and can be represented by a linear combination of those dimensions (e.g., Janković, 2000a, 2015; Osgood et al., 1957; Russell, 2003). Dimensional models have a long tradition in psychology. In early studies from the late 19th century, Wilhelm Wundt (1896) suggested that all affective experiences are based on three bipolar dimensions: pleasure–displeasure, tension–relaxation, and arousal–calmness. In the mid-20th century, Charles Osgood suggested the existence of three dimensions: (1) evaluation, (2) potency, and (3) activity (Osgood et al., 1957). James Russell (1980) proposed a circumplex model of affect consisting of two orthogonal bipolar dimensions, valence (pleasure) and arousal (activity), and all individual affective experiences can be represented by their values on the coordinates of such two-dimensional affective space. In addition to Russell's valence and arousal model, other two-dimensional models with differently conceptualised dimensions have been proposed: among others tension and energy (Thayer, 1996); positive affect, negative affect (Watson et al., 1999); and approach and withdrawal (Lang et al., 1998).

With respect to emotional experiences of music, there is still a lack of a broader consensus on the structure of music-induced affective responses. In an early study on the structure of affective experiences of music (Nordenstreng, 1968), participants rated their affective experiences of musical stimuli on 32 semantic differential scales that included emotional attributes. Exploratory factor analysis of the participants' responses to the musical stimuli revealed four factors, which were interpreted as softness, colourfulness, relaxation, and magnitude. In the study that followed, Lage Wedin (1972) suggested that music emotions can be accounted for by three bipolar factors: tension–energy (vehement, violent, furious); gaiety–gloom (playful, exuberant, glad); and solemnity–triviality (solemn, sublime, grand). In a more recent study on the structure of subjective experiences of classical music (Živanović et al., 2018), results suggested that descriptors of music experience are best represented by five interrelated dimensions: aesthetic experience, affective tone, tension, content-fullness, and structure. The lack of a broader consensus on the structure of music-induced affective reactions directed a number of researchers to rely on a two-dimensional model of emotion, in accordance with widespread recognition of valence and arousal as basic dimensions of affective experience. However, numerous studies have also suggested that the two-dimensional model is not able to account for all the variance in music-induced affective experiences and that two dimensions may not be enough (e.g., Collier, 2007; Fontaine et al., 2007).

In previous research (Trkulja & Janković, 2012), we analysed the latent structure of affective experiences of music through a comprehensive approach that included a large collection of music-evoked affective responses and a wide range of musical stimuli. The results suggested that affective experiences of music are best represented by three underlying dimensions: affective valence (pleasant-unpleasant, attractive-unattractive), arousal (interesting-boring, exciting-calming), and cognitive evaluation (familiar-unfamiliar, expected-unexpected). These results shed light on cognitive evaluation as a possible third dimension underlying the affective experiences. In this three-dimensional model, cognitive evaluation is understood as one of the basic evaluative mechanisms that, along with valence and arousal, contributes to the formation of affective experiences. The role of cognitive processes in the formation of affective experiences has received considerable attention in all modern cognitive theories of emotion, which assume that a certain type of cognitive processing is an inevitable component of emotions (e.g., Lazarus, 1991; Scherer, 2001). Cognitive evaluation as a dimension is partially similar to the concept of cognitive appraisal from appraisal theories of emotion (e.g., Scherer, 2001) in the sense that it influences the formation of emotional experience, but has a somewhat narrower meaning and includes only attributes related to the cognitive evaluation of objects and events (e.g., novelty, familiar-unfamiliar, clear-unclear, meaningful-meaningless, expected-unexpected, etc.). Cognitive evaluation as an additional dimension in the affective space offers the possibility of overcoming some of the main objections to previous dimensional models, which relate to the inability of valence and arousal dimensions to adequately distinguish some of the basic emotions such as fear and anger, as well as a group of knowledge emotions such as surprise, interest, confusion, and awe, which are highly relevant to aesthetic experience (Silvia, 2010).

Aesthetic experience is often understood as a complex process that seems to involve not only emotions but also a combination of perceptual and cognitive factors (e.g., Brattico & Pearce, 2013; Leder et al., 2004). Some authors have recently argued that aesthetic experience relates to the formation of meaning, interpretation, and understanding (e.g., Cespedes-Guevara & Eerola, 2018; Janković, 2014; Leder et al., 2004). The idea that meanings (associations) play an important role in the formation of our aesthetic experiences dates back to the beginnings of experimental aesthetics as a field. According to the aesthetic association principle proposed by Gustav Fechner in his paper from 1866, aesthetic choices are largely shaped by the observer's learning history (associative factors) rather than by the formal properties of an object (direct factors; Ortlieb et al., 2020). However, the various perceptual, cognitive, and affective factors involved in the formation of our aesthetic experience are not independent and isolated, but rather highly interrelated. Recent studies that tested this interrelationship in the visual art domain showed that the affective experience of different meanings activated in the mind of beholders while observing the artworks explained 98% and 95% of the variance in the aesthetic experience of paintings and photographs, respectively (Janković, 2014; Janković et al., 2019). The term 'meanings' here refers to the sum of the various perceived stimulus features, associations from episodic memory, knowledge, emotions, and cognitive interpretations that are activated or constructed in the viewer's mind when viewing the artwork. In the studies presented in this chapter, we will examine the relevance of cognitive evaluation as an affective dimension alongside emotional valence and arousal in the domain of music.

Aims

Emotion is a fundamental aspect of our aesthetic experience and understanding the involvement of emotions in the aesthetic evaluation of music is an essential question within the field of music psychology. Regardless of the great variety of emotional reactions that music can evoke in the listeners, as well as whether we are talking about everyday emotions, aesthetic emotions, or music-specific emotions, an assumption derived from dimensional theories of emotion would be that all of them include an underlying core affect represented by affective dimensions. In this chapter, we will present two studies in which we analysed the role of evaluative/affective dimensions in the aesthetic experiences of music.

The aim of the first study was to analyse the relation between three dimensions of affective experience: valence, arousal, and cognitive evaluation (Janković, 2000a, b; Trkulja & Janković, 2012) with the aesthetic experience of music. In the second study, we implemented a novel procedure, similar to the one employed in Dragan Janković's (2014) study in the field of visual arts, to further explore where the affective experience of music originates from and in what way it affects the aesthetic experience of music. We hypothesized that the aesthetic experience of music actually results from the affective experience of various meanings that are activated or constructed in the listener's mind when listening to music (e.g., associations from episodic memory, knowledge, cognitive interpretations, etc.), rather than merely from the affective experience of music as a physical stimulus and its objective characteristics.

Both studies examined the role of affective dimensions in the aesthetic experience of music. The difference between the two is that in the first study, the aesthetic experience of music was investigated using the affective experience of musical stimuli (directly rated by the participants), whereas in the second study, the aesthetic experience of music was investigated via the affective experience of (verbally expressed) meanings (associations) that the participants had in mind while listening to music.

Study 1: Relation between affective dimensions and aesthetic experience of music

Materials and methods

Forty-two first-year psychology students aged 18 to 20 years ($M = 18.95$, $SD = .66$, 81% female) from the Department of Psychology, University of Belgrade, participated in the study and received course credit for their participation. The authors and participants were from the same academic institution, and the authors were not involved in teaching any courses to the first-year psychology students who participated in the study.

The selection of music stimuli was conducted in two phases. First, a collection of 275 music excerpts (each part of existing music compositions, and 4–5 seconds long) was prepared. Excerpts were then rated by an additional group of participants ($N = 13$) on three dimensions of affective experience: valence (pleasantness), cognitive evaluation (familiarity), and arousal (impressiveness). In the second phase, 60 music excerpts were selected for the main study. Stimuli were selected to cover a wide range of genres (classical music, pop, rock, electronic, jazz, folk, ambient, etc.), themes, instruments, and affective experiences. Stimuli included both unfamiliar and familiar pieces of music (the average familiarity rating on a seven-point scale was $M = 4.45$, $SD = 1.27$).

In order to measure the affective experience of music we used an instrument consisting of nine seven-point bipolar scales measuring three dimensions of the affective experience (with three scales for each dimension) (Trkulja & Janković, 2012): valence (unpleasant–pleasant, bad–good, unattractive–attractive); arousal (boring–interesting, unimpressive–impressive, calming–exciting); and cognitive evaluation (unfamiliar–familiar, unclear–clear, incomprehensible–comprehensible). As a measure of aesthetic experience, a seven-point bipolar ugly–beautiful scale was used.

The questionnaire was administered via a computer interface employing an online survey form using Qualtrics software. Participants were asked to rate their own aesthetic and affective experience of each of the presented musical stimuli on seven-point bipolar scales with opposite attributes at each end (e.g., ranging from –3 = unpleasant, to 3 = pleasant). The order of the presented music stimuli was fixed for all participants and the scales were presented in randomised order for each stimulus and for each participant. The total duration of the study was around 30 minutes.

Results

This study was conducted to determine the relation between basic dimensions of affective experience and aesthetic experience of music. First, we calculated the average valence, arousal, and cognitive evaluation ratings from three representative scales for each of the affective dimensions. Results of the Pearson correlation indicated that there was a significant positive association between valence and aesthetic preference, $r(58) = .97$, $p < .001$, arousal and aesthetic preference, $r(58) = .57, p < .001$, and cognitive evaluation and aesthetic preference, $r(58) = .87, p < .001$.

In addition, we hypothesised that the aesthetic experience of music could be substantially explained by valence, arousal, and cognitive evaluation as basic dimensions of affective experience. To test this hypothesis, we used multiple regression analysis. The results showed that 96.3% of the variance of aesthetic preference could be explained by three affective predictors, $F(3, 56) = 507.30, p < .001$ (Figure 2.1).

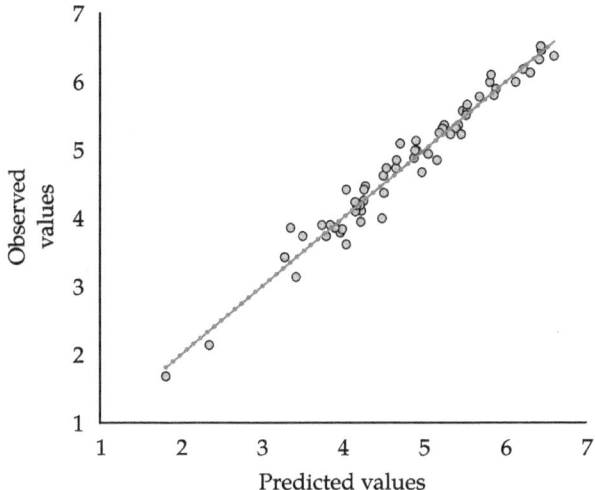

Fig. 2.1 Regression plot between observed values (ratings of aesthetic experience) versus predicted values (aesthetic experience predicted by the model)

Looking at the unique individual contributions of the predictors, the results indicated that all three affective dimensions showed a significant contribution to the prediction of aesthetic preference, with the largest contribution of affective valence ($\beta = .88$, $t = 16.00$, $p < .001$), followed by cognitive evaluation ($\beta = .22$, $t = 3.16$, $p < .001$) and arousal ($\beta = -.16$, $t = -3.88$, $p < .001$).

Study 2: The role of the affective experience of meanings activated in the listener's mind during the aesthetic evaluation of music

Materials and methods

Participants consisted of two groups made up according to music expertise: one group of music non-experts ($n = 33$) and one group of music experts ($n = 30$). The group of music non-experts included volunteers and undergraduate psychology students ($M_{age} = 24.1$, $SD = 2.2$, 66.7% female and 33.3% male) from the Faculty of Philosophy, University of Belgrade. All participants from this group stated that they had no formal music education and did not engage in music professionally. The group of music experts ($M_{age} = 24.3$, $SD = 3.6$, 76.7% female and 23.3% male) consisted of participants who had completed a university degree in music or music production and sound design ($n = 25$) or had been professionally involved in music for more than five years ($n = 5$).

The pre-testing and selection of music stimuli followed the same procedure as in Study 1. A total of 24 new music excerpts (4–5 seconds long, and part of existing music compositions that were not included in Study 1) were selected to cover a wide spectrum of genres, instruments, and subjective experiences. The research session consisted of two phases in which the same respondents participated. In the first phase, music stimuli were presented to the respondents one by one, and their task was to rate on a seven-point bipolar scale how much they liked or disliked the musical stimulus they had heard (ranging from $-3 =$ I don't like it, to $3 =$ I like it). Respondents were then asked to report what they had in mind while making their aesthetic evaluation of each musical stimuli (i.e., to write down at least two and at most five associations they had in mind while making their aesthetic evaluation). Participants were free to write down any thoughts that occurred to them during the aesthetic evaluation of the music (e.g., perceived musical features, associations from episodic memory, prior knowledge, experienced or perceived emotions, formal features of the music, its cognitive interpretation, etc.). In the second phase of the same research session, all participants were shown on a screen the associations (verbal responses) they had reported in the first phase, and below each response, three seven-point bipolar scales were presented for them to rate their affective experience of that response: unpleasant–pleasant (valence), unimpressive–impressive (arousal), and unfamiliar–familiar (cognitive evaluation). For instance, if a participant rated a musical stimulus in the initial phase and reported having thoughts of 'mystical', 'summer', and 'Kyoto' during the aesthetic evaluation of the music, in the subsequent phase, the participant was asked to rate their affective experience of 'mystical', 'summer', and 'Kyoto'. Music stimuli and scales were presented in randomised order for each participant. The total duration of the study was between 25 and 35 minutes.

Results

The basic hypothesis in this study was that the aesthetic experience of music would be related to the affective experience of the meanings (associations) that a given piece of music evoked in the listeners. Additionally, we wanted to examine this phenomenon independently in groups of music experts and non-experts. First, we calculated the average valence (pleasantness), arousal (impressiveness), and cognitive evaluation (familiarity) of all the meanings (verbal responses) that a certain musical stimulus evoked in the respondents. The data were analysed separately for music experts and non-experts. Results of the Pearson correlation indicated a strong positive association between the valence of verbal responses and aesthetic preference for music, both in non-experts, $r(22) = .87, p < .001$, and experts, $r(22) = .86, p < .001$. Statistically significant positive correlations were also obtained between cognitive evaluation of verbal responses and aesthetic preference for music, both in non-experts, $r(22) = .70, p < .001$, and experts, $r(22) = .62, p < .001$, and also for arousal both in non-experts, $r(22) = .72, p < .001$, and experts, $r(22) = .85, p < .001$.

In addition, we analysed whether the aesthetic experience of music could be substantially explained by valence, arousal, and cognitive evaluation of the meanings that music evokes, using multiple regression analysis separately for the music experts and non-experts. The results for the experts showed that a linear combination of three dimensions of affective experience of verbal responses explained 90.6% of the variance in aesthetic preference of music, $F(3, 20) = 64.05, p < .001$ (Figure 2.2). The results also indicated that valence ($\beta = .54, t = 6.21, p < .001$) and arousal ($\beta = .56, t = 4.55, p < .001$) showed significant contributions to the prediction of aesthetic experience in the regression model, while the contribution of cognitive evaluation did not reach statistical significance ($\beta = -.05, t = -.47, p = .641$).

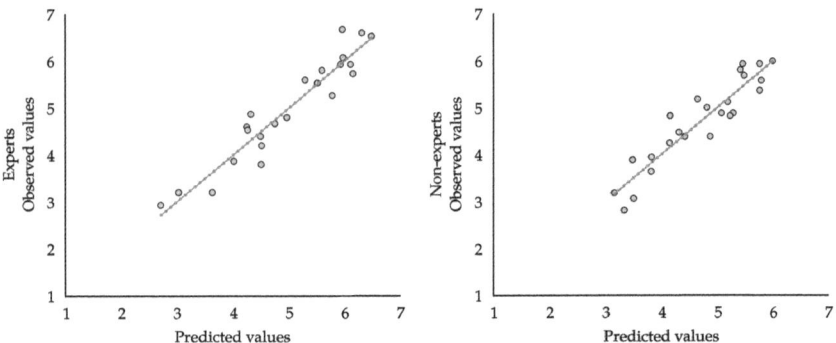

Fig. 2.2 Regression plots between observed values (ratings of aesthetic experience) versus predicted values (aesthetic experience predicted by the model) for music experts and non-experts

Similarly, the results for the non-experts showed that linear combination of three dimensions of affective experience of verbal responses explained 86.4% of the variance in aesthetic preference, $F(3, 20) = 42.47, p < .001$. The results also indicated that valence ($\beta = .66, t = 6.47, p < .001$) and arousal ($\beta = .31, t = 2.55, p = .02$) showed significant contributions to the prediction of aesthetic preference, while the contribution of cognitive evaluation did not reach statistical significance ($\beta = .10, t = .83, p = .415$).

Discussion

In two studies, we analysed the role of affective dimensions in the aesthetic experience of music. The results of the first study where participants evaluated their affective responses to the music indicated a positive association between all three affective-cognitive dimensions and the aesthetic experience. Valence showed the strongest association with aesthetic experience, followed by cognitive evaluation and finally arousal. These findings are in line with previous research and theories that have highlighted the positive effect that certain individual dimensions of subjective, affective experience have on our aesthetic experience. First of all, an aesthetic experience is understood as a state of pleasure or satisfaction (e.g., Leder et al., 2004; Reber et al., 2004). Secondly, numerous studies have shown that the intensity of arousal is associated with the intensity of music preference (e.g., Salimpoor et al., 2009). Thirdly, previous experimental studies suggested that familiarity is one of the most important factors that influence our aesthetic judgments (Brattico

& Pearce, 2013). The contribution of the present study in relation to previous research is that the various components of affective experience that were previously individually associated with aesthetic experience are now integrated into one coherent dimensional model of emotion that is able to explain 96% of the variance of aesthetic experience of music by the combined effect of the three dimensions of affective experience.

In the second study, we tested whether the aesthetic experience of music can be substantially explained by the affective experience of meanings activated while listening to that music. The results showed a strong positive correlation between the valence of activated meanings (verbal responses) and the aesthetic experience of music, both in non-experts and experts. Significant positive correlations were also obtained for both groups between the other two dimensions of cognitive evaluation and arousal and the aesthetic experience. These results suggest that for both non-experts and experts, musical preference is related to the activation of pleasant, arousing, and familiar associations. Indeed, the linear combination of the three dimensions of affective experience of the activated meanings explained a high proportion of the variance in the aesthetic experience of music for both groups, suggesting further parallels between the groups.

In the first study, cognitive evaluation showed a significant positive relationship with aesthetic experience and made a significant contribution to the explained variance of aesthetic experience in the regression model. In the second study, however, cognitive evaluation also showed a significant positive association with aesthetic experience, but the contribution of this predictor to the explanation of aesthetic experience in the regression model was not significant. The reason for this could be the lower variance in ratings of the familiarity of the associated meanings in the second study compared to the direct ratings of the familiarity of the music in the first study. Namely, participants largely rated the meanings they associated as familiar, whereas ratings of the familiarity of the music varied significantly more in the first study. Moreover, it is possible that the familiarity scale as a representative of the cognitive evaluation dimension in the second study was not the most appropriate solution for the task used in this study. In subsequent studies, it would be useful to test this result with another scale from the cognitive evaluation dimension (e.g., unclear-clear, incomprehensible-comprehensible, meaningful-meaningless, concrete-abstract, expected-unexpected) or with several of them used together, as was the case in the first study.

The results of the second study are in line with previous approaches that emphasized the role that the meanings (associations) evoked by artworks play in the formation of our aesthetic experiences (Cespedes-Guevara & Eerola, 2018; Fechner, 1866; Janković, 2014; Leder et al., 2004). These results are also consistent with findings of recent studies that used a similar approach in the visual art domain which showed that the affective experience of different meanings activated in the mind of beholders explained 95%–98% of the variance in the aesthetic experience of visual artworks (Janković, 2014; Janković et al., 2019). Similar findings obtained for music and visual artworks could suggest that music evokes aesthetic experiences through mechanisms that are common to different sensory modalities.

Based on the results of the studies presented in this chapter, we propose a Valence, Arousal, and Cognitive evaluation (VACe) model of the aesthetic experience of music. According to this model, the aesthetic experience of music is the result of affective experience (valence, arousal and cognitive evaluation) of specific meanings (perceived music characteristics, knowledge, emotions, associations from episodic memory, cognitive interpretations) activated or constructed in the mind of the person while listening to the music (Figure 2.3). Although we have focused on music in the present study, we believe that the model we propose could also be transferable to the aesthetic experiences of other forms of art.

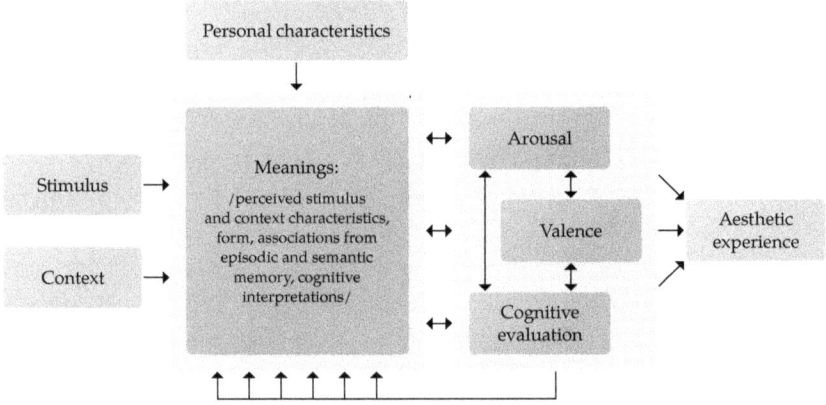

Fig. 2.3 Valence, Arousal and Cognitive evaluation (VACe) model of the aesthetic experience of music

According to the VACe model, aesthetic experience includes two broader constitutive components–meanings that are activated in the mind of the listener at the moment of perception of the music, and affective processing that is continuously executed on all activated meanings. Any meaning activated or constructed in the mind of the listener, whether it be perceptual (i.e., music characteristics), cognitive (i.e., knowledge, episodic memory, interpretation), or emotional (i.e., experiencing music as boring, happy, or sad) is automatically evaluated by three affective mechanisms. The meaning here is not conceptualised statically, in the sense of simply activating perceptual characteristics of stimuli or previously stored associations from episodic memory, but rather dynamically, as a result of the active construction of meaning that arises when the listener with particular characteristics interacts with a stimulus and context characteristics. Consequently, these meanings may be quite different in different individuals, in different age groups (Parsons, 1987), in experts and laymen, and even in the same person listening to the same piece of music on two different occasions. Moreover, as cognitive appraisal theorists have noticed, people can experience different emotions in response to the same eliciting event (Scherer, 2001) or in response to the same activated meaning, as this model suggests. Regardless, the assumption arising from the VACe model is that our aesthetic experience of music always depends on the affective experience of the meanings activated or constructed in the moment of perception of the stimulus, no matter what specific meanings, types of meanings, complexity, or number of meanings are generated.

There are a few potential limitations of these studies that need to be acknowledged. First, the results of the studies presented are based on correlations, which means that they do not themselves provide sufficient evidence for affective dimensions as causal mechanisms in the aesthetic experience of music. However, given the results of previous experimental studies that clearly demonstrated causal effects of valence, arousal, and cognitive evaluation (familiarity, clarity and meaningfulness) on aesthetic experience (Berlyne, 1971; Bornstein, 1989; Janković, 2014; Murphy & Zajonc, 1993; Reber et al., 2004), our assumption about their causal effects suggested in the VACe model was based on the results of previous studies. Another potential limitation is that, in the second study, participants expressed the meanings they had in mind during the aesthetic evaluation of music in verbal form, using a self-report. It is possible that some of the perceptual, cognitive, or emotional reactions that the participants had to the presented musical stimuli could either not at all or could not easily be transferred to the language modality and verbally expressed. For this reason, it is possible that the decline in the percentage of explained variance of aesthetic experience in the model from 96% in the first study to 90.6% and 86.4% in the second study, when meanings were verbally expressed, could be a consequence of participants' inability to express some aspects of the experience of music in words.

In terms of future research, it would be useful to extend the current findings by examining the structure of meanings activated and constructed in the mind of persons who listen to music. Namely, previous studies have suggested that the structure of activated meanings and the criteria participants use during aesthetic evaluation can vary considerably depending on age, level of expertise, or previous experience. Also, one of the open questions is whether the different types of meaning activated in the listener's mind while listening to music contribute differently to the aesthetic experience. We might ask, for example, whether the affective experiences of the sensory characteristics of music and the activated meanings from episodic memory equally contribute to the aesthetic experience.

Conclusion

In this chapter, we have presented the results of two studies whose aim was to examine the nature of the relation between affective dimensions and the aesthetic experience of music. We approached this from the framework of dimensional theories of emotions, more precisely from the framework of the three-dimensional model of affective experience (Janković, 2000a, 2014; Trkulja & Janković, 2012), where valence, arousal, and cognitive evaluation are conceptualised as three biologically based mechanisms whose role is evaluation of stimuli from the environment or organism. The results of the first study suggested that aesthetic experience is strongly related to affective valence (pleasantness) and cognitive evaluation (familiarity), and moderately related to arousal. The results of the second study suggested that the aesthetic experience of music can be substantially explained by the affective experience of meanings activated or constructed in the mind of the person while listening to that music. In other words, we like music that activates pleasant, arousing, and familiar meanings. Based on the results of these studies we proposed the Valence, Arousal, and Cognitive evaluation (VACe) model of aesthetic experience of music, where aesthetic experience is a result of affective experience of all individual meanings activated or constructed in the mind of the listener while listening to the music. The results of these studies suggested that studying the aesthetic experience of music from the perspective of core affective dimensions can provide a useful framework for understanding the role of different affective experiences in the aesthetic experience of music, and that cognitive evaluation is one of those dimensions. We also believe that the proposed VACe model can offer a useful theoretical framework for the interpretation of the results of previous studies, as well as offer hypotheses that encourage new studies in the field of the aesthetic experience of music.

Acknowledgement

This research was supported by the Ministry of Education, Science and Technological Development of the Republic of Serbia (grant number 179033; contract number: 451-03-9/2021-14/ 200163).

References

Augustin, M.D., Wagemans, J., & Carbon, C-C. (2012). All is beautiful? Generality vs. specificity of word usage in visual aesthetics. *Acta Psychologica, 139*(1), 187–201. https://doi.org/10.1016/j.actpsy.2011.10.004

Barrett, L.F., & Wager, T.D. (2006). The structure of emotion: Evidence from neuroimaging studies. *Current Directions in Psychological Science, 15*(2), 79–83. https://doi.org/10.1111/j.0963-7214.2006.00411.x

Berlyne, D.E. (1971). *Aesthetics and psychobiology.* Appleton-Century-Crofts.

Bornstein, R.F. (1989). Exposure and affect: Overview and meta-analysis of research, 1968–1987. *Psychological Bulletin, 106*(2), 265–289. https://doi.org/10.1037/0033-2909.106.2.265

Brattico, E., & Pearce, M. (2013). The neuroaesthetics of music. *Psychology of Aesthetics, Creativity, and the Arts, 7*(1), 48–61. https://doi.org/10.1037/a0031624

Cespedes-Guevara, J., & Eerola, T. (2018). Music communicates affects, not basic emotions—A constructionist account of attribution of emotional meanings to music. *Frontiers in Psychology, 9*, Article 215. https://doi.org/10.3389/fpsyg.2018.00215

Collier, G.L. (2007). Beyond valence and activity in the emotional connotations of music. *Psychology of Music, 35*(1), 110–131. https://doi.org/10.1177/0305735607068890

Ekman, P. (1992). An argument for basic emotions. *Cognition and Emotion, 6*(3–4), 169–200. https://doi.org/10.1080/02699939208411068

Fechner, G.T. (1866). Das Associationsprincip in der Aesthetik [The aesthetic association principle]. *Zeitschrift für bildende Kunst, 20*, 179–191.

Fontaine, J.R.J., Scherer, K.R., Roesch, E.B., & Ellsworth, P.C. (2007). The world of emotions is not two-dimensional. *Psychological Science, 18*(12), 1050–1057. https://doi.org/10.1111/j.1467-9280.2007.02024.x

Istók, E., Brattico, E., Jacobsen, T., Krohn, K., Müller, M., & Tervaniemi, M. (2009). Aesthetic responses to music: A questionnaire study. *Musicae Scientiae, 13*(2), 183–206. https://doi.org/10.1177/102986490901300201

Janković, D. (2000a). Konotativni aspekt značenja: Utvrđivanje latentnih dimenzija [Connotative aspect of meaning: Establishing the latent dimensions]. *Psihologija, 33*(1–2), 199–220. https://hdl.handle.net/21.15107/rcub_reff_334

Janković, D. (2000b). Konotativni aspekt značenja: Konstrukcija konotativnog diferencijala [Connotative aspect of meaning: Construction of the connotative differential]. *Psihologija, 33*(1–2), 221–238. https://hdl.handle.net/21.15107/rcub_reff_332

Janković, D. (2014). *Razvoj estetske preferencije slika* [Development of aesthetic preference of visual stimuli] (Publication No. 123456789/4956) [Doctoral dissertation, Faculty of Philosophy, University of Belgrade, Serbia]. National Repository of Dissertations in Serbia. https://hdl.handle.net/21.15107/rcub_nardus_4956

Janković, D. (2015). Cross-modal nature of evaluative meaning. In A. Galmonte & R. Actis-Grosso (eds), *Different psychological perspectives on cognitive processes: Current research trends in Alps-Adria region* (pp. 58–75). Cambridge Scholars Publishing.

Janković, D., Mađarev, M., & Živković, I. (2019). Aesthetic preference of photographs: The role of affective experience. In K. Damnjanović, O. Tošković, & S. Marković (eds), *Proceedings of the XXV scientific conference Empirical studies in psychology* (pp. 92–94). Faculty of Philosophy, University of Belgrade. http://empirijskaistrazivanja.org/wp-content/uploads/2019/12/proceedings_EIP_2019.pdf

Juslin, P.N., & Sloboda, J.A. (eds). (2010). *Handbook of music and emotion: Theory, research, applications*. Oxford University Press. https://doi.org/10.1093/acprof:oso/9780199230143.001.0001

Juslin, P.N., & Västfjäll, D. (2008). Emotional responses to music: The need to consider underlying mechanisms. *Behavioral and Brain Sciences, 31*(5), 559–575. https://doi.org/10.1017/S0140525X08005293

Konečni, V.J. (2005). The aesthetic trinity: Awe, being moved, thrills. *Bulletin of Psychology and the Arts, 5*(2), 27–44. http://konecni.ucsd.edu/pdf/2005%20Aesthetic%20Trinity,%20Bulletin%20of%20P.%20and%20A.pdf

Konečni, V.J. (2008). Does music induce emotion? A theoretical and methodological analysis. *Psychology of Aesthetics, Creativity, and the Arts, 2*(2), 115–129. https://doi.org/10.1037/1931-3896.2.2.115

Lang, P.J., Bradley, M.M., & Cuthbert, B.N. (1998). Emotion, motivation, and anxiety: Brain mechanisms and psychophysiology. *Biological Psychiatry, 44*(12), 1248–1263. https://doi.org/10.1016/s0006-3223(98)00275-3

Lazarus, R. S. (1991). *Emotion & adaptation*. Oxford University Press.

Leder, H., Belke, B., Oeberst, A., & Augustin, D. (2004). A model of aesthetic appreciation and aesthetic judgments. *British Journal of Psychology, 95*(4), 489–508. https://doi.org/10.1348/0007126042369811

Marković, S. (2012). Components of aesthetic experience: Aesthetic fascination, aesthetic appraisal, and aesthetic emotion. *i-Perception, 3*(1), 1–17. https://doi.org/10.1068/i0450aap

Murphy, S.T. & Zajonc, R.B. (1993). Affect, cognition, and awareness: Affective priming with optimal and suboptimal stimulus exposure. *Journal of Personality and Social Psychology, 64*(5), 723–739. https://doi.org/10.1037/0022-3514.64.5.723

Nordenstreng, K. (1968). A comparison between the semantic differential and similarity analysis in the measurement of musical experience. *Scandinavian Journal of Psychology, 9*(1), 89–96. https://doi.org/10.1111/j.1467-9450.1968.tb00521.x

Ortlieb, S.A., Kügel, W.A., & Carbon, C-C. (2020). Fechner (1866): The aesthetic association principle–A commented translation. *i-Perception, 11*(3). https://doi.org/10.1177/2041669520920309

Osgood, C.E., Suci, G.J., & Tannenbaum, P.H. (1957). *The measurement of meaning*. University of Illinois Press.

Parsons, M.J. (1987). *How we understand art: A cognitive developmental account of aesthetic experience*. Cambridge University Press.

Reber R., Schwarz, N., & Winkielman, P. (2004). Processing fluency and aesthetic pleasure: Is beauty in the perceiver's processing experience? *Personality and Social Psychology Review, 8*(4), 364–382. https://doi.org/10.1207/s15327957pspr0804_3

Russell, J.A. (1980). A circumplex model of affect. *Journal of Personality and Social Psychology, 39*(6), 1161–1178. https://doi.org/10.1037/h0077714

Russell, J.A. (2003). Core affect and the psychological construction of emotion. *Psychological Review, 110*(1), 145–172. https://doi.org/10.1037/0033-295X.110.1.145

Salimpoor, V.N., Benovoy, M., Longo, G., Cooperstock, J.R., & Zatorre, R.J. (2009). The rewarding aspects of music listening are related to degree of emotional arousal. *PLoS ONE, 4*(10), Article e7487. https://doi.org/10.1371/journal.pone.0007487

Scherer, K.R. (2001). Appraisal considered as a process of multilevel sequential checking. In K.R. Scherer, A. Schorr, & T. Johnstone (eds), *Appraisal processes in emotion: Theory, method, research* (pp. 92–120). Oxford University Press.

Scherer, K., & Zentner, M. (2008). Music evoked emotions are different–More often aesthetic than utilitarian. *Behavioral and Brain Sciences, 31*(5), 595–596. https://doi.org/10.1017/S0140525X08005505

Silvia, P.J. (2010). Confusion and interest: The role of knowledge emotions in aesthetic experience. *Psychology of Aesthetics, Creativity, and the Arts, 4*(2), 75–80. https://doi.org/10.1037/a0017081

Silvia, P.J. (2012). Human emotions and aesthetic experience: An overview of empirical aesthetics. In A.P. Shimamura & S.E. Palmer (eds), *Aesthetic science: Connecting minds, brains, and experience* (pp. 250–275). Oxford University Press. https://doi.org/10.1093/acprof:oso/9780199732142.003.0058

Thayer, R.E. (1996). *The origin of everyday moods: Managing energy, tension, and stress.* Oxford University Press.

Trkulja, M., & Janković, D. (2012). Towards three-dimensional model of affective experience of music. In E. Cambouropoulos, C. Tsougras, P. Mavromatis, & K. Pastiadis (eds), *Proceedings of the 12th International Conference ICMPC-ESCOM* (pp. 1016–1017). Aristotle University.

Watson, D., Wiese, D., Vaidya, J., & Tellegen, A. (1999). The two general activation systems of affect: Structural findings, evolutionary considerations, and psychobiological evidence. *Journal of Personality and Social Psychology, 76*(5), 820–838. https://doi.org/10.1037/0022-3514.76.5.820

Wedin, L. (1972). A multidimensional study of perceptual-emotional qualities in music. *Scandinavian Journal of Psychology, 13*(1), 241–257. https://doi.org/10.1111/j.1467-9450.1972.tb00072.x

Wundt, W. (1896). *Grundriss der Psychologie* [Outline of psychology]. Engelmann.

Živanović, M., Vukčević-Marković, M., & Bogunović, B. (2018). Structure of subjective experience of classical music. *Psihologija, 51*(4), 397–411. https://doi.org/10.2298/PSI170116009Z

3. Aesthetic Experiences of Contemporary Music from the Perspectives of a Composer, a Performer, and a Musicologist

Sanela Nikolić and Ivana Miladinović Prica

Introduction

Aesthetic experience presents 'one of the most poorly defined concepts in psychology and neuroscience' (Brattico et al., 2013, p. 1). Various terms are used to describe aesthetic experiences, including aesthetic processing, aesthetic emotion, aesthetic pleasure, aesthetic contemplation, or aesthetic judgments (Istók et al., 2009). The diversity of terms reveals the phenomenon's complexity, which contains both affective and cognitive components. Contemporary art in general, and contemporary classical music specifically, pose a challenge to psychological research into aesthetic experiences due to features that make them difficult to investigate and grasp. The high concentration of individualised styles and innovation in the creative process often results in significant departures from traditional canons. Indeed, aspects such as 'seeking out the new' and 'aesthetic curiosity' as immanent to contemporary art aesthetics raise questions about the communication capacities of contemporary music, and the possibility of it being understood by an audience (Pitts & Price, 2021; see Chapter 7 in this volume).

In previous studies, the aesthetic experience of music has primarily been equated with the emotions that music evokes (see Juslin & Västfjäll, 2008, p. 559). Yet the field of music and emotion studies is complex, reflecting the mutual inconsistency between many different research standpoints, terms used, conceptual solutions, and the defining relationships between everyday emotions, music-evoked emotions, aesthetic emotions, and judgments. The difference between perceived and felt emotions makes these considerations even more complicated. For example, Juslin and Västfjäll (2008) claimed that multiple mechanisms of the induction of musical emotions are not unique only to music, and that 'the study of musical emotions could benefit the emotion field as a whole' (p. 559). Konečni (2008) proposed the state of 'being moved' as a replacement for a category of musical emotions within his Aesthetic Trinity Theory (p. 582).

There are other theoretical alternatives, such as the insight that music-evoked emotions are somewhat different from real-life emotions, and more often aesthetic than utilitarian (Scherer & Zentner, 2008, p. 595); or the claims that 'music produces aesthetic pleasure, a sense of peace and relaxation and/or stimulation and arousal' and 'that music is about aesthetic pleasure linked principally to musical structure' (Rozin & Rozin, 2008, p. 594). The last claim connects the appearance of aesthetic emotion with a cognitive understanding of the musical structure. Here, questioning the role of expertise in the cognitive aspect of contemporary music perception is particularly important. Thus, some contemporary views presuppose that aesthetic judgments and aesthetic modes of engagement are vital elements of aesthetic emotions evoked primarily by cognitive mechanisms. In this case, the difference is made between causal inattentive listening, which may result in basic everyday emotions, and focused listening with an aesthetic attitude that can induce aesthetic emotions (Brattico & Pearce, 2013; see Chapter 4 in this volume).

Since we were focused on the question of how diverse classical music knowledge and expertise is integrated into aesthetic experiences, we transferred the perspective of aesthetic processing from the contemporary visual arts, where aesthetic processing is defined as 'the sensation-based evaluation of an entity with respect to the [...] conceptual system' (Jacobsen, 2006, p. 158). In this perspective, a perceiver's level of knowledge about the art is an important factor on which the outcome of a complex emotional and cognitive multistage process of aesthetic experience is based (Leder et al., 2004, p. 505). 'Consequently, the viewer's expertise is probably of ever-growing importance, because only through knowledge about stylistic devices and underlying ideas can the viewer dissolve the ambiguities an artwork poses' (Augustin & Leder, 2006, pp. 138–139). In line with this, some studies have examined the role of art knowledge and education as facilitators of aesthetic emotions in both the experience of music and painting (Miu et al., 2016), or investigated the differences between the aesthetic experience of trained musicians and non-trained listeners (Müller et al., 2010).

Gaver and Mandler (1987) observed that:

> to listen to a piece of music is to be engaged in a constant process of interpreting it by activating relevant schemas. [...] The number of schemas that may be active and the resulting richness of the interpretation reached depends on both the internal and external structure of the music and on the listeners' knowledge of the music, [and] the richness of their schematic representation. (pp. 264–265)

Deliège (1989) and Deliège and El Ahmadi (1990) gained interesting results in an experimental study where participants (musicians and non-musicians) identified the cues for segmentation of a musical piece during auditory perceptive analysis that coincided with the structure of the music, providing an important theoretical contribution to the cognitive psychology of contemporary art music forms.

Furthermore, as Krumhansl and Agres (2008) noted, contemporary 'empirical research extensively documents that listeners' knowledge about melody, harmony, and rhythm influences what they expect in a given musical context' (p. 584). Thus, in several theoretical models of the compositional process, music knowledge is considered a part of the composing system (Beauvois, 2018; Brown, 2003; Brown & Dillon, 2012; Dean, 2017; Sloboda, 1986). It is emphasised that from the perspective of the composer, music cannot be experienced without direct knowledge of music and engagement with the interactive elements of music material and structure, where the aesthetic experience relates to the meaningful engagement and analysis of the outcomes of compositional processes (Brown & Dillon, 2012, p. 79).

Certainly, the metacognitive strategies in generative and exploratory phases of the creative process (Finke et al., 1992), related to elaboration and hierarchical organisation and structuring of ideas, solving problems, and finding solutions (Bogunović & Popović Mlađenović, 2014), as well as the 'quality of the creative outcomes will be influenced by the extent of the person's knowledge and how the elements of that knowledge are accessed and combined' (Bogunović, 2019, p. 100).

When it comes to music performance studies, the opinion that the cognitive principle of structural interpretation is the determinant of performance expression, 'aesthetic necessity', and the basic source of expressiveness in performance is widely accepted (Clarke, 1991, p. 87; Doğantan-Dack, 2014, pp. 10–11; Juslin, 2003, p. 290). Some authors speak about 'structural expression' as part of the communication process during the performance (see Bogunović & Popović Mlađenović, 2014). This corresponds with the results of the newest research study, where musical properties are seen as the base on which the aesthetic experience of contemporary classical music processing starts and reflects its further cognitive and emotional processing (Mencke et al., 2023, p. 290). Understanding the musical structure is considered a prerequisite for the successful aesthetic experience of classical music. Music-specific knowledge is stressed as a crucial factor for the successful cognitive mastering of music material. Thus, in recent research, where the role of expert knowledge in professional music critics' experiences was analysed (Nikolić, 2020), it was proven that music-related expertise is an important variable that feeds the aesthetic experience of trained music professionals.

The role of expertise in art appreciation was inferred by Augustin and Leder (2006), who 'found evidence that the experts would categorise and interpret a piece of art based on style, while the non-experts would refer more to personal experiences regarding feelings' (pp. 150, 151). Interestingly, it has been pointed out that 'the possibility to use the linguistic labels of musical events enable musically trained listeners to encode musical structures in a more relevant way' (Bigand & Poulin-Charronnat, 2006, p. 102). Furthermore, Istók et al. (2009) concluded that musicians describe their listening experience using adjectives related to novelty and originality rather than to emotional characteristics (p. 199). So, we intend to stress the role of specialised music knowledge, presupposing that

> every time a subject generates a response (e.g., 'beauty' judgment or preference rating) to an artwork, the response reflects not only the proximal cognitive and emotional processes that underlie it, but also their distal developmental (including educational) histories. […] [P]recisely because expertise […] has been shown to be a strong determinant of art

perception [...] it has been incorporated as a critical variable in major contemporary theories of aesthetic judgment and creativity. (Vartanian & Kaufman, 2013, p. 161)

When it comes to the role of knowledge in emotional responses to musical stimuli, the generative role of music-related knowledge was stressed a long time ago in Meyer's (1956) grounding theoretical framework that binds perception, cognition, and emotional response to music. Namely,

> music produces emotions because listeners actively generate expectations and different degrees of tensions and relaxation from different sources of expectation, one of them being extra-opus knowledge or style knowledge, which does not depend strongly on explicit musical training; non-musicians internalise it through passive exposure. (Krumhansl & Agres, 2008, p. 584)

In other words, music-specific knowledge appears as a critical variable in forming expectations from music, as a constitutive element of the cognitive mastering of music, and, consequently, as a factor for positive or negative arousal and aesthetic judgment.

In the present study, our attention was concerned with the music-related knowledge and experience of contemporary music from the perspective of three music experts involved in creating a particular musical piece—from its composition to public performance and, finally, its critical reception. The research assumes that music-related knowledge is reflected in the communication of emotional and cognitive processes by musicians and embedded in musical structure expression and aesthetic responses.

Aims

This research aimed to: (1) analyse the verbalised aesthetic experiences of the three experts engaged in music creation, conceptualisation, and appreciation—that is, the composer, the performer (piano player), and the musicologist; (2) confirm how specialised music-related knowledge and proficiency are integrated into the participants' aesthetic experience of a contemporary music work; and (3) establish the differences in the participants' aesthetic experiences depending on their role in making music and, hence, in interpreting, understanding, and explicating the same musical piece.

We were interested in their experience of the piece of music, addressing it from the participants' different roles while not being focused on examining the specific life cycle of the piece's origination and the compositional process itself. The literature review shows that no prior studies have dealt with the phenomena of music professionals' aesthetic experience of contemporary classical music using the Interpretative Phenomenological Analysis (IPA). We believe this represents the novelty of this study. We anticipate that the insightful, in-depth statements about the aesthetic experience of contemporary music by these experts may contribute to the understanding of the aesthetics of contemporary music, and may facilitate communication between those who create and receive the music (see also Chapter 7 in this volume).

Method

Participants

Three musicians with expertise and long experience in contemporary music, especially its creation and performance, took part in the study from the point of view of the composer, performer, and musicologist.

Miroslav Miša Savić (b. 1954), one of the most significant Serbian contemporary composers (C) of the neo-avant-garde (Masnikosa, 2021), graduated from Vasilije Mokranjac's composition class at the Faculty of Music in Belgrade (see Serbian Academy of Sciences and Art, 2023). During the 1970s and 1980s, his work was radically innovative in Serbian and Yugoslav artistic circles (Šuvaković et al., 2016, p. 979). In addition to composing music, he is the author of various kinds of works in the domains of multimedia, video, performance, and computer installation. As a member and co-founder of the composer group Opus 4, and the director of the music programme of the Students' Cultural Centre in Belgrade (Miladinović Prica, 2021, p. 15), he advocated a new, 'open' approach to music. He had a significant role in originating Serbian minimalism, experimentalism, and electronic music (Emmery, 2021).

Nada Kolundžija (b. 1952) (Kolundžija, n.d.) is a distinguished Serbian pianist (P). For more than four decades, she has been introducing Belgrade and Serbian audiences to the works of the 20th century classics with great success (Miladinović Prica, 2021). She expanded her repertoire to include works by Serbian composers, many of whom have dedicated their work to her. As a professor at the Faculty of Music in Belgrade, she has inspired many young musicians to perform contemporary music. Since the mid-1970s, she has collaborated closely with Miroslav Miša Savić, among others, within the Ensemble for Different New Music [Ansambl za drugu novu muziku] (Ensemble for Different New Music, n.d.), founded in 1977 (Ensemble for Different New Music, 2023; Miladinović Prica, 2017). She is the winner of important awards including a Gold Medal at the Global Music Awards in 2020, the Aleksandar Pavlović Award from the Association of Composers of Serbia for lifetime achievements in the promotion of Serbian music in 2019, and a Lifetime Achievement Award from the Association of the Music Artists of Serbia in 2016. Kolundžija's recordings are available through five LP records, nine CDs, and numerous radio and television recordings.

Milan Milojković, PhD (b. 1986) is a musicologist (M) and Associate Professor at the Department of Musicology and Ethnomusicology, Academy of Arts in Novi Sad. He publishes articles and chapters in relevant Serbian publications concerning electronic music and new technologies in contemporary Serbian music (Milojković, 2018), and is author of the book *Digitalna tehnologija u srpskoj umetničkoj muzici* [Digital technology in Serbian art music] (Milojković, 2020). Milojković is also the music editor at the Third Program of Radio Belgrade, Serbia. He designs analogue and digital musical instruments and performs music with various, mostly chamber, ensembles.

Music material

The music piece *Oh Light, oh Tenderness, Oh Darkness, Fandango for Dušan* [O svetlosti, o nežnosti, o mraku, fandango za Dušana], for piano and virtual tape, was composed by Miroslav Miša Savić (Kolundžija, 2020). The work was performed for the first time in the Ceremonial Hall of Belgrade City Hall on 13 December 2019. The unique aspect of this composition lies in the fact that the pianist, Nada Kolundžija, played an essential part in the creative process, acting as co-composer. Her voice reading the poem 'Oh Light, Oh Tenderness, Oh Darkness', by the well-known Serbian poet Dušan Vukajlović (1948–1994; Vukajlović, 1995), was passed through the open source software Pure Data. The program monitored the amplitude and frequency of her voice and, based on this, generated an electronic MIDI recording, transposing the live voice into the electronic piano and voice sound. The tape with electronic (piano and voice) sound became the basis of the composition. In creating the piano part, the pianist combined aspects of Miroslav Miša Savić's composed piano material with selected excerpts (Figure 3.1) from *Fandango*, by the Spanish composer Antonio Soler (1729–1783), to create a final satisfactory version of the piano part (Savić, 2020). However, during the preparation of the performance, the composer and the pianist were not satisfied with certain solutions, so they changed the material and several iterations were exchanged between the co-authors before the final version of the piece came about. It is essential to recognise that Savić used computer algorithms, which are effective in terms of de-subjectivising music and suspending aesthetic judgment. Consequently, he invites the pianist to be active in composing, that is, to be responsible for choosing musical material. The pianist's interaction with the electronics as a virtual but coequal protagonist was vital for creating a specific amalgam that blurs the division between the composer and his performer, analogue, and digital mediums. The mutual challenges that piano and electronics set before each other, their joint play in illuminating and transforming each other, create a dynamic and imaginative sonic universe. Therefore, the sounds' origin, identity, and the difference between the piano/acoustic and electronic components are sometimes difficult to distinguish.

Data collection procedure

As to the methodological approach, we decided to use a qualitative method which has great value when 'a process of searching for meaning and understanding, seeking to illuminate participants' realities' (Williamon et al., 2021, p. 231) is the aim of the research study. We gathered qualitative data using short, semi-structured interviews conducted two years after the composition had its premiere performance. All three participants were asked to verbalise their impressions concerning their aesthetic experiences, emotional responses, and reflections while composing, performing, and listening to the musical composition. The participants were prompted in the following way: 'Please verbalise your aesthetic experience of the composition *Oh Light, oh Tenderness, Oh Darkness, Fandango for Dušan* in two ways: How do you reflect on/ understand the musical piece and how do you emotionally react to it?'

Questions and answers were given in written form and sent via email. Participants preferred writing down their narratives instead of having live conversations. The intention was to get personally salient in-depth contributions that would capture the core of their experience in a way that enabled us to work analytically with a detailed written narrative. After responding to the first round of questions, the piano player returned her narrative but needed additional, more concrete, and directed questions. Based on her initial narrative, we provided additional questions and opened a written dialogue to stimulate a more precise verbalisation of her thoughts and experiences. The other two participants did not need further encouragement to express their reflections. The average narrative we received from each participant was about 600 words long.

Data analysis

For qualitative data analysis, we chose IPA, which focuses on understanding the lived experiences of individual participants and, often, how these relate to or differ from those of others (Williamon et al., 2021, p. 236), trying to obtain in-depth comprehension. The idiographic focus of this method means that IPA aims to offer insights into how a person makes sense of a given phenomenon, making this method meaningful for our exploration (Eatough & Smith, 2008; Smith, 2004). Thus, the participants' narratives were treated as a window into their music experience. The first author performed the IPA.

The data analysis sequence of steps was as follows. Firstly, the pianist's, composer's, and musicologist's written narratives were read multiple times to extract meanings. The clusters of meanings were noted down, those relevant to each participant as well as to the data set as a whole (see Williamon et al., 2021, pp. 245–246). The identified significant elements were related to the content of words that participants used (what is being reflected upon), language use (features such as key phrases, metaphors, symbols, and explanations), descriptions of emotional responses, and the presence of specific terminology and concepts. Secondly, after completing the initial noting, a more interpretative stage of meta-critical analysis and grouping of identified meaningful elements was implemented to generate themes for each participant. The next step was to search for emerging, superordinate themes across all participants' narratives, actively interpreting clusters of participants' words. Each of the themes was supported by extracts from the verbal data made by the participants (see Williamon et al., 2021, p. 246). Finally, the third step of data analysis was related to the IPA's focus on convergence and divergence within a participant's experiences in such a way as to connect and compare themes. Thus, a comparative analysis was made to identify the mutual connections and differences within the generated themes concerning the specific musical roles and expertise participants have regarding composing, performing, and critical listening.

Findings

The results presented here are organised in two parallel ways: systematically, following the three identified themes presented within the perspective of each participant; and comparatively, highlighting the commonalities and differences that the themes reflect among the participants.

First theme: Aesthetic experience as a feeling of 'music completeness'

The first theme arose from participants' descriptions of the aesthetic experiences as 'feeling' music, but not in the way of some specific 'simple' feeling, but rather in generalised terms of music as an aesthetic event that is related to cognitive and perceptual processes, as the feeling of 'music completeness'. For example, the piano player formulated her initial narrative on aesthetic experience by talking about the process of collaborating on the creation of the piece and identifying the moments when she felt that she should stop working on it any further and that 'everything is in its place'. Her answers suggest that the pianist perceives music as a primarily experiential phenomenon, that is, auditory, sensational, and nonverbal, which is not possible to transfer into other systems of expression, such as language. Conclusions about music are guided by the feeling of aesthetic completeness, that something is 'good and in the right place', when inner auditory representations are in congruence with the external sound of the music. There are numerous narrative segments where the performer articulates her aesthetic experience as determined by the feelings retrieved from the current and past involvement with performing and listening to music. In the participants' quotes, certain phrases have been bolded for emphasis by the first author.

> It is hard for me to answer all these questions. I never ask them myself. Talking about music that is so abstract seems impossible to me. The answers I get **through playing** are not the ones that can be translated into words. During work preparation, conscious thinking has a role to play. It does help to reach the goal faster, which is 'to put everything where it belongs'. The place is **felt**. It is comfortable, and there is no need to look for anything else. This is preceded by [musical] work, listening, searching... (P)

> The decision to shape the musical piece was a process driven by **intuition and experience**. Like cooking. Spices are added, we try the taste, and we go on until we reach—mmmmmmmmmmmmm, it is delicious. (P)

> Fandango is a dance, so, in this case, I tried to get that dancing **feeling** while playing some segments of the composition. (P)

> I started listening to various fandangos to bring that **feeling** into the score. However, the music sheet was great and interesting, but I couldn't **feel** it like a fandango. And so, while still listening, I came across Soler's fandango and started playing it. [...] I took scissors and began to cut parts from both scores from which the material with the tape could be further built and aligned. I arranged those parts until it **seemed** to me that nothing needed to be changed anymore. (P) [Figure 3.1]

> [...] I did all this in parallel while listening to the tape. And really, **everything was placed where it belonged**. Although a new score was made, there was still room for me to **feel** when I 'entered' the tape sound, so it kept the energy of freshness and the power of spontaneity... (P)

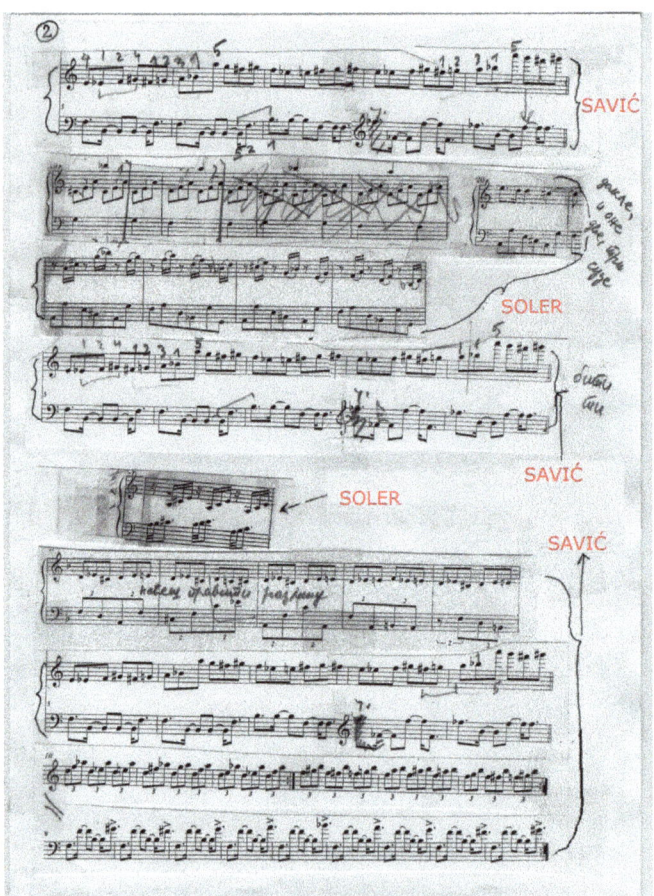

Fig. 3.1 The performer's presentation of 'finding the right feeling' for the musical piece through combining parts of Savić's original and parts of Soler's score (the names of the two composers are indicated in red colour)

When it comes to the composer's narrative, a description of the aesthetic experience as generated from feelings is not expressed, probably due to the compositional strategy of 'using computer algorithms, which are effective in de-subjectivising music and suspending aesthetic judgment'.

In the musicologist's narrative, the 'emotional effect' of music is tackled and defined as 'pleasure in sound'. Two equivalent ways to describe satisfaction felt by music are pointed out: (1) enjoying a piece of music as a 'beautiful object', in terms of admiring the composer's skilful handling and structuring of sound material, and (2), equivalent to that, a feeling of 'euphoria and optimism' caused by the effect of 'musical surprise' that occurs when discovering an unexpected music system. The latter is known in the cognitive psychology of music as a trigger of emotional response, as the unexpected musical event that is not in agreement with the 'expectations' built up by experience and knowledge (Huron, 2006; Juslin, 2019; Juslin & Västfjäll, 2008; Meyer, 1956).

> The **emotional effect** was the pleasure 'in sound', above all, since the work of music can be enjoyed as a 'beautiful object' of music art, only based on modelling its sound content, which, in addition to establishing complex (and therefore satisfactory) relationships with the past and contemporary music scene, is skilfully composed, and directed towards the settled goal. The second **feeling** I could describe is in connection with the nature of electro-acoustic sound, i.e., manners of using, in this case, digital musical tools. The equivalent of that **feeling** may be found in writing and listening to (tonal or atonal) counterpoint compounds according to pre-set rules, which on the one hand, manifest as music limitations, but on the other, the limitations arise from a person's insufficient knowledge of physical laws. Every moment of overcoming one system's rules by discovering another, new one, evokes a **feeling** of euphoria and optimism. (M)

Second theme: Imagery and metaphors as expressions of experience

The second superordinate theme was drawn from the examples of the participants' deliberate description of the music experience through specific metaphors and almost literary-oriented language style and terminology. For example, the cognitive elaboration of the relationship between performer and computer is experienced as if the computer program is a living machine resisting cooperation:

> The computer program that Miša used was a partner in creating the work. Unpredictable, uncontrollable, surprising... [...] The result of the poetry reading passed through the computer program was amazing. Although the program reacted to my voice, its reactions were utterly unexpected and unpredictable. There, it was not possible to achieve the interaction I expected. I changed the reading tempo, stretched the words, took breaks, and changed the pitch of the voice. I tried to somehow be in the community with the program, but it was still **completely independent**

and non-cooperative. I was appalled by this **unpredictable 'cooperation'** with the machine. (P)

From the composer's perspective, this theme expressed his continuous challenge in 'constructing' the piece's architecture and solving problems he faced on the way. Again, here we meet the need for 'aesthetic completeness', as in the pianist's reports of the process of searching for the right form and sound of the interpretation:

> I built my aesthetics like a tower of cards, which was increasingly threatened with the danger of collapsing by adding new cards (the aesthetics of a new musical piece). That is why creating new works challenges me with increased risk and difficulty. I thought of each new piece as the last one composed. However, the remaining deck of unallocated cards and the **feeling of incompleteness** forced me to take risks repeatedly. (C)

The narrative of the musicologist lacks the literary writing style, namely, the personal imagery provoked by the musical piece. The musicologist avoids poetic metaphors, maintaining their evaluative approach by using professional, stylistic terms and music expectations based on expert knowledge, which belongs to the third theme.

Third theme: Aesthetic experience and prevalence of musical knowledge

The aesthetic experience of the musical piece and its relationship to specific expertise is present within the narratives of all three participants, especially those of the composer and musicologist. However, the type of knowledge that is required and relied on is not only theoretical knowledge *per se*, but also the knowledge acquired by music-specific training and education as a deliberate mix of personal music preferences, expert attention, critical reflection on style, structure, and the application of aesthetic concepts, including what is shared and what is new for a particular composer:

> This composition is very special and layered. Various layers are involved in it. Sound-transformed poetry is its basis. The actuality is present through the score of the composer and the past through the score of Antonio Soler. Aleatoric elements were very present in its creation, in all layers, from reading the song, 'the piano that speaks', and both scores.

The composition is 'tailored' on elements of aleatoric. That's how it got structured. (P)

My aesthetic ideal consisted of a minimum of change that allows repetitiveness of dramatic tension, increase and/or decrease of tension, but also consistency. It was based on an increased aversion to those music patterns that were far from the proportions of pitch and rhythm and that made an unpleasant noise or clamour. In this way, I established a special non-aesthetic, the beauty of dislike. This non-aesthetic for me was a clear boundary that separated the acceptable from the unacceptable and by the nature of things, what was acceptable was more or less undefined, indefinite. Formal aesthetics such as Eduard Hanslick, Carl Dahlhaus, Ivan Foht, Dragan Jeremić, and others did not help establish my aesthetic theory. (C)

The difficulty of this challenge was partly influenced by the prejudice I always had towards the combination of poetry and music. For me, reciting poetry accompanied by music has always been at the lowest aesthetic level, on the unbearably pathetic scale of emotional understanding of sound. And that is exactly what I took as a topic or an **aesthetic challenge** to be solved. The reciting piano performer, her voice 'playing' the piano thanks to a computer program, and a whole series of shifted roles served to turn a non-aesthetic situation into a new and possibly, acceptable aesthetic. The element of improvisation included in all dimensions of the work further complicates this task. (C)

Collecting **non-aesthetic** criteria was especially valuable to me in algorithmic composition, when a computer program would generate, in part or whole, a music structure, and when the proposed material should be rejected or changed. As that experience increased, so did the role of the computer program. The compass of **positive aesthetic criteria** was a reliable tool for navigating an unknown space. (C)

I understand composition as a significant contribution to the development of sonification practice in our [Serbian] electro-acoustic music and as a welcome effort to further automate and implement music information retrieval (MIR) as part of a composition practice. Although there were similar aspirations in our musical past (such as Vladimir Jovanović's *Ornithophony* or Miroslav Miša Savić's *White Angel*; Milojkovic, 2020) this work differs from the previous ones primarily in instrumentation since it is a concert piece for piano and recorded electronic part, while earlier this type of work was related to the studio conditions or gallery installations. (M)

The first impression of listening is that this is 'real' Miroslav Miša Savić, the sound quality of the work is like that of my favourite compositions from his earlier works, especially for piano. The second impression was a surprise at how much vivacity the sonification process resulted in [...]. I similarly experienced extended techniques at the end of the composition, which was a welcome contrasting segment, 'refreshing' the overall sound result. (M)

Discussion

The final aim of the analysis was to compare superordinate themes between the narratives of the three participants. The condensed presentation of the IPA results contains the aesthetic and cognitive layer of the findings seen through the perspective of specialised knowledge and experience of music (Figure 3.2).

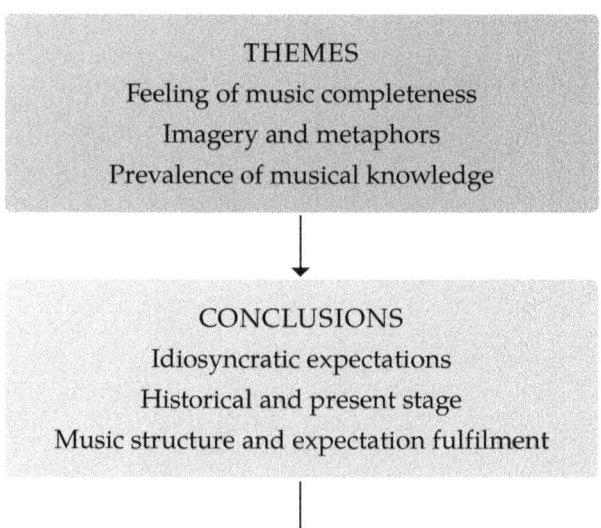

Fig. 3.2 Overview of research outcomes

The discussion focuses on three points:

Firstly, the perception of the aesthetic quality and character of the musical piece is driven by expectations that are idiosyncratic and based on the aesthetic experiences and expert knowledge of each participant. The performer's aesthetic experience is driven by her intuitive feeling for music and long-term experience of performing and listening to music. For example, to reach the fandango character of the composition, the performer compared and tried to match this new aesthetic experience with the previous aesthetic experiences of a particular type of music for dancing—the listening and performing experience of fandango.

On the other hand, the composer showed a tendency to achieve the consistency of his conceptual set-up, and elaborated compositional rules within the newly created composition as *differentia specifica* of his poietics. The composer's narrative of the aesthetic experience is presented as a theoretical elaboration of his attitudes towards the combination of poetry and music, the 'aesthetic challenge', and the technique of 'shifted roles' that could turn a 'non-aesthetic situation' into a new one that is aesthetically acceptable. The composer's narrative is marked by cognitive elaboration and decision-making concerning generating music material and structure. It presents a consistent personal aesthetic theory of transforming the non-aesthetic into the aesthetic through applying the appropriate poietic—conceptual and technical—compositional procedures.

Interestingly, both the criteria of the composer and performer appear in the narrative of the musicologist. Thus, the word 'fandango' in the composition's title directed both the performer and the musicologist to base a positive aesthetic evaluation on expecting and reaching the feeling—in creation and reception—of the fandango character. On the other hand, the composer and the musicologist expected sound expression of theoretically explicated compositional procedures, noted in the recorded composition's accompanying note (Savić, 2020). In both examples, the aesthetic experience was directed by expectations and references outside the music itself—by the verbally formulated dancing character of the composition and the theoretically explained compositional procedures that should be perceived in music through the experience of listening.

Secondly, the aesthetic experience of music is a process that operates in a circular progression involving two stages. These are the *historical stage*, based on past individual emotional and cognitive experiences, and the *present stage*, based on the musical structure of the current aesthetic object. These two stages are present in a circular relationship with different degrees of intensity. In the case of the composer, the deliberate cognitive processing of music based on conceptually founded and elaborated individual artistic poietics, and the expectation to 'hear' this in the sound, are dominant. In the case of the pianist, the previous personal auditory experiences of music as musical completeness are dominant.

In the case of the musicologist, the auditory experience passes through cognitive processing of specific classical music knowledge and training, with a transition towards emotional experiences. Emotional experiences are the result of deliberate cognitive mastering of music, in terms of surprise and satisfaction derived from the logic and expectations of musical material structuring. Thus, it seems that both the pianist and musicologist feel the logic of music both intuitively and deliberately simultaneously. However, emotion of the musicologist is aesthetic, where the emotional reaction to music is founded on the idea of experiencing beauty through the recognition and evaluation of the music's structure, characteristics, and properties of music material. This corresponds with the previous empirical research conclusions that 'the adjective "beautiful" was the most frequently used term to describe the aesthetic values of music', both by music experts and laymen (see Istók et al., 2009, pp. 191, 195). What is prominent is that in the cases of all three participants, the musical expertise is strongly grounded within the historical stage, not only in the form of knowledge about music, but also as expertise that has been acquired by long-term experiential training in creating and performing, that is, in listening to music.

Thirdly, and consequently, the findings showed that the mechanism of *music expectancy* (Huron, 2006; Meyer, 1956) has a crucial role in forming the aesthetic response to a music piece. This concerns expectancy that is fulfilled by the music material and structure, and by the induced emotions that belong to the category of aesthetic emotions. As already noted, music expectancy is important when considering how music elicits emotions, and was initially explained in Meyer's theoretical framework on musical expectancy and emotion:

> [An] important aspect of Meyer's theory is that it de-emphasises the general mood (such as happy, sad, or peaceful) engendered by passages, movements, or entire musical pieces and emphasises instead the moment-to-moment response to the ongoing music flow. The theory's essential claim is that music produces emotions because listeners actively generate expectations (mostly unconsciously) for what is to follow [...], and the response depends on how expectations are fulfilled, perhaps in a particularly artful way or at an unexpected delay. (Krumhansl & Agres, 2008, pp. 584)

Regarding Meyer's sources of music expectation, expertise was a primary source of anticipation among our participants, firmly integrated and developed within the aesthetic experiences, and accompanied by the development of style-related processing. Expertise as a source of expectation (from both composer and musicologist) is why the dominant criterion for making positive aesthetic judgments is established by evaluating music structure from the standpoint of stylistic and poietic conceptualisations. Next, an emphasis on the value of originality and novelty in structuring music expectation fulfilment had a significant role. The narratives of the composer and musicologist reflect the potential for cognitive music mastering through acquiring expertise: knowledge of musical structure, formal properties, and style. Successful cognitive mastering induces positive aesthetic emotions. Even in the case of the pianist and her description of intuitive music completeness as 'feeling', the experience is based on the artistic music expertise that determines what should be expected and heard in a piece of music, including musical structure and the properties of music components and form.

To summarise, the three conceptualisations of music or three types of music expectation that interweavingly induce the aesthetic experience of music experts are: (1) that music is an aesthetic object that is meant for listening to, feeling, and judging based on the expectations driven by the long-term experience of performing and listening to classical music structures; (2) that music as an aesthetic object is expected to reflect a composer's individual and theoretically elaborated concepts of how the piece of classical music should be made and (3) that music is an aesthetic object with autonomous structural characteristics that is expected to reflect its specific place within the history of classical music and its relations with other music pieces.

Conclusion

In conclusion, specialised art knowledge can play a salient role in experiencing art by acting as an underlayer of aesthetic experience and aesthetic emotions, and it has the power to put into operation, through an individual pattern, both emotional and cognitive aspects of aesthetic experience. Let us suppose that everyone is defined by specific self-developmental history (Vartanian & Kaufman, 2013). In that case, specialised art knowledge is not something other than the phenomena of aesthetic experience but is immanent to it, an essential factor that makes each person's developmental history unique. The comparison of the three narratives reflects the fact that the nature of specialised classical music knowledge is *doubled* and that dual core comes from the different developmental histories of the participants in terms of their music education and various types of involvement with music.

Namely, we may conclude that one type of expertise as a layer of aesthetic music experience is a type of *theoretical knowledge*—learning and knowledge acquisition through which models of music structure and style are integrated and developed within the aesthetic experiences. The other type of expertise could be named *experiential knowledge*—the knowledge that comes from experience and training in creating, performing, and listening to music, and is related to the person's mastery of skills in the appreciation of music acquired by their long-term lived experiences with music. Thus, the piano performer draws on her experience intuitively, based on internalised, automated knowledge about music, just as the other two respondents do. However, we should not neglect the fact that the performer talked about 'notes falling into place', the composer about 'dislike', and the musicologist about 'euphoria and optimism'. This means that even when the double nature of expertise is developed to its full potential, the cognitive processing of aesthetic music experience and music expectations always leads to the expression of a unique emotional response. This emotional response, as aesthetic emotion, is attached to and inseparable from the effects of both theoretical and experiential knowledge. This conclusion corresponds with current findings that the aesthetic experience brought about by contemporary music is mainly related to the successful cognitive mastering of music's formal properties (Brattico et al., 2013). We can see this as inherent in the aesthetic responses of all three participants.

Our findings further confirm existing insights that the perception of contemporary music results from conscious immersion in music, where the individual dedicates attention to perceptual, cognitive, and affective interpretation based on the *formal properties* of music (Brattico et al., 2013; Brattico & Pierce, 2013). The aesthetic experience of contemporary classical music is brought about by the mutual interplay of music expectation, experiential and theoretical knowledge, and, primarily, from immersive engagement with musical properties and structure.

Acknowledgements

We are very grateful to Miroslav Miša Savić, Nada Kolundžija, and Milan Milojković, who kindly agreed to participate in this research and gave their written consent to be the subjects and named interviewees of this study.

References

Augustin, M.D., & Leder, H. (2006). Art expertise: A study of concepts and conceptual spaces. *Psychological Science, 48*(2), 135–156.

Beauvois, M.W. (2018). Alkan's 'Petits Préludes' for organ: A case study of composition by constraints. *Music & Science, 1*, 1–19. https://doi.org/10.1177/2059204317733107

Bigand, E., & Poulin-Charronnat, B. (2006). Are we 'experienced listeners'? A review of the musical capacities that do not depend on formal musical training. *Cognition, 100*(1), 100–130. https://doi.org/10.1016/j.cognition.2005.11.007

Bogunović, B. (2019). Creative cognition in composing music. *New Sound: International Journal of Music, 53*(1), 89–117. http://ojs.newsound.org.rs/index.php/NS/article/view/No.53_89-117

Bogunović, B., & Popović Mlađenović, T. (2014). Emotion, cognition, and imagery. In T. Popović Mlađenović, B. Bogunović, & I. Perković (eds),

Interdisciplinary approach to music: Listening, performing, composing (pp. 191–227). Faculty of Music, University of Arts in Belgrade.

Brattico, E., Bogert, B., & Jacobsen, T. (2013). Toward a neural chronometry for the aesthetic experience of music. *Frontiers in Psychology, 4*, Article 206. https://doi.org/10.3389/fpsyg.2013.00206

Brattico, E., & Pearce, M. (2013). The neuroaesthetics of music. *Psychology of Aesthetics, Creativity, and the Arts, 7*(1), 48–61. https://doi.org/10.1037/a0031624

Brown, A.R., & Dillon, S. (2012). Meaningful engagement: Creative experiences with music composition. In D. Collins (ed.), *The act of musical composition: Studies in the creative process* (pp. 79–110). Routledge.

Brown, M. (2003). *Debussy's 'Iberia': Studies in musical genesis and structure*. Oxford University Press.

Clarke, E. (1991). Expression and communication in musical performance. In J. Sundberg, L. Nord, & R. Carlson (eds), *Music, language, speech, and brain. Wenner-Gren Center international symposium series* (pp. 184–193). Palgrave. https://doi.org/10.1007/978-1-349-12670-5_17

Dean, R.T. (2017). Creating music: Composition. In R. Ashley & R. Timmers (eds), *The Routledge companion to music cognition* (pp. 251–264). Routledge. https://doi.org/10.4324/9781315194738

Deliège, I. (1989). A perceptual approach to contemporary musical forms. *Contemporary Music Review, 4*(1), 213–30. https://doi.org/10.1080/07494468900640301

Deliège, I., & El Ahnmadi, A. (1990). Mechanisms of cue extraction in musical groupings: A study of perception on 'Sequenza VI' for viola solo by Luciano Berio. *Psychology of Music, 18*(1), 18–44. https://doi.org/10.1177/0305735690181003

Doğantan-Dack, M. (2014). Philosophical reflections on expressive music performance. In D. Fabian, R. Timmers, & E. Schubert (eds), *Expressiveness in music performance: Empirical approaches across styles and cultures* (pp. 3–21). Oxford University Press. https://doi.org/10.1093/acprof:oso/9780199659647.003.0001

Eatough, V., & Smith, J.A. (2008). Interpretative phenomenological analysis. In C. Willig & W. Stainton-Rogers (eds), *The SAGE handbook of qualitative research in psychology* (pp. 179–194). SAGE Publications Ltd. https://doi.org/10.4135/9781848607927

Emmery, L. (2021). Serbian twentieth- and twenty-first-century musical avant-gardes: An introduction. *Contemporary Music Review, 40*(5–6), 471–481. https://doi.org/10.1080/07494467.2021.2022884

Ensemble for Different New Music. (2023). *Keyboard ensemble Ensemble for Different New Music*. https://adnmbg.com/en/

Ensemble for Different New Music (n.d.). Home [YouTube Channel]. Retrieved from https://www.youtube.com/@ensemblefordifferentnewmus7997

Finke, R.A., Ward, T.B., & Smith, S.M. (1992). *Creative cognition: Theory, research and applications*. MIT Press.

Gaver, W.W., & Mandler, G. (1987). Play it again, Sam: On liking music. *Cognition and Emotion*, 1(3), 259–282. https://doi.org/10.1080/02699938708408051

Huron, D. (2006). *Sweet anticipation: Music and the psychology of expectation*. MIT Press. https://doi.org/10.7551/mitpress/6575.001.0001

Istók, E., Brattico, E., Jacobsen, T., Krohn, K., Müller, M., & Tervaniemi, M. (2009). Aesthetic responses to music: A questionnaire study. *Musicae Scientiae*, 13(2), 183–206. https://doi.org/10.1177/102986490901300201

Jacobsen, T. (2006). Bridging the arts and science: A framework for the psychology of aesthetics. *Leonardo*, 39(2), 155–162. https://doi.org/10.1162/leon.2006.39.2.155

Juslin, P.N. (2003). Five facets of musical expression: A psychologist's perspective on music performance. *Psychology of Music*, 31(3), 273–302. https://doi.org/10.1177/03057356030313003

Juslin, P.N. (2019). What comes next? Musical expectancy. In P.N. Juslin (ed.), *Musical emotions explained: Unlocking the secrets of musical affect* (pp. 343–363). Oxford University Press. https://doi.org/10.1093/oso/9780198753421.003.0024

Juslin, P.N., & Västfjäll, D. (2008). Emotional responses to music: The need to consider underlying mechanisms. *Behavioral and Brain Sciences*, 31(5), 559–575. https://doi.org/10.1017/S0140525X08005293

Kolundžija, N. (n.d.). *Home* [YouTube Channel]. Retrieved from https://www.youtube.com/@nadakolundzija7196/featured

Kolundžija, N. (2020, January 15). *Nada Kolundžija plays Miroslav Miša Savić 'Oh Light, Oh Tenderness, Oh Darkness'* [Video]. YouTube. https://www.youtube.com/watch?v=Rkh6ND_ZltA

Konečni, V.J. (2008). A skeptical position on 'musical emotions' and an alternative proposal. *Behavioral and Brain Sciences*, 31(5), 582–584. https://doi.org/10.1017/S0140525X08005372

Krumhansl, C.L., & Agres, K.R. (2008). Musical expectancy: The influence of musical structure on emotional response. *Behavioral and Brain Sciences*, 31(5), 584–585. https://doi.org/10.1017/S0140525X08005384

Leder, H., Belke, B., Oeberst, A., & Augustin, D. (2004). A model of aesthetic appreciation and aesthetic judgments. *British Journal of Psychology*, 95(4), 489–508. https://doi.org/10.1348/0007126042369811

Masnikosa, M. (2021). Serbian late twentieth-century neo-avant-garde: Minimalist music by Vladimir Tošić and Miroslav Miša Savić. *Contemporary*

Music Review, *40*(5–6), 626–649. https://doi.org/10.1080/07494467.2021.2022892

Mencke, I., Seibert, C., Brattico, E., & Wald-Fuhrmann, M. (2023). Comparing the aesthetic experience of classic–romantic and contemporary classical music: An interview study. *Psychology of Music*, *51*(1), 274–294. https://doi.org/10.1177/03057356221091312

Meyer, L.B. (1956). *Emotion and meaning in music*. University of Chicago Press.

Miladinović Prica, I. (2017). (ed.). *Breathing in/breathing out: A little anthology of piano music, 1914–2014* [Book accompanying three CDs]. Belgrade, Vertical Jazz.

Miladinović Prica, I. (2021). The Cage effect from a Serbian perspective. *Contemporary Music Review*, *40*(5–6), 595–625. https://doi.org/10.1080/07494467.2021.2022891

Milojković, M. (2018). Procesualnost u ostvarenjima Miroslava Miše Savića [Processuality in the works of Miroslav Miša Savić]. *INSAM: Journal of Contemporary Music, Art and Technology*, *1*(1), 39–55. https://insam-institute.com/wp-content/uploads/2018/12/5.-INSAM-Journal-Milan-Milojkovi%C4%87-Procesualnost-39-55-1.pdf

Milojković, M. (2020). *Digitalna tehnologija u srpskoj umetničkoj muzici* [Digital technology in Serbian art music]. Matica Srpska.

Miu, A.C., Simina, P., & Szentágotai-Tătar, A. (2016). Aesthetic emotions across arts: A comparison between painting and music. *Frontiers in Psychology*, *6*, Article 1951. https://doi.org/10.3389/fpsyg.2015.01951

Müller, M., Höfel, L., Brattico, E., & Jacobsen, T. (2010). Aesthetic judgments of music in experts and laypersons–An ERP study. *International Journal of Psychophysiology*, *76*(1), 40–51. https://doi.org/10.1016/j.ijpsycho.2010.02.002

Nikolić, S. (2020). Model of artistic music aesthetic experience in music criticism broadcasted on the Radio Belgrade 2 in 2017. In B. Bogunović & S. Nikolić (eds), *Proceedings of PAM-IE Belgrade 2019* (pp. 196–204). Faculty of Music, University of Arts in Belgrade. https://www.fmu.bg.ac.rs/wp-content/uploads/2020/12/psychology-and-music-proceedings-sa-koricama-1.pdf

Pitts, S.E., & Price, S.M. (2021). 'It's okay not to like it'. The appeal and frustrations of the contemporary arts. In S.E. Pitts & S.M. Price (eds), *Understanding audience engagement in the contemporary arts* (pp. 131–151). Routledge. https://doi.org/10.4324/9780429342455

Rozin, A., & Rozin, P. (2008). Feelings and the enjoyment of music. *Behavioral and Brain Sciences*, *31*(5), 593–594. https://doi.org/10.1017/S0140525X08005487

Savić, M. (2020). *Oh Light, Oh Tenderness: Contemporary Serbian Composers* [Performed by Nada Kolundžija; Accompanying note for CD]. Belgrade, Vertical Jazz.

Scherer, K., & Zentner, M. (2008). Music evoked emotions "are" different–more often aesthetic than utilitarian. *Behavioral and Brain Sciences, 31*(5), 595–596. https://doi.org/10.1017/S0140525X08005505

Serbian Academy of Sciences and Art. (2023). *Vasilije Mokranjac (composer)*. https://www.sanu.ac.rs/en/member/mokranjac-vasilije/

Sloboda, J.A. (1986). *The musical mind: The cognitive psychology of music*. Oxford University Press. https://doi.org/10.1093/acprof:oso/9780198521280.001.0001

Smith, J.A. (2004). Reflecting on the development of interpretative phenomenological analysis and its contribution to qualitative research in psychology. *Qualitative Research in Psychology, 1*(1), 39–54. https://www.tandfonline.com/doi/abs/10.1191/1478088704qp004oa

Šuvaković, M., Daković, N., Vujanović, A., Ignjatović, A., & Novak, J. (2016). Umetnost XX veka u Srbiji: Dodatak [Twenty century art in Serbia: Appendix]. In H.V. Janson & E.F. Janson (eds), *Istorija umetnosti: Dopunjeno izdanje* (pp. 956–987). Begen Comerc d.o.o.

Vartanian, O., & Kaufman, J.C. (2013). Psychological and neural responses to art embody viewer and artwork histories. *Behavioral and Brain Sciences, 36*(2), 161–162. https://doi.org/10.1017/S0140525X12001823

Vukajlović, D. (1995). *O svetlosti, o nežnosti o mraku: izabrane i nove pesme* [Oh Light, Oh Tenderness, Oh Darkness: Selected and new poems]. BIGZ.

Williamon, A., Ginsborg, J., Perkins, R., & Waddell, G. (2021). *Performing music research: Methods in music education, psychology, and performance science*. Oxford University Press. https://doi.org/10.1093/oso/9780198714545.003.0009

4. Aesthetic Emotions in Music: Theory, Measurements, and Cross-cultural Comparison

Renee Timmers, Scott Bannister, and Thomas M. Lennie

Introduction

An important reason for listening to music relates to the emotions expressed and elicited by it (Schäfer et al., 2013), with some listeners describing strong emotional responses to music that are highly memorable (Gabrielsson, 2011). Music and emotion research has often focused on how emotions are perceived in music (Balkwill & Thompson, 1999) and what psychological mechanisms underlie emotions elicited by music (Juslin, 2016; Juslin et al., 2015). Much of this research has focused on a small set of basic emotions (Ekman, 1999), linked to adaptive functions, action readiness, and goal orientation, and on Western participants and listening contexts (Jacoby et al., 2020). More recently, a growing body of research is conducted cross-culturally, including in areas with little exposure to Western tonal music (e.g. Smit et al., 2022). Within this, few studies investigate the experience of aesthetic emotions. In this chapter, we discuss properties of aesthetic emotions, and reflect on expanding the main concepts to align with ecological perspectives, arguing this will also contribute to the usefulness of this research across cultural contexts.

Aesthetic vs. everyday emotions

It has been proposed that musical emotions, and emotions in aesthetic engagements broadly, may have distinct features and should be separated from 'everyday', basic adaptive emotions (Menninghaus et al., 2019; Zentner et al., 2008).

Kant (1790/2001) described the idea of aesthetic emotions as being 'disinterested'; such emotional responses have no utilitarian or survival purpose. Recent formulations of aesthetic experiences have developed this idea. For example, Konečni (2005) noted that whilst awe, a prototypical aesthetic response to the sublime, can be elicited in the face of physical grandeur, including elements of threat, an essential requisite for the experience is the guarantee of existential security. Frijda and Sundararajan (2007) differentiate between 'coarse' and 'refined' emotions, the latter being more detached from real-world concerns, involving more self-reflection and little associated action.

Whilst the distinction between aesthetic and utilitarian emotions is intuitive, it is hard to objectively separate them. Schubert (2024) found three aesthetic emotions to be reliably included in previous investigations without counterexamples, namely awe, (being) moved, and wonder. Even so these emotions may occur in non-aesthetic circumstances (Keltner & Haidt, 2003; Silvia, 2008). In a complementary view, Koelsch (2010) proposed that musical emotions are 'true' emotions, as they reflect brain region activity linked to emotional responses with action tendencies and goal-orientation.

Given these issues, a contemporary view is that aesthetic judgments and aesthetic modes of engagement are key elements of aesthetic emotions. Brattico and Pearce (2013) propose that, in a music-listening context, causal inattentive listening may result in everyday basic emotions, whereas focused listening with an aesthetic attitude can induce aesthetic emotions. Juslin (2016) suggests that instead of considering 'coarse' and 'refined' emotions (Frijda & Sundararajan, 2007) as distinct sets of emotions, we should consider the 'refined' category as a special mode of experiencing ordinary emotions, i.e., as an aesthetic mode of listening. In Juslin's BRECVEMA framework (2013), aesthetic judgment is included as one of the mechanisms of emotion induction, complementing other mechanisms derived from general adaptive functions. As it is possible that aesthetic judgments may precede aesthetic emotion responses, and vice versa (Huron, 2016), the causal directionality remains undetermined (Egermann & Reuben, 2020). In theoretical work related to various art forms, Menninghaus et al. (2019) emphasised the importance of aesthetic evaluation in the definitional scope of aesthetic emotion; for instance, being moved may be an everyday emotion, an art-elicited emotion (elicited by an art object), and an aesthetic emotion (elicited by aesthetic qualities of the art object, involving aesthetic evaluation). Thus, not all emotions elicited by art are aesthetic (Wassiliwizky & Menninghaus, 2021), and those emotions that are, involve an evaluation of and response to aesthetic qualities of the stimulus. Janković and Mađarev (see Chapter 2 in this volume) provide supporting evidence for the role of cognitive evaluation as a contributing component to aesthetic experiences of music in addition to emotional valence and arousal, corroborating their three-dimensional model of aesthetic emotions. Nikolić and Miladinović Prica (see Chapter 3 in this volume) provide rich insight into such cognitive evaluative processes as reported by music specialists engaging with contemporary music.

Aims

The aim of this chapter is to consider how characteristics of aesthetic emotions as defined in the research literature operate within cross-cultural studies of emotion and music, and to discuss how we believe the main concepts can be developed to better fit notions of music listening as embodied and embedded in cultural contexts. To do so, we discuss concepts, measurements, processes, and cross-cultural comparisons centralising the aesthetic affordances relevant to music-related emotions. This discussion takes us from aesthetic evaluation being relevant to aesthetic emotions and a level of disconnect from everyday consequences, to considerations of value and affordances of music to listeners, including functional uses, which we argue facilitate the translation of the notion of aesthetic emotions in music to diverse cultures.

Main discussion

Measurement scales and physiology

Emotion concepts and labels

Systematic characterisations of the emotions frequently associated with music have been conducted by various researchers, as early as Hevner's list of adjectives (1936). Of specific interest are those studies that have investigated emotional responses in ecologically valid listening situations. For example, the Geneva Emotional Music Scale (GEMS; Zentner et al., 2008) has been validated with audiences attending music festivals and concerts. This scale was later adapted to better capture responses to a range of musical genres. The updated Geneva Music-Induced Affect Checklist (GEMIAC) contains fourteen clusters of feeling terms ranging from being moved or touched, feeling joyful and wanting to dance, being filled with wonder and amazement, to feeling indifferent and bored or tense and uneasy (Coutinho & Scherer, 2017).

A broad examination of aesthetic emotions has been conducted by Schindler et al. (2017), who captured aesthetic emotions in various contexts. Emotion terms were collated from empirical, theoretical and philosophical research that describe responses to music, literature, theatre, film, and visual art. The terms were clustered into five factors: prototypical aesthetic emotions, pleasing emotions, epistemic emotions, negative emotions, and self-forgetful emotions, leading to the formulation of the Aesthetics Emotion Scale (AESTHEMOS). This scale comprises twenty-one subscales including beauty, fascination, awe, being moved, nostalgia, humour, vitality, joy, interest, intellectual challenge, ugliness, boredom, and sadness, amongst others.

These self-reporting tools provide opportunities for exploring emotional experiences found during engagements with music as well as in other aesthetic contexts. Nevertheless, having a specialised list does not yet tell us whether an emotion is aesthetic in nature, as most, if not all of these emotions might occur in non-aesthetic circumstances. It is also important to evaluate appraisal patterns that may link emotion categories with aesthetic judgments (Menninghaus et al., 2019) or, as Janković and Mađarev (see Chapter 2 in this volume) argue, cognitive evaluation more generally. For example, Juslin et al. (2015) asked participants to evaluate the mechanism that they deemed responsible for their emotional responses in addition to the responses themselves. A further avenue for the exploration of mechanisms and examination of the experience of emotion is to consider the physiological manifestations accompanying aesthetic emotions in addition to self-reporting.

Physiological manifestations: Chills and tears

Physiological measurements can be used to corroborate emotional responses and to offer insight into moment-to-moment developments (Benedek & Kaernbach, 2011). Such measurements aim to capture bodily experiences including chills, shivers, tension, excitement, or tearfulness.

Aesthetic chills have been described as emotional experiences accompanied by goosebumps, shivers, or tingling sensations (Bannister, 2020). Chills have been associated with increased skin conductance, heart rate, and pupil dilation (Laeng et al., 2016; Rickard, 2004; Sumpf et al., 2015); additionally, chills have been linked to brain activity associated with reward and pleasure (Ferreri et al., 2019; Salimpoor et al., 2011). Theoretically and empirically, chills reflect prototypical qualities of aesthetic emotions; they are pleasurable and rewarding, involve increases in arousal, and can often be linked to aesthetic features of the music (Bannister & Eerola, 2018; Grewe et al., 2007; Panksepp, 1995). Additionally, chills are associated with common aesthetic emotion concepts such as awe and being moved (Benedek & Kaernbach, 2011; Konečni, 2005; Schurtz et al., 2012), feelings of beauty (Gabrielsson, 2011), and nostalgia (Bannister, 2020).

Further physical reactions indicative of strong emotional experiences are crying or tears in response to music (Gabrielsson, 2011). Crying is a multifaceted phenomenon with several subtypes (Vingerhoets, 2013), and whilst adaptive accounts describe the function of tears in terms of signals to elicit social support during times of distress (Gračanin et al., 2018), crying also seems prevalent across aesthetic engagements (Eerola & Peltola, 2016; Pelowski, 2015) where these functions are less apparent. Cotter et al. (2018) explored experiences of crying and feeling like crying in relation to music, finding that these mostly occurred with familiar music, music that held special meaning for the listener, and when participants were listening alone; furthermore, whilst crying to music was sometimes linked to awe and being touched, inspired, and amazed, most accounts were linked to sadness and more distressing experiences, and to memories of events (Cotter et al., 2019).

Hanser et al. (2021) found in a large survey of over 2,000 participants that tears were most commonly reported in the context of being moved (65%), sadness (53%), and nostalgia (28%), followed by powerlessness (24%). Nearly 50% of crying-to-music episodes also involved goosebumps, suggesting that chills and tears may be related experiences in aesthetic contexts (though see Mori & Iwanaga, 2017).

Several methodological challenges remain when recording tears and chills, including measurements using physiological and muscle tension signals. But, together with self-reports of aesthetic emotions, these phenomena can be used to further investigate the musical and contextual characteristics in which aesthetic emotions occur, with the aim of linking them to emotion induction processes. These phenomena may afford investigations of aesthetic emotions as they happen, exploring concurrent physiological activity patterns and brain activity via neuroimaging approaches, reflecting a burgeoning area of work labeled 'neuroaesthetics' (for a review of methods that includes neuroimaging, see Timmers & Loui, 2019). The meaningfulness of strong physiological responses such as chills, tears and shivers underpins a notion of aesthetic emotions as heightened emotional experiences of music.

Relationships to musical material, context, and person

In ecological terms, it is not just a matter of who listens to what in what context, but of their interactions: preferences interact with personal characteristics and use (Račevska & Tadinac, 2019), and emotional meaning arises through listeners interacting with music in particular contexts for particular purposes (Lennie & Eerola, 2022). This means that context and person need to be considered in combination with relationships between experienced emotions and musical properties.

Musical and acoustical properties

Various psychoacoustic characteristics have been identified as important cues for emotional expression in music, drawing parallels with vocal expressions of emotions (Juslin & Laukka, 2003) and emotional movement (for a review, see Timmers & Loui, 2019). However, where research on aesthetic emotions is concerned, specific attention has been paid to dynamic properties of music: changes, surprises, and patterns of tension-relaxation. Tension has been associated with harmonic progressions (e.g., away from and return to the tonic), intensity fluctuations, pitch height, and consonance and dissonance (Arthurs et al., 2018; Farbood, 2012). Whilst primarily modelled in the context of the Western classical and romantic repertoire (Lerdahl & Krumhansl, 2007), Solberg and Dibben (2019) investigated a contemporary example, specifically the break routine in electronic dance music where the release of tension is associated with heightened pleasure and physiological responses, including chills.

Dynamic change, deviation, and probability

Seen from a dynamic perspective, emotional response arises by variation across and within pieces (e.g., Coutinho & Cangelosi, 2011; Sloboda, 1991; Warmbrodt et al., 2022). A key strand of research in this context is the attempt to model the information dynamics of music, specifically variations in predictability and uncertainty, which has been modeled using information entropy (Pearce, 2018). As Huron (2006) famously explained, such predictability concerns the what (e.g., what pitch) and when in time of musical events. Musical expectancy has been indicated as one of several mechanisms for felt emotion (Juslin, 2016). However, there is debate around its strength as an emotion induction mechanism. Expectation and violations thereof may give rise to micro-affects (Huron, 2006) that are nevertheless important for an engaging experience (see, e.g., Mekiš Recek, et al., 2021).

The link to strong aesthetic emotional response may be found at the intersection between two forms of prediction: Cheung et al. (2019) found that music is experienced as most rewarding or pleasurable when high predictability (a highly expected event) occurs in an uncertain context or, conversely, when low likelihood (an unexpected, surprising event) is combined with high predictability. The break routine (Solberg & Dibben, 2019) seems an effective example of the first combination: the return of the original groove is highly predictable, but the timing is uncertain and delayed. The classical appoggiatura in a recursive harmonic sequence can be seen as an illustration of the second combination: a dissonant non-chord tone with low probability occurs in a highly predictable manner and context. This is used, for example, in Barber's *Adagio for Strings*, which is experienced as strongly sadness-inducing (Krumhansl, 1997). Such interactions between predictability and surprise extend notions of 'deviation as expressive'. Deviation in performance may be particularly valued if operating in a close to predictable manner (Todd, 1995), and if done in ways familiar to listeners (Timmers, 2007). They also offer an interesting perspective on the well-known inverted-U curve between complexity and preference: it is not just about the appreciation of a balanced level of complexity (Berlyne, 1970), but specific affective tensions that afford affective responses: seeing something familiar in new ways or predicting the unexpected.

A special case of combining predictability and innovation may be the widespread tradition of ornamentation, variation, and partial improvisation that is so very common in many music traditions. Some evidence exists for the emotional effect of ornamentation (Timmers & Ashley, 2007), but further work in this area is warranted, including how the balance between predictability, uncertainty, and certainty shifts within and across musical phrases.

Musical affordances as aesthetic emotional response

An interactional perspective on relationships between music and aesthetic emotions takes into account what music may afford to listeners in particular contexts: music affords an opportunity to dance, celebrate, and socialise at a party; to mourn and share grief at a funeral; and to aid spiritual reflection or expression at religious gatherings. This aligns with identified emotion mechanisms such as entrainment and emotional contagion, or the 'sharing' of emotion (Juslin, 2016). Memory is another identified mechanism. Whilst recall may give rise to felt emotion due to a particular incidental association, this process of association and recall can also be seen as something that music affords, a positive attribute of music, as applications of music in therapy and dementia care illustrate.

An illustration of the complex relationship between music and aesthetic emotional responses is the appreciation of negative music and, indeed, the pleasurable experience of tears. People report that they enjoy listening to sad music (Garrido & Schubert, 2011), and a subgroup of listeners enjoy what could be characterised as 'violent music' (Olsen et al., 2022). Capturing some of this variety, Peltola and Eerola (2016) subdivided experiences of sad music into three subcategories labeled 'grief', 'melancholia', and 'sweet sorrow'. The last category of sweet sorrow was characterised by a positive experience of sad music, and included references to beauty and feeling moved; experiences of grief were sometimes also identified as cathartic. Olsen et al. (2022) also identify balancing positive and negative emotions as important to the liking of music with violent lyrics.

In their review, Eerola et al. (2018) used the distinction between hedonic and eudaemonic pleasure to account for positive experiences of sadness in musical contexts. Interpreting self-reported experiences, they infer that 'the pleasure of being moved [in relation to sad music] is far from being purely hedonistic; it is strongly intertwined with interpersonal aspects' (p. 108). Furthermore, they state that 'musical expression gives special meaning to the emotional states it portrays; it is not just pointless sadness, but there is some reason or meaning to it' (p. 189). It is not a matter of not feeling the emotion. In contrast, interpersonal empathy and the enjoyment of sad music seem to be linked, suggesting heightened experiences of emotion in these listeners. Variations in trait empathy do not seem relevant to the enjoyment of violent music. Instead, the motivations for listening to violent music are characterised by specific appraisals of what violent music offers, including experiences of power, joy, and peace (Thompson et al., 2019).

Empirical findings indicate that music is appreciated for its values in relation to listeners. Indeed, the effect of music and whether listeners use music to influence their emotions is correlated with the relevance of music for listeners (Granot et al., 2021). This correlation may clearly operate in either direction—if valued more, the influence is stronger, and vice versa. Such sensitivity to music varies strongly, ranging from little to no emotional response to peak experiences with music. What are experienced as aesthetic characteristics of music may depend on the values and meanings awarded to music in particular contexts, and the identification with those values and meanings in connection with the music. As many researchers have previously identified, aesthetic appreciation is historically and culturally situated.

Cross-cultural translations

Musical features, discrete emotions, and physiological responses

Cross-cultural music studies are sparse and concentrate almost exclusively on emotion perception using basic emotions or evaluations of emotional dimensions. To our knowledge, no cross-cultural study of felt aesthetic musical emotions has been conducted, although evidence suggests that broad discrete emotion categories can be inferred across cultures (Balkwill et al., 2004; Balkwill & Thompson, 1999; Egermann et al., 2015; Fritz et al., 2009;). However, the degree of accuracy and the number of emotion categories varies. There is also a clear in-group advantage to perceiving the correct emotion in one's own musical culture (Laukka et al., 2013; Laukka & Elfenbein, 2020). Limitations are noted in the design of studies. Nelson and Russell (2013) cite the 'forced-choice paradigm' and 'unbalanced' methodological designs, while Matsumoto and van de Vijver (2010) acknowledge problems of conceptual 'equivalence' and 'construct bias'.

Laukka et al. (2013) showed that *basic* emotion terms were better perceived than more complex (*aesthetic*) terms. Acoustic cues correlated with the intended emotional expression of excerpts. Of 26 features, 4 acoustic cues ('spectral novelty', 'rhythmic novelty', 'tonal novelty', and 'novelty in pitch register') correlated with nearly all emotion terms. The only other cues that showed such consistency for listeners across cultures and emotion terms were 'spectral flux' and 'attack time', providing tentative evidence for the importance of musical novelty cross-culturally, at least with respect to the examined cultural contexts.

Musical familiarity also plays a key role cross-culturally. The Mafa (Pygmy population) showed a greater dislike for tonally dissonant manipulations of their own music than for Western music (Fritz et al., 2009), highlighting familiarity as an important mediator of cues.

Unfamiliar music may be subject to stereotyping and associated with a smaller range of emotional experiences (Susino & Schubert, 2019, 2020).

One of the few cross-cultural studies using emotion dimensions and physiological measures (Egermann et al., 2015) studied the affective response to Western music and the native music of the Congolese Mbenzele Pygmy population. Six low-level acoustic cues were correlated with subjective ratings of arousal, valence, and physiological measures for Western music in both populations. The study suggests that the greater number of acoustic cues in Western music leads to greater cross-cultural recognition and similar physiological responses, while the stronger use of symbolic or associative meaning in Mbenzele Pygmy music requires a stronger reliance on enculturation.

A lack of focus on aesthetic emotional responses, combined with methodological limitations, leaves significant gaps in the research literature. Evidence converges on the conclusion that there are both universal and culture-specific cues (Balkwill & Thompson, 1999), many shared with an evolutionary history of vocal emotion communication (Juslin & Laukka, 2003), that allow listeners from different cultures to reliably perceive emotions at above chance levels (Laukka & Elfenbein, 2020), but below the universality threshold (Haidt & Keltner, 1999, p. 229). However, a singular focus upon stimulus-driven components can lead to reductive explanations, and future research must better acknowledge context (Jacoby et al., 2020).

Framing aesthetic emotions: Cross-cultural functions and affordances of music

Music's functions have been well documented in the Western context: for example, meaning enhancement (Hays & Minichiello, 2005), supporting behaviours (DeNora, 2000; Greasley & Lamont, 2011), and mood management (Juslin et al., 2008). Cross-culturally, anthropologist Alan Merriam (1964) documented 10 musical functions, including 'aesthetic enjoyment'. One key distinction Merriam offers is the differentiation between musical 'functions' (its broader purpose) and 'use' (in a specific situation; p. 210). Clayton (2016) notes the importance of this distinction, as a list of 'uses' would lead to a countless number of categories (e.g., lullabies, courtship, sports, trance, etc.). Since Merriam, a greater focus upon the underlying dimensions of these functions has emerged (Schäfer et al., 2013). Differences in functions have been linked with cultural distinctions in musical experiences including emotional differences (Saarikallio et al., 2020), emotion mechanisms and motivation (Juslin et al., 2016), behaviours (Mehr et al., 2019; Saarikallio, 2008a,b), preferences (Schäfer et al., 2012; 2013), and musical form (Mehr et al., 2019). Analogously, Stefanija (2007) argues for the relevance of musical functions and their conceptualisation in relation to uses and preferences, musicality and behaviours.

Saarikallio and colleagues (2020) compared music-evoked emotions and functions between Finland and India. The emotion factor 'peacefulness-transcendence', that captured several aesthetic terms, appeared more prominently in the Indian sample, suggesting a greater prevalence of aesthetic emotions in Indian listeners, and supporting findings in other aesthetic contexts (Sundararajan, 2010). The musical function 'aesthetic enjoyment', understood as a focus upon musical qualities, emerged as a single function with no subcategories. Whilst other music functions showed significant cultural differences, 'aesthetic enjoyment' showed similar moderate emergence and links to typical musical genres in both cultures.

Links between musical preferences and musical functions were investigated by Schäfer and colleagues (2012) in a comparison of German and Indian listeners. Musical functions were shown to correlate with preferences in both cultures. The function of 'diversion' was most closely linked with aesthetic satisfaction (p. 378), and appeared in both cultures as the second strongest predictor of musical preferences. Nevertheless, 'diversion' was operationalised differently in these two cultures. German participants placed a greater focus on dancing than on appraising the music's qualities, which was most relevant for Indian participants. The findings of Saarikallio (2008b) note the importance of dancing as a diversion for Kenyan teenagers. These differences relate to variations in 'uses' whilst serving a similar function. Apart from preferences for music that enables 'diversion', aesthetic enjoyment has been associated with reflective experiences, grouped under the factor of 'self-awareness' by Schäfer et al. (2013), including items with an inward focus (solace, escapism, absorption).

Juslin et al. (2016) compared emotional experiences of music across individualist and collectivist cultures. The 'aesthetic judgment' mechanism was found to be more prevalent in collectivist cultures although the effect size was small ($d = .18$). The strongest effects related to preferences in collectivist cultures for low arousal states (nostalgia-longing, spirituality-transcendence, love-tenderness) and socially orientated emotions. All functions appeared across cultures, although several functions showed significant differences in their prevalence. Individual and collectivist cultures also differed in listening motivations. The collectivist cultures included in the study placed greater importance on the motivations to 'relax', 'reflect', 'appreciate beauty', and 'enhance health'. Despite cross-cultural differences, to 'appreciate beauty' and 'interest in music' (important aesthetic items) appeared in the top three most highly rated motives for listening to music cross-culturally. This contrasts with findings by Mehr et al. (2019), who analysed a large ethnographic dataset. They found that vocal music from 60 societies could be collapsed into four types of behaviours (dancing, lullabies, healing, and love songs). Aesthetic experiences were not included in this analysis, at least not explicitly. Further analyses may generate insight how aesthetic appreciation and physiology may play a role in music to be experienced as 'healing' or expressing 'love'.

Whilst many musical functions appear cross-culturally relevant, differences relate to their prevalence and the cultural value associated with them. Aesthetic emotional responses are set within a complex and culturally bound process of meaning-making. Ultimately, a cross-cultural approach allows a better understanding of how music may afford meaningful experiences that have a functional significance, whether by affording a heightened intense emotional experience or a more reflective and contemplative one.

Conclusion

The notion that musical emotions result from the interaction between music, person, and context is not new. Yet it is important to revisit this understanding with respect to aesthetic emotions as illustrated in Figure 4.1: what is experienced as an aesthetic affordance and an aesthetic property of music is dependent on the interaction between music, listeners/users, and context. Moreover, we argue that, for the cross-genre, cross-cultural, and historical understanding of aesthetic emotions in response to music, it is important to consider what the meaningful encounters with music are for listeners. To find hedonic and eudaemonic pleasure in music is for that music to afford meaningful engagement, which relates to body, mind, and social and material context. This position brings musical functions and uses into the realm of aesthetic emotions, seemingly blurring the distinction with utilitarian emotions. However, the differences between aesthetic and utilitarian emotions lie in safety and relative control, as well as the close association with music-aesthetic properties. It is necessary to consider musical functions and affordances in order to go beyond the expectation that aesthetic emotions are confined to a sense of beauty, transcendence, or 'high art'.

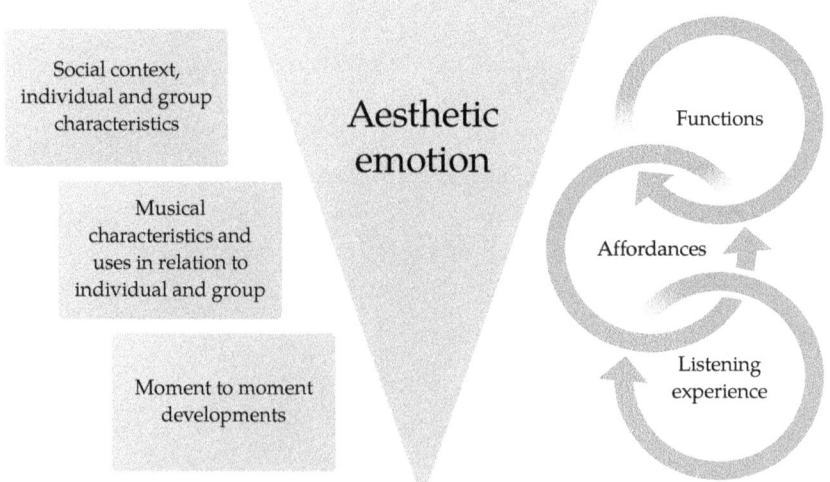

Fig. 4.1 Aesthetic emotions arise from the interaction between individuals, groups and musical characteristics in particular social contexts. The moment-to-moment developments and affordances of music are particularly relevant for aesthetic listening experiences

Of note here are the bodily, cognitive, and physiological expressions afforded by music in specific listening contexts, such as chills, tears, tension-release, predictability and unexpectedness, movement and dancing. The temporal aspect of music in the unfolding experience of emotions remains an important area for further investigation, whether this concerns the neurophysiological affordances of longer periods of entrainment with music, the effects of contrast and variation, or the effect of the sharing of experiences and facilitating relational behaviours such as synchronised movement.

Overall, we have shown why systematically investigating aesthetic emotions in a range of contexts (including cultures) must be a priority for future research. We claim that novel research methods with less emphasis on passive listening should be developed and be sufficiently sensitive to different contexts. Furthermore, cross-cultural research should start with the values and functions afforded to music combined with behavioural, bodily, and physiological engagement. These two perspectives may then offer a framework to understand how music and its properties fit together. We point towards functions as a culturally bound, 'goal-orientated' understanding of musical aesthetic emotions. Thus, we move away from the historically *disinterested* narrative, a notion that Huron (2016) identifies as difficult to 'reconcile with biology' (p. 242), and instead acknowledge aesthetic experience as a situated cognitive process. This is in line with recent theoretical constructs of aesthetic (Menninghaus et al., 2019) and musical (Lennie & Eerola, 2022) emotions that note the importance of goals, situation, and context. Finally, as to the meaningfulness of the term aesthetic emotions in music, what we have offered here is a perspective that notes the move of aesthetics from a philosophical construction to an empirical one. This change has led to a broader construction of the concept of aesthetics and aesthetic emotions. Aesthetic emotions may be distinguished from everyday emotions by functional context, close interaction with musical properties, and the functions and engagements they afford that listeners value and experience as meaningful.

References

Arthurs, Y., Beeston, A.V., & Timmers, R. (2018). Perception of isolated chords: Examining frequency of occurrence, instrumental timbre, acoustic descriptors and musical training. *Psychology of Music, 46*(5), 662–681. https://doi.org/10.1177/0305735617720834

Balkwill, L.-L., & Thompson, W.F. (1999). A cross-cultural investigation of the perception of emotion in music: Psychophysical and cultural cues. *Music Perception: An Interdisciplinary Journal, 17*(1), 43–64. https://doi.org/10.2307/40285811

Balkwill, L.-L., Thompson, W.F., & Matsunaga, R. (2004). Recognition of emotion in Japanese, Western, and Hindustani music by Japanese listeners. *Japanese Psychological Research, 46*(4), 337–349. https://doi.org/10.1111/j.1468-5584.2004.00265.x

Bannister, S. (2020). A survey into the experience of musically induced chills: Emotions, situations and music. *Psychology of Music, 48*(2), 297–314. https://doi.org/10.1177/0305735618798024

Bannister, S., & Eerola, T. (2018). Suppressing the chills: Effects of musical manipulation on the chills response. *Frontiers in Psychology, 9*, Article 2046. https://doi.org/10.3389/fpsyg.2018.02046

Benedek, M., & Kaernbach, C. (2011). Physiological correlates and emotional specificity of human piloerection. *Biological Psychology, 86*(3), 320–329. https://doi.org/10.1016/j.biopsycho.2010.12.012

Berlyne, D.E. (1970). Novelty, complexity, and hedonic value. *Perception & Psychophysics, 8*(5), 279–286. https://doi.org/10.3758/BF03212593

Brattico, E., & Pearce, M. (2013). The neuroaesthetics of music. *Psychology of Aesthetics, Creativity, and the Arts, 7*(1), 48–61. https://doi.org/10.1037/a0031624

Cheung, V.K.M., Harrison, P.M.C., Meyer, L., Pearce, M.T., Haynes, J.-D., & Koelsch, S. (2019). Uncertainty and surprise jointly predict musical pleasure and amygdala, hippocampus, and auditory cortex activity. *Current Biology, 29*(23), 4084–4092. https://doi.org/10.1016/j.cub.2019.09.067

Clayton, M. (2016). The social and personal functions of music in cross-cultural perspective. In S. Hallam, I. Cross, & M.H. Thaut (eds), *Oxford handbook of music psychology* (2nd ed., pp. 47–59). Oxford University Press. https://doi.org/10.1093/oxfordhb/9780198722946.013.8

Cotter, K.N., Prince, A.N., Christensen, A.P., & Silvia, P.J. (2019). Feeling like crying when listening to music: Exploring musical and contextual features. *Empirical Studies of the Arts, 37*(2), 119–137. https://doi.org/10.1177/0276237418805692

Cotter, K.N., Silvia, P.J., & Fayn, K. (2018). What does feeling like crying when listening to music feel like? *Psychology of Aesthetics, Creativity, and the Arts, 12*(2), 216–227. https://doi.org/10.1037/aca0000108

Coutinho, E., & Cangelosi, A. (2011). Musical emotions: Predicting second-by-second subjective feelings of emotion from low-level psychoacoustic features and physiological measurements. *Emotion, 11*(4), 921–937. https://doi.org/10.1037/a0024700

Coutinho, E., & Scherer, K.R. (2017). Introducing the GEneva Music-Induced Affect Checklist (GEMIAC): A brief instrument for the rapid assessment of musically induced emotions. *Music Perception: An Interdisciplinary Journal, 34*(4), 371–386. https://doi.org/10.1525/mp.2017.34.4.371

DeNora, T. (2000). *Music in everyday life*. Cambridge University Press. https://doi.org/10.1017/CBO9780511489433

Eerola, T., & Peltola, H.-R. (2016). Memorable experiences with sad music: Reasons, reactions and mechanisms of three types of experiences. *PLoS ONE, 11*(6), Article e0157444. https://doi.org/10.1371/journal.pone.0157444

Eerola, T., Vuoskoski, J.K., Peltola, H.-R., Putkinen, V., & Schäfer, K. (2018). An integrative review of the enjoyment of sadness associated with music. *Physics of Life Reviews, 25*, 100–121. https://doi.org/10.1016/j.plrev.2017.11.016

Egermann, H., Fernando, N., Chuen, L., & McAdams, S. (2015). Music induces universal emotion-related psychophysiological responses: Comparing Canadian listeners to Congolese Pygmies. *Frontiers in Psychology, 5*, Article 1341. https://doi.org/10.3389/fpsyg.2014.01341

Egermann, H., & Reuben, F. (2020). 'Beauty is how you feel inside': Aesthetic judgments are related to emotional responses to contemporary music. *Frontiers in Psychology, 11*, Article 510029. https://doi.org/10.3389/fpsyg.2020.510029

Ekman, P. (1999). Basic emotions. In T. Dalgleish & M.J. Power (eds), *Handbook of cognition and emotion* (pp. 45–60). John Wiley & Sons Ltd. https://doi.org/10.1002/0470013494.ch3

Farbood, M.M. (2012). A parametric, temporal model of musical tension. *Music Perception: An Interdisciplinary Journal, 29*(4), 387–428. https://doi.org/10.1525/mp.2012.29.4.387

Ferreri, L., Mas-Herrero, E., Zatorre, R., Ripollés, P., Gomez-Andres, A., Alicart, H., Olivé, G., Marco-Pallarés, J., Antonijoan, R.M., Valle, M., Riba, J., & Rodriguez-Fornells, A. (2019). Dopamine modulates the reward experiences elicited by music. *Proceedings of the National Academy of Sciences, 116*(9), 3793–3798. https://doi.org/10.1073/pnas.1811878116

Frijda, N.H., & Sundararajan, L. (2007). Emotion refinement: A theory inspired by Chinese poetics. *Perspectives on Psychological Science, 2*(3), 227–241. https://doi.org/10.1111/j.1745-6916.2007.00042.x

Fritz, T., Jentschke, S., Gosselin, N., Sammler, D., Peretz, I., Turner, R., Friederici, A.D., & Koelsch, S. (2009). Universal recognition of three basic emotions in music. *Current Biology, 19*(7), 573–576. https://doi.org/10.1016/j.cub.2009.02.058

Gabrielsson, A. (2011). *Strong experiences with music: Music is much more than just music.* Oxford University Press. https://doi.org/10.1093/acprof:oso/9780199695225.001.0001

Garrido, S., & Schubert, E. (2011). Individual differences in the enjoyment of negative emotion in music: A literature review and experiment. *Music Perception: An Interdisciplinary Journal, 28*(3), 279–296. https://doi.org/10.1525/mp.2011.28.3.279

Gračanin, A., Krahmer, E., Rinck, M., & Vingerhoets, A.J.J.M. (2018). The effects of tears on approach–avoidance tendencies in observers. *Evolutionary Psychology, 16*(3), 1–10. https://doi.org/10.1177/1474704918791058

Granot, R., Spitz, D.H., Cherki, B.R., Loui, P., Timmers, R., Schäfer, R.S., Vuoskoski, J.K., Cárdenas-Soler, R.-N., Soares-Quadros, J.F.Jr., Li, S., Lega, C., La Rocca, S., Martínez, I.C., Tanco, M., Marchiano, M., Martínez-Castilla, P., Pérez-Acosta, G., Martínez-Ezquerro, J.D., Gutiérrez-Blasco, I.M., ... & Israel, S. (2021). "Help! I need somebody": Music as a global resource for obtaining wellbeing goals in times of crisis. *Frontiers in Psychology, 12*, Article 1038. https://doi.org/10.3389/fpsyg.2021.648013

Greasley, A.E., & Lamont, A. (2011). Exploring engagement with music in everyday life using experience sampling methodology. *Musicae Scientiae, 15*(1), 45–71. https://doi.org/10.1177/1029864910393417

Grewe, O., Nagel, F., Kopiez, R., & Altenmüller, E. (2007). Listening to music as a re-creative process: Physiological, psychological, and psychoacoustical correlates of chills and strong emotions. *Music Perception: An Interdisciplinary Journal, 24*(3), 297–314. https://doi.org/10.1525/mp.2007.24.3.297

Haidt, J., & Keltner, D. (1999). Culture and facial expression: Open-ended methods find more expressions and a gradient of recognition. *Cognition and Emotion, 13*(3), 225–266. https://doi.org/10.1080/026999399379267

Hanser, W.E., Mark, R.E., & Vingerhoets, A.J.J.M. (2021). Everyday crying over music: A survey. *Musicae Scientiae.* Advance online publication. https://doi.org/10.1177/1029864920981110

Hays, T., & Minichiello, V. (2005). The meaning of music in the lives of older people: A qualitative study. *Psychology of Music, 33*(4), 437–451. https://doi.org/10.1177/0305735605056160

Hevner, K. (1936). Experimental studies of the elements of expression in music. *The American Journal of Psychology, 48*(2), 246–268. https://doi.org/10.2307/1415746

Huron, D. (2006). *Sweet anticipation: Music and the psychology of expectation.* MIT Press. https://doi.org/10.7551/mitpress/6575.001.0001

Huron, D. (2016). Aesthetics. In S. Hallam, I. Cross, & M.H. Thaut (eds), *The Oxford handbook of music psychology* (2nd ed., pp. 151–159). Oxford University Press. https://doi.org/10.1093/oxfordhb/9780198722946.013.19

Jacoby, N., Margulis, E.H., Clayton, M., Hannon, E., Honing, H., Iversen, J., Klein, T.R., Mayr, S.A., Pearson, L., Peretz, I., Perlman, M., Polak, R., Ravignani, A., Savage, P.E., Steingo, G., Stevens, C.J., Trainor, L., Trehub, S., Veal, M., & Wald-Fuhrmann, M. (2020). Cross-cultural work in music cognition: Challenges, insights, and recommendations. *Music Perception: An Interdisciplinary Jounal, 37*(3), 185–195. https://doi.org/10.1525/mp.2020.37.3.185

Juslin, P.N. (2013). From everyday emotions to aesthetic emotions: Towards a unified theory of musical emotions. *Physics of Life Reviews, 10*(3), 235–266. https://doi.org/10.1016/j.plrev.2013.05.008

Juslin, P.N. (2016). Emotional reactions to music. In S. Hallam, I. Cross, & M.H. Thaut (eds), *The Oxford handbook of music psychology* (2nd ed., pp. 197–213). Oxford University Press. https://doi.org/10.1093/oxfordhb/9780198722946.013.17

Juslin, P.N., Barradas, G., & Eerola, T. (2015). From sound to significance: Exploring the mechanisms underlying emotional reactions to music. *The American Journal of Psychology, 128*(3), 281–304. https://doi.org/10.5406/amerjpsyc.128.3.0281

Juslin, P.N., Barradas, G.T., Ovsiannikow, M., Limmo, J., & Thompson, W.F. (2016). Prevalence of emotions, mechanisms, and motives in music listening: A comparison of individualist and collectivist cultures. *Psychomusicology: Music, Mind, and Brain, 26*(4), 293–326. https://doi.org/10.1037/pmu0000161

Juslin, P.N., & Laukka, P. (2003). Communication of emotions in vocal expression and music performance: Different channels, same code? *Psychological Bulletin, 129*(5), 770–814. https://doi.org/10.1037/0033-2909.129.5.770

Juslin, P.N., Liljeström, S., Västfjäll, D., Barradas, G., & Silva, A. (2008). An experience sampling study of emotional reactions to music: Listener, music, and situation. *Emotion, 8*(5), 668–683. https://doi.org/10.1037/a0013505

Kant, I. (2001). *Critique of the power of judgment* (P. Guyer & E. Matthews, Trans.). Cambridge University Press. (Original work published 1790)

Keltner, D., & Haidt, J. (2003). Approaching awe, a moral, spiritual, and aesthetic emotion. *Cognition and Emotion, 17*(2), 297–314. https://doi.org/10.1080/02699930302297

Koelsch, S. (2010). Towards a neural basis of music-evoked emotions. *Trends in Cognitive Sciences, 14*(3), 131–137. https://doi.org/10.1016/j.tics.2010.01.002

Konečni, V. (2005). The aesthetic trinity: Awe, being moved, thrills. *Bulletin of Psychology and the Arts, 5*(2), 27–44. http://konecni.ucsd.edu/pdf/2005%20Aesthetic%20Trinity,%20Bulletin%20of%20P.%20and%20A.pdf

Krumhansl, C.L. (1997). An exploratory study of musical emotions and psychophysiology. *Canadian Journal of Experimental Psychology, 51*(4), 336–353. https://doi.org/10.1037/1196-1961.51.4.336

Laeng, B., Eidet, L.M., Sulutvedt, U., & Panksepp, J. (2016). Music chills: The eye pupil as a mirror to music's soul. *Consciousness and Cognition, 44*, 161–178. https://doi.org/10.1016/j.concog.2016.07.009

Laukka, P., Eerola, T., Thingujam, N.S., Yamasaki, T., & Beller, G. (2013). Universal and culture-specific factors in the recognition and performance of musical affect expressions. *Emotion, 13*(3), 434–449. https://doi.org/10.1037/a0031388

Laukka, P., & Elfenbein, H. A. (2020). Cross-Cultural emotion recognition and in-group advantage in vocal expression: A meta-analysis. *Emotion Review, 13*(1), 175407391989729. https://doi.org/10.1177/1754073919897295

Lennie, T.M., & Eerola, T. (2022). The CODA model: A review and skeptical extension of the constructionist model of emotional episodes induced by music. *Frontiers in Psychology, 13*, Article 822264. https://doi.org/10.3389/fpsyg.2022.822264

Lerdahl, F., & Krumhansl, C.L. (2007). Modeling tonal tension. *Music Perception: An Interdisciplinary Journal, 24*(4), 329–366. https://doi.org/10.1525/mp.2007.24.4.329

Matsumoto, D., & Van de Vijver, F.J. (eds). (2010). *Cross-cultural research methods in psychology.* Cambridge University Press. https://doi.org/10.1017/CBO9780511779381

Mehr, S.A., Singh, M., Knox, D., Ketter, D.M., Pickens-Jones, D., Atwood, S., Lucas, C., Jacoby, N., Egner, A.A., Hopkins, E.J., Howard, R.M., Hartshorne, J.K., Jennings, M.V., Simson, J., Bainbridge, C.M., Pinker, S., O'Donnell, T.J., Krasnow, M.M., & Glowacki, L. (2019). Universality and diversity in human song. *Science, 366*(6468), Article eaax0868. https://doi.org/10.1126/science.aax0868

Mekiš Recek, Ž., Rojs, Z., Šinkovec, L., Štibelj, P., Vogrin, M., Zamrnik, B., & Slana Ozimič, A. (2021). Which chord progressions satisfy us the most? The effect of expectancy, music education, and pitch height. *Interdisciplinary Description of Complex Systems: INDECS, 19*(4), 578–588. https://doi.org/10.7906/indecs.19.4.9

Menninghaus, W., Wagner, V., Wassiliwizky, E., Schindler, I., Hanich, J., Jacobsen, T., & Koelsch, S. (2019). What are aesthetic emotions? *Psychological Review, 126*(2), 171–195. https://doi.org/10.1037/rev0000135

Merriam, A.P. (1964). *The anthropology of music.* Northwestern University Press.

Mori, K., & Iwanaga, M. (2017). Two types of peak emotional responses to music: The psychophysiology of chills and tears. *Scientific Reports, 7*, Article 46063. https://doi.org/10.1038/srep46063

Nelson, N.L., & Russell, J.A. (2013). Universality revisited. *Emotion Review, 5*(1), 8–15. https://doi.org/10.1177/1754073912457227

Olsen, K. N., Powell, M., Anic, A., Vallerand, R. J., & Thompson, W. F. (2022). Fans of Violent Music: The Role of Passion in Positive and Negative Emotional Experience. *Musicae Scientiae, 26*(2), 364–387. https://doi.org/10.1177/1029864920951611

Panksepp, J. (1995). The emotional sources of 'chills' induced by music. *Music Perception, 13*(2), 171–207. https://doi.org/10.2307/40285693

Pearce, M.T. (2018). Statistical learning and probabilistic prediction in music cognition: Mechanisms of stylistic enculturation. *Annals of the New York Academy of Sciences, 1423*(1), 378–395. https://doi.org/10.1111/nyas.13654

Pelowski, M. (2015). Tears and transformation: Feeling like crying as an indicator of insightful or 'aesthetic' experience with art. *Frontiers in Psychology, 6*, Article 1006. https://doi.org/10.3389/fpsyg.2015.01006

Peltola, H.-R., & Eerola, T. (2016). Fifty shades of blue: Classification of music-evoked sadness. *Musicae Scientiae, 20*(1), 84–102. https://doi.org/10.1177/1029864915611206

Račevska, E., & Tadinac, M. (2019). Intelligence, music preferences, and uses of music from the perspective of evolutionary psychology. *Evolutionary Behavioral Sciences, 13*(2), 101–110. https://doi.org/10.1037/ebs0000124

Rickard, N.S. (2004). Intense emotional responses to music: A test of the physiological arousal hypothesis. *Psychology of Music, 32*(4), 371–388. https://doi.org/10.1177/0305735604046096

Saarikallio, S. (2008a). Music in mood regulation: Initial scale development. *Musicae Scientiae, 12*(2), 291–309. https://doi.org/10.1177/102986490801200206

Saarikallio S. (2008b). Cross-cultural investigation of adolescents' use of music for mood regulation. In Miyazaki K., Hiraga Y., Adachi M., Nakajima Y., Tsuzaki M. (eds), *Proceedings of the 10th International Conference on Music Perception and Cognition, Sapporo, Japan* (pp. 328–333). ICMPC.

Saarikallio, S., Alluri, V., Maksimainen, J., & Toiviainen, P. (2020). Emotions of music listening in Finland and in India: Comparison of an individualistic and a collectivistic culture. *Psychology of Music*. Advance online publication. https://doi.org/10.1177/0305735620917730

Salimpoor, V.N., Benovoy, M., Larcher, K., Dagher, A., & Zatorre, R.J. (2011). Anatomically distinct dopamine release during anticipation and experience of peak emotion to music. *Nature Neuroscience, 14*(2), 257–262. https://doi.org/10.1038/nn.2726

Schäfer, T., Sedlmeier, P., Städtler, C., & Huron, D. (2013). The psychological functions of music listening. *Frontiers in Psychology, 4*, Article 511. https://doi.org/10.3389/fpsyg.2013.00511

Schäfer, T., Tipandjan, A., & Sedlmeier, P. (2012). The functions of music and their relationship to music preference in India and Germany. *International Journal of Psychology, 47*(5), 370–380. https://doi.org/10.1080/00207594.2012.688133

Schindler, I., Hosoya, G., Menninghaus, W., Beermann, U., Wagner, V., Eid, M., & Scherer, K.R. (2017). Measuring aesthetic emotions: A review of the literature and a new assessment tool. *PLoS ONE, 12*(6), Article e0178899. https://doi.org/10.1371/journal.pone.0178899

Schubert, E. (2024). The aesthetic emotion Lexicon: A literature review of emotion words used by researchers to describe aesthetic experiences. *Empirical Studies of the Arts, 42*(1), 3–37. https://doi.org/10.1177/02762374221143728

Schurtz, D.R., Blincoe, S., Smith, R.H., Powell, C.A.J., Combs, D.J.Y., & Kim, S.H. (2012). Exploring the social aspects of goose bumps and their role in awe and envy. *Motivation and Emotion, 36*(2), 205–217. https://doi.org/10.1007/s11031-011-9243-8

Silvia, P.J. (2008). Interest: The curious emotion. *Current Directions in Psychological Science, 17*(1), 57–60. https://doi.org/10.1111/j.1467-8721.2008.00548.x

Sloboda, J.A. (1991). Music structure and emotional response: Some empirical findings. *Psychology of Music, 19*(2), 110–120. https://doi.org/10.1177/0305735691192002

Smit, E.A., Milne, A. J., Sarvasy, H.S., & Dean, R.T. (2022). Emotional responses in Papua New Guinea show negligible evidence for a universal effect of major versus minor music. *PLoS ONE, 17*(6), e0269597. https://doi.org/10.1371/journal.pone.0269597

Solberg, R.T., & Dibben, N. (2019). Peak experiences with electronic dance music: Subjective experiences, physiological responses, and musical characteristics of the break routine. *Music Perception: An Interdisciplinary Journal, 36*(4), 371–389. https://doi.org/10.1525/mp.2019.36.4.371

Stefanija, L. (2007). Functions of music: a survey of research vocabularies. *Muzikos funkcijos: tyrimø terminologijos apžvalga, 7*, 6–17. https://xn--urnalai-cxb.lmta.lt/wp-content/uploads/2007/2007_6-17_Leon.pdf

Sumpf, M., Jentschke, S., & Koelsch, S. (2015). Effects of aesthetic chills on a cardiac signature of emotionality. *PLoS ONE, 10*(6), Article e0130117. https://doi.org/10.1371/journal.pone.0130117

Sundararajan, L. (2010). Two flavors of aesthetic tasting: 'Rasa' and savoring a cross-cultural study with implications for psychology of emotion. *Review of General Psychology, 14*(1), 22–30. https://doi.org/10.1037/a0018122

Susino, M., & Schubert, E. (2019). Cultural stereotyping of emotional responses to music genre. *Psychology of Music, 47*(3), 342–357. https://doi.org/10.1177/0305735618755886

Susino, M., & Schubert, E. (2020). Musical emotions in the absence of music: A cross-cultural investigation of emotion communication in music by extra-musical cues. *PloS ONE, 15*(11), e0241196. https://doi.org/10.1371/journal.pone.0241196

Thompson, W.F., Geeves, A.M., & Olsen, K.N. (2019). Who enjoys listening to violent music and why? *Psychology of Popular Media Culture, 8*(3), 218–232. https://doi.org/10.1037/ppm0000184

Timmers, R. (2007). Perception of music performance on historical and modern commercial recordings. *The Journal of the Acoustical Society of America, 122*(5), 2872–2880. https://doi.org/10.1121/1.2783987

Timmers, R., & Ashley, R. (2007). Emotional ornamentation in performances of a Handel sonata. *Music Perception: An Interdisciplinary Journal, 25*(2), 117–134. https://doi.org/10.1525/mp.2007.25.2.117

Timmers, R., & Loui, P. (2019). Music and emotion. In P.J. Rentfrow & D. Levitin (eds), *Foundations in music psychology: Theory and research* (pp. 783–825). MIT Press.

Todd, N.P.M. (1995). The kinematics of musical expression. *The Journal of the Acoustical Society of America, 97*(3), 1940–1949. https://doi.org/10.1121/1.412067

Vingerhoets, A. (2013). *Why only humans weep: Unravelling the mysteries of tears.* Oxford University Press. https://doi.org/10.1093/acprof:oso/9780198570240.001.0001

Warmbrodt, A., Timmers, R., & Kirk, R. (2022). The emotion trajectory of self-selected jazz music with lyrics: A psychophysiological perspective. *Psychology of Music, 50*(3), 756–778. https://doi.org/10.1177/03057356211024336

Wassiliwizky, E., & Menninghaus, W. (2021). Why and how should cognitive science care about aesthetics? *Trends in Cognitive Sciences, 25*(6), 437–449. https://doi.org/10.1016/j.tics.2021.03.008

Zentner, M., Grandjean, D., & Scherer, K.R. (2008). Emotions evoked by the sound of music: Characterization, classification, and measurement. *Emotion, 8*(4), 494–521. https://doi.org/10.1037/1528-3542.8.4.494

PART II

MUSIC LISTENING IN CONTEXT

5. Sound Experience and Imagination at Early School Age: An Opportunity for Unleashing Children's Creative Potential

Mirsada Zećo, Marina Videnović, and Lejla Silajdžić

Introduction

This study describes a novel approach to facilitating children's musical development, creativity, and imagination with the use of vibrational percussive instruments in early music education. These musical instruments have been used in therapeutic techniques called sound bath or sound healing (Goldsby et al., 2022; Stanhope & Weinstein, 2020) and as tools for relaxation, meditation, and stress reduction (e.g., Benton, 2008; Crowe & Scovel, 1996; Lee-Harris et al., 2018; Trivedi & Saboo, 2019). We trialled the introduction of these instruments in early musical education to support children's imagination as a crucial element of creativity (Duffy, 2006; National Advisory Committee on Creative and Cultural Education, 1999). The Vernon Howard continuum of imagination (Howard, 1992) was used as an instrument for validating our assumptions and analysing sound experiences triggered by listening and playing these instruments. The pedagogical aims of this approach are to arouse interest in music-related experiences and promote a long-term appreciation of sounds and music.

Music has already been proven as beneficial for various aspects of children's development, starting from prenatal musical development (Welch, 2014). Early experiences of sound are related to the construction of subjective meanings in the pattern of sound and silence (Welch, 2006). However, loud noises, stress, and the cacophony present in contemporary society may narrow the space for developing this ability (Nadilo, 2013). Children need a supportive environment for their native musical abilities to flourish (Welch, 2014) as well as other cognitive, emotional, and social capacities for music development (Stepanović & Videnović, 2012). Research has shown that, alongside the stimulation of the family environment, early music education can facilitate musical development (Schellenberg, 2015). Moreover, there are non-musical benefits that can be derived from early music education through later development, including improvements to cognitive (Schellenberg, 2004) and socio-emotional skills (Stepanović et al., 2019; Stepanović Ilić et al., in press; see Chapter 6 in this volume) as well as to linguistic (Degé & Schwarzer, 2011; Gromko, 2005) and visuospatial abilities (Rauscher & Zupan, 2000).

While there have been some attempts to introduce the sound of vibrational instruments into education, the focus has been on vulnerable children. Peter Hess (2008) in his pedagogical work aimed to give young people with behaviour disorders equal opportunities for education and an individualised approach to support their development. During his journey to Nepal, Hess was inspired to conceptualise the use of sound as a medium for relaxation and a mechanism to release different blockages in the body, in therapeutic as well as educational settings.

Designing successful early music education for all children (not only for gifted ones) that would broaden their experiences in creative activities related to music and contribute to their early musical development is a challenging task. A sharp focus on the formal curriculum has led to limitations in creative engagement with music, which could be overcome by an informal music education that enhances new ideas and extends experiences (Georgii-Hemming & Westvall, 2010). Some think that returning to sound and the production of sound as the beginning of music experiences could be an appropriate starting point (e.g., Schiavio et al., 2017).

In this applied interdisciplinary study, we traced the sound experiences of a group of six-year-olds during specifically created musical activities. We expected the selected vibrational instruments to be a means whereby children's imaginative processes could be enhanced.

We assimilated musical activities into the daily school schedule and researched how much and in what way holistic sound can stimulate a creative and positive social and musical environment.

Musical vibrational instruments and early education

We have argued that every child should benefit from early musical education, regardless of their talent, background, musical knowledge, or interest. It is well documented that children intuitively discover different qualities of sound, timbres, melodic and rhythmic patterns before starting their formal musical education (Blacking, 1974; Tafuri, 1995), and that these sound-oriented musical actions appear in infancy (Schiavio et al., 2017). Children are generally able to describe sounds verbally, and to anticipate and describe changes in music and differences between musical genres by the end of the preschool period (Burke, 2018; Stepanović & Videnović, 2012;). However, a child needs support to develop these skills, as well as the ability to listen attentively. Teaching music in preschool by ear, or 'aural learning', is an important mode of learning at various levels of music education (Bačlija Sušić et al., 2019; Zećo et al., 2023).

Children can learn musical conventions and structures through environmental exposure to music (Tafuri et al., 2003). Children spontaneously differentiate sound qualities during free imaginative play, where there are no strict rules and they are not foreseeing what they still 'do not know'. In this way, children sensitise themselves and develop listening skills as preconditions for music education.

Vibrational musical instruments could be a powerful didactic tool in early childhood education for several reasons. The soft, resonant, and subtle sound of these instruments prompts one to listen to their qualities in a quiet manner. This is particularly important because growing up in noisy, stressful environments interferes with a child's language development (White-Schwoch et al., 2015), increases the risk of academic failure (Kraus et al., 2014), and can reduce the quality of life (Klatte et al., 2017). Raising children's awareness of sounds provides a basis for enjoying music (Swanwick & Tillman, 1986). It is also a way to increase children's sensitivity to the sound coming from the environment (Zhou, 2015) and their more general phonological awareness (Degé &

Schwarzer, 2011). We furthermore expect that exposure to different, interesting sounds will trigger the process of imagination as an inevitable part of a child's play.

The beginning of formal education can be a very stressful and demanding period for some children in the areas of communication, language acquisition, and social adjustment (Crowe & Scovel, 1996; Videnović et al., 2018). However, listening to vibrational instruments can have a relaxation effect and potentially reduce anxiety and stress (Goldsby et al., 2022; Stanhope & Weinstein, 2020). One of the advantages of these instruments is that it is relatively easy for children to produce a rich and harmonious sound that is novel to them, different from other sounds or instruments, and they can then improvise and produce their own music. Children can very quickly become involved in music-making regardless of their previous knowledge and musical affinity. Research data has shown that children often find playing vibrational instruments more attractive than any other music-related activity (Temmerman, 2000). Hence, playing such instruments in class can enhance students' motivation to engage in musical activities during early music education. Moreover, when children play in a group, they also learn to collaborate in the process of creating meaning through sound. This kind of engagement contributes to their social and collaborative skills development, which is an important objective of education in general (Baucal et al., 2023).

Imagination and improvisation to foster musical creativity

Cognitive processes of improvisation and imagination have a role even in the early years in promoting the development of musical creativity, as was shown in a school context in Croatia (Bašić, 1973) and confirmed in later music research (Koutsoupidou & Hargreaves, 2009). Improvisation implies the simultaneous making and performing of music without much previous preparation (Campbell, 2009; Young, 2002, 2008). Playing with sounds by improvising or exploring could be considered something that any child can do and that should be supported as part of music education (Hickey, 2009). It is expected that six-year-olds are able to make the first steps towards playing musical instruments and devising rhythmical patterns (Burke, 2018). Research shows that creating opportunities for improvising significantly affects the development of musical creative thinking, by promoting musical flexibility, originality, and syntax in children's music-making (Koutsoupidou, 2008). Improvisation in a group as a medium for non-verbal dialogue can support social development and communication skills (MacDonald et al., 2002; Major & Cottle, 2010) and foster emotional expression (Duffy, 2006).

The idea that early music education needs a different approach is pretty old. Émile Jaques-Dalcroze noticed that by teaching children to play and sing, we avoid teaching them to hear and listen (Jaques-Dalcroze, 1932). He designed a well-known approach to music education that aims to support students' innate musicality by introducing rhythmic movement (often called eurhythmics), improvisation and spontaneous expression (Anderson, 2012; Jaques-Dalcroze, 1930). His idea was that music education should encourage the expression of the somatic experience of rhymes before introducing intellectual explanation. The tension in contemporary music education also lies between teaching children musical skills, techniques, and rules, while at the same time leaving space for spontaneous music-making. Playing vibrational instruments does not require a particular mastering of skills for it to be sonically rewarding. It could be a useful didactic tool for encouraging a child's creative growth through spontaneous improvisation.

Spontaneous improvisation can include various artistic areas where the child can express their story through sound and art, and the use of motor skills (Bašić, 1985), including body movements (Burnard, 1999). When children are given the opportunity to choose an instrument for improvisation, they will often select percussion instruments that allow unrestricted body-use, with no need for precise instrumental technique during playing.

A child's imagination and fantasies may support spontaneous music-making in response to sounds, which are considered crucial spontaneous aspects of musical experience (Reichling, 1997). Imagination bridges children's play and musical engagement. Imagination has also been the focus of contemporary arts education as the source of creative expression (e.g., Sungurtekin & Kartal, 2020; Wagner, 2014). Imagination emerges early in childhood development, first in pretend play and later in role play (Harris, 2000). A child's fantasy life is not something trivial or useless. It is a valuable resource for a child's cognitive and socio-emotional development (e.g., Kushnir, 2022). Connecting music with the world of fantasy at an early age may increase the likelihood that a child will later engage in music as an extracurricular activity or hobby. Furthermore, engaging in music in their free time has a multitude of positive effects on students' development (Videnović et al., 2010). Research shows that formal music education in primary school often does not adequately support children's musical creativity and imagination (Sungurtekin, 2021). Formal educational activities are often perceived as mentally demanding, tedious, and boring, frequently provoking anxiety (Pešić et al., 2013; Radišić et al., 2015). The importance of imagination was recognised in Lev Vygotsky's theoretical writings a long time ago. He argued that education should be oriented towards developing children's imaginative abilities (Vygotsky, 1967/2004). Imagination was treated as a basis for all creative activities. Children's experience of music is in many ways different from that of adults or professional musicians (Gardner, 1982).

Howard proposed a way to trace a child's imagination in relation to music (Sungurtekin, 2021). He constructed a scale labelled 'continuum of imagination', which is rarely used, but in our opinion the only available method that considers specific qualitative differences in the child's responses to sounds. The Howard continuum of imagination has four points: 'Beginning with fantasy, imagining the non-existent, imagining what exists but is not present, having an image and imposing it on something, imagining X as Y and ending with perceiving things in general and recognising them' (summarised by Reichling, 1997, p. 43). These points do not imply a particular age or stage of development but are considered milestones in the continuum. The further the child's imagination progresses along the continuum, the greater is their ability to recognise and include concrete sonic characteristics in the imagination process. Reichling (1997) chose this scale to investigate the role of imagination in play and music and to develop a framework for music grounded in play theory. The first point is named *fantasy or imagining the non-existent*. This kind of imagination is the most similar to children's play, when substitutes for the perceivable world are created (e.g., monsters, fairy tales, heroes). At the second point—*imagining what exists but is not present*—things that are part of the imagination exist in the real world, but they are not part of the child's current situation

(Reichling, 1997). The third point describes 'figurative imagination'—*imagining X as Y*—when a metaphoric relationship between present and imagined is created (Reichling, 1997). The final point, labelled 'literal imagination', includes *perceiving things in general and recognising them*. This type of imagination is thoroughly grounded in the sense-world. It includes improvisation with sound elements to construct a new musical performance combination. A child should be able to recognise and preserve sound elements like volume, intensity, harmony, and the colour of the sound.

Aims

Following on from this theoretical background, this empirical study had two related aims. The main aim was to create a series of workshops with intensive musical activities, demonstrations, and active participation, working with selected vibrational instruments in the first year of primary school. The second aim was to investigate students' imaginative processes instigated by listening to and playing vibrational instruments. We assumed that the opportunity for spontaneous improvisation with these instruments would foster a sensitivity to sound qualities.

Method

Participants

Four groups of students attending the first year of primary school, aged 6 to 7, participated in the sound workshops. There were 15 children in each group, 34 boys and 26 girls, totalling 60 children. The workshop leader (WL) was the first author, a music teacher with experience and expertise working with young children. A technical assistant (TA) was involved in supporting the workshops. The research was carried out in a primary school in the Canton of Sarajevo in the academic year 2016/17, with extensive support and collaboration from the headmaster, school counsellors, teachers, and parents. Parents were informed about the content of the workshops and gave informed consent for their children's participation in workshops and research.

Materials

Three types of vibrational instruments were used in all the workshops: gongs, Himalayan Singing Bowls, and Koshi Chimes. All instruments were of East Asian origin. In the workshops, we used the Planetary gong Venus, similar to the Symphonic gong (Cousto, 2015). The gong is about 66 cm high, and it produces a rich, warm bass tone, with a frequency of 221.23 Hz. Children played it while they were on their knees, with the gong placed in front of them (on the right in Figure 5.1).

Fig. 5.1 Photograph of the workshop setting. The faces of the participants are blurred to preserve their privacy. Photo from Mirsada Zećo's private collection

Himalayan Singing Bowls, or small gongs, also have a long-standing tradition (Perry, 2016). Three different bowls were used (Figure 5.1, in the middle) that are often part of sound therapies (Hess, 2008). The small bowl weighs about 600 grams and has a high sound (200–1,200 Hz). The medium bowl weighs about 900 grams and has a wide sound spectrum (100–1,000 Hz). The large sonic bowl weighs 1,500 grams and produces a deep sound (100–2,800 Hz). Therefore, each bowl emanates numerous sounds and aliquots depending on the place where it is touched. A special wooden or leather-coated stick (puja) was used to produce the sound waves by rubbing the instrument. Chimes are also used in classical music as percussion instruments (Pesek & Bratina, 2016). The

Koshi Chimes that were used have a specific sound and contain eight tones in a resonant bamboo tube (held by the children at the left of Figure 5.1).

Procedure

A series of twelve workshop sessions with different content was realised over a period of four months. The workshops were held once a week, lasting forty minutes each. Workshops were scheduled during Music Culture lessons, which is an obligatory subject in general primary school and hence all the children in the class were present. The schedule was adapted according to the children's school timetable and other curricular activities. The developmental characteristics of the age group, such as attention span and the ability to concentrate, including individual differences in abilities and knowledge, were considered when planning the workshop session activities. A technical assistant recorded videos and wrote down children's verbal responses and observations of children's behaviour in the pre-prepared protocols. After each workshop, the workshop leader and assistant collated their observations about the children's behaviours.

Guided fantasy was used to enhance the imaginative process in these workshops. A regular part of some workshops was a fantasy trip with vibrational instruments as the background sound, providing a relaxed and non-threatening environment as a solid ground for creative processes (Anderson, 1980). Children lay on the floor with their eyes closed during guided fantasy, listening to sounds and building up the fantasy stories related to them. In this way the atmosphere, pleasure, state of mind, and mood was created. The leader/researcher delivered spontaneous sound improvisations along with a story. The stories that were intended to inspire fantasy were about natural elements, such as the symbols associated with the vibrational instruments. Children were guided to travel 'through the sky' and listen to the story about a 'water drop', or else an 'imaginary doll' took them on a trip to the land of dreams and play. A brief description of the workshops' content is presented in Table 5.1.

Table 5.1 Content of the workshops

Workshop number	Activities and tasks
W1	Listening to the sound of Himalayan Singing Bowls
	A guided fantasy story about travelling through the sky
	Discussion on auditory experience and drawing the images
W2	Touching the Himalayan Singing Bowls and sensing the vibration
	Discussion on kinaesthetic and auditory experience
W3	Active listening to the sound of the Gong
	Drawing impressions using leaves and fingerprints on the paper
W4	Listening to the sound of the Koshi Chimes
	A guided fantasy story about the drop of water and the fire's flicker
W5	Connecting breathing with the sound of the Himalayan Singing Bowls
	Voice improvisation by children and enhancing awareness of breathing rhythm
W6	Breathing techniques and voice improvisation
	Children playing on Himalayan Singing Bowls
W7	Listening to the story 'Birds on a String' along with a gong sound and dramatisation
	Expressing creative ideas by drawing and touching instruments
W8	Guided fantasy with the doll along with WL's improvisation
	Drawing impressions with 'magic powder' (using solt and chock)
	Children imitating sounds of instruments
W9	Guided fantasy with the doll's travel along with WL's improvisation
	Children improvising on instruments
W10	Guided fantasy about Native Americans and strange beings from the wood along with WL's improvisation
	Children playing instruments and dancing
W11	Improvisation with the voice by children along with the sounds of instruments
W12	Making forms out of plasticine while listening to the improvisation of WL
	Children improvising on instruments

Children at this age cannot accurately express their sound experience solely through words (Lefevre, 2004). With that in mind, children were encouraged to reflect on their sound experience (Workshops 1–5) using different symbolic systems (drawing, movement, or dance). Children were encouraged in the early sessions to fantasise about the sounds, but they did not play the instruments or improvise. For example, having been assigned into groups, children were asked to draw their impressions after different musical activities. Also, they were encouraged to verbally describe the colour of the instruments or to use movement to express their imagination. This method is in line with recent empirical research showing that sensory systems (e.g., touch, smell, the auditory system) interact, producing multimodal or cross-modal experiences (Eitan & Granot, 2006).

In the next set of workshops, children had the opportunity to produce or act out sounds, followed by playing the instruments, in addition to listening and guided fantasy. Namely, children were encouraged to imitate the instruments' sounds with their voices or movements like in the first set, and then they played instruments and improvised with them (Workshops 6–12). The gong's position was lowered to the children's height so they could play more easily, and it was suggested that they 'do not play too hard because the hidden heart is in the instrument's middle'.

The additional thirteenth workshop took place without instruments, and the aim of the session was evaluation; specifically, we were interested to hear children's impressions about the whole process. The workshop leader told the children the instruments had returned to their homeland. Children were invited to share their experiences about the activities or the instrument they enjoyed the most or to tell the story about the homeland of the instruments. A brief questionnaire (four multiple-choice questions and the opportunity to add additional insights) was created to assess parents' perspectives on the workshops (e.g., did the children talk about the workshops, participate in them, describe instruments, or imitate instruments at home). Also, two teachers described their impressions of the workshops and their impact on the children's behaviour.

Data analysis

Qualitative analysis was conducted using the transcriptions of children's verbal reactions from the video recordings. Children's responses during the discussion phase of the workshops, their guided fantasy stories, and spontaneous comments produced during activities (Table 5.1) were included as material for analysis. We used Thematic Analyses (Braun & Clarke, 2006) and combined deductive and inductive methods. Two authors read each child's verbal response, analysing, in particular, their relationship with Howard's four-point classification. Less than 10% of the answers remained unclassified.

Statements were coded by hand on one of the four points of the continuum. Two authors independently coded the transcripts. The statements were mixed up so that the coder could not see in which workshops they had appeared. The differences between codes (less than 10%) were discussed in detail. In case of disagreement, final codes were created collaboratively. We paid particular attention to statements that appeared in the process of the workshops related to whether the children's imagination was stimulated through guided fantasy (Workshops 1–5), and to responses after instruments were introduced and played in the workshop (Workshops 6–12).

Results

Figure 5.2 shows the percentage of responses children gave that were classified to be at a certain point of Howard's continuum across the two workshop phases. Responses to the first five workshops were considered as one phase or group, namely, fantasies induced by the WL's storytelling and playing the instruments. Workshops where the practice of playing and improvisation was introduced (6–12), constituted the second group of responses. We analysed 131 responses in total: 69 were produced during the first five workshops, and the remaining 62 were from the second group of workshops. The results showed that children's imagination reached each point of the Howard continuum of imagination.

5. Sound Experience and Imagination at Early School Age

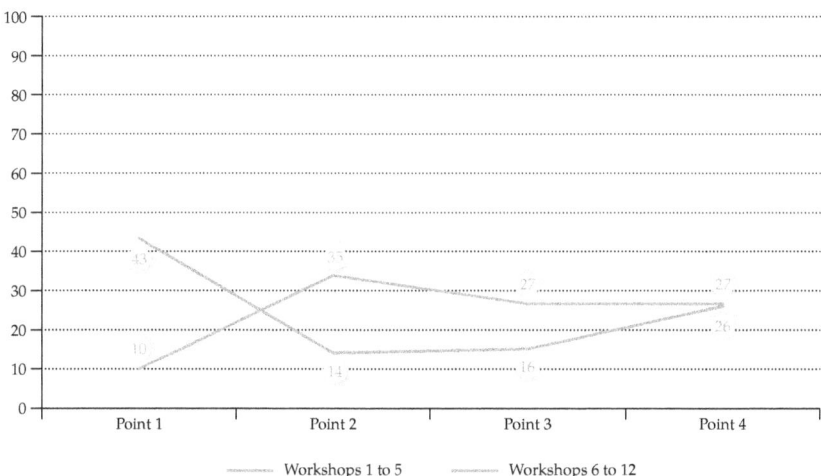

Note. Imagining the non-existing (Point 1), Imagining what exists but is not present (Point 2), Figurative imagination (Point 3), Literal imagination (Point 4).

Fig. 5.2 Percentage of the responses at each point of the Howard continuum of imagination

The biggest difference between the two phases (groups) is in terms of Point 1 of the continuum. At the beginning, the children's imaginative processes were oriented towards the non-existing world when they were exposed to listening to improvisation and guided fantasy. They described the visions they created in their minds as: 'Clouds [that] whisper a secret or a story or take you to the dragon castle'. Sometimes they were emotionally involved: 'A ghost came to our classroom, and I was very scared.' To attribute life to inanimate objects (like clouds) is a well-known characteristic of this developmental stage (e.g., Klingensmith, 1953; Piaget, 1926). It was expected to occur during guided fantasy.

The fantasies sometimes took the form of quite a complex story. For example, a child created a fairy tale about the instruments' homeland during the last workshop:

> Once upon a time there were three instruments, one was big and called a gong, and the other was small, and it was called a bowl. And then they walked until they saw the house and went inside. And the gong says, 'Is this your house or are we going round?' The small bowl says, 'We're just playing!', And the gong says, 'We're not playing after all.' Then something black came, they didn't know what it was, but it was a stick

called 'little black'. When they met that stick, they joined it and followed it. The stick took them to a dark place. When they came into the scary, big house, they met a great spirit and the spirit fulfilled their three wishes to play loud or a little quieter. When they told them what their wishes were, they went on a picnic. The story is over!

The second kind of fantasy with real-life elements was the dominant one in the second group of workshops. Children were 'travelling to Africa, Japan, Paris', or they included their relatives, parents, or friends in their imagination ('My aunt and I walked into the park'; 'I saw a stork and a chicken—a very small stork'; 'My parents were drinking tea, while I was playing').

Figurative imagination (Reihling, 1997) included metaphors to describe sounds. The percentage of these statements increased in the second group of workshops. Our results show that children construct verbal metaphors spontaneously when they try to express their sound experiences. Improvisation tasks seemed to support this process. They compared the sound of the therapeutic instrument with another sound in nature or their environment. For example, 'The sound is like the heart', or 'It is the sound of an elephant movement', or 'The sound of an insect or laser'.

At the final point of the Howard continuum of imagination, the students were able to describe sound characteristics: intensity, volume, rhythm, and harmony. They showed their sensitivity by comparing sounds; for example, 'a better sound than the gong instrument, softer sound' (Literal imagination). Students used their sound experience as a tool to describe something beyond music and the world of sound ('The sound of Earth will be like this'). They also made a connection between different sensory systems. The sound was ascribed a colour, smell, and tactile characteristics: the sound is 'cold', 'sweet', 'heavy', 'soft'. These statements occurred from the first to the last workshop. It is important to notice that the children were not selected based on their musical talent. This shows that children's ability to listen and fantasise based on sounds is better than is often assumed. Introducing vibrational instruments into their education would be one way to stimulate the further development of their imaginative capacities. Table 5.2 presents examples of children's comments from each point.

Table 5.2 Examples of the children's answers

Imagining the non-existing	Imagining what exists but is not present	Figurative imagination	Literal imagination
	It's a volcano!	The sound is like ice.	
The cloud was singing TU, TU, TU.	.... I am an Indian and I light a fire... the fire crackles ...	The bowl has a heart beating in the wood!!!	The sound of the biggest bowl is the deepest! It has both a medium sound and a high sound.
I saw a white cloud and hung out with it.			
I was flying. I was dreaming high.	We are the 'Flowering Tribe' and we are invisible in the forest ... we are very quiet, we listen to the wind.	The sound of a bee.	I'm light from music.
		The sound is a stampede of elephants.	
I went to Mount Jupiter.			I felt a sound, a heavy sound, a deep sound.
	I went to Dubrovnik.	The sound of surprise.	

During the workshops, we took care not to leave any children behind and to include them all in the designed activities. All children had an equal opportunity to participate according to their wishes at the time. Our impression was that children accepted the activities, easily developed their imagination, and were happy to participate. The last workshop was dedicated to the children's evaluation of their experience with this type of work. They had the opportunity to talk about the workshops while drawing with watercolours. For example, a child drew a house for the instruments while saying: 'Their house is somewhere in the air since the instruments go somewhere up there when we play the notes!' They were very enthusiastic about enrolling again on the workshop.

Besides investigating the children's experiences, we also asked parents and teachers to share their impressions with us. Our results show that children shared with their parents their experiences relating to the workshops. Most parents (71%) described instruments and their sounds correctly. Only two parents (out of 42) did not talk with their children about the workshops' activities. Almost all the parents (91% present) reported that their children gladly participated in the workshops' activities. Teachers also described the positive effects of the workshops. They reported that the children looked forward to each workshop with great impatience. They would return to the classroom full of impressions, happy and ready to talk about everything they heard, saw, and learned. As one teacher said: 'After the workshops, they would return to the classroom relaxed, rested, and full of energy for the next wave of teaching.'

Discussion

Research in music pedagogy emphasises the importance of a child's spontaneous improvisation and imagination during musical education (Clennon, 2009; Goncy & Waehler, 2006; Hickey, 2009). Music is a powerful medium for invoking these processes (Ritter & Ferguson, 2017). However, educators experience difficulties implementing and developing activities that are dedicated to these goals. Traditional teaching in the form of 'learning to sing children's songs' has not fostered enough of children's inner creative competencies (Anderson, 2012; Georgii-Hemming & Westvall, 2010). In light of its interdisciplinary and innovative approach to early music education, this study intended to draw attention to underused possibilities relevant to facilitating children's creativity.

The study represents a unique attempt to enhance children's spontaneity, imagination, curiosity, and openness towards new ideas by implementing unconventional vibrational music instruments into music classes. Émile Jaques-Dalcroze, in his pioneer works, used classical musical instruments to foster improvisation with sounds through spontaneous movement (Jaques-Dalcroze, 1930). The sound colour and tone qualities of vibrational musical instruments differ from classical ones, producing uncommon aesthetic experiences. The results suggest that the deliberately planned workshops acted as catalysts for the children's imaginative processes, with these fantasies gradually evolving in their properties, adopting forms of figurative or literal imagination over time. The children were sometimes able to describe sound characteristics and use them to guide their imagination (Howard, 1992). Furthermore, the children expressed sensitivities to sound qualities, particularly in later workshops when playing the instruments was introduced. However, differences between the two sets of workshops do not imply that certain activities, like playing, will better foster sound sensitivity and imagination. This study's methodology only suggests that designed workshops will eventually provoke figurative imagination and sophisticated perception of sound quality among preschool students.

The study results are in line with previous research indicating the significance of children's improvisatory music-making, which can be a tool for fostering creative processes (Koutsoupidou & Hargreaves, 2009) and cognitive development (Duffy, 2006; Pešić & Videnović, 2017). Furthermore, giving children the chance to use imagination and play freely may make them better listeners. In our research, we developed a method to scaffold improvisatory play with musical instruments. This was facilitated by emphasising imaginative ideas evoked by sounds, and modelling improvisatory play to support imagery provided by the workshop leader before inviting children to have a go. The emphasis on sounds and their qualities may have offered a safe environment for play and improvisation.

The practical implication suggests that an effort should be made to introduce listening to simple sounds before singing or instrument learning in early music education. Challenging children to express their experiences will foster their ability to pay attention to and identify sound qualities. Guided fantasy and other art forms (like drawing) can be powerful tools for enhancing the imagination. The important point is that the workshop participants were not selected based on their musical talents or prior knowledge. Indeed, we believe that musical pedagogy should start from the notion that every child could be creative in music (Goncy & Waehler, 2006; National Advisory Committee on Creative and Cultural Education, 1999), rather than musical education being reserved for talented children only. However, organising education following this principle is still a challenge. We argue that this important pilot study on the introduction of vibration instruments into general education could be the way to unlock every child's creative potential.

Limitations of the study

This research design could not separate the effects of workshop activities (including, e.g., guided fantasy) from the effects of being more familiar with the sound of the instruments. It is possible that a change in the type of imagination during the workshop might be related to children becoming more familiar and relaxed in the new activity, and should not be exclusively attributed to the workshop activities. It is important to keep in mind that no control group or elimination of confounding factors were used, which limits the inference about the effects of the pedagogical intervention. Furthermore, we did not formally assess the skill development outcomes of the workshops. Our observations do point to the inclusivity of the methods and the qualitative benefits that the children reported.

Conclusion

As a result of our research, we can state that vibrational musical instruments can play an important role in music education classes, in the early years and possibly beyond. They can be included successfully in combination with guided fantasy, drawing, dancing, and improvisation activities. The benefits are directed towards increasing children's sound sensitivity and making them better music listeners, which was facilitated by the fact that children did not have prior expectations of how these instruments sound. Moreover, it was easy for them to play the instruments and make rich sounds. In that way, every child had an equal opportunity to be a musician regardless of their abilities and previous knowledge. This represents a good start for further implementations made for developing musical skills in general education without excluding anyone.

We are aware that this practice can sometimes be a challenge to incorporate into existing research paradigms and music education. These activities require significant resources. However, this action research was essential for gaining new insights into the opportunities to make music in childhood in a new setting. Clearly, teachers are the gatekeepers and can have a powerful influence on access to music: 'From a Vygotskian sociocultural perspective, it is clear that children's development is shaped and guided by "more competent others"' (Lamont, 2017, p. 180). The implementation of workshops with unconventional sound instruments and related practice in regular schools can serve as an incentive for adopting this flexible model. Such instruments have a place in enhancing the imagination, aural skills, and cognitive development. The practice of 'playing with music' opens new ways of understanding music and building up 'music in identity' (Hargreaves et al., 2012). This trial opens the possibility of applying theory and practice from the music therapy domain to the future work of music educators. It presents a challenge and a contribution for further use and exploration.

References

Anderson, R.F. (1980). Using guided fantasy with children. *Elementary School Guidance and Counseling, 15*(1), 39–47.

Anderson, W.T. (2012). The Dalcroze approach to music education: Theory and applications. *General Music Today, 26*(1), 27–33. https://doi.org/10.1177/1048371311428979

Bačlija Sušić, B., Habe, K., & Mirošević, J.K. (2019). The role of improvisation in higher music education. In L. Gómez Chova, A. López Martínez, & I. Candel Torres (eds), *ICERI2019 12th International Conference of Education, Research and Innovation, Seville, Spain: Conference Proceedings* (pp. 4473–4482). IATED Academy. https://library.iated.org/view/BACLIJASUSIC2019ROL

Bašić, E. (1973). Improvizacija kao kreativni čin [Improvisation as an act of creativity]. *Umjetnost i dijete, 26*(5), 44–69.

Bašić, E. (1985). Sinkretizam u muzikalnom izražavanju djeteta [Syncretism in children's musical expression]. *Umjetnost i dijete, 17*(1), 21–33.

Baucal, A., Jošić, S., Stepanović Ilić, I., Videnović, M., Ivanović, J., & Krstić, K. (2023). What makes peer collaborative problem solving productive or unproductive: A qualitative systematic review. *Educational Research Review,* 100567. https://doi.org/10.1016/j.edurev.2023.100567

Benton, M. (2008). *Gong yoga: Healing and enlightenment through sound.* Bookshelf Press.

Blacking, J. (1974). *How musical is man?* University of Washington Press.

Braun, V., & Clarke, V. (2006). Using thematic analysis in psychology. *Qualitative Research in Psychology, 3*(2), 77–101. https://doi.org/10.1191/1478088706qp063oa

Burke, N. (2018). *Musical development matters in the early years.* The British Association for Early Childhood Education. https://early-education.org.uk/wp-content/uploads/2021/12/Musical-Development-Matters-ONLINE.pdf

Burnard, P. (1999). Bodily intention in children's improvisation and composition. *Psychology of Music, 27*(2), 159–174. https://doi.org/10.1177/0305735699272007

Campbell, P.S. (2009). Learning to improvise music, improvising to learn music. In G. Solis, & B. Nettl (eds), *Musical improvisation: Art, education, and society* (pp. 119–142). University of Illinois Press.

Clennon, O.D. (2009). Facilitating musical composition as 'contract learning' in the classroom: The development and application of a teaching resource for primary school teachers in the UK. *International Journal of Music Education, 27*(4), 300–313. https://doi.org/10.1177/0255761409344373

Cousto, H. (2015). *The cosmic octave: Origin of harmony*. Mendocino, California, EUA: LifeRhythm.

Crowe, B.J., & Scovel, M. (1996). An overview of sound healing practices: Implications for the profession of music therapy. *Music Therapy Perspectives, 14*(1), 21–29. https://doi.org/10.1093/mtp/14.1.21

Degé, F., & Schwarzer, G. (2011). The effect of a music program on phonological awareness in preschoolers. *Frontiers in Psychology, 2*, Article 124. https://doi.org/10.3389/fpsyg.2011.00124

Duffy, B. (2006). *Supporting creativity and imagination in the early years* (2nd ed.). Open University Press.

Eitan, Z., & Granot, R.Y. (2006). How music moves: Musical parameters and listeners' images of motion. *Music Perception: An Interdisciplinary Journal, 23*(3), 221–248. https://doi.org/10.1525/mp.2006.23.3.221

Jaques-Dalcroze, E. (1930). Eurhythmics and its implications (F. Rothwell, Trans.). *The Musical Quarterly, 16*, 358–365. https://doi.org/10.1093/mq/XVI.3.358

Jaques-Dalcroze, E. (1932). Rhythmics and pianoforte improvisation (F. Rothwell, Trans.). *Music and Letters, 13*, 371–380.

Gardner, H. (1982). *Art, mind, and brain: A cognitive approach to creativity*. Basic Books.

Georgii-Hemming, E., & Westvall, M. (2010). Music education—a personal matter? Examining the current discourses of music education in Sweden. *British Journal of Music Education, 27*(1), 21–33. https://doi.org/10.1017/S0265051709990179

Goldsby, T.L., Goldsby, M.E., McWalters, M., & Mills, P.J. (2022). Sound healing: Mood, emotional, and spiritual well-being interrelationships. *Religions, 13*(2), Article 123. https://doi.org/10.3390/rel13020123

Goncy, E.A., & Waehler, C.A. (2006). An empirical investigation of creativity and musical experience. *Psychology of Music, 34*(3), 307–321. https://doi.org/10.1177%2F0305735606064839

Gromko, J.E. (2005). The effect of music instruction on phonemic awareness in beginning readers. *Journal of Research in Music Education, 53*(3), 199–209. https://doi.org/10.1177/002242940505300302

Hargreaves, D. J., Hargreaves, J. J., & North, A. C. (2012). Imagination and creativity in music listening. In D. Hargreaves, D. Miell, & R. Macdonald (eds), *Musical imaginations: Multidisciplinary perspectives on creativity, performance and perception*. Oxford University Press.

Harris, P.L. (2000). *The work of the imagination*. Blackwell Publishing.

Hess, P. (2008). *Singing bowls for health and inner harmony through sound massage according to Peter Hess. Tension reduction, creativity enhancement, history, rituals.* (T. Hunter, Trans). (Original work published 1999). Verlag Peter Hess.

Hickey, M. (2009). Can improvisation be 'taught'?: A call for free improvisation in our schools. *International Journal of Music Education, 27*(4), 285–299. https://doi.org/10.1177/0255761409345442

Howard, V.A. (1992). *Learning by all means: Lessons from the arts.* Peter Lang.

Klatte, M., Spilski, J., Mayerl, J., Möhler, U., Lachmann, T., & Bergström, K. (2017). Effects of aircraft noise on reading and quality of life in primary school children in Germany: Results from the NORAH study. *Environment and Behavior, 49*(4), 390–424. https://doi.org/10.1177/0013916516642580

Klingensmith, S.W. (1953). Child animism: What the child means by 'alive'. *Child Development, 24,* 51–61.

Koutsoupidou, T. (2008). Effects of different teaching styles on the development of musical creativity: Insights from interviews with music specialists. *Musicae Scientiae, 12*(2), 311–335. https://doi.org/10.1177/102986490801200207

Koutsoupidou, T., & Hargreaves, D.J. (2009). An experimental study of the effects of improvisation on the development of children's creative thinking in music. *Psychology of Music, 37*(3), 251–278. https://doi.org/10.1177/0305735608097246

Kraus, N., Hornickel, J., Strait, D.L., Slater, J., & Thompson, E. (2014). Engagement in community music classes sparks neuroplasticity and language development in children from disadvantaged backgrounds. *Frontiers in Psychology, 5,* Article 1403. https://doi.org/10.3389/fpsyg.2014.01403

Kushnir, T. (2022). Imagination and social cognition in childhood. *Wiley Interdisciplinary Reviews: Cognitive Science, 13*(4), Article e1603. https://doi.org/10.1002/wcs.1603

Lamont, A. (2017). Musical identity, interest, and involvement. In R. McDonald, D.J. Hargreaves, & D. Miell (eds), *Handbook of musical identities* (pp. 176–196). Oxford University Press. https://doi.org/10.1093/acprof:oso/9780199679485.003.0010

Lee-Harris, G., Timmers, R., Humberstone, N., & Blackburn, D. (2018). Music for relaxation: A comparison across two age groups. *Journal of Music Therapy, 55*(4), 439–462. https://doi.org/10.1093/jmt/thy016

Lefevre, M. (2004). Playing with sound: The therapeutic use of music in direct work with children. *Child & Family Social Work, 9*(4), 333–345. https://doi.org/10.1111/j.1365-2206.2004.00338.x

MacDonald, R.A.R., Miell, D., & Mitchell, L. (2002). An investigation of children's musical collaborations: The effect of friendship and age. *Psychology of Music, 30*(2), 148–163. https://doi.org/10.1177/0305735602302002

Major, A.E., & Cottle, M. (2010). Learning and teaching through talk: Music composing in the classroom with children aged six to seven years. *British Journal of Music Education, 27*(3), 289–304. https://doi.org/10.1017/S0265051710000240

Nadilo, B. (2013). Definiranje i zakonsko određivanje buke: Mnogo nepreciznosti i nejasnoća [Definitions and legal determination of noise: A lot of vagueness and ambiguity]. *Građevinar, 64*(9), 857–863. http://casopis-gradjevinar.hr/assets/Uploads/JCE_65_2013_9_8_Zastita-oklisa.pdf

National Advisory Committee on Creative and Cultural Education (1999). *All our futures: Creativity, culture and education*. DfEE Publications. https://sirkenrobinson.com/pdf/allourfutures.pdf

Perry, F. (2016). *Himalayan sound revelations: The complete Singing bowl book*. Polair Publishing.

Pesek, A., & Bratina, T. (2016). Gong and its therapeutic meaning. *Muzikološki zbornik/ Musicological Annual, 52*(2), 137–161. https://doi.org/10.4312/mz.52.2.137-161

Pešić, J., & Videnović, M. (2017). Slobodno vreme iz perspective mladih: kvalitativna analiza vremenskog dnevnika srednjoškolaca [Leisure from the youth perspective: A qualitative analysis of high school students' time diary]. *Zbornik Instituta za pedagoška istrazivanja, 49*(2), 314–330. https://doi.org/10.2298/ZIPI1702314P

Pešić, J., Videnović, M., & Plut, D. (2013). How high-schoolers perceive educational activities: A qualitative analysis of time recordings. *Nastava i vaspitanje, 62*(3), 407–420. https://scindeks.ceon.rs/article.aspx?artid=0547-33301303407P

Piaget, J. (1926). *La représentation du monde chez l'enfant* [The child conception of the world]. Félix Alcan.

Radišić, J., Videnović, M., & Baucal, A. (2015). Math anxiety—contributing school and individual level factors. *European Journal of Psychology of Education, 30*(1), 1–20. https://doi.org/10.1007/s10212-014-0224-7

Rauscher, F.H., & Zupan, M.A. (2000). Classroom keyboard instructions improve kindergarten children's spatial-temporal performance: A field experiment. *Early Childhood Research Quarterly, 15*(2), 215–228. https://doi.org/10.1016/S0885-2006(00)00050-8

Reichling, M.J. (1997). Music, imagination, and play. *Journal of Aesthetic Education, 31*(1), 41–55. https://doi.org/10.2307/3333470

Ritter, S.M., & Ferguson, S. (2017). Happy creativity: Listening to happy music facilitates divergent thinking. *PloS ONE, 12*(9), Article e0182210. https://doi.org/10.1371/journal.pone.0182210

Schellenberg, E.G. (2004). Music lessons enhance IQ. *Psychological Science, 15*(8), 511–514. https://doi.org/10.1111/j.0956-7976.2004.00711.x

Schellenberg, E.G. (2015). Music and nonmusical abilities. In G. McPherson (ed.), *The child as musician: A handbook of musical development* (2nd ed., pp. 149–176). Oxford University Press. https://doi.org/10.1093/acprof:oso/9780198744443.003.0008

Schiavio, A., van der Schyff, D., Kruse-Weber, S., & Timmers, R. (2017). When the sound becomes the goal: 4E cognition and teleomusicality in early infancy. *Frontiers in Psychology, 8,* Article 1585. https://doi.org/10.3389/fpsyg.2017.01585

Stanhope, J., & Weinstein, P. (2020). The human health effects of singing bowls: A systematic review. *Complementary Therapies in Medicine, 51,* Article 102412. https://doi.org/10.1016/j.ctim.2020.102412

Stepanović Ilić, I., Krnjaić, Z., Videnović, M. & Krstić, K. (in press). How do adolescents engage with music in spare time? Leisure patterns and their relation with socio-demographic characteristics, wellbeing and risk behaviours. *Psychology of Music.*

Stepanović, I., & Videnović, M. (2012). Intelektualni (saznajni) razvoj [Intellectual (cognitive) development]. In A. Baucal (ed.), *Standardi za razvoj i učenje dece ranih uzrasta u Srbiji* [Standards for the development and learning of early-age children in Serbia] (pp. 23–39). Filozofski fakultet.

Stepanović Ilić, I., Videnović, M., & Petrović, N. (2019). Leisure patterns and values in adolescents from Serbia born in 1990s: An attempt at building a bridge between the two domains. *Serbian Political Thought, 66,* 99–123. https://doi.org/10.22182/spm.6642019.5

Sungurtekin, S. (2021). Classroom and music teachers' perceptions about the development of imagination and creativity in primary music education. *Journal of Pedagogical Research, 5*(3), 164–186. http://doi.org/10.33902/JPR.2021371364

Sungurtekin, S., & Kartal, H. (2020). Listening to colourful voices: How do children imagine their music lessons in school? *International Online Journal of Primary Education, 9*(1), 73–84. https://www.iojpe.org/index.php/iojpe/article/view/40

Swanwick, K., & Tillman, J. (1986). The sequence of musical development: A study of children's composition. *British Journal of Music Education, 3*(3), 305–339. https://doi.org/10.1017/S0265051700000814

Tafuri, J. (1995). *L'educazione musicale: Teorie, metodi, pratiche* [Music education. Theories, methods, practices] (Vol. 1). EDT srl.

Tafuri, J., Baldi, G., & Caterina, R. (2003). Beginnings and endings in the musical improvisations of children aged 7 to 10 years. *Musicae Scientiae, 7*(1), 157–174. https://doi.org/10.1177/10298649040070S108

Temmerman, N. (2000). An investigation of the music activity preferences of pre-school children. *British Journal of Music Education, 17*(1), 51–60. https://ro.uow.edu.au/edupapers/6

Trivedi, G.Y., & Saboo, B. (2019). A comparative study of the impact of Himalayan singing bowls and supine silence on stress index and heart rate variability. *Journal of Behavior Therapy and Mental Health, 2*(1), 40–50. https://doi.org/10.14302/issn.2474-9273.jbtm-19-3027

Videnović, M., Pešić, J., & Plut, D. (2010). Young people's leisure time: Gender differences. *Psihologija, 43*(2), 199–214. https://doiserbia.nb.rs/img/doi/0048-5705/2010/0048-57051002199V.pdf

Videnović, M., Stepanović Ilić, I., & Krnjaić, Z. (2018). Dropping out: What are schools doing to prevent it? *Serbian Political Thought, 17*(1), 61–77. https://www.ips.ac.rs/wp-content/uploads/2018/07/spt17_12018-4.pdf

Vygotsky, L.S. (2004). Imagination and creativity in childhood (M.E. Sharpe, Trans.). *Journal of Russian and East European Psychology, 42*(1), 7–97. https://doi.org/10.1080/10610405.2004.11059210 (Original work published 1967)

Wagner, T. (2014). *The global achievement gap: Why our kids don't have the skills they need for college, careers, and citizenship—and what we can do about it*. Hachette UK.

Welch, G.F. (2006). Singing and vocal development. In G. McPherson (ed.), *The child as musician: A handbook of musical development* (pp. 311–330). Oxford University Press. https://doi.org/10.1093/acprof:oso/9780198530329.003.0016

Welch, G.F. (2014). The musical development and education of young children. In B. Spodek & O.N. Saracho (eds), *Handbook of research on the education of young children* (pp. 269–286). Routledge. https://doi.org/10.4324/9781315045511

White-Schwoch, T., Davies, E.C., Thompson, E.C., Carr, K.W., Nicol, T., Bradlow, A.R., & Kraus, N. (2015). Auditory-neurophysiological responses to speech during early childhood: Effects of background noise. *Hearing Research, 328*, 34–47. https://doi.org/10.1016/j.heares.2015.06.009

Young, S. (2002). Young children's spontaneous vocalizations in free-play: Observations of two- to three-year-olds in a day-care setting. *Bulletin of the Council for Research in Music Education, 152*, 43–53.

Young, S. (2008). Collaboration between 3- and 4-year-olds in self-initiated play on instruments. *International Journal of Educational Research, 47*(1), 3–10. https://doi.org/10.1016/j.ijer.2007.11.005

Zećo, M., Videnović, M., & Žmukić, M. (2023). Sound improvisation through image and shape. *Facta Universitatis, Series Visual Arts and Music, 9*(2), 101-112. https://doi.org/10.22190/FUVAM231002009Z

Zhou, J. (2015). The value of music in children's enlightenment education. *Open Journal of Social Sciences, 3*(12), 200–206. https://doi.org/10.4236/jss.2015.312023

6. Adolescent Musical Preferences and their Relationship with Schwartz's Basic Values

Ivana Stepanović Ilić, Marina Videnović, Zora Krnjaić, and Ksenija Krstić

Introduction

This chapter investigates the structure of music preferences in Serbian adolescents with the aim of comparing the results with studies in other countries, mostly in Western Europe, Australia, and the USA, as well as with previous Serbian findings and surveys conducted in neighbouring Balkan countries. The other important objective of this study is to explore the relationship between music preferences and values, which is rarely investigated although it is frequently understood that musical taste reflects one's ethics and worldview. As a theoretical model with cross-cultural aspirations, Schwartz's taxonomy of ten basic values distinguished by their motivational goals was applied (Schwartz, 1994).

Music preferences in adolescence

Numerous studies indicate that a large proportion of adolescents' spare time and many activities are dedicated to music (López-Sintas et al., 2017; Piko & Vazsonyi, 2004; Stepanović Ilić et al., 2019). Listening to music in adolescence can be a solitary activity, but it is also frequently practised with friends, and it takes place in a variety of contexts (Franken et al., 2017; North et al., 2004). Particular music preferences are associated with different developmental outcomes and those related to mental health. Amongst other aspects, music influences social identity construction, emotional regulation, and socialisation (Abrams, 2009; Hargreaves et al., 2015; Lonsdale, 2021; Miranda, 2013; Miranda et al., 2015; North & Hargreaves, 1999; Saarikallio & Erkkilä, 2007). Miranda and Gaudreau (2011) have found higher scores on well-being scales and better psychological adaptation in adolescents who experience stronger positive emotions while listening to music. Although studies (Franken et al., 2017; Miranda & Claes, 2009; Mulder et al., 2010) have established a link between listening to loud and energetic music (Heavy Metal, intense forms of Rap, Rock, and Dance) and an inclination towards externalising behaviours (aggression, delinquency, substance use), recent research (Olsen et al., 2022; Slade et al., 2021) has shown that youngsters can experience a variety of emotions when listening to music with violent lyrics, depending on their particular passion for it and their state of mind at the time.

Adolescence is a period of stabilisation and crystallisation of musical preferences. Children are open to different music genres while adolescents have narrower, better-defined, and longer-lasting musical preferences (Delsing et al., 2008; Hargreaves et al., 2015; Thomas, 2016). Mid-adolescence is commonly marked by an inclination towards popular music, while older adolescents develop preferences for complex genres (Hargreaves et al., 2015; Reić Ercegovac & Dobrota, 2011; Reić Ercegovac et al., 2017). Mulder et al. (2010) explain the cause of such a tendency as progressive cognitive development, which allows a change in preferences and an understanding of sophisticated genres (see Chapter 7 in this volume).

Structure of adolescents' music preferences

The music preferences of young people have been extensively investigated in the past two decades (Miranda et al., 2015), mostly in relation to personality, but also to psychological arousal and social identity (Rentfrow & Gosling, 2003). The Short Test of Musical Preferences (STOMP) is a famous comprehensive questionnaire for analysing affinity for music, developed by Rentfrow and Gosling (2003, 2020), which includes fourteen music genres (Blues, Jazz, Classical, Folk, Rock, Alternative, Heavy Metal, Country, Soundtracks, Religious, Pop, Rap/Hip-hop, Soul/Funk, Electronic/Dance). Rentfrow and Gosling determined four factors describing wider dimensions: Reflective and Complex (including Classical, Jazz, Folk, Blues), Intense and Rebellious (Rock, Alternative, Heavy Metal), Upbeat and Conventional (Country, Pop, Soundtracks, Religious), and Energetic and Rhythmic (Rap, Soul, Electronic). That these dimensions might be universal became evident after they were replicated in many Western and South American countries (Miranda et al., 2015). Using a different methodology (ratings of given genre excerpts), Rentfrow et al. (2011) later established a five-factor MUSIC model: Mellow, representing smooth and relaxing music; Urban, described as rhythmic and percussion music; Sophisticated, composed of music styles perceived as complex, intelligent, and inspiring; Intense, including loud, fierce, and energetic music; and Campestral, defined as country and singer-songwriter music.

Reviewing the studies about music preferences of adolescents, Miranda et al. (2015) state that a four- or five-factor structure is common. The four-factor solution (Rock, Elite, Urban, Pop/Dance), similar to Rentfrow and Gosling's, is found in Dutch (Delsing et al., 2008) and South African (Rock, African, Academic, Party) adolescents (Getz et al., 2012). In Canada, Miranda and Claes (2009) identified Metal, Soul, Electronic, Pop, and Classical dimensions. The five-factor model (Urban, Rock, Pop, Dance, Highbrow) is also found across ten European countries (Miranda et al., 2015). Although these music preferences are comparable, researchers detected specific cultural/ethnic tastes (Delsing et al., 2008; Miranda et al., 2015). In the case of Balkan countries, a specific cultural influence could be recognised in one of the identified factors that represents a mixture of national pop and folk music (Gardikiotis & Baltzis, 2012; Petrović & Kuzmanović, 2009; Reić Ercegovac et al., 2017; Tekman, 2009).

In Serbia, only one study (Petrović & Kuzmanović, 2009) has examined adolescents' music preferences among 13 genres (using a yes/no scale) and discovered four factors. The first factor, labelled as Folk after the highest loading of this genre, has negative loadings on Rock, Heavy Metal, and Punk in particular, suggesting dislike of these genres. The second factor comprises Hip-hop, R&B, Techno, and Pop, and is called Club music by the authors, who claim that it is usually played at nightclubs. The Sophisticated factor includes Jazz, Blues, Classic, Alternative, and Reggae. The Conventional factor is predominantly defined by Pop, less by Rock, and even less by Folk. These results are akin to the findings from Western societies, but they also show some characteristics that are inherent in Balkan countries, indicating the need to conduct studies that compare different cultures.

Music preferences and values

Values are relatively persistent broad goals, reflecting one's worldview and influencing a person's behaviour, attitudes, and interests (Rokeach, 1985; Schwartz, 1994). Researchers emphasise that adolescents' musical tastes express their personality and values (Franken et al., 2017; Hargreaves et al., 2015). Musical preferences are thought to reflect an adolescent's inner nature, which is important for social bonding and consequently for identity development (Boer et al., 2011; North & Hargreaves, 1999). Thus, it is usually assumed that the value system determines the musical choices and taste of young people (Gardikiotis & Baltzis, 2012; Petrović & Kuzmanović, 2009). It is likely, however, that music preferences influence the value system itself in adolescence. Musicians are often adolescents' role models (Miranda, 2013; Stepanović, Pavlović Babić, & Krnjaić, 2009; Stepanović Ilić et al., 2017), so one can expect that they might easily adopt the lifestyles and values associated with their favourite genres and authors.

With the previous discussion in mind, it is surprising that investigations into the relationship between adolescents' music preferences and values are sparse. Although Petrović and Kuzmanović (2009) identified four music factors and examined 36 personal and social goals, they did not group value orientations to relate them to the music factors. Instead, they only tested the difference between adolescents who listened to a particular genre and those who did not regarding each social/personal aspiration, and they found a weak relationship between value orientations and music preferences. Greek (Gardikiotis & Baltzis, 2012) and Turkish studies (Tekman et al., 2012) only connect music preferences to Schwartz's (1992) values, namely with four higher-level factors. The Greek study shows that Self-transcendence (with the highest loadings on Universalism and Benevolence values) is related to complex, rebellious, and traditional Greek folk preferences. Turkish findings relate this value to a preference for local Turkish music and a sophisticated musical taste, including Classical, Jazz & Blues, Samba, and World music. Self-enhancement (with the highest loadings on Power and Achievement values) in the Greek study is associated positively with sentimental/sensational music (Soul, R&B, Rap, Greek pop and rap) and negatively with Rock and Greek folk. Similarly, the Turkish study connects this value with contemporary music, i.e., mainly with Pop and Hip-hop. Openness to change (with the highest loadings on Self-direction, Stimulation, and Hedonism values) is linked with rebellious and non-mainstream music genres in Greece, as well as with intense (Metal, Electronic, Rock) and sophisticated music in Turkey. Conservation (with the highest loadings on Security and Conformity values), similarly to Self-enhancement, correlates positively with sentimental/sensational Greek and contemporary Turkish genres, and negatively with complex and non-mainstream styles of music in Greece and intense ones in Turkey. Examining values as mediators between musical taste and friendship, Boer et al. (2011) found similar results. Rebellious music was positively associated with Openness and negatively with Conservation. Pop music is preferred by adolescents inclined to Self-enhancement and Openness, while those listening to complex genres appreciate Self-transcendence values.

Aims

The first aim of this study is to establish a structure of music preferences in Serbian adolescents and to compare it with findings obtained in Western countries. Furthermore, we deem it important to enrich this field by tracking cultural variations in the musical preferences of young people. Hence, we intend to juxtapose our results with an earlier Serbian investigation (Petrović & Kuzmanović, 2009) as well as with research from other Balkan countries (Gardikiotis & Baltzis, 2012; Reić Ercegovac & Dobrota, 2011; Tekman, 2009) which share a similar socio-cultural context. The second aim is dedicated to the underestimated relation between music preferences and values in adolescence. Adolescence is a developmental period in which a system of values and particular music preferences become a defining feature of young people (Boer et al., 2011; North & Hargreaves, 1999), and it is reasonable to expect these domains to be connected.

Method

Participants

The quota sample included 1,358 adolescents (56% female) from the first year (51%, aged 15) and third year (49%, aged 17) of 26 secondary schools (62% vocational and 38% grammar) in 10 cities in three regions of Serbia (north, central, and south).

Materials

Music preferences were assessed by a 5-point scale (1 = never, 5 = often) measuring the frequency of listening to 12 genres: Pop, Rock, Folk, Techno/Electronic, Hip-hop/Rap, Punk, Heavy Metal, House, Rhythm & Blues, Reggae, Jazz, and Classical. The selected genres are very similar to the STOMP test (Rentfrow & Gosling, 2003, 2020).

Ten Schwartz values (Security, Conformity, Tradition, Benevolence, Universalism, Self-direction, Stimulation, Hedonism, Achievement, Power) were measured by a 6-point scale, and the scores were standardised according to the European Social Survey instruction (Schwartz, 2003).

Procedure

The data was collected via a survey on adolescents' everyday life that was administered in 2018 by specially trained school psychologists. Informed consent was obtained from school principals and the respondents' parents. The students were assured that their data would remain anonymous. The research was approved by the local Institutional Review Board.

Data analysis

Factor analysis, i.e. principal axis factoring (Oblimin rotation) was used to identify adolescents' wider music preferences. To examine the relationship between these music preferences and Schwartz's values, canonical correlation analysis was carried out with musical preferences as one set of variables and Schwartz's ten values as the other set.

Results

The Kaiser-Meyer-Olkin measure of sampling adequacy (.76), and Bartlett's test of sphericity, $\chi^2(66) = 4016.94, p < .01$, indicated that factor analysis was adequate for the obtained data. According to the Kaiser-Guttman criterion and the scree plot, the four-component solution best describes the data explaining 46% of the variance.

Table 6.1 Musical preferences: Structure matrix

Musical preferences	Factors			
	Rebellious	Energetic	Sophisticated	Conventional
Heavy Metal	**.877**		.360	
Punk	**.740**		.389	
Rock	**.681**		.357	
Folk	−.321			
Techno and Electronic		**.722**		
House		**.661**		
Hip-hop and Rap		**.533**		
Jazz	.361		**.865**	
Rhythm & Blues	**.417**		**.746**	
Reggae	.340	.350	**.506**	
Classical music			.390	
Pop				**.604**

Note. Factor loadings lower than .30 were suppressed. Structure coefficients higher than .40 are bolded.

The Rebellious factor, explaining 25% of the variance, shows adolescents' interest in Heavy Metal, Punk, and Rock music, and to a lesser extent in Rhythm & Blues, Jazz, and Reggae (Table 6.1). It is also characterised by a negative attitude towards Folk music. Note that Folk in the Serbian context represents a mixture of Serbian ethnic music, Turkish and Greek folk music, as well as electronic rhythms, and it cannot be considered a complex genre according to the terms of Western countries (Rentfrow & Gosling, 2003). We named this factor Rebellious, after Rentfrow and

Gosling's very similar Intense and Rebellious preference that includes Rock, Heavy Metal, and Alternative.

The Energetic factor (9% of the variance), is related dominantly to a preference for Techno, House, and Hip-hop, but also to some extent to Reggae. This factor is analogous to Rentfrow and Gosling's Energetic and Rhythmic preferences.

The Sophisticated factor (7% of the variance) is defined with Jazz, Rhythm & Blues, Reggae music, and to a lesser extent to genres predominant in the Rebellious factor (see Table 6.1). It is comparable to the factor of the same name within the five-factor MUSIC model (Rentfrow et al., 2011). The correlation between the Sophisticated factor and the Rebellious factor is moderate (around .46), which justifies the use of Oblimin rotation.

The Conventional factor (4% of the variance) is strongly loaded by Pop, while loadings on other genres are lower than .30. It is similar to the factor found by Serbian researchers Petrović and Kuzmanović (2009), and to the one identified by Rentfrow and Gosling (2003).

The canonical correlation analysis was conducted to examine the relationship between Schwartz's values and music preference components, in order to explore which values are associated with particular musical tastes. This analysis revealed three statistically significant pairs of canonical factors indicating that adolescents' music preferences and their values represent related phenomena. The full model across all functions is statistically significant, $Wilks's\ \lambda = .850$, $F(40, 4775.84) = 5.212, p < .001$. For the set of four canonical functions, the $r^2\ (1 - \lambda)$ type effect size is .15 showing that 15% of the variance is shared between the two sets. Apart from the full model (Functions 1 to 4), Functions 2 to 4, $F(27, 3880.49) = 4.18, p < .001$, and 3 to 4 were also statistically significant, $F(16,2522) = 2.90, p < .001$. Function 4 did not meet the statistical significance criteria $(p > .01)$.

Table 6.2 Canonical solution for Values and Musical preferences:
The structure coefficients

Values	Function 1	Function 2	Function 3
Security	−.140	**−.413**	.209
Conformity	.058	**−.646**	−.163
Tradition	.103	**−.565**	−.101
Benevolence	.086	.249	**.467**
Universalism	**−.792**	−.024	.254
Self-direction	−.391	**.516**	**−.466**
Stimulation	.167	**.677**	.196
Hedonism	**.608**	.353	.062
Achievement	.229	−.068	.125
Power	.394	.112	**−.574**
Rebellious	**−.745**	.345	**−.438**
Sophisticated	.222	**.901**	−.373
Energetic	**−.669**	.247	−.358
Conventional	−.274	.392	**.873**

Note. Structure coefficients higher than .40 are bolded.

The structure coefficients are presented in Table 6.2. Correlations higher than .40 were considered significant for interpretation. The results show that adolescents who don't prefer Rebellious and Energetic music have lower scores on Universalism and higher on Hedonism (Function 1). The Sophisticated music preference is positively related to Self-direction and Stimulation values, and negatively to Conformity, Tradition, and Security (Function 2). The structure coefficients for Function 3 show that the Conventional music preference is negatively related to Power and Self-direction values and positively to Benevolence. The Rebellious music preference has the opposite relation to these values. Thus, adolescents who do not appreciate these genres have lower scores on Power and Self-direction, but higher on Benevolence (Function 3).

Previously reported findings are summarised in Table 6.3, primarily to enhance understanding of the relationship between the obtained music preferences and Schwartz's values. Thus, the right-hand column presents extracted factors, and the left contains signs reflecting the nature of their relationship with relevant values and the description of those values provided by Schwartz and Boehnke (2004, p. 239).

Table 6.3 Results regarding the relation between musical preferences and values

Musical preferences	Values
Rebellious (+) Heavy Metal, Rock, Punk (−) Folk	(+) Universalism—Understanding, appreciation, tolerance, and protection for the welfare of all people and nature (−) Hedonism—Pleasure or sensuous gratification for oneself (+) Power—Social status and prestige, control or dominance over people and resources (+) Self-direction—Independent thought and action: choosing, creating, exploring (−) Benevolence—Preservation and enhancement of the welfare of people one is in frequent personal contact with
Energetic (+) Techno, House, Hip-hop	(+) Universalism—Understanding, appreciation, tolerance, and protection for the welfare of all people and nature (−) Hedonism—Pleasure or sensuous gratification for oneself
Sophisticated (+) Jazz, Rhythm & Blues, Reggae	(+) Stimulation—Excitement, novelty, change in life (+) Self-direction—Independent thought and action: choosing, creating, exploring (−) Security—Safety, harmony, and stability of society, of relationships and of self (−) Conformity—Restraint of actions, inclinations, and impulses likely to upset or harm others and violate social expectations/norms (−) Tradition—Respect, commitment, and acceptance of the customs and ideas that traditional culture or religion provide
Conventional (+) Pop	(−) Power—Social status and prestige, control or dominance over people and resources (−) Self-direction—Independent thought and action: choosing, creating, exploring (+) Benevolence—Preservation and enhancement of the welfare of people one is in frequent personal contact with

Discussion

Our results show that the musical taste of Serbian adolescents could be represented by four musical preferences, very similar to the factors obtained in several Western and Western Balkan countries (Delsing et al., 2008; Getz et al., 2012; Miranda et al., 2015; Petrović & Kuzmanović, 2009; Reić Ercegovac & Dobrota, 2011; Tekman, 2009). The similarity would be even more obvious if we had used the statistical analysis that presumes an independent relationship between extracted factors, as was the case in much previous research into musical preferences (Getz et al., 2012; Mulder et al., 2010; Rentfrow et al., 2011). Thus, the labels assigned to the obtained musical preferences are chosen to highlight a similarity with the results of the related studies.

As mentioned before, the Rebellious factor is very similar to the Intense and Rebellious preference present in Western countries within the four-factor model (Rentfrow & Gosling, 2003). Our Rebellious factor includes Heavy Metal, Rock, and Punk music and, to a lesser extent, an appreciation of Rhythm & Blues, Jazz, and Reggae. A rejection of Folk music is characteristic of this musical taste. The opposition between Folk and other genres, however, is specific to the Serbian socio-political context. Petrović and Kuzmanović (2009) found the same pattern but with opposite loadings: positive on Folk and negative on the other three genres. Namely, the tendency to despise folk music in Serbian youth inclined towards rebellious genres could be explained by common criticisms of folk as kitsch and being related to criminals and to the war ideology of the 1990s (Archer, 2012; Gordy, 2001).

The Energetic factor, incorporating Techno, House, and Hip-hop, unites powerful dance rhythms like the Energetic and Rhythmic dimension in Rentfrow and Gosling's four-factor model (2003) and the Urban orientation in the five-factor MUSIC model (Rentfrow et al., 2011). Like the Rebellious factor, this very dynamic preference seems to be universal across different cultural contexts.

The Sophisticated factor, comprising Jazz, Rhythm & Blues, and Reggae, is analogous to the Reflective and Complex factor within the four-factor model detected in Western countries (Rentfrow & Gosling, 2003) and the Sophisticated factor in the five-factor MUSIC model (Rentfrow et al., 2011). Namely, Jazz and Classical music, which almost reached significant loading of 0.4 (See Table 6.1) are similar to the Reflective and Complex factor in Rentfrow & Gosling's four-factor model, while Rhythm & Blues are more like the Mellow factor in the five-factor MUSIC model. Petrović and Kuzmanović (2009) found a comparable Serious factor consisting of Jazz, Blues, Classical, Alternative, and Reggae. These results show that older adolescents from various cultures develop a taste for complex genres and become similar to adults in their preferences. It is possible that such orientation is not influenced only by cognitive development, as Mulder et al. (2010) suggested, but also by schooling, when we consider that classical music is introduced early within the school context. Our results show that a Sophisticated musical preference correlates with the Rebellious factor.

The Conventional factor, with the highest loading on Pop, is similar to the contemporary music preference found in Turkey (Tekman et al., 2012) and it is the factor in earlier Serbian research (Petrović & Kuzmanović, 2009) that is mostly dominated by Pop and much less by Rock and Folk. It could also be related to Rentfrow and Gosling's (2003) Upbeat and Conventional preference within the four-factor model revealed in Western countries, where Pop and Country sit together, alongside Soundtracks and Religious music.

Our second aim was to examine potential links between adolescents' music preferences and their values. Canonical correlation analysis highlights the association of these domains, as was the case in research by Gardikiotis and Baltzis (2012) and Tekman et al. (2012), and in a Serbian study about the relation between adolescents' leisure patterns, found to be defined predominantly by their music preferences, with social and individual goals (Stepanović, Videnović, & Plut., 2009; Stepanović Ilić et al., 2017).

We established that the Rebellious factor (Heavy Metal, Rock, Punk, and avoidance of Folk) is positively associated with Universalism, i.e., with one's wish to contribute to the welfare of all people and nature, which resonates with previous findings of a relationship between adolescents' leisure patterns and values (Pavlović & Stepanović Ilić, 2022). This is also in line with Gardikiotis and Baltzis's (2012) finding of an association between the rebellious music preference and a Self-transcendent higher-order value that includes Universalism and Benevolence. However, our results show a negative relation with

Benevolence, instead of a positive one. Furthermore, it is demonstrated that the Rebellious factor is associated with Power, which is not confirmed in other studies. This value, together with a negative relation with Benevolence, reflects a tendency to dominate over others and a negative attitude towards social surroundings. Carpentier et al. (2003) report that musical styles featuring defiant messages (often present in Heavy Metal and Hard Rock) can be connected with dominance and antisocial feelings. Perhaps this could enrich our understanding of the relationship between the Rebellious musical preference and the aforementioned values, but it also explain our finding that such a musical taste does not go along with a hedonistic lifestyle. Still, the opposition between an inclination towards Universalism on the one hand and towards Benevolence on the other remains unclear and needs to be confirmed by future studies. Investigations in this field (Boer et al., 2011; Gardikiotis & Baltzis, 2012; Tekman et al., 2012) have discovered that an appreciation of rebellious musical genres is positively related to the Openness value dimension, which could be associated with our finding that the same preference is correlated with Self-direction, which together with Stimulation is most significant for defining the Openness factor (Schwartz & Boehnke, 2004).

The results of our study show that adolescents who appreciate Energetic music genres have higher scores on Universalism and lower on Hedonism. This means that young people listening to Techno and Electronic music, and to House as well as Hip-hop and Rap, are orientated towards the welfare of all people and the protection of nature, and that they do not seek pleasure and sensual gratification. Unfortunately, other studies (Gardikiotis & Baltzis, 2012; Tekman et al., 2012) examining the relationship between values and musical preferences have not established such a musical taste in their respondents, which makes a comparison with our findings impossible.

The Sophisticated factor is positively associated with Stimulation and Self-direction, referred to above as constituting the Openness to change value dimension. At the same time, it is negatively correlated with Security, Conformity, and Tradition belonging to the Conservation value dimension (Schwartz & Boehnke, 2004). This suggests that adolescents whose listening styles are commonly perceived as complex and intellectually demanding (Schäfer & Sedlmeier, 2009) focus on excitement and challenges, and do not appreciate tradition, the status quo, or being under somebody else's influence. Tekman et al. (2012) also discovered that Openness was a positive predictor of the Sophisticated musical preference. The relationship between Openness to new experiences and an interest in sophisticated musical genres is well established in research on personality and musical preferences (Manolika & Baltzis, 2021; Rentfrow & Gosling, 2003). However, we did not find a correlation between a preference for sophisticated and complex music and the Self-transcendence higher-order value (Universalism and Benevolence) revealed by the Greek and Turkish research (Gardikiotis & Baltzis, 2012; Tekman et al., 2012).

The Conventional factor, defined by Pop music, negatively correlates with Self-direction and Power. Hence, youngsters favouring Pop music are not prone to independence and social status and do not want to have control over others. Notions such as independence, status, and power are usually associated with the adult world, so it seems that adolescents with Conventional music tastes reject such values and do not want to grow up. Seemingly our results contradict the findings of other researchers (Boer et al., 2011; Gardikiotis & Baltzis, 2012; Tekman et al., 2012), who determined a positive relation between similar musical tastes and Openness (incorporating Self-direction) and Self-enhancement (including Power).

Summarising the previously discussed results regarding the relationship between music preferences and values, it can be stated that some of our findings are in accordance with the few studies that have empirically investigated this topic (Boer et al., 2011; Gardikiotis & Baltzis, 2012; Tekman et al., 2012). However, many differences are also noticeable. These may be attributable to specific statistical techniques and to the fact that the genres contributing to musical factors in these studies were not exactly the same. Moreover, our respondents were slightly younger than participants in the other two studies from the Balkans region. Keeping in mind that adolescence is characterised by intensive development (Krstić, 2016)), this can be reflected in both musical taste and one's value system (Hargreaves et al., 2015; Petrović & Kuzmanović, 2009; Reić Ercegovac et al., 2017), but also in the relationship between them. The impact of cultural specificities on adolescents' everyday life should also not be discarded (Baucal & Krstić, 2020; Videnović et al., 2010).

Conclusion

This study has identified four factors, Rebellious, Energetic, Sophisticated, and Conventional, that describe music preferences in Serbian adolescents analogous to the music preferences found across Western countries. It has also discovered antagonisms between the inclination towards music often labelled as rebellious and an appreciation of the folk genre, specific to the Serbian socio-historical context, determined in earlier national research, with the majority of findings replicated in our investigation. Besides, resemblances regarding music preferences of this kind are also detected in other Balkan countries sharing a similar cultural heritage.

Our results have revealed that each identified music preference in adolescents is related to a certain set of values from Schwartz's taxonomy. The significance of these findings is corroborated as they confirm the relevance of a system of values for the development of adolescents' musical taste that has previously been highlighted by scholars (Boer et al., 2011; Franken et al., 2017; Hargreaves et al., 2015). However, as we stated before, this might also imply that specific music choices have a possible influence on one's system of values, whose formation occurs in adolescence, bearing in mind that musicians are amongst the favourite role models of adolescents, with whom they can have very close parasocial relationships (Gleason et al., 2017, Stepanović Ilić et al., 2017, 2023). Our study rediscovered previously established relationships between particular musical tastes and values, although differences have also arisen, especially regarding the rebellious preference and its relation to apparently antagonistic values. This suggests that further examinations of the adolescent population are needed with an international perspective. Furthermore, such investigations should consider values and take into account the specific role of music as a protective factor (Krnjaić et al., 2023; Stepanović Ilić et al., in press), as well as the utilisation of music in relation to emotions, as advocated by contemporary literature in this field (Manolika & Baltzis, 2021). This aspect is particularly significant in adolescence, which is commonly considered a sensitive period with intensive emotional growth (Krstić, 2016; Videnović et al., 2010; Videnović et al., 2018).

References

Abrams, D. (2009). Social identity on a national scale: Optimal distinctiveness and young people's self-expression through musical preference. *Group Processes & Intergroup Relations, 12*(3), 303–318. https://doi.org/10.1177/1368430209102841

Archer, R. (2012). Assessing turbofolk controversies: Popular music between the nation and the Balkans. *Southeastern Europe, 36*(2), 178–207. https://doi.org/10.1163/187633312X642103

Baucal, A., & Krstić, K. (2020). Searching for an integrative theoretical framework for psychology: Evolutionary psychology is needed, but not sufficient. *Integrative Psychological and Behavioral Science, 54*, 579–588. https://doi.org/10.1007/s12124-020-09551-2

Boer, D., Fischer, R., Strack, M., Bond, M.H., Lo, E., & Lam, J. (2011). How shared preferences in music create bonds between people: Values as the missing link. *Personality and Social Psychology Bulletin, 37*(9), 1159–1171. https://doi.org/10.1177/0146167211407521

Carpentier, F.D., Knobloch, S., & Zillmann, D. (2003). Rock, rap, and rebellion: Comparisons of traits predicting selective exposure to defiant music. *Personality and Individual Differences, 35*(7), 1643–1655. https://doi.org/10.1016/S0191-8869(02)00387-2

Delsing, M.J.M.H., ter Bogt, T.F.M., Engels, R.C.M.E., & Meeus, W.H.J. (2008). Adolescents' music preferences and personality characteristics. *European Journal of Personality, 22*(2), 109–130. https://doi.org/10.1002/per.665

Franken, A., Keijsers, L., Dijkstra, J.K., & ter Bogt, T. (2017). Music preferences, friendship, and externalizing behavior in early adolescence: A SIENA examination of the music marker theory using the SNARE study. *Journal of Youth and Adolescence, 46*(8), 1839–1850. https://doi.org/10.1007/s10964-017-0633-4

Gardikiotis, A., & Baltzis, A. (2012). 'Rock music for myself and justice to the world!': Musical identity, values, and music preferences. *Psychology of Music, 40*(2), 143–163. https://doi.org/10.1177/0305735610386836

Getz, L.M., Chamorro-Premuzic, T., Roy, M.M., & Devroop, K. (2012). The relationship between affect, uses of music, and music preferences in a sample of South African adolescents. *Psychology of Music, 40*(2), 164–178. https://doi.org/10.1177/0305735610381818

Gleason, T.R., Theran, S.A., & Newberg, E.M. (2017). Parasocial interactions and relationships in early adolescence. *Frontiers in Psychology, 8*, Article 255. https://doi.org/10.3389/fpsyg.2017.00255

Gordy, E.D. (2001). *The culture of power in Serbia: Nationalism and the destruction of alternatives*. Pennsylvania State University Press.

Hargreaves, D.J., North, A.C., & Tarrant, M. (2015). How and why do musical preferences change in childhood and adolescence? In G.E. McPherson (ed.), *The child as musician: A handbook of musical development* (2nd ed., pp. 303–322). Oxford University Press. https://doi.org/10.1093/acprof:oso/9780198744443.003.0016

Krnjaić, Z., Grujić, K., & Vuletić, T. (2023). How students report about their education experiences during the first year of Covid-19 pandemic? *Andragoške studije, 1*, 125–149. https://doi.org/10.5937/AndStud2301125K

Krstić, K. (2016). Attachment to parents and friends as a context for development of self-concept in adolescence: The personality traits as mediators. *Psihologija, 49*(4), 335–355. https://doi.org/10.2298/PSI1604335K

Lonsdale, A.J. (2021). Musical taste, in-group favoritism, and social identity theory: Re-testing the predictions of the self-esteem hypothesis. *Psychology of Music, 49*(4), 817–827. https://doi.org/10.1177/0305735619899158

López-Sintas, J., Ghahraman, A., & Pérez Rubiales, E. (2017). Young people's leisure patterns: Testing social age, social gender, and linguistic capital hypotheses. *Journal of Youth Studies, 20*(2), 180–199. https://doi.org/10.1080/13676261.2016.1206863

Manolika, M., & Baltzis, A. (2021). The interplay of personal values and uses of music in explaining music listener preferences. *Psychology of Music, 50*(2), 596–610. https://doi.org/10.1177/03057356211005850

Miranda, D. (2013). The role of music in adolescent development: Much more than the same old song. *International Journal of Adolescence and Youth, 18*(1), 5–22. https://doi.org/10.1080/02673843.2011.650182

Miranda, D., Blais-Rochette, C., Vaugon, K., Osman, M., & Arias-Valenzuela, M. (2015). Towards a cultural-developmental psychology of music in adolescence. *Psychology of Music, 43*(2), 197–218. https://doi.org/10.1177/0305735613500700

Miranda, D., & Claes, M. (2009). Music listening, coping, peer affiliation and depression in adolescence. *Psychology of Music, 37*(2), 215–233. https://doi.org/10.1177/0305735608097245

Miranda, D., & Gaudreau, P. (2011). Music listening and emotional well-being in adolescence: A person- and variable-oriented study. *European Review of Applied Psychology, 61*(1), 1–11. https://doi.org/10.1016/j.erap.2010.10.002

Mulder, J., ter Bogt, T.F.M., Raaijmakers, Q.A.W., Gabhainn, S.N., Monshouwer, K., & Vollebergh, W.A.M. (2010). Is it the music? Peer substance use as a mediator of the link between music preferences and adolescent substance use. *Journal of Adolescence, 33*(3), 387–394. https://doi.org/10.1016/j.adolescence.2009.09.001

North, A.C., & Hargreaves, D.J. (1999). Music and adolescent identity. *Music Education Research, 1*(1), 75–92. https://doi.org/10.1080/1461380990010107

North, A.C., Hargreaves, D.J., & Hargreaves, J.J. (2004). Uses of music in everyday life. *Music Perception: An Interdisciplinary Journal, 22*(1), 41–77. https://doi.org/10.1525/mp.2004.22.1.41

Olsen, K. N., Powell, M., Anic, A., Vallerand, R. J., & Thompson, W. F. (2022). Fans of violent music: The role of passion in positive and negative emotional experience. *Musicae Scientiae, 26*(2), 364–387. https://doi.org/10.1177/1029864920951611

Pavlović, Z., & Stepanović Ilić, I. (2022). Basic values as predictors of leisure-time activities among adolescents. *Primenjena psihologija, 15*(1), 85–117. https://doi.org/ 10.19090/pp.v15i1.2349

Petrović, N., & Kuzmanović, B. (2009). Životni ciljevi kao činioci muzičkih preferencija srednjoškolaca [Life aspirations as musical preference factors among high school students]. *Nastava i vaspitanje, 58*(4), 523–539. https://reff.f.bg.ac.rs/handle/123456789/864

Piko, B.F., & Vazsonyi, A.T. (2004). Leisure activities and problem behaviours among Hungarian youth. *Journal of Adolescence, 27*(6), 717–730. https://doi.org/10.1016/j.adolescence.2004.02.004

Reić Ercegovac, I., & Dobrota, S. (2011). Povezanost između glazbenih preferencija, sociodemografskih značajki i osobina ličnosti iz petofaktorskoga modela [The relationship between musical preferences, socio-demographic characteristics and Big Five personality model]. *Psihologijske teme, 20*(1), 47–65.

Reić Ercegovac, I., Dobrota, S., & Surić, S. (2017). Listening to music and music preferences in early adolescence. *Metodički obzori: Časopis za odgojno-obrazovnu teoriju i praksu, 12*(24), 6–23.

Rentfrow, P.J., Goldberg, L.R., & Levitin, D.J. (2011). The structure of musical preferences: A five-factor model. *Journal of Personality and Social Psychology, 100*(6), 1139–1157. https://doi.org/10.1037/a0022406

Rentfrow, P.J., & Gosling, S.D. (2003). The do re mi's of everyday life: The structure and personality correlates of music preferences. *Journal of Personality and Social Psychology, 84*(6), 1236–1256. https://doi.org/10.1037/0022-3514.84.6.1236

Rentfrow, P.J., & Gosling, S.D. (2020, 9 September). *Short Test of Music Preferences (STOMP)*. Measurement Instrument Database for the Social Sciences. https://gosling.psy.utexas.edu/scales-weve-developed/short-test-of-music-preferences-stomp/

Rokeach, M. (1985). Inducing change and stability in belief systems and personality structures. *Journal of Social Issues, 41*(1), 153–171. https://doi.org/10.1111/j.1540-4560.1985.tb01123.x

Saarikallio, S., & Erkkilä, J. (2007). The role of music in adolescents' mood regulation. *Psychology of Music, 35*(1), 88–109. https://doi.org/10.1177/0305735607068889

Schäfer, T., & Sedlmeier, P. (2009). From the functions of music to music preference. *Psychology of Music, 37*(3), 279–300. https://doi.org/10.1177/0305735608097247

Schwartz, S.H. (1992). Universals in the content and structure of values: Theoretical advances and empirical tests in 20 countries. In M. Zanna (ed.), *Advances in experimental social psychology* (pp. 1–65). Academic Press.

Schwartz, S.H. (1994). Are there universal aspects in the structure and contents of human values? *Journal of Social Issues, 50*(4), 19–45. https://doi.org/10.1111/j.1540-4560.1994.tb01196.x

Schwartz, S.H. (2003). *Computing scores for the 10 human values.* European Social Survey. https://www.europeansocialsurvey.org/news/article/findings-human-values-scale

Schwartz, S.H., & Boehnke, K. (2004). Evaluating the structure of human values with confirmatory factor analysis. *Journal of Research in Personality, 38*(3), 230–255. https://doi.org/10.1016/S0092-6566(03)00069-2

Slade, A., Olsen, K. N., & Thompson, W. F. (2021). An investigation of empathy in male and female fans of aggressive music. *Musicae Scientiae, 25*(2), 189–211. https://doi.org/10.1177/1029864919860169

Stepanović Ilić, I., Krnjaić, Z., Videnović, M. & Krstić, K. (in press). How do adolescents engage with music in spare time? Leisure patterns and their relation with socio-demographic characteristics, well-being and risk behaviours. *Psychology of Music.*

Stepanović, I., Pavlović Babić, D., & Krnjaić, Z. (2009). Ispitivanje uzora i idola srednjoškolaca u Srbiji [The analysis of actual and symbolic models of secondary school students in Serbia]. *Zbornik Instituta za pedagoška istraživanja, 41*(2), 401–417. https://reff.f.bg.ac.rs/handle/123456789/838

Stepanović, I., Videnović, M., & Plut, D. (2009). Obrasci ponašanja mladih tokom slobodnog vremena [Youth spare time: Typical patterns of behavior]. *Sociologija, 51*(3), 247–261. https://reff.f.bg.ac.rs/handle/123456789/924?locale-attribute=sr_RS

Stepanović Ilić, I., Blažanin, B., & Mojović, K. (2017). Public figures as role models of Serbian adolescents: Who are idols and why? *Serbian Political Thought, 15*(1), 5–20. https://www.ips.ac.rs/en/magazine_editions/serbian-political-thought-1-2017eng/

Stepanović Ilić, I., Nikitović, T., Blažanin, B., & Mojović Zdravković, K. (2023). Media figures as adolescent role models: (Dis)similarities between millennials and generation Z. *Psihološka istraživanja, 26*(2), 239–267. https://doi.org/10.5937/psistra26-45395

Stepanović Ilić, I., Videnović, M., & Petrović, N. (2019). Leisure patterns and values in adolescents from Serbia born in 1990s: An attempt at building a bridge between the two domains. *Serbian Political Thought, 66*(4), 99–123. https://doi.org/10.22182/spm.6642019.5

Tekman, H.G. (2009). Music preferences as signs of who we are – Personality and social factors. In J. Louhivuori, T. Eerola, S. Saarikallio, T. Himberg, & P.S. Eerola (eds), *Proceedings of the 7th Triennial Conference of European Society for the Cognitive Sciences of Music* (pp. 592–595). Jyväskylä, Finland. https://jyx.jyu.fi/handle/123456789/20138

Tekman, H.G., Boer, D., & Fischer, R. (2012). Values, functions of music, and musical preferences. In E. Cambouropoulos, C. Tsougras, P. Mavromatis, & K. Pastiadis (eds), *Proceedings of the 12th International Conference on Music Perception and Cognition and the 8th Triennial Conference of the European Society for the Cognitive Sciences of Music* (pp. 372–377). Aristotle University of Thessaloniki, Greece. http://icmpc-escom2012.web.auth.gr/files/papers/372_Proc.pdf

Thomas, K.S. (2016). Music preferences and the adolescent brain: A review of literature. *Update: Applications of Research in Music Education, 35*(1), 47–53. https://doi.org/10.1177/8755123315576534

Videnović, M., Pešić, J., & Plut, D. (2010). Young people's leisure time: Gender differences. *Psihologija, 43*(2), 199–214. https://doiserbia.nb.rs/img/doi/0048-5705/2010/0048-57051002199V.pdf

Videnović, M., Stepanović Ilić, I., & Krnjaić, Z. (2018). Dropping out: What are schools doing to prevent it? *Serbian Political Thought, 17*(1), 61–77. https://www.ips.ac.rs/wp-content/uploads/2018/07/spt17_12018-4.pdf

7. How Professional Musicians Can Better Connect to Audiences for Live Classical Music: Assessing Theory And Practice in the Light of the COVID-19 Crisis

John Sloboda

Introduction

Attendance at live classical music events in many countries has been steadily declining for decades, both in absolute terms and relative to other arts. For instance, the USA National Endowment for the Arts has periodically surveyed public participation in the arts. Attendance at classical music concerts has steadily declined over the period 1982–2017, whereas other participation, such as gallery attendance or attendance at pop concerts has not declined. Specifically, in 1982, 13% of the US population had attended at least one classical concert in the year. By 2017 this percentage had fallen to 8%.

One of the most striking contributors to this decline is the changing age profile of audiences. The average classical music audience is getting older, as is shown clearly in the 2017 data from the USA (National Endowment for the Arts, 2018) and also the UK. Data from the UK Office for National Statistics (Sigurjonsson, 2005) showed that while 16% of the 55–64 age group had attended a classical concert, the figure for under 35s was around 5%. This compares with 90% attendance from that same cohort for films and pop concerts.

Since live performance is at the heart of classical performance training and practice, this decline presents challenges for the profession, and an urgent need for greater understanding of its causes and how it might be reversed. One potential line of explanation is that classical concerts have been failing to give contemporary audiences, particularly the under-50s, what they seek. In support of this, Dobson (2010) analysed the responses of culturally aware young adults attending their first classical concerts and found that they valued inclusion and participation highly, and sought the sense that their attendance mattered to the performers, who wanted to co-create with them a unique encounter, not just exposure to works they could have heard at home.

In response to such findings, Sloboda and Ford (2019) have articulated four key dimensions on which live events may vary and which may help to explain why classical music concerts have experienced such difficulties.

The first dimension is *established work versus new work*, and in what proportion. Established work means work that belongs to a repertoire of tried-and-tested value, often by authors or composers no longer alive. In general, the programmes of major classical venues concentrate on established work, particularly of dead composers. In contrast, programmes of major theatres have a very high proportion of new work alongside the established. Even art galleries that build their reputation on established work and the work of dead artists, tend to have major exhibitions of relatively recent work by living artists, or work not exhibited before. For instance, 25% of the special exhibitions at London's National Gallery in 2018 were of living artists, although its main collection focuses on works from the thirteenth to the early twentieth centuries. And at pop concerts it is virtually unknown for the work of dead artists to be performed. As was the case for classical concerts before the mid-19th century, audiences for popular music are primarily interested in the work of living artists with whom they can have a direct encounter, and from whom they can eagerly anticipate the production of further new songs in the future. In general, in the 18th and early 19th centuries, once a composer was dead, his music held little further interest for audiences (Weber, 1984).

The second dimension is *predictable versus unpredictable*. This is determined by such factors as the nature and order of the programme, whether known in advance or not, and the level of improvisatory or ad-libbing moments to be found. Very often there is no advance programme at a pop, folk, or jazz concert. In theatres, productions typically vary sets, lighting, and costume. Classical concerts, by contrast, are often highly predictable. The programme specifies exactly what will be played, in what order, and the degrees of freedom for the performers are quite limited. What they play, how they are arranged on the stage, how they behave, what they wear, is very similar from event to event. Ad libs are minimal and often squeezed to the margins, as in encores, which in some ways could be seen as acknowledgements from the performers that the main event has failed to meet some important audience need. The more predictable, the less easy it is to generate the sense of an event—something special. Dobson's (2010) research on younger audiences for classical music provides the example of the 'Night Shift' series of classical concerts by the London-based Orchestra of the Age of Enlightenment. She documents how staging concerts at nightclubs, with no advance written programme, with the audience and players standing and moving around the space and impromptu conversations taking place between the players, all create a sense of occasion through their unpredictability and disruption of conventions.

The third dimension is *impersonal versus personal*. This relates to the level of personal engagement in the projection of performers. There are considerable differences across performances regarding how far performers stay in strict performer roles, or step outside the role and project themselves as people. One kind of projection is talking directly to the audience, either from the stage, or more informally, before or after the performance. This is not a traditional part of the classical performers' persona, but is increasingly being adopted by both soloists and ensembles (for instance, the Orchestra of the Age of Enlightenment; see Sawer, 2018). Another kind of projection relates to the degree of self-conscious acting: for example, the projection of emotional and other qualities through such things as body movement, facial expressions, or vocalisations. In classical music this is often restrained or idiosyncratic. Either performers try to be neutral and invisible, or, as in the case of some well-known soloists, they engage in exaggerated gestures, which are often highly similar across different performances—a kind of gestural personal signature. The piano commentator Frances Wilson (2015) observes that 'the spectrum of gesture in piano playing is very broad, from almost complete concentrated stillness at the piano (Marc-André Hamelin, Stephen

Hough) to exaggerated flamboyance bordering on the ridiculous'. In theatre these things are generally highly consciously managed as part of the stagecraft, an awareness that has prompted pedagogical innovations where musicians work alongside actors to learn this skill (e.g., Rea, 2015).

The fourth dimension is *passive versus active*. This concerns the level of audience behaviour and communication. Live arts vary considerably in what is permitted or expected of the audience in terms of active engagement. In some events active behaviour is allowed or encouraged. In some forms, such as pop, opera, or jazz, it is perfectly acceptable to clap or cheer at points where an audience member feels someone has done something particularly excellent or moving. In classical concerts it is generally expected that audience members wait until the end of a work, even if the work has multiple movements, and will restrict movement to a minimum. In other contexts, more usually associated with popular music, it is permitted or encouraged to move, be it dancing, moving in one's seat, or actually moving around the space. The traditional classical concert places an audience member in the position of a humble viewer, coming into the presence of greatness. In this mode, an audience may feel it has nothing to give, only to receive (an observation articulated influentially by Small, 1998).

It is evident that in general, classical music events are established, predictable, impersonal, and passive in comparison to what else people can pay to go to in contemporary culture. However, the experience of inclusion and participation that contemporary audiences seek is more likely to occur at events which contain elements of the new, the unpredictable, the personal, and the active. Sloboda and Ford (2019) outline some potential historical and sociological explanations as to why classical concerts lag behind other live art forms in these respects, but the question posed here is how can more of what audiences seek be added to live classical events? A working hypothesis is that this can be achieved by shifting the event along one or more of the dimensions identified above, towards an emphasis on the new, the unpredictable, the personal, and the active.

Aims

This chapter aims to increase understanding of how artists and promoters can respond to audience needs through practical but theoretically grounded adjustments to the concert experience. It does this through drawing out key elements of an artist-led series of research projects which brought musicians and researchers together to explore how more of what audiences seek can be added to live classical events through principled innovations in programme design, content, and presentation. These projects drew on the dimensional analysis provided by Sloboda and Ford (2019) to devise concerts which explicitly shifted the audience experience along one or more of the dimensions identified, i.e., towards an emphasis on the new, the unpredictable, the personal, and the active.

These projects were undertaken at Guildhall School of Music & Drama from 2010 onwards within a programme entitled Understanding Audiences. This has allowed practical initiatives within the framework described above to be devised by artists, and the effects to be assessed in collaboration with researchers. These projects have been described in more detail in a series of publications (see Dobson & Sloboda, 2014; Dolan et al., 2013, 2018; Ford & Sloboda, 2013; Halpern et al., 2017; O'Neill et al., 2016; Sloboda, 2013, 2015; Sloboda & Ford, 2019; Sloboda & Wise, 2016; Toelle & Sloboda, 2021).

Here, an overview is provided, illustrating this approach with four case studies from this programme, each case study focusing primarily on one of the four dimensions in the framework, with summary accounts of methodology, findings, and implications.

In the context of the global COVID-19 pandemic where live concerts were initially not allowed, but where there was much online activity, the discussion then turns to a consideration of how the understanding gained previously might be adapted and enlarged to reflect the experiences, challenges, and opportunities faced by musicians during the COVID-19 restrictions, drawing on examples of concerts performed at the height of the global lockdown (March–May 2020). It concludes by assessing some advantages and limitations of the approach taken here and outlining some areas for future investigation.

Main discussion

Dimension 1—Established versus new: Repeating the same work in a concert

Classical concert promoters and programme makers are often reluctant to introduce new or unfamiliar music into concert programmes (Price, 2022). This is because core classical audiences are believed to prefer 'tried-and-tested' familiar works. As a result, programmes of major orchestras and major concert halls are very conservative (Beethoven and Mozart dominate; see Marín, 2018).

Studies using recorded music show that repeated hearings increase enjoyment and understanding of a piece (Margulis, 2014). But there is little evidence regarding the effects of repetition during live concerts. Spontaneous encores have long been a documented feature of live concerts. Planned and programmed repetitions are rarer, but have been featured (see Anderson, 2017), and they mainly feature new, or unfamiliar, work. This study aimed to examine the effects on listener response of deliberately programming repeats of unfamiliar works within the same concert.

In two separate concerts of new music performed by staff and students at the Guildhall School, planned repeats of some performances were introduced into the programme (some pre-announced, others not). After each performance, audience members ($N = 63$, age range 18–84, median 19.5) were asked to complete a four-item questionnaire probing both cognitive and affective variables. The key quantitative items were Likert-scale ratings (two for cognitive and two for affective). Participants were also invited to elaborate on their reactions in free-field responses. For further details see Halpern et al. (2017).

There was a statistically significant increase in ratings of the piece on a second hearing. Audience members liked the piece more on a second hearing and felt they understood it better. This suggests that a good way to increase 'tolerance' for new music amongst more traditional audiences could be to make the practice of repetition a more normal part of concert protocols. This could make such concerts more attractive to those seeking the new rather than the familiar.

Dimension 2—Predictable versus unpredictable: Effects on audience of classical improvisation

Classical improvisation represents a radical challenge to the notion that faithfulness to the score is a core or abiding value. Until the late nineteenth century, improvisation was considered to be a core attribute of live performance. Mozart and Beethoven would have been astonished with the contemporary reverence accorded to their music. They expected performers to take liberties with the score, as they did themselves in performance (Dolan, Sloboda, et al., 2013). It could be argued that a historically authentic performance of much classical repertoire requires (rather than invites) an improvisatory approach, which may be defined as a spontaneous, in the moment, musically informed variation in expressive parameters of timing, loudness, and timbre, along with actual new notes.

Not only is such an approach more historically authentic, it arguably has the power to provide a more intense experience for all concerned in live performance. This is because improvised performances are newer, more unpredictable, more personal, and—arguably—invite more audience engagement.

We evaluated the impact of such an improvisatory approach in a series of experiments exploring the hypothesis that improvisation, and an improvisational state of mind on the part of the performer during performance, is associated with a heightened musical experience in terms of both the performers' engagement and audience response (Dolan, Jensen, et al., 2018; Dolan, Sloboda, et al., 2013). These studies involved musicians playing the same piece twice within a concert, once with a prepared interpretation, and once with improvisation. Three levels of measurement of effects were employed: behavioural (actual sound parameters of performance), experiential (subjective judgement of listeners), and physiological (electroencephalography [EEG] response).

Our specific predictions were for the improvised versions to show (1) increased (more varied) and more 'risky' use of performance-related parameters (timing, tempi, rhythms, dynamics, timbre, and actual extemporised notes) by the musicians; (2) increased ratings by audience members of performance quality; and (3) increased activation of certain brain areas in both performers and audience, and increased synchronisation in brain activity between performers and listeners. In a live concert by Trio Anima (Dolan, Sloboda, et al., 2013), attended by fourteen individuals, a mixture of students and staff from UK academic institutions, as well as outside guests and casual concert-goers (age not recorded), five pieces were each performed twice in two modes: 'prepared' and 'improvised'. The order of the two modes was varied from piece to piece and was unknown to the audience and any co-author other than the first. On objective performance parameters, the performances displayed clear differences. Greater expressive variation was found in the improvised version than in the prepared version, and also embellishments of the score.

Audience reactions were obtained by asking each audience member to rate each performance on five separate dimensions: improvisatory in character, innovative in approach, emotionally engaging, musically convincing, and risk-taking. A free-response box was also provided for comments on each performance. On all rating dimensions the improvised interpretations scored substantially and significantly higher than the prepared interpretations. The ratings were supported by written comments which exemplify the very different feel of the two types of performance. Prepared: 'Pleasantly played, though tame and conventional.' Improvised: 'It was very intense. Musically a lot happened. The musicians were really making music and telling a story together.'

Brain measurements (EEG) from performers and two audience members showed substantial differences between prepared and improvised performances, for both performers and listeners. One particularly striking finding was a contrast between performers, whose brain centres for focused attention were less active during improvisation, and listeners, who showed more activity in these areas (signalling a greater attentive involvement). A second finding was that improvisation yielded greater activation in areas of motor control for both performers and listeners, even though listeners remained very still. It seems as if improvisation was particularly effective in allowing listeners to mirror the movements of the musicians in their imagination. This adds a specific dimension to the wider body of research linking music listening to brain activation in the motor areas (Gordon et al., 2018)

Thus, there is consistent evidence that improvised classical performances are experienced as significantly different by participants, as indicated through both conscious verbal and unconscious brain responses, as well as the musical features of the performances. This is a part of the case for suggesting that improvisatory elements will enhance audience engagement.

Dimension 3—Impersonal versus personal: Effects of attending an open rehearsal

The audience experience of a live event is not solely determined by the experience of the concert itself. The surrounding context—before, during, and after—can shape the experience in a number of ways. Rather than altering some aspect of the concert itself, some artists have chosen to enhance the experience through events planned to accompany the concert. One such event is the open rehearsal.

As part of a project on audience development in a professional chamber orchestra (collaborators Helena Gaunt, John Rink, Karen Wise, and Britten Sinfonia), an opportunity arose to examine the effects of attending an open rehearsal on audience experience. Seventy-two audience members (age data not collected) attended an open rehearsal given by a professional chamber orchestra, followed later that day by the concert. During the open rehearsal, audience members were able to witness conversations between the musicians, and the consequent adjustment of performance details. The concert contained new works including a world premiere. Audience reactions were probed by a post-concert questionnaire. One focus looked at how attendance at the rehearsal had affected the concert experience. Thematic analysis on the free-form responses yielded evidence of three main influences on the concert experience.

The first influence was one of orientation towards the music, creating familiarity and recognition when in the concert itself. One respondent wrote: 'Both rehearsal and discussion helped towards enjoyment of the concert as growing familiarity breeds enjoyment.' Another wrote: 'Having been in the rehearsal, it was wonderful to have these moments of recognition in the concert.' This is another indication that repeated hearing is a key route to greater enjoyment.

The second influence was one of connecting with the process of artistry, and therefore feeling more a part of the artistic journey. One respondent wrote:

> Having listened to the rehearsals/behind the scenes, I felt more connected in some way. Even if they were rehearsing snippets, I felt more involved. I loved hearing them discuss and talk about the process that went towards this concert. I enjoyed it more, having listened to their process, and I felt like I was part of a journey.

The third influence was one of connecting with the musicians, thereby seeing artists as fallible and human. One respondent wrote:

> I found the rehearsal interesting. It made the performers seem more human in the sense of being fallible and subject to variation and imperfection. This made the occasion of the concert feel more unique and special, and in fact I felt more empathy with the performers (with them being less like untouchable perfect gods) and because of that more involved with the whole event.

These findings suggest that audiences seek a more personal relationship to musicians, and being let in 'behind the scenes' makes for a stronger and deeper experience. This contrasts quite markedly with the traditional training of classical musicians, which encourages process to be hidden in favour of a 'perfect' end product. Allowing the audience into the process involves a degree of risk-taking for which many classical musicians have not been prepared. Even more risk attaches to improvisation on stage which, in crucial respects, cannot be prepared in advance.

Dimension 4—Passive versus active: The audience as artist

One strong, but rarely adopted, method of bringing an audience into active engagement is to involve them as performers. Such a direct participatory role has been offered to audiences in some works by composers such as Iannis Xenakis, François-Bernard Mâche, Malcolm Williamson, Luc Ferrari, Mauricio Kagel, John Cage, Dieter Schnebel, Louis Andriessen, and Cornelius Cardew. However, no systematic data collection has ever been undertaken on audience members regarding the effects of this on their engagement and satisfaction. Toelle and Sloboda

(2019) rectified these gaps through a study of audience reaction to two new works commissioned by the Art Mentor Foundation Lucerne, which were performed in four European cities by four different professional new music ensembles. The method of investigation was a questionnaire completed by audience members in the concert hall at the end of the performance.

The works were by composers Huang Rao and Christian Mason, and audience data was collected at three of the four performances (by the London Sinfonietta, Ensemble Modern Frankfurt, and Asko Schönberg Ensemble Amsterdam). The pieces were composed with parts written for the audience to play instruments, make sounds (including reading poetry extracts), and move. In publicity material, the artistic rationale was described as to 'inspire composers to experiment with the idea of shared curation, encourage musicians to lead public participation, and empower audiences to play their own role in great art' (Press release Art Mentor Foundation Lucerne, 2015). Audiences performed under guidance (visual and sonic cues) using voice, gongs, bells, harmonica, and so on. There were also rehearsals and warm-ups (some in the concert, some optional at advance sessions).

There were 638 attendees over the 3 venues (50 attended preparatory workshops) and 273 (43%) participated in the research. The age of the participants was not recorded. The key data came from open-ended questions asking for positive ('best thing about the performance') and negative ('was there anything you did not like or find difficult?') opinions.

Responses were predominantly positive. Thematic analysis yielded four main categories of audience reflection. First was the Special group experience (e.g., 'sharing the experience with composer, performer, audience'; 'musicians around the room made it feel like we were in the piece'). Second was the Interactive musical experience (e.g., 'seeing how the music came together through rehearsal'; 'participating gave me a greater appreciation of the structure behind the two pieces'). Third was the Evaluation of the participatory situation (e.g., 'it was wonderful to engage with poetry again, inspired me to read some poetry to my hospitalized mother'; 'participating made me watch and listen closely: more than I usually do'). The fourth category was the Experience of shifting power relationships. Here, some respondents were more cautious (e.g., 'child-like participation in the Mason';

'I think the audience could have managed a bigger/more complex part. This would avoid the "cameo" sensation'; 'it did feel more like an experiment than a performance, which was rather weird as an audience member'). This was an indication, perhaps among the more musically advanced audience members, that audience participation was too tokenistic, with the real artistic interest remaining with the professional performers. This could be a difficult balance to strike with a mixed-ability audience.

Nonetheless, this first extensive study of audience reactions to a participatory composition demonstrates a high level of engagement (both with the activity and the research on it) and a variety of benefits of taking part. In particular, such participation heightens appropriate attentiveness and connection to the musicians and each other, and validates the uniqueness of the live concert experience.

As this example shows, one means of involving audiences actively is to proactively seek their feedback after the event, either through dialogue or through written feedback. A range of interventions outlined in Dobson and Sloboda (2014) showed that post-concert feedback events increased a sense of agency in the audience, and also the artists' sense of connection to the audience, with a levelling of the traditional power relationship.

Adapting concerts to the constraints of the COVID-19 pandemic: Audience experience through the dimensional lens

From March 2020 the world was plunged into a new and unprecedented situation of social isolation in which concerts were suddenly stopped or disrupted. The situation changed very rapidly over successive months and may further change in the future. It is worthwhile, however, to look at early reactions to the pandemic when artists and researchers were struggling to make some immediate but focused responses to their new circumstances. The analysis here was developed in a series of three online practice-based seminar-recitals presented with singer Rafael Montero during April and May 2020.[1]

---

1   Hosted by the Instituto Katarina Gurska, Segovia (17 April 2020), the Maastricht Centre for the Innovation of Classical Music (14 May 2020), and the Guildhall School of Music & Drama (26 May 2020).

Even under strict lockdown the impulse for live face-to-face performance was strong. Small groups of co-quarantined musicians immediately started to perform in the streets and on balconies. One UK example was a husband-and-wife duo who performed music in the street near the homes of quarantined families, described as 'Cuppa Concerts' (World Harmony Orchestra, n.d.). But unless asked for and pre-agreed, these audience members didn't choose to be the audience—therefore this was more like busking (street entertainers) than a mutually agreed concert.

Very quickly, many musicians began live-streaming concerts from their homes. This was possible for solo performers or musicians who happened to live in the same house. An early UK example of this was Stephen Isserlis's children's concerts for solo cello (Tutti.space, 2020). He talked between pieces and answered children's questions posted online. This set-up required a 'live-in' cameraman producer—who happened to be his son.

More common than live-streamed concerts were pre-recorded concerts with each performer in a separate home. In such performances the sense of 'liveness' was lost as audience members were not co-present in time or space with the performers. However, audience response was possible post-performance, for example from the comment facility in platforms such as YouTube. An early and now famous example of this was the Rotterdam Philharmonic Orchestra's (2020) recording of Beethoven's *Ode to Joy* on 25 March. Within a few days there were more than 2,500 viewer comments—some highly emotional; for example, 'I haven't cried like that since my father died. I'm a nurse in the National Health Service. We need art like this right now. Thank you.' However, there was little opportunity for audience-artist dialogue, or artist response to such comments.

Another type of concert that appeared was a hybrid model, where performances were pre-recorded but curated/presented in real time by performers, or by a host in real-time communication with pre-registered audience members, through conferencing software such as Zoom. This allowed immediate real-time comments and questions, to which performer/hosts could respond. This was the model we adopted in our seminar-recitals, a model which also allowed a global audience from several continents to interact with us and with each other, in discussion about the music and the modality of its presentation, thereby giving audience members considerable agency. In these new forms of concert, how does this new situation impact on the four dimensions of live events discussed earlier? Can the priorities of delivering new, unpredictable, personal, and active experiences still be upheld, and if so, how?

In relation to *established versus new*, virtuality imposes no restrictions on the familiarity/unfamiliarity of the repertoire. Repeated hearings of performances remain possible.

In relation to *predictable versus unpredictable*, new formats in experimentation made concerts under COVID-19 potentially more unpredictable. At least initially, there was a sense of shared adventure under adversity. However, 'standard' formats quickly became dominant, drawing on established models such as that used by the Virtual Choir (Whitacre, n.d.), founded in 2010. These formats were substantially determined by the functionality of common online platforms, to the point where a screen full of heads and shoulders became almost a cliché and highly predictable. Other dimensions of unpredictability, such as those introduced by improvisation, became technically problematic when performers were communicating with one another over the Internet, although institutions that could afford it invested in low-latency technology, requiring ultra-fast broadband, to eliminate the typical internet-induced delay between people performing in different locations.

On the *impersonal versus personal* dimension, it was noticed that the pandemic crisis gave more opportunity for musicians to be seen as human, performing in their own homes, wearing informal clothes, and backgrounded by their personal effects. Often the situation would inspire musicians to talk about why they were offering the performance, with unusual intensity (for example, on 15 March 2020 the operatic soprano Joyce DiDonato offered an impromptu concert in her New York apartment of arias from the recently cancelled Metropolitan Opera performance; DiDonato, 2020). However, such events were usually one-way with no opportunity for an audience to respond in real time.

On the *passive versus active* dimension, although remote feedback/dialogue is possible, both spoken and written, interpersonal signalling is limited (e.g., body language, group laughter, and applause are all absent, or highly compromised). Audience/audience interactions are possible, but a remote concert experience is not easily socially embedded. Audience participation in the music is possible (e.g., sing-along) but normally each person will only hear themselves, thus missing the embedded communal experience.

Devising, executing, and publishing peer-reviewed research is a process that generally requires a greater timespan than was possible after the onset of the global lockdown. Thus, at the time of writing (September 2021), little published peer-reviewed research exists that can directly inform the design of online classical concerts. However, Swarbrick et al. (2021) provide an extensive analysis of 661 respondents' experience of a wide variety of online concerts across the world; and Onderdijk et al. (2021) devised online and socially distanced live concerts which allowed them to manipulate variables which could affect experience of agency, presence, and social connectedness amongst 83 concert attenders. We can expect significantly more findings to emerge in 2022, and beyond, through a range of research initiatives and networks of researchers which have been set up, many becoming active within weeks of the curtailment of normal concert life. These networks include Music Across the Balconies (Davidson, 2020), a resource which documents a large number of specific online initiatives taken by musicians since March 2020. Musicovid (Hansen & Wald-Fuhrmann, 2021) is an international network of researchers who have initiated projects assessing various aspects of the impact of COVID-19 on musical production, experience, and effects. These networks provide information on upcoming conferences and calls for contributions to publications, including special issues of journals, and these initiatives can be expected to bear fruit over time. Since the vast majority of live concerts are of popular—not classical—music, much of the new research (e.g., Rendell, 2021) is similarly focused. In research, as well as in life, classical music occupies a particular niche, and it remains important to be cautions in extrapolating from one genre to another in drawing conclusions.

Conclusion

This chapter has drawn together the findings from artist-involved research into audience experience, where artists play an equal role in the research alongside researchers, thus assessing innovations in concert practice which are meaningful and relevant to their practice. Practice-based, or practice-led research is becoming an increasingly significant feature of the music research environment, where in-depth understanding of a particular artistic practice or context—with all its individuality—can provide a challenge to the scientific imperative towards generality. This chapter has provided one attempt to outline a conceptual framework of some generality which is, nonetheless, sufficiently flexible to encompass a wide variety of artistic and organisational initiatives around concerts.

However, most of the research described has taken place in the UK (the remainder in north-western Europe), and much of it in the context of just one higher music education (HME) institute. HMEs have the advantage of allowing more freedom and experimentation than is sometimes possible in the commercial arts world, and HMEs are also natural homes for researchers. Embedding research-informed innovation within commercial or municipal arts organisations is a greater challenge, but one which may have more profound effects on the industry, if achieved.

Another challenge is to define more concretely the impact of such research on artistic practice going forward. Although the musicians in our studies were very engaged in the research process at the time, it is less easy to discover and document how the research influenced practice over the longer term, when the immediate collaboration ended.

Concert-going, and the socio-cultural underpinnings which sustain it, also varies quite considerably from country to country. Although the decline in classical concert attendance may be a global phenomenon, its rate and causes may be substantially different from country to country. It would be a productive future development to conduct more comparative research into experiences of, and motivations for, concert attendance in different countries, which could tailor artistic and organisational responses more closely to socio-cultural realities in different countries. There are also other demographic factors which could benefit from a more detailed analysis, and which may interact with location. Age and prior experience of concert attendance are clearly important variables which are not as well understood as they might be; particularly, which differences are generational and thus relate to different social and cultural contexts in different eras, and which are more internal (related to biological, cognitive, and aesthetic maturation, for example).

References

Anderson, J. (2017). On the practice of repeating concert items in concerts of modern or contemporary music: Historical precedents and recent contexts. *Participations: Journal of Audience & Reception Studies, 14*(2), 116–134. https://www.participations.org/14-02-08-anderson.pdf

Art Mentor Lucerne Foundation (2015). *Press Release: CONNECT, the audience as artist*. https://artmentor.ch/wp-content/uploads/2016/04/20151117_EN_Press-release.pdf

Davidson, J.W. (ed.). (2020). *Music Across the Balconies*. https://research.unimelb.edu.au/strengths/initiatives/interdisciplinary/hallmark/creativity-and-wellbeing/news/music-across-the-balconies

DiDonato, J. (2020, March 17). *Werther excerpts—Joyce DiDonato & Piotr Beczała* [Video]. YouTube. https://www.youtube.com/watch?v=tikkN3z145Q

Dobson, M. C. (2010). New audiences for classical music: The experiences of non-attenders at live orchestral concerts. *Journal of New Music Research, 39*(2), 111–124. https://doi.org/10.1080/09298215.2010.489643

Dobson, M., & Sloboda, J.A. (2014). Staying behind: Explorations in post-performance musician-audience dialogue. In K. Burland & S.E. Pitts (eds), *Coughing and clapping: Investigating audience experience* (pp. 159–173). Ashgate/SEMPRE Studies in the Psychology of Music. https://doi.org/10.4324/9781315574455

Dolan, D., Jensen, H.J., Mediano, P.A.M., Molina-Solana, M., Rajpal, H., Rosas, F., & Sloboda, J.A. (2018). The improvisational state of mind: A multidisciplinary study of an improvisatory approach to classical music repertoire performance. *Frontiers in Psychology, 9*, Article 1341. https://doi.org/10.3389/fpsyg.2018.01341

Dolan, D., Sloboda, J.A., Jensen, H.J., Crüts, B., & Feygelson, E. (2013). The improvisatory approach to classical music performance: An empirical investigation into its characteristics and impact. *Music Performance Research, 6*, 1–38. https://www.semanticscholar.org/paper/The-improvisatory-approach-to-classical-music-An-Dolan-Sloboda/bcb8007dccb604a87120fe93aff621aaf03b6348

Ford, B., & Sloboda, J.A. (2013). Learning from artistic and pedagogical differences between musicians' and actors' traditions through collaborative processes. In H. Gaunt & H. Westerlund (eds), *Collaborative learning in higher music education* (pp. 27–36). Ashgate. https://doi.org/10.4324/9781315572642

Gordon, C.L., Cobb, P.R., & Balasubramaniam, R. (2018). Recruitment of the motor system during music listening: An ALE meta-analysis of fMRI data. *PloS ONE, 13*(11), Article e0207213. https://doi.org/10.1371/journal.pone.0207213

Halpern, A.R., Chan, C.H.K., Müllensiefen, D., & Sloboda, J.A. (2017). Audience reactions to repeating a piece on a concert programme. *Participations: Journal of Audience & Reception Studies* (14)2, 135–152. https://research.gold.ac.uk/id/eprint/22524/1/7b.pdf

Hansen, N.C., & Wald-Fuhrmann, M. (eds). (2021, September 25) *Musicovid— An international research network*. https://www.aesthetics.mpg.de/forschung/abteilung-musik/musicovid-an-international-research-network.html

Margulis, E.H. (2014). *On repeat: How music plays the mind*. Oxford Scholarship Online. https://doi.org/10.1093/acprof:oso/9780199990825.001.0001

Marín, M.Á. (2018). Challenging the listener: How to change trends in classical music programming. *Resonancias*, 22(42), 115–130. https://resonancias.uc.cl/n-42/challenging-the-listener-how-to-change-trends-in-classical-music-programming/

National Endowment for the Arts. (2018, September). *The 2017 survey of public participation in the arts*. https://www.arts.gov/impact/research/arts-data-profile-series/adp-18

Onderdijk, K.E., Acar, F., & Van Dyck, E. (2021). Impact of lockdown measures on joint music making: Playing online and physically together. *Frontiers in Psychology, 12*, Article 642713. https://doi.org/10.3389/fpsyg.2021.642713

O'Neill, S., Edelman, J., & Sloboda, J.A. (2016). Opera and emotion: The cultural value of attendance for the highly engaged. *Participations: Journal of Audience & Reception Studies, 13*(1), 24–50. https://e-space.mmu.ac.uk/617206/

Price, S. M. (2022). In defence of the familiar: Understanding conservatism in concert selection amongst classical music audiences. *Musicae Scientiae, 26*(2), 243–258. https://doi.org/10.1177/1029864920940034

Rea, K. (2015). What classical musicians can learn from working with actors: Conceptual and pedagogic foundations and outcomes of bringing musicians to integrate in a drama training environment. *British Journal of Music Education, 32*(2), 195–210. https://doi.org/10.1017/S0265051715000108

Rendell, J. (2021). Staying in, rocking out: Online live music portal shows during the coronavirus pandemic. *Convergence: The International Journal of Research into New Media Technologies, 27*(4), 1092–1111. https://doi.org/10.1177/1354856520976451

Rotterdam Philharmonic Orchestra. (2020, March 20). *From us, for you: Beethoven Symphony No. 9* [Video]. YouTube. https://www.youtube.com/watch?v=3eXT60rbBVk

Sawer, P. (2018, November 9). Classical musicians to break with tradition and speak to the audience. *The Telegraph*. https://www.telegraph.co.uk/news/2018/11/09/classical-musicians-break-tradition-speak-audience/

Sigurjonsson, N. (2005). Young audience development and aesthetics: John Dewey's pragmatist philosophy and its implications for orchestra management. http://neumann.hec.ca/aimac2005/PDF_Text/Sigurjonsson_Niordur.pdf

Sloboda, J.A. (2013, April 4–7). *How does it strike you? Obtaining artist-directed feedback from the audience at a site-specific performance of a Monteverdi opera* [Paper presentation]. CMPCP Performance Studies Network 2nd Conference, Cambridge, UK. https://www.cmpcp.ac.uk/wp-content/uploads/2015/11/PSN2013_Sloboda.pdf

Sloboda, J.A. (2015). The composer and the audience. In P. Weigold & G. Kenyon (eds), *Beyond Britten: The composer and the community* (pp. 175–189). Boydell & Brewer, Boydell Press. https://doi.org/10.2307/j.ctv136c1vj

Sloboda, J.A., & Ford, B. (2019). Classical music borrowing from other arts: New strategies for audience building through performance. In A. F. Corrêra (ed.), *Music, speech, and mind* (pp. 187–212). Brazilian Association of Cognition and Musical Arts.

Sloboda, J.A., & Wise, K. (2016). Going to a classical concert: The relationship between audience perceptions of artistic identity and motivation for future attendance. *Creative Works London Working*. http://www.creativeworkslondon.org.uk/wp-content/uploads/2016/07/28-BrittenSinfoniaWorkingPaperJun2016.pdf

Small, C. (1998). *Musicking: The meanings of performing and listening*. Wesleyan University Press.

Swarbrick, D., Seibt, B., Grinspun, N., & Vuoskoski, J.K. (2021). Corona concerts: The effect of virtual concert characteristics on social connection and *Kama Muta*. *Frontiers in Psychology, 12*, Article 648448. https://doi.org/10.3389/fpsyg.2021.648448

Toelle, J., & Sloboda, J.A. (2021). The audience as artist? The audience's experience of participatory music. *Musicae Scientiae, 25*(1), 67–91. https://doi.org/10.1177/1029864919844804

Tutti.space. (2020, March 29). *Steven Isserlis' children's concert over Facebook live* [Video]. YouTube. https://www.youtube.com/watch?v=xtSY0LVV3qg

Weber, W. (1984). The contemporaneity of eighteenth-century musical taste. *The Musical Quarterly, 70*(2), 175–194. https://doi.org/10.1093/mq/LXX.2.175

Whitacre, E. (n.d.). *Eric Whitacre's Virtual Choir*. Retrieved September 25, 2021, from https://ericwhitacre.com/the-virtual-choir

Wilson, F. (2015, November 23). *Gestures in piano playing: Seeing and hearing. The Cross Eyed Pianist*. https://crosseyedpianist.com/tag/gestures-in-piano-playing/

World Harmony Orchestra. (n.d.). *Cuppa Concerts*. Retrieved June 24, 2022, form https://www.worldharmonyorchestra.com/

PART III

MUSIC COGNITION IN PERFORMANCE AND PRACTICE

8. Influences of Physical and Imagined Others in Music Students' Experiences of Practice and Performance

Andrea Schiavio, Henrique Meissner, and Renee Timmers

Introduction

Most musical activities can be carried out either individually, such as practicing with a musical instrument by oneself, or in a more social context, such as rehearsing or performing with an ensemble. These situations showcase different characteristics which bring particular pressures, challenges, and rewards. Nevertheless, offering clear-cut distinctions between social and individual contexts may be more difficult than expected. On the one hand, the felt presence of 'others' in solitary contexts could transform the individual nature of certain musical actions into a more intersubjective experience; on the other hand, a strengthened awareness of the 'self' in group situations can reveal in a clearer fashion the different subjectivities that contribute to the collective work. Music-making itself is strongly intersubjective: musicians may experience a 'dialogue' with the composer and assign agency to the music as represented by the score (Mak et al., 2022), in addition to experiencing the dialogue with other musicians happening in real-time, or in the past (Clarke et al., 2016). The social context of performance is often strongly felt by musicians, and seems to contribute to emotional peak experiences in the form of intense positive experiences of felt connection with the audience, and to emotional challenges and apprehension in

©2024 A. Schiavio, H. Meissner & R. Timmers, CC BY-NC 4.0   https://doi.org/10.11647/OBP.0389.08

reports of music performance anxiety (e.g., Perdomo-Guevara, 2014). In this chapter, we investigate this intersubjective dimension that often permeates musical performance and practice. We are interested in how social presence shapes and becomes part of the experience of performers and learners, and how different ways of engagement between musicians and 'others' are formed and qualitatively felt. To explore these aspects, we operationalised intersubjectivity[1] as two main modes of social presence, namely physical presence and imagined presence. By doing so, we assume that we can also observe intersubjectivity when musicians engage with others who are only present in their thoughts, creating inner dialogues and establishing social relationships that take an imaginative form. This conjecture is in line with recent scholarship on interactive cognition and musical creativity, which increasingly places emphasis on the social components of mental life (Di Paolo & De Jaegher, 2012; Schilbach et al., 2013), as well as on the imaginative capacities that are central to thinking and acting musically (Hargreaves, 2012; Kratus, 2017). At the crossroads of these approaches lies research positing an intersubjective framing also in seemingly solitary contexts (Høffding & Satne, 2019). This work, in a nutshell, suggests that settings in which agents operate by themselves (e.g., when practising or composing music alone) should not be conceived of as separate from the broader network of cultural, social, and historical influences that drive and inspire musical activity (Clarke et al., 2016; Folkestad, 2011; Schiavio et al., 2022).

With this in mind, imagining others can be seen to stand between the two connected levels of intersubjectivity described by Fusaroli et al. (2012), where the latter is understood as '1. [...] the articulation of continuous interactions *in praesentia* between two or more subjects. [... and] 2. As sedimented socio-cultural normativity: i.e., of habits, beliefs, attitudes, and historically and culturally sedimented morphologies' (p. 2). Imagining others, indeed, displays a rather ambiguous status in that—at least in certain cases of vivid imaginative activity—it can feel as if interaction were *in praesentia*; as if, in other words, the imagined other(s) were physically present. This makes such a phenomenon

---

1   We understand intersubjectivity as the sense of individuals sharing meaning with others and functioning as part of a larger whole that has been described as a powerful experience in a range of musical contexts (see, e.g., Rabinowitch et al., 2012; Sawyer, 2003).

particularly fascinating in the musical domain, where the role of others (e.g., listeners, co-players, teachers, etc.) is crucial for music's various manifestations (see, e.g., Small, 1998). Specifically, we ask (1) in what sense can relevant musical 'others' (whether physically present or not) shape music-making activity? And (2) how does the influence of others vary depending on whether we are considering a performing or practising context? In what follows, we aim to address such questions by reporting on a qualitative study conducted with a small group of music higher education (MHE) students, whose verbal descriptions can help to increase understanding of intersubjectivity in musical contexts.

Method

Participants

Ethical approval was obtained through the Department of Music at the University of Sheffield. Following ethics approval, a total of 17 adult music students responded to a recruitment email. They were studying music performance at postgraduate level at MHE institutions of the second and third author in the Netherlands and in the UK, respectively. Taking part in this study was voluntary, and participants gave their written consent. Two individuals were excluded as they either did not give their consent or answered in an insufficient manner. This reduced the sample to 15 participants (7 women; 8 men), playing different musical instruments and genres (see Table 8.1). Their ages ranged between 21 and 32 years ($M = 26.2$ years; $SD = 3.1$). Each respondent was assigned a pseudonym (P1, P2, etc.) to ensure anonymity.

Table 8.1 Overview of the participants

Pseudonym	Gender	Age	Musical instrument	Musical genre played
P1	M	25	Classical guitar	Classical
P2	F	26	Voice	Classical
P3	M	27	Percussion	Various
P4	M	28	Drums	Rock and Jazz
P5	F	31	Piano	Classical
P6	F	32	Piano	Jazz, Pop, and Blues
P7	F	23	Voice	Jazz
P8	M	28	Violin	Classical
P9	M	24	Organ	Classical
P10	F	25	Cello	Classical
P11	M	21	Electric bass	Metal
P12	M	27	Saxophone	Rock
P13	M	30	Guitar	Jazz and Classical
P14	F	22	Bass clarinet	Classical
P15	F	24	Violin	Classical

Materials and procedure

The research team developed an open-ended questionnaire to explore the responses of music students when asked about the range of intersubjective experiences felt during practice and performance. Participants accessed the questionnaire online and were invited to type their answers on a Google form anonymously. The instrument comprised a first section dedicated to demographics and musical background, and a second one featuring eleven questions, to which respondents answered without a word limit. With these questions we invited participants to share their perspectives on practice and performance both as a solitary activity and in the presence of others. This involved exploring the differences between such situations and offering examples illustrative of the influence of others on emotions, feelings, and thoughts. Accordingly, we focused on the following modes of presence: (i) physical presence, that is, when someone else is present, whether passively or playing together (e.g., in the same room as the musician), and (ii) imagined presence, that is, when this 'someone else' is only present in the mind of the musician. To make sure the written responses could capture the continuities and differences between these types of presence, as well as elicit a variety of subjective characterisations of both phenomena, we developed deliberately broadly interpretable questions that could resonate with each musician and invite personal reflections about the (intersubjective) experiences permeating their musical practice and performance. The main part of the questionnaire can be found in the Appendix of this chapter.

Data analysis

Given the exploratory nature of the research, data analysis was performed via a grounded theory approach (Oktay, 2012). This allows the researcher to look for meaningful units of analysis (i.e., codes referring to distinctive ideas, concepts, or experiences) directly in the data, and to systematise them into categories relating to more general dimensions. The analysis began with an immersion phase, where the raw data were read multiple times to gain familiarity with their content. Preliminary interpretations were noted through informal memos, so that the units of analysis could be generated contextually and, if necessary, modified. This gave rise to eleven codes. Subsequently, all raw data were merged into a single Word document, with each participant's answers being segmented into shorter quotes. Where possible, these quotes were organised around the codes developed earlier on, assessed for intra-code coherence, and either kept, discarded, or moved to another code. During this phase, three codes were eliminated since many of the quotes associated with them could be submerged under other codes. This process was re-examined in a third phase of the analysis, where codes were systematically grouped into four broad categories with two codes each. The initial coding was done by the first author and independently verified by the second and third authors. The resulting coding scheme is depicted in Figure 8.1.

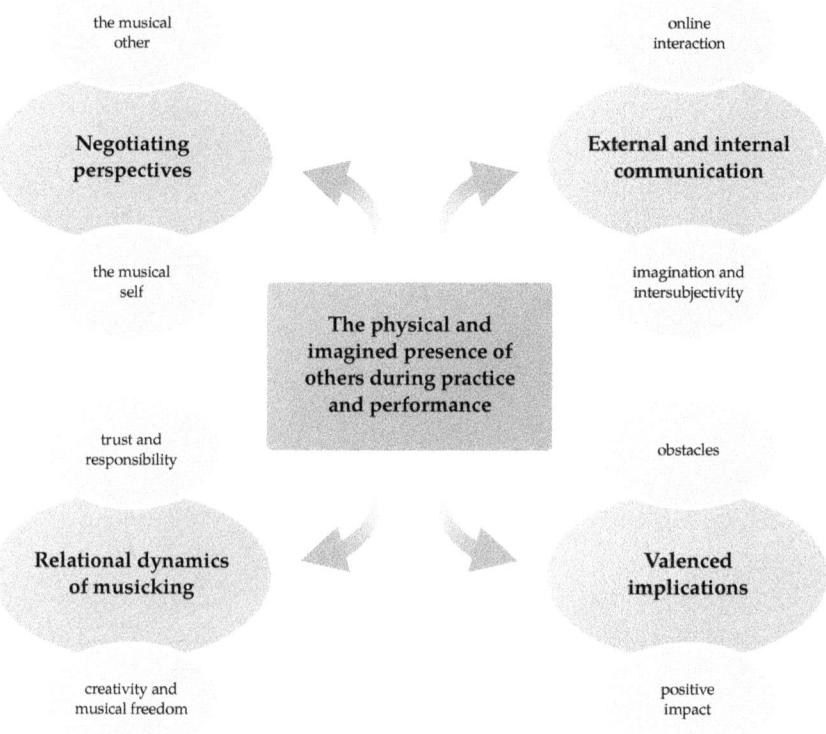

Fig. 8.1 Coding scheme

Results and discussion

Negotiating perspectives

This category includes statements referring to the way our respondents distinguish and negotiate between social-focused and individual-centred perspectives. It includes the codes 'the musical other' and 'the musical self'.

The musical other

Not only is social participation a defining feature of music-making; it is also seen by one participant as a defining feature of who we are as a species:

> We can only define ourselves as humans through other people. This also goes for the fact of being a musician. (P13)

This aspect of defining oneself in relation to others (or 'the musical other', as we will call it when stressing its musical connotations) is further elaborated by another participant:

> I think our behaviour is strongly determined by how we interact with others and how we think the other sees us. I therefore think it's impossible to not be impacted by others in practising, performing and any other things. (P1)

The same respondent also explains why such an investigation can reveal an important, yet often underplayed dimension; that is, the self-other dialectics that emerge in the musical moment:

> It's interesting to think about the concept of 'the other'. In performances you cannot really see how the other sees you, you only have your own perspective, so you see your version of the other and you fill in how the other would see you. In that sense there might not be a big difference between a physical audience and an imagined audience. (P1)

One aspect at the heart of this form of self-other interplay, as the quotation suggests, is represented by a continuous change of perspective. Intersubjective experience appears to be systematically filtered by one's own agency and subjectivity. Accordingly, the physical or imagined presence of others may, in a sense, feel the same: what matters is not primarily how the others manifest themselves, but rather how we react to their presence. This resonates with a reflection offered by another participant:

> I think whether the presence of others affects you or not depends on your personality and the way you take things. If you feel affected [by] thinking about what others can say about your performance, their presence during your performance could affect you, but if you are confident enough with yourself and your performance, others' opinions cannot cause you any problem. (P3)

Nevertheless, several participants mentioned that they are affected by the presence of others during practice or performance, and that this is very much dependent on the situation and on how they perceive the musical others, and whether they are seen as friendly and supportive or critical and evaluating:

> It depends on how they react. For example, if there are friends and they enjoy what I practise, I feel good. On the other hand, if they judge my play, I feel very uncomfortable, and I don't want to practise in front of them anymore. (P6)

While 'the musical other' manifests itself in a variety of forms, how this might affect one's musicking seems to depend on the situation and on how one is attuned to it. Developing this view, the role of intersubjective presence in musical settings might be better understood if we re-orient the discussion towards a more self-centred perspective.

The musical self

As we have just seen, the focus on 'the musical other' lends itself naturally to a consideration of its complementary pole of interaction, that is, the (musical) self. This dimension emerges strongly when respondents are asked to define what performing music means to them. Consider the following statements from three different participants:

> Performing music is presenting your musical voice, either in solo or in harmony with those you're performing with, towards an audience. (P11)

> 'Performing music' means letting myself be carried away by the feelings and emotions that music produces in me. I perform to feel and to convey these feelings to the audience. (P5)

> [Performing music is] showing myself and inviting [the] audience to my world; comforting myself and someone. (P6)

Note how these participants place emphasis on their personal perspectives (i.e., their own 'musical voice'; 'letting myself be carried away'; 'inviting [the] audience to my world'), before letting others join in. *Prima facie*, this could be taken for a one-way communication model, in which the musician sends a musical message to an otherwise passive audience. However, as the last quote suggests, there is also a more active role for the latter: they are 'invited' to enter a personal space, one in which musicians and others can share something meaningful in the musical moment. This arguably gives rise to a less static process of give-and-take, where the presence of others can shape musical activity—including practice:

> If I am thinking of others while practising, it will often be a motivator. Mainly this is of my teachers and how they motivate me to work on the things I may not [...] want to practise in the moment. (P11)

However pervasive the presence of others may be, it should be clear that musicians do not 'suffer' from it passively. Instead, they are able to use their mental resources to adapt to it and to optimise their musicking accordingly:

> I think it is not about the presence of others during practice or [performance], but rather the kind of thoughts I have and how I perceive the situation. When I started to realise that anxiety was not created by others but by the thoughts I had about them, I could focus more on music and started to enjoy what I was doing. (P5)

According to P5, it is important to work on a robust and confident musical self that can be informed or inspired by others, being at the same time defined by a strong sense of agency and competence. We explore these inner-outer dialectics in the next section.

External and internal communication

This category includes descriptions of how one can communicate with others when they are physically present, and when these latter are only constructed internally in the imagination. We use here the distinction between 'online' and 'offline' social cognition proposed by Schilbach (2014). The former term describes social cognition from an interactor's point of view, whereas the latter focuses on the observer. It includes the codes 'online interaction' and 'imagination and intersubjectivity'.

Online interaction

Despite the previously mentioned fuzzy or porous distinctions between the impact of imagined and actual others, some participants do highlight an important difference between such modes of presence:

> With others physically present you are communicating your story to the others, and you will get a genuine reaction from them, [while] with others in your imagination you are just interacting with yourself and with your idea of the other. (P1)

Participants also explain how they adjust to others and foster communication:

> [When] performing with others [...] I often feel that I can be more focused on expressive and communicative intent because I have more contact with them on the stage and their physical presence reminds me that the performance is not only about technical competency. (P2)

This dimension of openness to others, importantly, also emerges during practice:

> practising music with others [...] means more teamwork: taking into account other people's opinions, expressing yours and being more flexible. (P10)

It appears that this self-other dialogue when others are physically present gives rise to a range of explicit, intuitive forms of communication. These may arguably be associated with a more direct involvement of both parties when compared to situations where others are only imagined. The next code includes reflections that address the latter case.

Imagination and intersubjectivity

Experience teaches us that imagination can be extremely vivid. As such, within the musical settings being considered here, it might be hard to distinguish how others can impact on musical experience and behaviour based only on their mode of presence:

> The feeling is the same if others are physically present or in my imagination. There have been times when while I was practising, I have thought that a certain person is listening to me, and I have noticed the

nerves in my stomach. Suddenly my feelings change, and I worry about what that person might think. (P5)

This point is echoed in another example provided by a different respondent:

Sometimes [during performance] I try to remember someone whose smile brings me ease. If I think about the people who are watching in an evaluation context, I tend to get more tense and start losing control of what I'm doing. (P10)

It should be noted that the concrete consequences of engaging in such an imaginative practice may go beyond influencing one's musical experience, reaching instead to a deeper dimension:

In practice, [imagining others] can [make me] feel quite safe but also a bit vulnerable because there is a recognition that this person really wants to understand your thoughts and imaginative ideas and that can be quite a personal thing. (P2)

This last statement suggests a subjective form of communication with the imagined other, as if the latter were not a product of the musician's imaginative activity, but rather an independent sentient being. Of particular interest is the reported effect of such a peculiar, inner dialogue, in which the presence of the imagined other is felt as almost intruding upon the intimate spheres of one's mental life. This could be a manifestation of anxiety. However, this was not further explained in the written responses. Perceiving others in the mind or in the surrounding environment, as we have seen, can thus give rise to different forms of inter- and intra-personal dialogue.

Relational dynamics of musicking

Recurring themes in the data are related to 'trust and responsibility' and 'creativity'. This category explores how both dimensions play out in a social context, shaping relational dynamics.

Trust and responsibility

A great sense of responsibility was perceived both in solo and ensemble situations. As stated by one respondent: '[performing music is about] responsibility, having fun, and transmitting emotions' (P4). And both forms of performance bring high responsibility in subtly different ways:

> [Playing with others] feels safer because you are not in the spotlight and yet at the same time more compromising because of the responsibility of being only one part of the whole. (P10)

> When I am playing with others, the group itself forces me [...] to keep doing what I am doing better. (P3)

> When I perform music alone, I feel like I have all the responsibilities such as drummer, bassist, and other melodic instrument players. (P6)

> When performing alone all the responsibility is on you to play well. In a way that is nice because you know what you are capable of and if something goes wrong it is usually easier to fix because you are the only person involved. (P9)

These responses indicate a sharing of responsibility with others, which requires trust and a reliance on others. Often such sharing makes both performance and practice more enjoyable, as one participant illustrates in two different quotes:

> I think when others are physically present in performance it's much more likely to be able to enter a flow state. When I performed in Le Nozze di Figaro I feel like that happened also because we began to trust each other more through the rehearsals and we get real response and communication between the characters, rather than just repeating musical lines that are written in the score. (P2)

> [When others are physically present while I'm practising], I feel like there is more trust in the room and less judgement. I've found that especially during opera rehearsals when people are physically present there can be more playfulness and curiosity and willingness to take more risks. When this hasn't happened, and I notice that they are concerned about remembering lines or feeling a bit stuck in their body, it becomes harder to create a performance and feels that you can't be as free in your freedom of expression and ideas. (P2)

Across all responses, there was no mention of the role played by imagined others in shaping trust and responsibility. Instead, rich descriptions were offered of how the physical presence of others contributes to creating a sense of shared responsibility. In addition, several participants mention how performing with others helps them feel safe and enhances their confidence (see below). Overall, positive experiences are reported when it comes to communicating and trusting others in music-making. As the last quotation also suggests, however, if joint musicking does not work properly, the presence of others might be detrimental for musical creativity and expression. In the next code, we explore these aspects in more detail.

Creativity and musical freedom

While the attribution of trust and responsibility to others often requires their physical presence, creative thought and action appear to be less constrained by such a mode of engagement with musical others. With respect to practice, one of the participants explains:

> If you are practising technique, [imagining others] is not positive because this means that you are losing concentration. But if you are working on improvisation, for instance, it can inspire you. (P4)

The separation between practising technique and improvisation delineated here, where the influence of imagined others is considered as positive only for the latter, contrasts with a previously reported statement by P11—in which the mental presence of others is understood as a 'motivator'. In a similar vein, imagining others might drive creativity:

> In performance, I feel that when others are present in my imagination then it is possible to create a kind of spiral of ideas and have more possibility of risk-taking and being spontaneous. (P2)

The final line about risk-taking is particularly interesting, as one would expect more creativity to flourish when openly communicating with other musicians or audience members who are physically present. However, as the same participant explains: 'Alone I feel like I can take a bit more time for the exploration of body and music' (P2). The point is echoed by another music student as follows: 'I feel more freedom when I practise alone' (P1). It seems, then, that while responsibility and trust are particularly relevant when others are physically present (possibly due to direct musical exchanges occurring in real time), creativity and expressivity appear to be associated with self-focused attention (see Berkowitz & Ansari, 2010), where a quasi-interpersonal form of communication unfolds between the musicians themselves and their imagined others. As such, this code highlights a special role for imagined interaction with others in the relatively flexible setting of solo performance and practice.

Valenced implications

The implications of the thought processes and musicking with others were regularly negatively valenced, which we code as 'obstacles'. This is contrasted with instances in which the presence of others did have a positive impact.

Obstacles

A prominent theme we touched upon in the code 'The musical self' is that of tension and anxiety—a sensation that musicians can feel intensely across a variety of contexts (see, e.g., Papageorgi & Welch, 2020). It is sometimes difficult to avoid being affected by someone else's presence, particularly when they might assess and judge the performance, or when they have a strong emotional bond with the musicians. The following example speaks about the influence of the imagined presence of others:

> I think having others present in your thoughts and imaginations can create a lot of pressure you put upon yourself. There you can feel the need to prove yourself and impress upon people what you can do and as those others are often the ones you feel a closer emotional connection to, you want to do the best you can. This can create a lot more unnecessary performance anxiety in contrast to being able to see them present in the room and their live reactions. (P11)

This point is restated by another participant as follows:

> I normally feel uncomfortable when I imagine someone listening to my practice. This is because they are mostly the people who judge me in my thoughts. (P6)

Also, when looking at the physical presence of others during a performance—audience members particularly—a similar sense of tension arises in relation to their level of familiarity. For instance, one participant admits that 'it all very much depends on how well I know the people' (P1). Another participant explains:

> In a more relaxed concert setting with an unknown audience, I may become more relaxed and comfortable in my physicality and therefore my performance. In a more formal environment (such as with juries, competitions etc.) this may add tension. If I am performing to an audience that features people I know, I feel more pressure to perform to a higher level. (P12)

This situation is not specific to performance, but can also occur during practice:

> When I practise playing the piano, a little thought about someone watching makes me stumble and I will make a mistake for sure. (P7)

Getting rid of such daunting sensations is no easy task, and musicians might therefore try to reduce moments where they actively think of others. That said, it is generally more difficult to avoid situations where others are physically present, so musicians may use various techniques to feel more at ease:

> During the group lessons, the fact that I feel observed and listened to attentively makes me feel nervous and my breathing is interrupted. I physically weaken and lose my grip on the keyboard. I must be very aware of my breathing and do a 'bodyscan' before playing to be able to control these sensations. (P5)

This last example aligns well with one of the major themes of our analysis, namely the focus on a self-centred view used as a resource to adapt to external perturbations. Nevertheless, many participants also describe the presence of others as a positive driver of performance and practice.

Positive impact

While the imagined or physical presence of others are understood as distinct situations with distinct phenomenologies and nuances, they arguably share more properties than one might expect. Amongst others, we have seen how they both have a real impact on the musicians as well as a particular relation with their emotional sphere:

> I often use the imagery in my practice, so this—[...] depending on the circumstance—generally positively impacts my playing. It's easier for me to play with feeling and emotion if I'm imagining/remembering something emotional. (P12).

If we assume that imagining others while musicking may give rise to a sort of inner dialogue, as we pointed out in the code 'Imagination and intersubjectivity', it appears that such an intra-personal experience may also facilitate musical expression and emotion, similarly to how it facilitates the generation of novel and valuable musical ideas and outcomes (see code 'Creativity and musical freedom'). Furthermore, one of the positive aspects of the physical presence of others concerns the musician's confidence:

> I've noticed over time that the presence of others while practising has gone from placing a pressure on me to perform to a high standard to giving me confidence in showing an audience what I am able to do. (P11)

The same participant further elaborates on this idea, extending the same insight from practice to performance settings:

> I think the presence of others has a great impact upon my confidence as a musician. Firstly, if you see the audience enjoying what you're playing then it affirms what you've been doing and therefore your confidence can grow massively. Also, while the presence of others can create a form of pressure it can also give you the encouragement you need to perform in the best way you can at that moment. (P11)

Several participants report that performing together with others can also provide a feeling of safety, thus enhancing confidence:

> [Performing] alone feels quite naked but you have the time for yourself and together you have the feeling that the others can provide a safety net. (P14)

> Interpreting in a group I feel more sheltered. Eye contact and a smile while playing gives me peace. (P5)

A possible way to boost confidence, which we believe many musicians are familiar with, is described as follows:

> You can fake a live situation at home by imagining very strongly that you have to play in front of people. Your heart beats faster when you do this. Practising this really works when you find it hard to perform. (P13)

As we have seen earlier, the presence of others is never purely passively perceived. Rather, it triggers a more or less explicit response—an evaluation, or a coping mechanism that is often self-centred (e.g., a 'bodyscan' in the words of P5, or a reflection on the emotional components involved in musicking). Musicians seem to be open and receptive to the presence and actions of others, being at the same time ready to react in the most efficient way through reliance on a strong inner self.

Conclusion

Music is an intrinsically participatory phenomenon (Turino, 2008), but this is by no means confined to purely physical interaction. The imagined co-production of musical parts played by others has been shown to causally contribute to synchronisation (Novembre et al., 2014) and accuracy of turn-taking (Hadley et al., 2015). Furthermore, imagining an audience has been advocated as a technique to prepare for public performance (Connolly & Williamon, 2004), and mental rehearsal through listening and imagining one's own and others' parts is a known strategy to advance practice and performance (Clark et al., 2011). In the present chapter, we have contributed to such research areas by exploring how social presence shapes and becomes part of the experience of a group of advanced music performers and learners, and how different modes of social engagement (i.e., physical and imagined presence) are qualitatively felt.

In response to our first research question—in what sense can relevant musical 'others' (whether physically present or not) shape music-making activity—we note that participants often focused on those shifts between attention oriented inward and outward which, in many cases, accompany the presence of others. Respondents combined socially oriented descriptions with analyses of self-centred processes. Such an inner-outer dialectic aligns well with the notion of 'dual intentionality of music-making' (Høffding & Schiavio, 2019), which examines how making music is both directed towards external (social) domains, and towards a more intimate dimension, strongly associated with agency and selfhood. This dialectic between internal and external focus was felt in relation to responsibility and agency, a sense of competence and vulnerability where others were seen as either motivators and supporters, or as judges, or a source of distraction. Inner strength and competence ('my voice') was felt to be important in this context of high-performance demands. In other descriptions, such a dialectic gave way to a more integrated sense of self and other, with references to 'our energy', group creativity, and sheltered performance. This was primarily described in the context of performing with others, but imagined others could, for some, also play a role in promoting creativity or sharing responsibility.

Engaging with others musically, we suggest, involves a continuous renegotiation of individual focus, involving both internal and external aspects, regardless of the nature (i.e., physical or imagined) of the other(s) being present. This relates to the sense of communication that our participants reported to be part of their musicking, and that includes others who are imagined or physically present. Internal and external focus are closely associated, in line with explanations by participants of the narrow distinctions between physical others and imagined others: one cannot fully know what others think even if they are present, and since imagination can be extremely vivid, concrete (positive or negative) implications are physically experienced even in the absence of others. This proximity also works the other way around: an external focus on audiences as judges can be strongly internally oriented, as they may represent personal fears and developed processes of self-evaluation. The seeking of approval was seen as unavoidable, but also something that many participants sought to free themselves from, both in practice and performance.

This brings us to our second research question: how does the influence of others vary depending on whether we are considering a performing or practising context? In general, performing together with other musicians was seen by most as an enjoyable and creative experience, in which co-players provide safety and confidence. Conversely, imagining others during practice was seen by most as a sign of intrusive thoughts or distraction, which could lead to feeling vulnerable when playing. However, imagining others could also serve a variety of positive functions, including pre-experiencing performance situations during practice and inspiring expressivity and creativity. Whilst the presence of an observing audience often leads to considerable negative feelings, as known from the extensive literature on performance anxiety (see Chapter 15 in this volume), the goal of performance has been described as to share one's 'story' and musical interpretation with others. And, indeed, musicians who focus on communication with imagined or physically present audiences may enjoy their musicking more than those who see the latter as evaluators. But while it might be liberating to focus on communication and expression in such cases, the references to tension in several responses suggest that this is not easy and requires practice. One participant, for example, refers to the detrimental effects of recurring negative feedback:

> Sometimes the things people have said or done to you can resonate with you as you're playing. [...] I know many great musicians [who] have the negative words of past teachers 'ringing in their ear' as they play and practise. The continuous negativity impacts their confidence, playing, and thus their ability to enjoy music. (P12)

This vivid description highlights the importance of raising awareness of the risks connected to a 'pedagogy of correction' (Bull, 2022) in music education. It is important to foster safe learning environments where musicians can focus on connection and communication rather than perfection and evaluation (Meissner et al., 2022). Future research could build on the method and findings of this chapter to encourage musicians to make explicit their thought processes and perspectives on self and others during practice and performance. This may involve exploring shifts of attention between internal and external focus, examining their associated subjective experiences, and investigating how a sense of joint effort and intersubjectivity can be described and enhanced when musicking. This chapter has highlighted the multitude of roles of the self and others in music performance and practice, and the relevance of these perspectives on the felt experiences of a cohort of music students.

Acknowledgements

We are grateful to the students who took part in this study.

References

Berkowitz, A.L., & Ansari, D. (2010). Expertise-related deactivation of the right temporoparietal junction during musical improvisation. *Neuroimage, 49*(1), 712–719. https://doi.org/10.1016/j.neuroimage.2009.08.042

Bull, A. (2022). Equity in music education: Getting it right: Why classical music's "Pedagogy of Correction" is a barrier to equity. *Music Educators Journal, 108*(3), 65–66. https://doi.org/10.1177/00274321221085132

Clarke, E., Doffman, M., & Timmers, R. (2016). Creativity, collaboration and development in Jeremy Thurlow's 'Ouija' for Peter Sheppard Skærved. *Journal of the Royal Musical Association, 141*(1), 113–165. https://doi.org/10.1080/02690403.2016.1151240

Clark, T., Williamon, A., & Aksentijevic, A. (2011). Musical imagery and imagination: The function, measurement, and application of imagery skills for performance. In D.J. Hargreaves, D.E. Miell, & R.A.R. MacDonald (eds), *Musical Imaginations: Multidisciplinary perspectives on creativity, performance, and perception* (pp. 351–365). Oxford University Press. https://doi.org/10.1093/acprof:oso/9780199568086.003.0022

Connolly, C., & Williamon, A. (2004). Mental skills training. In A. Williamon (ed.), *Musical excellence: Strategies and techniques to enhance performance* (pp. 221–245). Oxford University Press. https://doi.org/10.1093/acprof:oso/9780198525356.001.0001

Di Paolo, E., & De Jaegher, H. (2012). The interactive brain hypothesis. *Frontiers in Human Neuroscience, 6*, Article 163. https://doi.org/10.3389/fnhum.2012.00163

Folkestad, G. (2011). Digital tools and discourse in music: The ecology of composition. In D.J. Hargreaves, D.E. Miell, & R.A.R. MacDonald (eds), *Musical Imaginations: Multidisciplinary perspectives on creativity, performance, and perception* (pp. 193–205). Oxford University Press. https://doi.org/10.1093/acprof:oso/9780199568086.001.0001

Fusaroli, R., Demuru, P., & Borghi, A.M. (2012). The intersubjectivity of embodiment. *Journal of Cognitive Semiotics, 4*(1), 1–5. https://www.degruyter.com/document/doi/10.1515/cogsem.2012.4.1.1/html?lang=en

Hadley, L.V., Novembre, G., Keller, P.E., & Pickering, M.J. (2015). Causal role of motor simulation in turn-taking behavior. *Journal of Neuroscience, 35*(50), 16516–16520. https://doi.org/10.1523/JNEUROSCI.1850-15.2015

Hargreaves, D.J. (2012). Musical imagination: Perception and production, beauty and creativity. *Psychology of Music, 40*(5), 539–557. https://doi.org/10.1177/0305735612444893

Høffding, S., & Satne, G. (2019). Interactive expertise in solo and joint musical performance. *Synthese, 198*(1), 427–445. https://doi.org/10.1007/s11229-019-02339-x

Høffding, S., & Schiavio, A. (2019). Exploratory expertise and the dual intentionality of music-making. *Phenomenology and the Cognitive Sciences, 20*, 811–829. https://doi.org/10.1007/s11097-019-09626-5

Kratus, J. (2017). Music listening is creative. *Music Educators Journal, 103*(3), 46–51. https://doi.org/10.1177/0027432116686843

Mak, S.Y., Nishida, H., & Yokomori, D. (2022). Agency in ensemble interaction and rehearsal communication. In R. Timmers, F. Bailes, & H. Daffern (eds), *Together in music: Coordination, expression, participation* (pp. 35–43). Oxford University Press. https://doi.org/10.1093/oso/9780198860761.003.0004

Meissner, H., Timmers, R., & Pitts, S.E. (2022). *Sound teaching: A research-informed approach to inspiring confidence, skill, and enjoyment in music performance.* Routledge. https://doi.org/10.4324/9781003108382

Novembre, G., Ticini, L.F., Schütz-Bosbach, S., & Keller, P.E. (2014). Motor simulation and the coordination of self and other in real-time joint action. *Social Cognitive and Affective Neuroscience, 9*(8), 1062–1068. https://doi.org/10.1093/scan/nst086

Oktay, J.S. (2012). *Grounded theory.* Oxford University Press. https://doi.org/10.1093/acprof:oso/9780199753697.001.0001

Papageorgi, I., & Welch, G.F. (2020). 'A bed of nails': Professional musicians' accounts of the experience of performance anxiety from a phenomenological perspective. *Frontiers in Psychology, 11*, Article 605422. https://doi.org/10.3389/fpsyg.2020.605422

Perdomo-Guevara, E. (2014). Is music performance anxiety just an individual problem? Exploring the impact of musical environments on performers' approaches to performance and emotions. *Psychomusicology: Music, Mind, and Brain, 24*(1), 66–74. https://doi.org/10.1037/pmu0000028

Rabinowitch, T.-C., Cross, I., & Burnard, P. (2012). Musical group interaction, intersubjectivity, and merged subjectivity. In D. Reynolds & M. Reason (eds), *Kinesthetic empathy in creative and cultural practices* (pp. 109–120). Intellect Press. https://www.researchgate.net/publication/290857650_Musical_group_interaction_intersubjectivity_and_merged_subjectivity

Sawyer, K.R. (2003). *Group creativity: Music, theater, collaboration.* Erlbaum.

Schiavio, A., Ryan, K., Moran, N., van der Schyff, D., & Gallagher, S. (2022). By myself but not alone. Agency, creativity, and extended musical historicity. *Journal of the Royal Musical Association, 147*(2) 533–556. https://doi.org/10.1017/rma.2022.22

Schilbach, L. (2014). On the relationship of online and offline social cognition. *Frontiers in Human Neuroscience, 8,* Article 278. https://doi.org/10.3389/fnhum.2014.00278

Schilbach L., Timmermans, B., Reddy, V., Costall, A., Bente, G., Schlicht, T., & Vogelay, K. (2013). Toward a second-person neuroscience. *Behavioral and Brain Sciences, 36*(4), 393–462. https://doi.org/10.1017/S0140525X12000660

Small, C. (1998). *Musicking: The meanings of performing and listening.* Wesleyan University Press.

Turino, T. (2008). *Music as social life: The politics of participation.* University of Chicago Press.

Appendix

Questionnaire

1. What does practising music mean to you?
2. What does performing music mean to you?
3. What are the main differences for you between practising music alone or together with others*?
4. What are the main differences for you between performing music alone or together with others?
5. How do you feel (in terms of emotions or physical sensations) during your musical practice when others are physically present? Please provide examples based on your personal experience.
6. How do you feel (in terms of emotions or physical sensations) during your musical performance when others are physically present? Please provide examples based on your personal experience.
7. How do you feel (in terms of emotions or physical sensations) during your musical practice when others are present in your imagination or thoughts? Please provide examples based on your personal experience.
8. How do you feel (in terms of emotions or physical sensations) during your musical performance when others are present in

your imagination or thoughts? Please provide examples based on your personal experience.

9. Do others (whether they are physically present or not) have an impact on your musical interpretation? Please explain.

10. Do others (whether they are physically present or not) have an impact on your confidence as a musician? Please explain.

11. Would you like to add anything else about your thoughts about others or the relevance of the presence of others for your musical performance and practice?

* Others may include teachers, ensemble members, other students, friends, audience, family members, etc.

9. 4E Music Cognition in Theory and Practice

Andrea Schiavio and Dylan van der Schyff

Introduction

The last few decades have witnessed a shift in focus in research on musical experience and cognition. Existing frameworks that emphasise on information-processing, as well as approaches interested in the neural or behavioural correlates of musical experience, have been complemented by a novel perspective that offers a broader synthesis of psychological, physiological, neural, and ecological levels. This orientation, known as 'embodied music cognition' (e.g., Leman, 2007), has provided fascinating insights into current discourses in music research. According to this view, the cognitive processes underlying musical activities such as perceiving a melody, imagining a tonal cadence, learning to play a guitar solo, composing a song, or performing with a band, are thought to emerge from a variety of bodily-based (e.g., motor, visceral, affective) factors, suggesting that musical minds are grounded in low-level processes much more than previously assumed. For instance, research has shown that musical perception is shaped by instrument-specific motor expertise (Overy & Molnar-Szakacs, 2009); that making music together often relies on non-verbal forms of communication and reciprocal bodily adaptations (Badino et al., 2014); and that our capacity to remember musical stimuli is facilitated by previous sensorimotor familiarisation with the musical material (Schiavio & Timmers, 2016). In brief, this orientation explores the processes and mechanisms that underlie our ability to participate in musical activities—whether by actively making music or listening—from a wide-ranging, body-based perspective that decentres the more traditional focus on the information-processing of individual cognisers. Recently, this broadening view has extended beyond the body to include the social and material environment in which bodies are situated. To account for the complex patterns of reciprocal causation unfolding between brains, bodies, and environments, musical minds are now conceived of as Embodied, as well as Embedded, Extended, and Enactive (or 4E).

Aims

While the 4E framework offers a promising addition to music research, it was first developed in other scholarly domains. As such, its implications for our understanding of music and its experience are still not yet fully developed. The aim of this chapter is thus to introduce this orientation to readers who may not be familiar with it and who are interested in music. In particular, we offer a series of musical examples that speak to each 'E' distinctly, spanning musical domains such as perception, (remote) learning, performance, and development. Our intention here is to suggest that the 4E framework can provide a clearer view (when compared to more traditional frameworks) on how bodily interaction with an environment shapes musical experience and learning, and how this perspective reveals a continuum between musical activity and human flourishing more generally. We first illustrate the main principles of the 4E approach by tracing its origins in the fields of philosophy, psychology, and cognitive science. We then turn to explore what each E entails for musical cognition. We should note that our analysis is meant to offer only a preliminary overview of the rich variety of conceptual resources and possible applications stemming from a 4E approach to musicality; it is not intended to provide a complete account of the whole framework as it applies to other domains.

Main discussion

The 4E framework

One of the main assumptions of the multi-disciplinary school of thought developed under the umbrella term of 4E cognition is that mental life is best understood as a dynamic unity between bodily (neural, motor, emotional) and environmental (social, physical, cultural) factors (see Newen et al., 2018). We say 'dynamic unity' because the emerging organism-world network is instantiated by a recurrent interplay of factors inherent to three main components—brain, body, and environment—giving rise to multiple states and configurations (e.g., thoughts, behaviours, etc.). Accordingly, we may understand the 4E orientation as an exploration of the various relationships formed between organisms and the world. Fuchs (2020) addresses this reciprocity in terms of what he labels the 'circular structure of embodiment'. This involves sets of downward and upward processes between (1) brain and body as well as (2) brain-body systems and the world. To address the first point, we may consider empirical research showing that bodily states can alter one's perceptual experience: when feeling tired or carrying a heavy weight, for example, hills are seen as steeper, and distances are experienced as greater (Bhalla & Proffitt, 1999). Perceptual experiences are here understood to depend on what Johnson (2007) labels 'visceral connection with the world' (p. 12), which originates in our bodily sensations. Other examples come from the domain of linguistics, where a wealth of empirical studies suggest that different abstract concepts are mapped into bodily-based knowledge (see Casasanto, 2009; Gibbs, 2006). As reported by Hostetter and Alibali (2008), for instance, recent experimental work has shown that the understanding of metaphorical sentences such as 'grasping a concept' is primed by experiencing a related action (e.g., grasping something) before reading the sentence (Wilson & Gibbs, 2007). In the next section, we will centre our discussion on the corporeal roots of musical perception, suggesting that bodily knowledge plays a primary role in driving musical experience and that it shapes how we acquire musical competencies in learning settings.

The second point raised by Fuchs (2020)—the reciprocal interplay of organisms and the world—is best understood when considering how bodily feelings, motor activity, and sensorimotor experiences play out in ecological settings that go beyond the individual subject. The rich variety of bodily aspects that permeates our mental life, in other words, is always contextual and open to the diverse contingencies that make up the world we inhabit. As such, we can widen the dynamics of *embodied* cognition to include environmental factors. This means that cognition can also be conceived of as *embedded*. Our bodies are immersed in environmental dynamics, beginning at the earliest stages of life. And these dynamics involve histories of interaction with people, things, places, and events that shape our possibilities for thought and action as well as our socio-cultural presence (see Chemero, 2009). The co-dependencies between living systems and the environment have been studied both ontogenetically and phylogenetically (see Malafouris, 2013; Oyama, 2000), leading to richer understandings of how brain-body systems function when coupled with a given ecological niche. We discuss this embedded dimension from a musical perspective in the next section, where we offer some examples from pedagogical settings.

The claim that cognition is *extended* aims to increase our comprehension of what the organism-world nexus described above entails (see Clark, 2008). Consider how living systems often manipulate objects and exploit the structures of the world when a task is particularly demanding. Musical notation, for instance, helps people remember, teach, perform, and reproduce music more easily. To account for such internal-external integration, extended approaches often rely on a principle of functional similarity. This involves the idea that external structures may play a functional role akin to those structures that are internal to the cogniser (Clark & Chalmers, 1998). A classic example used to illustrate this is when someone uses a tool—say, a notepad—to remember something. In this case, it can be argued that the role of the tool is functionally similar to the person's biological memory. Accordingly, memory need not be limited to the biology of the agent; cognition can thus extend into the environment where it shapes and is shaped by socio-material interactions. When applied to musical contexts, this extended dimension can be approached from different angles. In the next section, we will specifically focus on music performance, exploring how instruments and other external (e.g., social) factors may contribute to drive music-making.

The idea that cognition is *enactive* connects with insights from the previous embodied-embedded-extended claims to describe the set of interactions between agent-environment that contribute to bringing forth a world of meaning (Varela et al., 1991). The basic idea here is that to survive and flourish, living beings must develop viable patterns of interactivity with their world, regulated by their needs and physiology as they adjust to ecological contingencies (Di Paolo et al., 2017). These interactions allow for the emergence of a world of salience, where things and other agents become meaningful in relation to the organism's concerned point of view on the world (its self). Importantly, this approach highlights a deep continuity between biological and mental processes, as well as the active role living systems play in shaping the worlds they live through (Thompson, 2007). Shortly, we consider musical development from this enactive perspective, suggesting that the acquisition of musical competencies reflects the sense-making dynamics associated with human flourishing more generally.

4E music cognition

To summarise our discussion above, the 4E view holds that the mind is *embodied*, as cognition is grounded in sensorimotor experience; *embedded*, as our being-in-the-world is immersed within wider ecological dynamics; *extended*, as tools and other features of the environment may be functionally integrated with cognition; and *enactive*, as mind and life compose a unity based on a variety of adaptive sensorimotor couplings whereby a world of salience and meaning is brought forth.

Before we move on, we should note that each of the Es connects with thought and research in different domains of cognitive science, which converge and diverge in various ways. For example, conceptions of what embodied cognition entails differ with regard to the role that should be ascribed to the active body in cognition. Some consider the body as an important mediating domain between inner and outer realities, as it provides the basis for instantiation of the corporeally-based representations in the brain that are fundamental to cognition (Shapiro, 2010). Others see the body as a cognitive domain in its own right, arguing that the role of mental representation has been overemphasised (Chemero, 2009). Additionally, there is ongoing discussion over the degree to which cognition can be properly understood as *extended*. Some theorists argue that while the body plays a central role in cognition (e.g., in the generation of corporeal and action-based representations), cognition should not be understood as extending beyond the body and brain (Adams & Aizawa, 2009). By contrast, other authors have made compelling arguments that some cognitive tasks are impossible to realise without the incorporation of environmental factors. For example, Louise Barrett (2011) explains how creatures with relatively simple neural structures (e.g., insects and spiders) are able to perform surprisingly complex cognitive acts (such as building webs, hunting, and finding mates) by including environmental features as integrated aspects of their cognitive domain.

Although aspects of the 4E approach are under debate, this orientation is nevertheless gaining traction across various domains as a useful framework for research and theory—it offers an important interdisciplinary meeting point for scholars interested in studying mental life from a distributed, relational perspective (Newen et al., 2018). Most importantly, a 4E perspective shifts the focus from individual agents and neural processes to brain-body systems and their histories of co-specification with the world. This approach has inspired a number of new perspectives on music-related areas of cognition such as emotion, empathy, and creativity. Whereas these aspects of mental life have often been studied in terms of responses, predispositions, and processes that play out within the domain of individual agents, 4E approaches have shown that these domains can be understood in terms of histories of dynamic interactivity between agents and the socio-material environments they inhabit and shape (Krueger & Szanto, 2016; Schiavio et al., 2017a; van der Schyff & Krueger, 2019). In what follows, we explore how these interactive dynamics play out in musical contexts, with an emphasis on perception, learning, performance, and development. It should be noted that while we treat each E separately, each subsection should not be considered independent from the others. In fact, because there are necessary overlaps between all 4Es, insights associated with one can also be relevant for others.

Embodied music cognition: From music perception to learning

Music listening is an activity that plays a crucial part in a musician's life and often permeates the lives of non-musicians as well. While 'the perception of pitch and consonance are among the oldest topics in Western science' (Large, 2017, p. 5), giving rise to multiple perspectives and theories, recent literature has shown a special interest in models based on prediction (see, e.g., Huron, 2006; Koelsch et al., 2018). One of the central ideas here is that predictions about the musical stimulus are internally generated by a listener via learned statistical regularities, so that the sensory input can be judged in terms of its violation or confirmation of such predictions. Accordingly, internal representations are supposed to govern perceptual activity through a variety of deliberate or spontaneous associations developed through exposure (see also Pearce, 2018).

An embodied approach to music perception can complement similar models by highlighting the role of body and action in shaping perceptual experience. This move has two main consequences. The first concerns what is emphasised in explaining music perception, while the second involves how the actual process plays out. The former point is best understood when considering that perceptual ability is shaped not only by (e.g., passive) exposure to musical culture, but also by the active engagements one has experienced in music-making activities. Indeed, a range of empirical studies has shown that expert musicians display strong activation of the motor cortex during listening tasks, reflecting their ability to associate specific actions with the music being listened to (see D'Ausilio et al., 2006; Haueisen & Knösche, 2001). The development of these neural connections through practice and learning, it has been suggested, plays a critical part in how music perception works, which leads to the second point listed above. This involves the idea that the motor schemata one has learned through musical practice are re-enacted during listening, leading to an enhanced perceptual experience, as if one were actually playing the music itself (Cox, 2016; Overy & Molnar-Szakacs, 2009).

This active process has been described as embodied simulation (see Gallese, 2005). The theory holds that learned repertoires of action not only drive our behaviour, but also shape our perception of actions (and sounds) performed by others. As Gallese and Sinigaglia note (2011), many studies have shown that performing a particular action activates the same parieto-premotor areas recruited when observing that very same action executed by someone else. This mechanism is based on the firing of a neural population known as mirror neurons, and has important implications for our understanding of musical perception. For example, it has been argued that simulation-like processes influence our capacity to predict the beat of a perceived musical stimulus through interactions between auditory and motor-planning regions of the brain (Patel & Iversen, 2014). According to this view, bodily factors are seen to constrain our predictive ability. Another fascinating contribution in this area involves the study of music-colour synaesthesia[1] from a sensorimotor account proposed by Caroline Curwen (2018; 2020), who argues that such a phenomenon might be best understood as fundamentally continuous with our real-life engagements with the world. Her research posits a profound unity between imaginative and perceptual processes, where both are seen as rooted in bodily experience. More generally, the idea that action underlies our perceptual and imaginative ability echoes earlier insights developed by the French philosopher Maurice Merleau-Ponty (1945/1962). While his work focused mostly on visual perception, many of his observations are also applicable to music. Merleau-Ponty notes that to acquire a way of perceiving involves a new use of one's own body, enriching and recasting the body image. Accordingly, the living body is not an object among others—it is a 'grouping of lived through meanings which moves towards its equilibrium' (p. 153, emphasis added, quoted in Crossley, 2015). This insight has important consequences for activities such as musical learning, where students often perceive and imitate the actions of other people in their environment. As Merleau-Ponty suggests, this requires a style of perceiving that makes use of the bodily power of action, rather than an acquisition of external knowledge through exposure. Of particular interest here is recent work that emphasises the role of the teacher's body in helping students acquire their musical skills (Simones et al., 2015; 2017). Such contributions examine how gestures, interaction, and other modes of

---

1   Generally speaking, this can be defined as a type of synaesthesia where the perception of certain sounds immediately evokes an experience of colour (see Ward et al., 2006).

virtual online communication can facilitate the learning process, and how specific musical behaviours are optimised through participation, improvisation, active experience, and dialogue (see, e.g., Borgo, 2005; 2007). This is further examined in recent research from Bremmer and Nijs (2020), who provide an illuminating perspective on how music teachers use their bodily resources to actively construct a meaningful learning environment. Here, actions, adaptations, and collaborations are seen as integral parts of the pedagogical space—they encourage creative interaction whereby learners can develop the patterns of action-as-perception involved in musical expression and communication (see also Laroche & Kaddouch, 2015).

These examples begin to illustrate how the embodied approach to cognition has important implications for music research, highlighting the body as a fundamental source of significance and meaning-making. In what follows, we expand on these insights to explore how the processes described here may include a broader social milieu.

Embedded music cognition: The case of remote musical learning

In this section, we outline some possibilities concerning how the embedded dimension of cognition can help us think about the dynamics of interactive learning environments, with a focus on remote learning contexts. Indeed, while the embedded dimension might be most obvious in face-to-face contexts—where performers or students and teachers interact in the same physical space—recent technological developments have made it possible for musicians to work together online in real time. And with the advent of the COVID-19 pandemic, virtual learning environments have become especially important. With this in mind, we will first look at these kinds of environments through the embedded lens before moving on to consider extended and enactive aspects in turn.

The idea of 'remote learning' is often closely connected with technology-based pedagogical settings. However, as indicated by Dabbagh (2007), this phenomenon taps into a long tradition that stretches back to pre-internet and pre-digital distance education formats based on correspondence and home study (see Hanson et al., 1997). But whereas older forms of distance learning were teacher-centred and focused on a relatively fixed curriculum and delivery, recent models involve more joint musicking activities, as well as a range of technology-enhanced possibilities intended to stimulate collaborative learning (Ehrmann & Collins, 2001). Ideally, these kinds of approaches may produce a community of interacting individuals, which may be conceived of as:

> a dynamic whole that emerges when a group of people share common practices, are interdependent, make decisions jointly, identify with something larger than the sum of their individual relationships, and make long-term commitment to well-being (their own, one another's, and the group's). (Shaffer & Anundsen, 1993, p. 26)

Remarkably, this collaborative aspect presents important similarities with the kinds of relationships built in face-to-face settings, suggesting that remote interaction may not be less meaningful than in person forms. Recently, Schiavio et al. (2020) explored the range of perspectives and thoughts that music teachers working in different settings shared with regard to learning and ensemble skills. They found that one of the most common factors discussed in enhancing such skills was the ability to listen and respond to others, highlighting the collaborative dimension of learning and making music. In addition, it emerged that 'comparing yourself to the class' was deemed a fundamental factor among other learning abilities, suggesting that open dialogue and reciprocal feedback can play a key role in nurturing talent and learning. This aligns with research by Wu et al. (2014), who have shown that students who learn in web-based environments can achieve more satisfying results when compared to learners with fewer opportunities for interactive study.

The types of community-building that develop in physical spaces can also emerge in settings where collaboration is virtual, providing important benefits for students who are geographically distant from each other. Here, learners can offer support, share thoughts, beliefs, and ideas through virtual educational platforms, as well as complement existing pedagogical methods more or less informally. This is a distinctive attribute of the virtual environment in which participants are immersed. As individuals engage and interact with one another, they can actively shape the digital landscape, thereby forging novel synergies that may surpass what is possible in traditional settings. Although the end results may resemble those attainable in face-to-face interactions, the modes of engagement within this specific digital realm are uniquely crafted, enabling types of interactions that are inherently digital, such as simultaneous contributions from geographically dispersed participants, one-to-many discussions, and dynamic multimedia integration.

Of course, these possibilities proved exceptionally valuable during the recent COVID-19 pandemic, facilitating the transition of music lessons into virtual settings given the necessary restrictions imposed in numerous countries. But while technologically mediated learning afforded many opportunities during this period, the necessity of online teaching during the pandemic also revealed the difficulties that can arise when students' social 'embeddedness' in a pedagogical environment is (almost) entirely virtual. This issue sparked a wealth of scholarly exploration dedicated to analysing the challenging pedagogical dynamics inherent in online music learning contexts (e.g., Adam & Metljak 2022; Biasutti et al., 2022, 2023; Novković Cvetković, 2023). To take one example, a study of online instrumental teaching at the Faculty of Music at University of Arts in Belgrade during the pandemic (Mutavdžin et al., 2021) revealed that, to be successful, online music environments need to foster students' ability to engage in self-regulated learning. However, to achieve this, students need to feel supported in virtual learning contexts – it is necessary that they are embedded within an interactional social environment that supports and guides their emotional, technical, and creative development; that demonstrates care for their progress and well-being; and where they can develop meaningful relationships with their peers and teachers, and with the technologies they use. Self-regulated learning, in other words, is not isolated learning; it is motivated, given meaning and context, and flourishes only when it is situated within a broader ecology of learning. Due to the inherent 'remoteness' of virtual environments, attaining a such interaction and support requires additional levels of care and guidance. This means that the development and maintenance of an online learning environment 'requires a conscious commitment to it and careful planning of the teaching/learning process' (p. 292)—where are ongoing attention is given to the perspectives of the teacher and the students, and the broader socio-cultural and technological context in which they are embedded.

As noted by Crow (2006), many performers, teachers, and learners often find it helpful to work with computers to support specific musical needs. This ranges from platforms that assist the trained musician in writing complex scores to more intuitive loop-based sequencers and accompaniment generators. Because such tools also allow users to interact remotely, they are particularly useful for educational purposes: students can form communities of practice through these resources (Makrakis, 2014), assisting each other in various ways—through brainstorming, peer feedback, and so on. Consider, for example, how constructive dialogues in online forums, or similar platforms, have proved useful to enhance both basic and advanced psychological skills such as the investigation of new ideas as well as high-order decision-making (Biasutti, 2011).

From an embedded perspective, it is important to note that the kinds of learning environments described here are not fixed but rather evolve in a symbiotic relationship with the individuals that populate them. Indeed, there is a bidirectional dependency between the users and the shared worlds of practice they create. This intersubjective network involves adaptations that require the development of problem-solving skills and empathy, and encourages the fluid integration of individual and collective aspects that stand at the basis of an inclusive learning environment. As such, it can foster cultural and social understandings that drive various musical dynamics. For instance, sharing a particular musical issue in an online forum (say, how to arrange a piece for lute for a modern orchestra) may stimulate others to explore their creative potential and find novel outcomes. In this case, the learning space can be transformed by innovative musical solutions reflecting different cultural and musical needs, expertise, and taste. Creative possibilities can be negotiated and developed contextually, giving rise to a circle of reciprocal influences where individual and social dimensions inform one another. In the next section, we explore this aspect in more detail by focusing on the kind of relationships musicians often develop with their instrument and ecological surroundings.

Extended music cognition: Mutual incorporation and music performance

In most cases, performing music alone or with other individuals involves the use of analogue or digital musical instruments. It has been argued that musicians form important relationships with these instruments in the contexts of improvisation or score-reproduction. Nijs et al. (2013; see also Nijs, 2017), for example, address this point in terms of incorporation and transparency: instruments may be transparent to the musicians because they become part of one's cognitive ecology. Consider, for example, how the flow and structure of musical passages during improvisation are developed in the process of performing, and are built upon through the act of playing. To do this, the musician relies on the possibilities of the body in close interaction with the instrument, which have been refined over practice. Because the instrument is a central aspect of the creative process, it can be argued that it plays a crucial role in improvisatory activity (see Ryan & Schiavio, 2019; van der Schyff, 2019). The instrument, in other words, becomes part of the performer's 'extended' cognitive system as it serves the specific function to generate (and not simply reproduce) musical expressions.

The physical relationships musicians establish with their instruments are not the only types of connection that emerge here. Musicians regularly build emotional relationships with the unique sonic and physical characteristics of a specific violin, cymbal, guitar, and so on. Instruments also have histories, which include their use in particular repertoires, the development of the physical materials and design properties required to produce the sounds they do,[2] as well as various communities of musicians who have exploited different aspects of their sonic potential in shared musical events. This connects the extended dimension with a broader embedded socio-cultural environment. Examining these extended-embedded relationships can also frame how we think about other material and cultural relationships, for example where artefacts are used to store musical information and guide practice. For instance, the practice of re-producing a musical score, as is common

---

2   Consider, for instance, the addition of octaves in modern pianos, or a (lower) seventh string in some electric guitars. Another example could be the 'preparation' of instruments where additional objects are placed on the strings or body of the instrument to alter its tonal characteristics (e.g., John Cage's music for prepared piano; this practice is also common in contexts of free improvisation).

in Western contexts, often involves developing a relationship with the composer and the style and historical period they are associated with, as well as recordings of previous performances, to inform an individual's interpretation. These social, historical, and aesthetic aspects of the performer-instrument relationality can be further modulated on the basis of particular contextual contingencies, where, for example, instruments might require a modification to better accommodate the expressive needs of a given style, or where a score or musical practice is reinterpreted.

Musical activity involves a continuous negotiation between bodily, external (tools, instruments), and embedded (socio-cultural) dimensions, where instruments, other people, as well as cultural and historical factors, participate in guiding one's musical activity in various ways. The example of remote learning discussed above offers an interesting example of how these Es intersect. The technology serves to facilitate perceptual and communicative faculties, while also allowing the participants to meet in a virtual space where local agent-environment systems extend into and influence each other. While the Es do overlap with each other, they can provide different perspectives and insights on the same phenomena. To take another example, musical notation can be seen, from an extended perspective, as a tool that facilitates performance in real-time situations, serving a function similar to that of musical memory. Viewed from the embedded perspective, however, music notation is also a cultural product that necessarily involves norms and narratives framed relative to certain historical periods.

Enactive music cognition: The flourishing of human musicality

These embodied, embedded, and extended aspects involve the active creation of meanings that span and shape personal, social, and cultural worlds. This is highlighted by the enactive dimension of the 4Es, which explores how living systems bring forth (or 'enact') domains of meaning—most fundamentally, through the development of (survival-relevant) repertoires of perception-as-action. This activity is driven by a natural tendency for living systems to actively explore the world and its contingencies. The development of human musicality, we suggest, follows a similar trajectory when (since early infancy) it involves an impulse to regulate and optimise a behavioural attunement with the environment through sonic discovery (Malloch & Trevarthen, 2018). As infants manipulate things (e.g., objects, toys) in their peripersonal space to gain familiarity with their properties, they also improve their own motor and perceptual capacities—including those linked with the association of sounds and movements. In other words, they start to develop a repertoire of basic music-related actions that drive and motivate their further musical discoveries, allowing them to play with things and produce sounds that can be further reorganised in various ways (Schiavio et al., 2017b).

These early musical behaviours are transformed and optimised through a series of perception-action loops, leading towards specific goals and outcomes. For instance, the squeezing of a toy may produce a unique sound that infants could associate with a behavioural configuration (e.g., the 'squeezing' grip) and its experiential results (e.g., a feeling of surprise). In this process, various pragmatic understandings of the environment and their own motor possibilities are acquired, which may serve further musical and non-musical actions. The latter, for example, include possibilities to improve perceptual capacities related to the control and prediction of various behaviours, thereby minimising sensations of surprise or fear when a sound is produced contextually (e.g., when a toy falls from a table and hits the floor). But when adopted to achieve musical goals, these actions may lead to more complex and satisfying ways of playing in which sonic outcomes are produced with increased precision.

This vignette captures one key tenet of the enactive approach, namely the understanding of cognitive life as situated action: organisms generate rolling patterns of interactivity with their niches, which in turn constitute a 'sensorimotor self' (Di Paolo et al., 2017). Importantly, the relationships with the world infants establish through these sonic discoveries do not arguably adhere to a predetermined agenda, but rather emerge within a synergistic nexus of ecological and biological factors. Musical minds and musical life are continuous with each other, as both musical and personal growth are understood to include embodied, embedded, and extended aspects.

From an embodied perspective, it could be suggested that the range of musical activities described here originate in an active attunement with the environment, where the body plays a major role in discovering novel behaviours and experiences. The body drives discovery because it is at the same time a means (manipulating objects is necessary for exploratory activity) and an end (the infant's repertoire of action is shaped by its adaptive behaviours). As such, this natural inclination to explore the environment can also be seen, from an embedded perspective, as an early manifestation of the transforming dialogue between organisms and the world. When objects and things are manipulated, they may reveal novel characteristics that could invite new engagements and trigger further motivated actions. By rotating a toy, infants may be fascinated by its hidden side, thereby acting to explore its various (e.g., sonic) properties. When adequate expertise is gained, and infants can use objects to produce and play with sounds—for example, by hitting a toy car on the floor—there is a strong sense in which the object becomes 'transparent', resulting in the incorporated extended dynamics that prefigure those discussed above with regard to musical instruments. The object, in line with such a perspective, becomes part of the infant's cognitive system, serving a musical function that facilitates the task of producing sounds in a specific way. In this threefold characterisation, musical development might be understood as an enactive phenomenon rooted in exploratory meaning-making: infants establish sensorimotor relationships with their milieu, giving rise to basic behavioural configurations constituting an early repertoire of musical actions.

Conclusion

An understanding of the musical mind as embodied, embedded, extended, and enactive provides new angles to look at the concrete dynamics in which musicking takes place. It eschews the dichotomies between mind and body and between body and world, placing renewed emphasis on the continuity between biological and cognitive processes at the heart of human musicality (see also Honing, 2018). In this chapter, we have examined different musical contexts to articulate parallels between the general 4E framework and its musically relevant contexts. We have highlighted how the whole brain-body system affects music perception, showing how it can help us re-examine its role in pedagogical contexts. Drawing on recent literature in the field, we have then considered cases of remote pedagogies. Here, agents compensate for the lack of close bodily connection (as in individual teaching) by actively participating in each other's learning. They co-create, modify, and optimise their environment, giving rise to circular dynamics where individuality and collectivity are synergistically transformed. This organism-world coupling has been further discussed when observing how musicians develop unique connections with their instruments to facilitate their musicking in various ways. As we saw lastly, exploring musical development from an enactive perspective brings together the embodied, embedded, and extended dimensions by conceiving skill acquisition as a sense-making process rooted in action and exploration. In all, 4E accounts of music cognition can help us approach different musical contexts from a perspective that conceives the (musical) mind as a relational phenomenon, based on an adaptive coupling between organisms and the world. Future work may build on this intuition to study how more exploratory activities in pedagogical settings can be implemented, examining the behavioural, emotional, and neural trajectories at the basis of various musically relevant brain-body-world synergies; how these synergies involve things and other people; how cultural norms may affect one's exploratory impulse; and how bodily factors drive musical creativity and discovery.

References

Adam, T. B., & Metljak, M. (2022). Experiences in distance education and practical use of ICT during the COVID-19 epidemic of Slovenian primary school music teachers with different professional experiences. *Social Sciences & Humanities Open, 5*(1), 100246. https://doi.org/10.1016/j.ssaho.2021.100246

Adams, F., & Aizawa, K. (2009). Why the mind is still in the head. In P. Robbins & M. Aydede (eds), *The Cambridge handbook of situated cognition* (pp. 78–95). Cambridge University Press. https://doi.org/10.1017/CBO9780511816826

Badino, L., D'Ausilio, A., Glowinski, D., Camurri, A., & Fadiga, L. (2014). Sensorimotor communication in professional quartets. *Neuropsychologia, 55*, 98–104. https://doi.org/10.1016/j.neuropsychologia.2013.11.012

Barrett, L. (2011). *Beyond the brain: How body and environment shape animal and human minds*. Princeton University Press. https://doi.org/10.2307/j.ctt7rvqf

Bhalla, M., & Proffitt, D.R. (1999). Visual-motor recalibration in geographical slant perception. *Journal of Experimental Psychology: Human Perception and Performance, 25*(4), 1076–1096. https://doi.org/10.1037/0096-1523.25.4.1076

Biasutti, M. (2011). The student experience of a collaborative e-learning university module. *Computers & Education, 57*(3), 1865–1875. https://doi.org/10.1016/j.compedu.2011.04.006

Biasutti, M., Antonini Philippe, R., & Schiavio, A. (2022). Assessing teachers' perspectives on giving music lessons remotely during the COVID-19 lockdown period. *Musicae Scientiae, 26*(3), 585–603. https://doi.org/10.1177/1029864921996033

Biasutti, M., Antonini Philippe, R., & Schiavio, A. (2023). E-learning during the COVID-19 lockdown. An interview study with primary school music teachers in Italy. *International Journal of Music Education, 41*(2), 256–270. https://doi.org/10.1177/02557614221107190

Borgo, D. (2005). *Sync or swarm: Improvising music in a complex age.* Continuum.

Borgo, D. (2007). Free jazz in the classroom: An ecological approach to music education. *Jazz Perspectives, 1*(1), 61–88. https://doi.org/10.1080/17494060601061030

Bremmer, M., & Nijs, L. (2020). The role of the body in instrumental and vocal music pedagogy: A dynamical systems theory perspective on the music teacher's bodily engagement in teaching and learning. *Frontiers in Education, 5*, Article 79. https://doi.org/10.3389/feduc.2020.00079

Casasanto, D. (2009). Embodiment of abstract concepts: Good and bad in right- and left-handers. *Journal of Experimental Psychology: General, 138*(3), 351–367. https://doi.org/10.1037/a0015854

Chemero, A. (2009). *Radical embodied cognitive science.* MIT Press. https://doi.org/10.7551/mitpress/8367.001.0001

Clark, A. (2008). *Supersizing the mind: Embodiment, action and cognitive extension.* Oxford University Press. https://doi.org/10.1093/acprof:oso/9780195333213.001.0001

Clark, A., & Chalmers, D. (1998). The extended mind. *Analysis, 58*(1), 7–19. https://doi.org/10.1093/analys/58.1.7

Cox, A. (2016). *Music and embodied cognition: Listening, moving, feeling, and thinking.* Indiana University Press. https://doi.org/10.2307/j.ctt200610s

Crossley, N. (2015). Music worlds and body techniques: On the embodiment of musicking. *Cultural Sociology, 9*(4), 471–492. https://doi.org/10.1177/1749975515576585

Crow, B. (2006). Musical creativity and the new technology. *Music Education Research, 8*(1), 121–130. https://doi.org/10.1080/14613800600581659

Curwen, C. (2018). Music-colour synaesthesia: Concept, context and qualia. *Consciousness and Cognition, 61*, 94–106. https://doi.org/10.1016/j.concog.2018.04.005

Curwen, C. (2020). Music-colour synaesthesia: A sensorimotor account. *Musicae Scientiae*. Advance online publication. https://doi.org/10.1177/1029864920956295

Dabbagh, N. (2007). The online learner: Characteristics and pedagogical implications. *Contemporary Issues in Technology and Teacher Education, 7*(3), 217–226. https://citejournal.org/wp-content/uploads/2014/05/v7i3general1.pdf

D'Ausilio, A., Altenmüller, E., Olivetti Belardinelli, M., & Lotze, M. (2006). Cross-modal plasticity of the motor cortex while listening to a rehearsed musical piece. *European Journal of Neuroscience, 24*(3), 955–958. https://doi.org/10.1111/j.1460-9568.2006.04960.x

Di Paolo, E., Buhrmann, T., & Barandiaran, X. (2017). *Sensorimotor life: An enactive proposal*. Oxford University Press. https://doi.org/10.1093/acprof:oso/9780198786849.001.0001

Ehrmann, S.C., & Collins, M. (2001). Emerging models of online collaborative learning: Can distance enhance quality? *Educational Technology, 41*(5), 34–38. https://www.researchgate.net/publication/234716789_Emerging_Models_of_Online_Collaborative_Learning_Can_Distance_Enhance_Quality

Fuchs, T. (2020). The circularity of the embodied mind. *Frontiers in Psychology, 11*, Article 1707. https://doi.org/10.3389/fpsyg.2020.01707

Gallese, V. (2005). Embodied simulation: From neurons to phenomenal experience. *Phenomenology and the Cognitive Sciences, 4*, 23–48. https://doi.org/10.1007/s11097-005-4737-z

Gallese, V., & Sinigaglia, C. (2011). How the body in action shapes the self. *Journal of Consciousness Studies, 18*(7–8), 117–143.

Gibbs, R.W., Jr. (2006). Metaphor interpretation as embodied simulation. *Mind and Language, 21*(3), 434–458. https://doi.org/10.1111/j.1468-0017.2006.00285.x

Hanson, D., Maushak, N.J., Schlosser, C.A., Anderson, M.L., Sorensen, C., & Simonson, M. (1997). *Distance education: Review of the literature* (2nd ed.). Association for Educational Communications and Technology.

Haueisen, J., & Knösche, T.R. (2001). Involuntary motor activity in pianists evoked by music perception. *Journal of Cognitive Neuroscience, 13*(6), 786–792. https://doi.org/10.1162/08989290152541449

Honing, H. (2018). On the biological basis of musicality. *Annals of the New York Academy of Sciences, 1423*(1), 51–56. https://doi.org/10.1111/nyas.13638

Hostetter, A.B., & Alibali, M.W. (2008). Visible embodiment: Gestures as simulated action. *Psychonomic Bulletin & Review, 15*(3), 495–514. https://doi.org/10.3758/PBR.15.3.495

Huron, D. (2006). *Sweet anticipation: Music and the psychology of expectation*. MIT Press. https://doi.org/10.7551/mitpress/6575.001.0001

Johnson, M. (2007). *The meaning of the body: Aesthetics of human understanding*. University of Chicago Press. https://doi.org/10.7208/chicago/9780226026992.001.0001

Koelsch, S., Vuust, P., & Friston, K. (2018). Predictive processes and the peculiar case of music. *Trends in Cognitive Sciences, 23*(1), 63–77. https://doi.org/10.1016/j.tics.2018.10.006

Krueger, J., & Szanto, T. (2016). Extended emotions. *Philosophy Compass, 11*(12), 863–878. https://doi.org/10.1111/phc3.12390

Large, E.W. (2017). Music from the air to the brain and body. In R. Ashley & R. Timmers (eds), *The Routledge companion of music cognition* (pp. 3–11). Routledge. https://doi.org/10.4324/9781315194738

Laroche, J., & Kaddouch, I. (2015). Spontaneous preferences and core tastes: Embodied musical personality and dynamics of interaction in a pedagogical method of improvisation. *Frontiers in Psychology, 6*, Article 522. https://doi.org/10.3389/fpsyg.2015.00522

Leman, M. (2007). *Embodied music cognition and mediation technology*. MIT Press. https://doi.org/10.7551/mitpress/7476.001.0001

Makrakis, V. (2014). Transforming university curricula towards sustainability: A Euro-Mediterranean initiative. In K.D. Tomas & H.E. Muga (eds), *Handbook of research on pedagogical innovations for sustainable development* (pp. 619–640). IGI Global. https://doi.org/10.4018/978-1-4666-5856-1

Malafouris, L. (2013). *How things shape the mind: A theory of material engagement*. MIT Press. https://doi.org/10.7551/mitpress/9476.001.0001

Malloch, S., & Trevarthen, C. (2018). The human nature of music. *Frontiers in Psychology, 9*, Article 1680. https://doi.org/10.3389/fpsyg.2018.01680

Merleau-Ponty, M. (1962). *The phenomenology of perception* (C. Smith, Trans.; 1st ed.). Routledge. (Original work published 1945) https://doi.org/10.4324/9780203981139

Mutavdžin, D., Stančić, M., & Bogunović, B. (2021). To be connected: Supporting self-regulated learning in higher music education before and during the pandemic. *Psihološka Istraživanja, 24*(2), 277–301. https://reff.f.bg.ac.rs/handle/123456789/3431

Newen, A., De Bruin, L., & Gallagher, S. (2018). *The Oxford handbook of 4E cognition*. Oxford University Press. https://doi.org/10.1093/oxfordhb/9780198735410.001.0001

Nijs, L. (2017). The merging of musician and musical instrument: Incorporation, presence, and levels of embodiment. In M. Lesaffre, P.-J. Maes, & M. Leman (eds), *The Routledge companion to embodied music interaction* (pp. 49–57). Routledge. https://doi.org/10.4324/9781315621364

Nijs, L., Lesaffre, M., & Leman, M. (2013). The musical instrument as a natural extension of the musician. In M. Castellengo, H. Genevois & J.-M. Bardez (eds), *Music and its instruments* (pp. 467–484). Editions Delatour France.

Novković Cvetković, B., Mladenović, M., Spasić Stošić, A., Tasić Mitić, I., & Stojadinović, A. (2023). How pandemics like COVID-19 change education in early childhood: The music practice and tendencies in Serbia. *European Early Childhood Education Research Journal*, 1–13.

Overy, K., & Molnar-Szakacs, I. (2009). Being together in time: Musical experience and the mirror neuron system. *Music Perception, 26*(5), 489–504. https://doi.org/10.1525/mp.2009.26.5.489

Oyama, S. (2000). *The ontogeny of information: Developmental systems and evolution.* Duke University Press.

Patel, A.D., & Iversen, J.R. (2014). The evolutionary neuroscience of musical beat perception: The action simulation for auditory prediction (ASAP) hypothesis. *Frontiers in Systems Neuroscience, 8*, Article 57. https://doi.org/10.3389/fnsys.2014.00057

Pearce, M.T. (2018). Statistical learning and probabilistic prediction in music cognition: Mechanisms of stylistic enculturation. *Annals of the New York Academy of Sciences, 1423*(1), 378–395. https://doi.org/10.1111/nyas.13654

Ryan, K., & Schiavio, A. (2019). Extended musicking, extended mind, extended agency: Notes on the third wave. *New Ideas in Psychology, 55*, 8–17. https://doi.org/10.1016/j.newideapsych.2019.03.001

Schiavio, A., Küssner, M.B., & Williamon, A. (2020). Music teachers' perspectives and experiences of ensemble and learning skills. *Frontiers in Psychology, 11*, Article 291. https://doi.org/10.3389/fpsyg.2020.00291

Schiavio, A., & Timmers, R. (2016). Motor and audiovisual learning consolidate auditory memory of tonally ambiguous melodies. *Music Perception, 34*(1), 21–32. https://doi.org/10.1525/mp.2016.34.1.21

Schiavio, A., van der Schyff, D., Céspedes-Guevara, J., & Reybrouck, M. (2017a). Enacting musical emotions: Sense-making, dynamic systems, and the embodied mind. *Phenomenology and the Cognitive Sciences, 16*(5), 785–809. https://doi.org/10.1007/s11097-016-9477-8

Schiavio, A., van der Schyff, D., Kruse-Weber, S., & Timmers, R. (2017b). When the sound becomes the goal: 4E cognition and teleomusicality in early infancy. *Frontiers in Psychology, 8*, Article 1585. https://doi.org/10.3389/fpsyg.2017.01585

Shaffer, C.R., & Anundsen, K. (1993). *Creating community anywhere: Finding support and connection in a fragmented world.* Tarcher; Perigee Books.

Shapiro, L. (2010). *Embodied cognition.* Routledge. https://doi.org/10.4324/9780203850664

Simones, L., Rodger, M., & Schroeder, F. (2015). Communicating musical knowledge through gesture: Piano teachers' gestural behaviours across different levels of student proficiency. *Psychology of Music, 43*(5), 723–735. https://doi.org/10.1177/0305735614535830

Simones, L., Rodger, M., & Schroeder, F. (2017). Seeing how it sounds: Observation, imitation, and improved learning in piano playing. *Cognition and Instruction, 35*(2), 125–140. https://doi.org/10.1080/07370008.2017.1282483

Thompson, E. (2007). *Mind in life: Biology, phenomenology, and the sciences of mind.* Harvard University Press.

Van der Schyff, D. (2019). Improvisation, enaction, and self-assessment. In D.J. Elliott, M. Silverman, & G.E. McPherson (eds), *The Oxford handbook of philosophical and qualitative assessment in music education* (pp. 319–346). Oxford University Press. https://doi.org/10.1093/oxfordhb/9780190265182.001.0001

van der Schyff D., & Krueger J. (2019). Musical empathy: From simulation to 4E interaction. In A.F. Corrêa (ed.), *Music, speech, and mind* (pp. 73–108). Associação Brasileira de Cognição e Artes Musicais (ABCM). https://www.researchgate.net/publication/326998297_Musical_Empathy_From_Simulation_to_4E_Interaction

Varela, F. J., Thompson, E., & Rosch, E. (1991). *The embodied mind: Cognitive science and human experience.* MIT Press. https://doi.org/10.7551/mitpress/6730.001.0001

Ward, J., Huckstep, B., & Tsakanikos, E. (2006). Sound-colour synaesthesia: To what extent does it use cross-modal mechanisms common to us all? *Cortex, 42*(2), 264–280. https://doi.org/10.1016/S0010-9452(08)70352-6

Wilson, N.L., & Gibbs, R.W., Jr. (2007). Real and imagined body movement primes metaphor comprehension. *Cognitive Science, 31*(4), 721–731. https://doi.org/10.1080/15326900701399962

Wu, C.-H., Hwang, G.-J., & Kuo, F.-R. (2014). Collab-Analyzer: An environment for conducting web-based collaborative learning activities and analyzing students' information-searching behaviors. *Australasian Journal of Educational Technology, 30*(3), 356–374. https://doi.org/10.14742/ajet.998

10. Memorisation of Twentieth-Century Piano Music: A Longitudinal Case Study

Valnea Žauhar, Dunja Crnjanski, and Igor Bajšanski

Introduction

Multiple memory systems are involved in learning and memorising a new piece of music. Practising notated music includes a large amount of repeating passages and longer sections that appear in serial order. During practice, auditory and procedural (or motor-based) memory are inevitably spontaneously activated (Chaffin et al., 2016). The playing of each passage is influenced by the preceding and following passages, and performing music is firmly based on serial cueing (Chaffin et al., 2023). However, auditory and motor-based memory are activated implicitly, without conscious awareness. These memories are not reliable enough to allow for a performance to be entirely successful if something goes wrong (Chaffin et al., 2016).

To perform efficiently, musicians need to integrate different types of memory: implicit or spontaneous and explicit or declarative. Declarative memory is activated when memorisation is deliberate and conscious. Research has shown that expert musicians deliberately, repeatedly, and systematically pay attention to particular locations in the music. If these locations remain relevant for monitoring the memorised performance, they are called performance cues (PCs). PCs may refer to aspects of the music that musicians pay attention to during a performance, such as basic technical issues (e.g., fingering, technical difficulties), interpretation, expression, and structure. Musicians form their mental map of the piece as they start practising at different locations during the memorisation process (Chaffin et al., 2002; Ginsborg & Chaffin, 2011), and PCs become retrieval cues that they can use efficiently during a performance. The mental map provides content-addressable access to the musician's memory for the piece once it is successfully memorised. When memory is content-addressable, the musician can start to perform the piece from the particular section or passage they are thinking of (Ginsborg et al., 2012). The function of PCs in a mental map is twofold. During a performance that unfolds smoothly, PCs are a source that allow the musician to perform spontaneously, expressively, and with conviction (Lisboa et al., 2018). At the same time, they are also landmarks where the musician can restart or continue the performance following a memory lapse or mistake (Chaffin et al., 2002). Research has shown that the use of PCs during performance is flexible and that not all PCs are always used during repeated performances. Core PCs are features that are identified during practice and retained as retrieval cues in each performance, while non-core PCs are the features retained as retrieval cues only in some performances. Spontaneous thoughts about the music being performed also appear and may be retained as PCs in subsequent performances (Ginsborg & Bennett, 2021; Ginsborg et al., 2012).

Memorisation strategies used by expert musicians (e.g., deliberate encoding of novel material) are similar to those used by experts in other domains (e.g., playing chess, memorising digit strings, acting, dancing; see Chase & Ericsson, 1982; Ericsson & Kintsch, 1995; Noice & Noice, 2006). In general, expert memorisation is characterised by three principles: meaningful encoding of new material, efficient use of a retrieval structure or mental map, and prolonged practice to ensure fast retrieval from long-term memory (Ericsson & Kintsch, 1995). These principles also apply to memorising music. Research has shown that expert musicians rely strongly on the formal structure of the piece from the earliest stages of practising, identify PCs within the formal structure, and use them when preparing for memorised performance (e.g., Chaffin et al., 2002; Ginsborg et al., 2006). Consequently, the mental map of the piece often corresponds to its hierarchical organisation into sections and subsections. Like experts in other areas, musicians engage in extended encoding and retrieval practice to achieve fast retrieval from declarative as well as motor and auditory memory (Chaffin & Imreh, 2002).

Longitudinal case studies revealed that memorisation follows similar patterns irrespective of the musical style of the piece that has to be memorised and performed by heart (e.g., Chaffin, 2007; Chaffin et al., 2023; Chaffin & Imreh, 2002; Ginsborg et al., 2006, 2012). Musicians memorise works of varying complexity in similar ways (Chaffin, 2007; Chaffin et al., 2013; Noice et al., 2008; Soares, 2015). However, when the piece is free-form or has a complex non-tonal structure, musicians have to develop their understanding of the musical structure in order to segment the piece into meaningful sections. In this way musicians impose a narrative or a musical story onto the piece. The musician's understanding of the musical structure informs their practice and memorisation (Chueke & Chaffin, 2016; Fonte, 2020; Soares, 2015).

The number of studies investigating the memorisation of 20th century and contemporary repertoire has begun to increase, but there are fewer studies involving non-tonal rather than tonal repertoire (Fonte, 2020). To expand the literature on the memorisation of 20th century and contemporary music, Žauhar et al. (2020) examined the process whereby a piano student learned and memorised a short piece by the Croatian composer Boris Papandopulo (1906–1991) for international competition: his Fourth Study for Piano composed in 1956. Although it has a formal structure that follows structural conventions of the Western classical tradition, it is polytonal and uses a wide range of harmonies (Detoni, 2008). Like the advanced students who took part in the case studies reported by Miklaszewski (1989) and Nielsen (1999, 2004), for example, the piano student relied on the formal structure and her segmentation of the piece from the earliest stages of practising, and used structurally relevant bars throughout the whole process of practice, as do experienced musicians (e.g., Chaffin et al., 2002). However, she also repeated structurally relevant and technically difficult bars more than other bars in each learning stage, suggesting that repetition was the primary practice strategy.

In this study, we wanted to explore the process whereby the student and the professional pianist learned and memorised the same piece of music, so we used the same procedure as described by Žauhar et al. (2020). To date, few multiple-case longitudinal studies comparing the memorisation of the same piece by two or more musicians have been reported (e.g., Fonte, 2020; Ginsborg, 2002; Williamon & Valentine, 2002). Because we have already published the study with the piano student (Žauhar et al., 2020), we present here only the results of the study with the professional pianist. In the discussion, however, we take the opportunity to compare the learning processes of the two performers, who had different proficiency levels, and the outcomes of those processes. The comparison aimed to gain insight into the similarities and differences between their strategies for mastering and memorising the music.

Aims

The study aimed to investigate the process whereby a professional pianist learned and memorised a short piece of 20th century music and to examine the effects of its formal structure and technical complexity on the amount of practice undertaken (starts, stops, and repetitions). We anticipated that the pianist would rely on the formal structure of the piece and the segmentation she made from the earliest stages of practising, as was shown in other studies with expert musicians (e.g., Chaffin, 2007; Chaffin & Imreh, 2002). Moreover, we expected that the use of the formal structure would be more pronounced than in the practice process of the piano student mentioned earlier (Žauhar et al., 2020) who learned the same piece. Unlike the student, who worked on difficult bars in each learning period, we expected the professional pianist to work on technical difficulties only early on in the process. However, we also expected her to pay attention to certain difficult bars in the later stages of practice so that they would become retrieval cues.

Method

The pianist

Dunja Crnjanski (the second author of this chapter) holds an MA in piano performance and specialises in chamber music, focusing on contemporary repertoire. Dunja regularly performs in public as a chamber musician and accompanist. She was not acquainted with the music of Papandopulo until she began to practise the Fourth Study for Piano within the framework of this research study.

The music

Papandopulo's Fourth Study for Piano (*Allegro Vivace*) (1956), in 3/8, is part of the cycle Eight Studies for Piano. The studies are in various styles, from the baroque toccata to tango and blues, and are also influenced by folk music (Kovacic, 1996). Each study is a miniature, exploring the sound possibilities of the piano. The Fourth Study is a scherzo form that parodies the waltz, enriched by polytonality and a more comprehensive range of harmonies than is typical in most classical traditions. Its main theme is the accompaniment, from which the melody emerges only intermittently in a sequence of repetitions coloured differently each time; these features produce its parodic quality. Heavily accented, the Study has to be played at a fast, precise tempo, requiring a skilful piano technique (Detoni, 2008) and efficient retrieval if it is to be performed effectively. It has 153 bars and a duration of 1:30 minutes.

Procedure

The pianist was asked to prepare the Fourth Study for Piano for a performance from memory. She made audio recordings of 20 practice sessions, which were subsequently transcribed (see Data preparation), and she completed a practice diary after each session by describing it briefly (e.g., 'I worked on putting together the whole composition. I practised certain parts by heart. I worked on difficult passages. I focused on memorising.' [Session 5]). In order not to interfere with the pianist's spontaneous process of practising, more detailed instructions were not given. The diary was used for the purpose of collecting short notes about practice that could be used when defining the learning periods once the whole process of practising had ended. The descriptions from the diary were also useful for integrating into the interpretation of the results.

At the end of the preparation process, the pianist performed from memory in front of the first author only, due to the COVID-19 pandemic restrictions. The performance was recorded but those data are not included in the analysis. After the pianist had given the performance from memory, she divided the practice sessions into four learning periods on the basis of the diary entries. The first author listened to the recordings of the practice sessions and transcribed them; on this basis, she also identified four learning periods, consistent with those identified by the pianist, and presented them in Table 10.1. The average duration of one session was 29:54 minutes, and the whole practice process took ten hours over seven weeks.

Table 10.1 Description of learning periods and practice sessions

Learning period[a]	Practice Session	Days from the start of practice	Practice session duration (min:sec)	Practice segment[b] length (bars) Mean	Range of segments length	Practice segments n
Section-by-section and putting together	1	1	32:12	3.53	1–31	320
	2	2	32:38	4.75	1–32	257
	3	3	31:26	6.06	1–77	228
	4	9	34:41	5.99	1–50	223
	5	10	32:55	6.39	1–65	213
	6	11	30:44	7.55	1–117	191
	7	12	30:04	7.06	1–60	203
Memorisation	8	13	31:20	6.27	1–40	235
	9	14	31:48	8.63	1–61	184
	10	15	28:10	6.34	1–61	261
	11	16	32:45	8.57	1–64	221
Improving fluency and consolidating	12	17	31:04	7.54	1–107	254
	13	18	30:44	7.10	1–84	261
	14	20	22:11	10.28	1–130	141
	15	31	30:26	6.24	1–60	323
	16	35	23:15	10.27	1–153	153
Polishing	17	37	30:20	8.18	1–108	282
	18	38	16:26	10.83	1–153	106
	19	46	30:23	7.87	1–153	268
	20	51	34:23	9.64	1–153	232

[a] Learning period included practice, memorising, and practising performance to demonstrate technical fluency, interpretation, and expressivity.

[b] One practice segment represents one episode of uninterrupted playing.

After the performance from memory, the pianist was also asked to mark on the score the bars that she had relied on during memorisation, and to note the aspects of the music that she paid attention to in each of the reported bars. She was further asked to mark the bars that she found technically difficult during practice. Finally, she described the other ways in which she prepared for practice and performance, such as listening to other pianists' recordings and reading the score without playing.

The study was conducted according to the Code of Ethics of the University of Rijeka.

Materials

Twenty recorded practice sessions were transcribed using the Study Your Music Practice software tool (Music Lab, University of Connecticut, 2020). The first author listened to the audio recordings of the practice sessions and made the transcriptions by noting the start and end bars of each practice segment in each session. These are illustrated in Figure 10.1 (Session 3: an early practice session with mainly short practice segments; and Session 16: a later practice session with longer, more integrated practice segments). The transcripts, which should be read from left to right and bottom to top, show how the practice unfolded. When all the practice segments had been transcribed, the number of starts, stops,[1] and repetitions of each bar were counted for each session.[2]

---

1   Only deliberate starts and stops were counted; those caused by technical or memory errors were not counted.
2   For more details about the methods used in this type of research, see Ginsborg (this volume, Chapter 11).

218 *Psychological Perspectives on Musical Experiences and Skills*

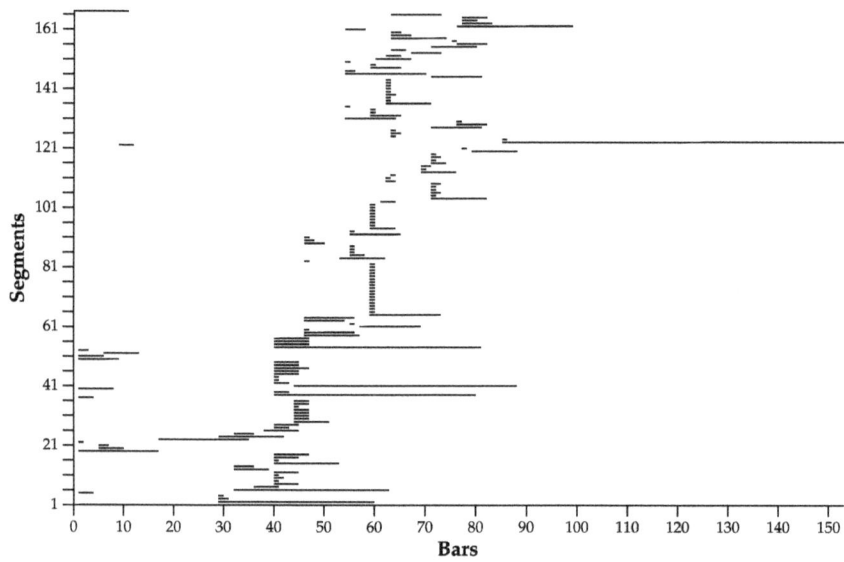

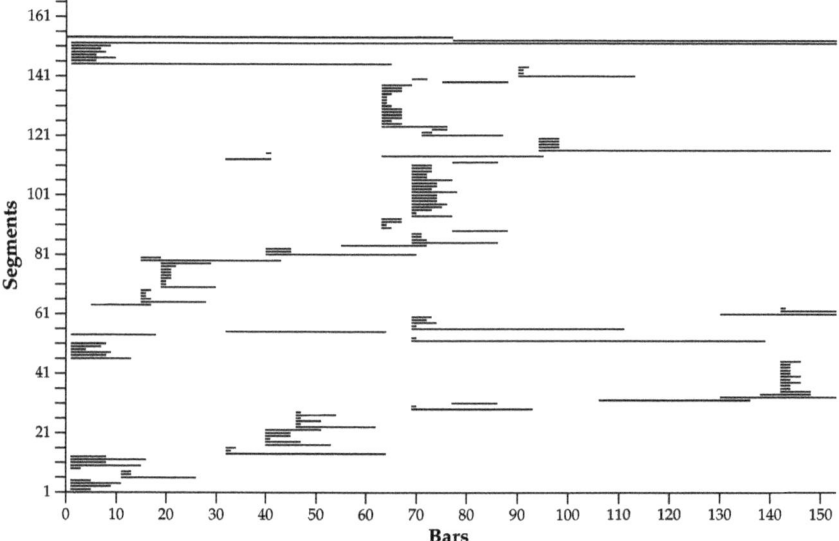

Fig. 10.1 (a) Session 3 (early) and (b) Session 16 (late)

Data analysis

Multiple regression analyses were performed to examine the effects of the formal structure of the piece, the pianist's segmentation of the piece, and technical difficulties, on the amount of practice (i.e., the numbers of starts, stops, and repetitions) during the four learning periods. The predictor variables were formal structure ('structural bars' at the beginnings and endings of sections) as determined by a music theorist (Žauhar et al., 2020); the pianist's segmentation of the piece in addition to its formal structure ('structurally relevant bars' at the beginnings and endings of sections she reported as relevant for memorisation); technical difficulty (bars reported as 'technically difficult'), and basic PCs (bars reported as 'technically difficult' as well as relevant for memorisation and monitoring of the performance).

The pianist's segmentation of the piece matched the formal structure only to some extent, $\varphi(151) = .47, p < .001$,[3] because she did not mark all the structural bars as relevant for memorisation and monitoring of the performance. However, she did mark additional shorter segments, such as bars containing harmony changes, as structurally relevant. These structurally relevant bars were included as a predictor variable to observe their contribution to the amount of practice. They were not correlated with the structural bars as defined by the music theorist, $\varphi(151) = -.06, p > .05$. There were no significant correlations between the four predictor variables, $\varphi(151)$ ranged from -.09 to .12, $p > .05$. Three outcome variables were used to represent the amount of practice: numbers of starts, repetitions, and stops. The first bar of the piece was not included in the analyses of starts, and the last bar was not included in the analyses of stops.

Results

Multiple regression analyses were performed to investigate the effects of formal structure, the pianist's segmentation of the piece, technical difficulties, and basic PCs on the amount of practice in the four learning periods (Table 10.2).

---

3   Phi (φ) correlation coefficients were calculated to check if the predictors were independent.

Table 10.2 Results of multiple regression analyses for four learning periods

Predictor variables	Section-by-section and putting together			Memorisation			Improving fluency and consolidating			Polishing		
	Starts	Repetitions	Stops	Starts	Repetitions	Stops	Starts	Repetitions	Stops	Starts	Repetitions	Stops
Formal structure												
Beginning of section	.33***	.06	.23**	.38***	.07	.17*	.28**	.13*	.11	.33***	.15	.03
End of section	.03	.07	.40***	−.02	−.04	.28***	.08	.04	.13	−.03	.02	.25**
Pianist's own segmentation												
Beginning of section	.68***	.23***	.26***	.49***	.10	.11	.67***	.18**	.14	.50***	.17	.05
End of section	−.02	.12	.15*	−.02	−.01	.12	−.01	−.04	.03	−.01	−.02	.19*
Technical difficulties	.03	.14*	.08	.05	.10	.03	.01	−.02	.07	−.02	.19*	−.08
Basic PCs (e.g., jumps)	.06	.53***	.11	.10	.31***	.02	.12*	.64***	.01	−.05	.22**	−.02
R^2	.53	.36	.28	.37	.12	.11	.52	.45	.04	.34	.14	.10
$F(6,145)$	28.11	14.01	9.92	14.05	3.28	3.06	26.61	19.83	1.27	12.66	3.81	2.77
p	<.001	<.001	<.001	<.001	<.01	<.01	<.001	<.001	ns	<.001	<.01	<.05

Note. For all predictors standardised coefficients are shown (β).

*p < .05; **p < .01; ***p < .001

A horizontal version of this table may be viewed online at https://hdl.handle.net/20.500.12434/46be45c0

The predictors together accounted for 10% to 53% of the variation in the amount of practice. The results of the regression analyses are interpreted below. Where applicable, comments from the practice diary are included to complement the interpretations, given that the pianist's short descriptions of the practice sessions are a helpful source of information.

The regression analyses showed that the pianist relied on the formal structure and her segmentation in four learning periods, that is, during the whole process of preparing for the performance from memory. As can be seen from Table 10.2, starts were predicted by the beginnings of sections within the formal structure and the pianist's segmentation. Beginnings in the pianist's segmentation were the main predictors of starts in each learning period. Stops were predicted by the beginnings and endings of sections within the formal structure and the pianist's additional segmentation in the first learning period. In the second learning period, stops were predicted only by structural bars, and in the fourth learning period by endings of sections.

In the first learning period (section-by-section and putting together), the pianist worked in short segments, as shown by her choice of beginnings of sections as starting places, and the beginnings and endings of sections as stopping places. According to her practice diary, she did this to master the musical material, and it can be inferred that she also did so to link landmarks in the piece together. Furthermore, she reported in her practice diary that she began to memorise some segments as early as the fourth practice session.

In the second learning period, the pianist focused on deliberate memorisation. From Table 10.2, it can be observed that she started more often at the beginnings of sections in the formal structure and according to her own segmentation. However, she stopped more often at the beginnings and endings of sections only within the formal structure. This result suggests that the pianist practised starting at multiple locations within larger segments corresponding to the formal structure.

In the third learning period, the pianist consolidated her memory for the music and improved the performance's fluency from memory. As can be seen from Table 10.2, starts were predicted by the beginnings of sections and basic PCs. This indicates that the pianist was encoding additional landmarks as starting points. In the practice diary, she reported working on phrases and/or sections as well as on details, directing her attention to locations that were demanding to memorise, and aiming to play without effort. In this period, she began to play the piece fluently from memory.

In the final learning period (polishing), starts were predicted by the beginnings of sections and stops by the endings (Table 10.2). The pianist reported that practice was intended to make her feel comfortable while playing and to prepare her for performing from memory.

Some effects of the beginnings of sections were also observed in repetitions. From Table 10.2 it can be observed that the pianist repeated bars at the beginnings of sections according to her own segmentation, more often in the first, third, and fourth learning periods. Beginnings of sections within the formal structure predicted repetitions only during the third, consolidation, period.

The effects of technically difficult bars on repetitions were observed in the first and the final learning periods, although basic PCs predicted repetitions in all four periods (Table 10.2). In the first period, the pianist repeated difficult bars to master them. In the fourth period, she repeated them to overlearn them or to feel more comfortable when playing them. As reported in the practice diary, she directed her attention towards PCs representing technically difficult bars throughout all four periods to ensure that she would ultimately perform them fluently and effortlessly.

Discussion

In this study we examined the process whereby a professional pianist learned and memorised a short piece of 20th century music, Papandopulo's Fourth Study for Piano. Several findings can be highlighted. Firstly, the results show that, in the process of preparing the Fourth Study, the pianist relied on its formal structure and her segmentation of the piece throughout the process of preparing to perform it from memory. Secondly, technically difficult bars affected repetitions in the initial and final learning period. Furthermore, bars including technical difficulties that were used as basic PCs and were relevant for memorisation predicted repetitions in all four learning periods. Below, we compare the learning processes of the professional pianist with those of the piano student who took part in the study by Žauhar et al. (2020) and highlight the similarities and differences between their strategies for mastering and memorising the music. The results are discussed with reference to studies carried out in Western Europe and the USA using a similar procedure, as few have been conducted in the Western Balkans.

One of the key findings of the present study is that the effects of the structure were identified from the earliest stages of practice. That is, the pianist used structural bars as starting and stopping places more often than the other bars. Moreover, when asked to describe her preparation for the process of practising, she reported that she read the score without playing it to gain an overall idea of the structure and technical complexity of the piece. She also estimated how difficult it would be for her to master the material and play the piece. Other experienced musicians have also been observed to form an overall idea of the structure of music they are to perform, its tempo, and any potential technical problems, before starting practice (Chaffin et al., 2003; Hallam, 1995). In the present study, the pianist reported that she tried to 'understand a structural and artistic idea of the piece', which corresponds to what Neuhaus (1961/2000) calls the 'artistic image'. Her practice, in learning and memorising a new work, was consistent with that of expert memorisers. These results corroborate the findings of other studies on the memorisation of music by, for example, Bach (e.g., Chaffin & Imreh, 2002; Lisboa et al., 2018), Debussy (Chaffin, 2007), and Stravinsky (e.g., Ginsborg et al., 2006), and show that similar memory processes occur during the memorisation of music pieces with a clear-cut formal structure, irrespective of the style of the music. The memorisation processes are similar also for music that has a complex and challenging structure (e.g., Chopin's *Barcarolle*, Op. 60, Chaffin et al., 2013). When the piece is free-form (e.g., Schoenberg's Op. 11, No. 3, Chueke & Chaffin, 2016) or has a complex non-tonal structure (e.g., Messiaen's *Oiseaux Exotiques* and other non-tonal pieces from the 20th and 21st centuries, Soares, 2015), the musician has to develop their own understanding of the musical structure to be able to segment the piece into sections. Once the musician has segmented the piece into sections that are meaningful for them, the process of memorisation is again similar to that observed with highly structured pieces (Chueke & Chaffin, 2016;

Fonte, 2020; Soares, 2015). Expert musicians use the structure of a piece to organise their practice and memorisation, regardless of its length and complexity and/or how long they have to prepare it for performance from memory (Chaffin, 2007; Ginsborg et al., 2006; Noice et al., 2008). In this way, the (formal) structure becomes a ready-made retrieval scheme when the piece is performed from memory.

In previous studies, the musicians who participated often determined the formal structure of the piece themselves (Chaffin & Imreh, 2002) or in discussion with other musicians (Žauhar & Bajšanski, 2012). In general, musicians tend to agree on the formal structure of a piece (Chaffin et al., 2016), although they may have different ways of segmenting it for memorisation, or other ways of analysing it and understanding its structure (Ginsborg et al., 2006). In the present study, as in Žauhar et al.'s (2020) study with a piano student, the formal structure was determined by the music theorist and the professional pianist. The segmentation of the piece by the pianists in both studies matched the formal structure identified by the music theorist to some extent, although the pianists were of different levels of expertise. Neither marked all the structural bars, and both marked other bars as relevant. According to their segmentations, they used their structurally relevant bars as starting and stopping places more often than other bars, which confirms that structuring the material during practice plays a vital role in preparing for performance from memory. Yet, while the student was aware of the formal structure from the earliest stages of practising and used structural bars as starting and stopping places, as observed in other studies involving students as participants (e.g., Williamon & Valentine, 2002), she repeated structural bars identified by the music theorist more often than other bars in each learning period. On the other hand, the professional pianist repeated structural bars defined by the music theorist more often only in one of the learning periods, when improving fluency and consolidating memory.

In the present study, the effects of the technical difficulties of the piece were observed in the initial and final stages of practice. The professional pianist reported, however, that few technically difficult bars became PCs. These bars needed attention throughout the whole learning process, as demonstrated by the number of times they were repeated. They were also bars at which the pianist started practice segments, but only at the consolidation stage, suggesting that she identified them as starting points on the mental map so that they would become retrieval cues. By contrast, the student who memorised the same piece worked on technically difficult bars throughout the learning process (Žauhar et al., 2020). The number of starts at and repetitions of difficult bars decreased over time, as observed in other studies involving students (e.g., Williamon & Valentine, 2002; Žauhar & Bajšanski, 2012). Nevertheless, unlike the professional pianist, the student needed to continue working on these bars to master their technical difficulties.

Another important finding is that the professional pianist who took part in the present study began to memorise early on, in the fourth practice session. Chaffin (2007) reported a similar finding in a study involving a concert pianist's memorisation of Debussy's *Clair de Lune*, a piece in a simple ABBA form; the pianist started playing from memory in the fourth practice session even though she had not yet completed the section-by-section learning period. Early memorisation characterises the practice of experienced musicians even when they prepare more complex pieces (Chaffin et al., 2003), as this means they can begin to develop their mental maps and practise retrieving at least some segments of the music. By memorising difficult passages early on in the learning process, they reduce the load on working memory and free up attentional resources for other aspects of the piece (Chaffin, 2007). Like other experienced musicians, the pianist in the present study devoted the second learning period to deliberate memorisation, and the third to consolidation and improving the fluency with which she played from memory. By contrast, the student in the parallel study (Žauhar et al., 2020) only started memorising after completing the section-by-section, whole-practice, and improving-fluency learning periods. Taken together, these findings suggest that using landmarks in the formal structure to memorise in the earliest stages of practice enables performers to focus on details while developing a mental map of the music. Research with singers of different proficiency levels also pointed out the importance of starting to memorise early on in the practice process, and highlighted that early strategic memorisation contributes to performance efficacy more than expertise (Ginsborg, 2002).

Specific teaching is necessary if musicians are to improve their practice by becoming aware of and using their knowledge of formal structure.

Expert musicians participating in longitudinal case studies have been asked to repeatedly report their thoughts and describe the strategies they use while practising. There is evidence that it is helpful for professional musicians to report their thoughts during practice, as this increases their conceptual understanding and improves memorisation (Lisboa et al., 2011). It can also be helpful for students (Lisboa et al., 2015, 2018; Timperman & Miksza, 2019) to identify the landmarks in a piece of music that have been shown as beneficial to more experienced musicians. It would contribute to the development of their own efficient memorisation strategies and help them to master new pieces of music. In a study investigating string students' immediate and delayed recall of memorised études, for example, verbalisations about learning were shown to be effective in later performances, once the pieces had been retained for some time in long-term memory (Timperman & Miksza, 2019). Chaffin et al. (2013) reported a longitudinal study examining the learning of Chopin's *Barcarolle*, Op. 60, by an experienced pianist who was also a music theorist, and who made a detailed Schenkerian analysis of the complex structure of the piece. Although carrying out this analysis did not have immediately observable effects, it was reported to be helpful in the learning process when the pianist subsequently came to prepare the piece for public performance. The ability to recognise formal patterns in music increases as students learn to analyse pieces and pay attention to the reasons why some places may be particularly useful when forming mental maps (Timperman & Miksza, 2019). Such strategies can help students develop a deeper understanding of the piece, and strengthen their ability to encode it securely and retrieve it when performing from memory.

Conclusion

The findings of this study confirm that the memorisation of Papandopulo's Fourth Study for Piano followed established patterns of music memorisation (e.g., Chaffin & Imreh, 2002) corresponding to general memory principles (Ericsson & Kintsch, 1995). The professional pianist who took part in the study relied on the formal structure and her own segmentation of the piece while preparing to perform it from memory. She deliberately developed a mental map of it to serve as a reliable retrieval structure. The results of this study corroborate the findings of previous studies with concert and jazz pianists (e.g., Chaffin & Imreh, 2002; Chueke & Chaffin, 2016; Fonte, 2020; Noice et al., 2008; Soares,

2015); a cellist (e.g., Lisboa et al., 2018); and a singer (e.g., Chaffin et al., 2023; Ginsborg & Chaffin, 2011; Ginsborg et al., 2006), and contribute to their generalisability. To date, memorisation of music pieces of different styles has been examined from late Baroque to contemporary music. This study expands the repertoire used to investigate the memorisation of 20th century and contemporary pieces to include music of Croatian heritage. It also represents an interdisciplinary collaboration between a performer and cognitive psychologists, established to investigate the memorisation of music.

Studies including participants of different levels of proficiency who learn the same piece of music (e.g., Ginsborg, 2002) are rarely conducted, so the comparison between the processes of memorisation of a professional pianist and a piano student offers an important contribution, even though the comparison is descriptive, which presents a limitation. Such comparisons have implications for the teaching of efficient practice. For example, Lisboa et al. (2015, 2018) have shown how a teacher may encourage their students to report thoughts during practice to improve its quality. Reporting thoughts helps students to develop content-addressable access to memory, and consequently, memorisation becomes more reliable. The metacognitive awareness of the musician's learning process and progress is also characteristic of the practice of expert musicians (Chueke & Chaffin, 2016). Detailed comments recorded during practice provide insight into the focus of a musician's attention during the learning process (Chaffin et al., 2003), and confirm that professional musicians have a good understanding of their learning strategies, the difficulties they encounter, the actions they must take to fix passages that go wrong, and how to improve their performance (Hallam, 1995). In the present study, we collected only brief descriptions of practice sessions, which were congruent with analysis of the amount of practice undertaken. Reporting thoughts during practice, and discussing them with the teacher, could also improve students' awareness of their strengths and weaknesses when preparing new pieces for performance.

It can be concluded that by deepening the understanding of the musical material being learned, and with the appropriate use of memorisation strategies, the quality of practice improves. Organising practice according to the principles of expert memory could speed up and improve the processes whereby students prepare repertoire for performance from memory.

Acknowledgements

The authors thank Jane Ginsborg, an anonymous reviewer, and the editors for their thorough reading and valuable comments on earlier versions of this chapter.

References

Chaffin, R. (2007). Learning Clair de Lune: Retrieval practice and expert memorisation. *Music Perception, 24*(4), 377–393. https://doi.org/10.1525/mp.2007.24.4.377

Chaffin, R., Demos, A., & Logan, T. (2016). Performing from memory. In S. Hallam, I. Cross, & M. Thaut (eds), *The Oxford handbook of music psychology* (2nd ed., pp. 559–71). Oxford University Press. https://doi.org/10.1093/oxfordhb/9780198722946.001.0001

Chaffin, R., Gerling, C., Demos, A.P., & Melms, A. (2013). Theory and practice: A case study of how Schenkerian analysis shaped the learning of Chopin's Barcarolle. In A. Williamon & W. Goebl (eds), *Proceedings of the International Symposium on Performance Science* (pp. 21–26). European Association of Conservatoires.

Chaffin, R., Ginsborg, J., Dixon, J., & Demos, A. P. (2023). Recovery from memory failure when recalling a memorized performance: The role of musical structure and performance cues. *Musicae Scientiae, 27*(1), 94–116. https://doi.org/10.1177/10298649211025491

Chaffin, R., & Imreh, G. (2002). Practicing perfection: Piano performance as expert memory. *Psychological Science, 13*(4), 342–349. https://doi.org/10.1111/j.0956-7976.2002.00462.x

Chaffin, R., Imreh, G., & Crawford, M. (2002). *Practicing perfection: Memory and piano performance.* Lawrence Erlbaum. https://doi.org/10.4324/9781410612373

Chaffin, R., Imreh, G., Lemieux, A.F., & Chen, C. (2003). 'Seeing the big picture': Piano practice as expert problem solving. *Music Perception, 20*(4), 465–490. https://doi.org/10.1525/mp.2003.20.4.465

Chase, W.G., & Ericsson, K.A. (1982). Skill and working memory. In G. H. Bower (ed.), *Psychology of learning and motivation: Vol. 16* (pp. 1–58). Academic Press.

Chueke, Z., & Chaffin, R. (2016). Performance cues for music 'with no plan': A case study of preparing Schoenberg's Op. 11, No. 3. In C. Mackie (ed.), *New thoughts on piano performance* (pp. 255–268). London International Piano Symposium.

Detoni, D. (2008). Note about the composer. In D. Cikojević, & F. Spiller (eds), *Boris Papandopulo: Osam studija za glasovir* [Boris Papandopulo: Eight studies for piano] (Revised ed., pp. 9–11). Croatian Music Information Centre.

Ericsson, K.A., & Kintsch, W. (1995). Long-term working memory. *Psychological Review, 102*(2), 211–245. https://doi.org/10.1037/0033-295X.102.2.211

Fonte, V. (2020). *Reconsidering memorisation in the context of non-tonal piano music* [Unpublished doctoral disseration]. Royal College of Music, London.

Ginsborg, J. (2002). Classical singers learning and memorising a new song: An observational study. *Psychology of Music, 30*(1), 58–101. https://doi.org/10.1177/0305735602301007

Ginsborg, J., & Bennett, D. (2021). Developing familiarity in a new duo: Rehearsal talk and performance cues. *Frontiers in Psychology, 12*, Article 590987. https://doi.org/10.3389/fpsyg.2021.590987

Ginsborg, J., & Chaffin, R. (2011). Preparation and spontaneity in performance: A singer's thoughts while singing Schoenberg. *Psychomusicology: Music, Mind & Brain, 21*(1–2), 137–158. https://doi.org/10.1037/h0094009

Ginsborg, J., Chaffin, R., & Demos, A.P. (2012). Different roles for prepared and spontaneous thoughts: A practice-based study of musical performance from memory. *Journal of Interdisciplinary Music Studies, 6*(2), 201–231. https://repository.rncm.ac.uk/111/

Ginsborg, J., Chaffin, R., & Nicholson, G. (2006). Shared performance cues in singing and conducting: A content analysis of talk during practice. *Psychology of Music, 34*(2), 167–194. https://doi.org/10.1177/0305735606061851

Hallam, S. (1995). Professional musicians' orientations to practice: Implications for teaching. *British Journal of Music Education, 12*(1), 3–19. https://doi.org/10.1017/S0265051700002357

Kovacic, L. (1996). *The piano music of Boris Papandopulo* [Unpublished doctoral dissertation]. Rice University, Houston, Texas.

Lisboa, T., Chaffin, R., & Demos, A.P. (2015). Recording thoughts while memorising music: A case study. *Frontiers in Psychology, 5*, Article 1561. https://doi.org/10.3389/fpsyg.2014.01561

Lisboa, T., Chaffin, R., & Logan, T. (2011). An account of deliberate practice: Thoughts, behaviour and self in learning Bach's Prelude 6 for cello solo. In A. Cervino, M. Lettberg, C. Laws, & T. Lisboa (eds), *The practice of practising* (pp. 9–31). Orpheus Research Centre in Music.

Lisboa, T., Demos, A.P., & Chaffin, R. (2018). Training thought and action for virtuoso performance. *Musicae Scientiae, 22*(4), 519–538. https://doi.org/10.1177/1029864918782350

Miklaszewski, K. (1989). A case study of a pianist preparing a musical performance. *Psychology of Music, 17*(2), 95–109. https://doi.org/10.1177/0305735689172001

Music Lab, University of Connecticut. (2020). *Study Your Music Practice* [Software]. https://musiclab.uconn.edu/study-your-own-music-performance/

Neuhaus, H. (2000). *O umjetnosti sviranja klavira* [The art of piano playing]. (2nd ed.). Naklada Jakša Zlatar.

Nielsen, S.G. (1999). Learning strategies in instrumental music practice. *British Journal of Music Education, 16*(3), 275–291. https://doi.org/10.1017/S0265051799000364

Nielsen, S.G. (2004). Strategies and self-efficacy beliefs in instrumental and vocal individual practice: A study of students in higher music education. *Psychology of Music, 32*(4), 418–431. https://doi.org/10.1177/0305735604046099

Noice, H., Jeffrey, J., Noice, T., & Chaffin, R. (2008). Memorisation by a jazz musician: A case study. *Psychology of Music, 36*(1), 63–79. https://doi.org/10.1177/0305735607080834

Noice, H., & Noice, T. (2006). Artistic performance: Acting, ballet and contemporary dance. In A. Ericsson, N. Charness, P. Feltovich, & R. Hoffman (eds), *The Cambridge handbook of expertise and expert performance* (1st ed., pp. 489–503). Cambridge University Press. https://doi.org/10.1017/CBO9780511816796

Soares, A. (2015). *Memorisation of atonal music* [Unpublished doctoral dissertation]. Guildhall School of Music and Drama, London.

Timperman, E., & Miksza, P. (2019). Verbalization and musical memory in string players. *Musicae Scientiae, 23*(2), 212–230. https://doi.org/10.1177/1029864917727332

Williamon, A., & Valentine, E. (2002). The role of retrieval structures in memorising music. *Cognitive Psychology, 44*(1), 1–32. https://doi.org/10.1006/cogp.2001.0759

Žauhar, V., & Bajšanski, I. (2012). Uloga formalne strukture i izvedbene zahtjevnosti glazbenoga djela kod upamćivanja notnoga teksta: Studija slučaja [The role of the formal structure and technical difficulties of a piece of music in memorising music score: A case study]. *Psihologijske teme, 21*(2), 225–247. https://hrcak.srce.hr/89528

Žauhar, V., Matić, A., Dražul, A., & Bajšanski, I. (2020). Memorising the contemporary piano piece of music: The effects of the formal structure, pianist's segmentation, and technical difficulties. In B. Bogunović & S. Nikolić (eds), *Proceedings of PAM-IE Belgrade 2019* (pp. 69–77). Faculty of Music, University of Arts in Belgrade. https://www.fmu.bg.ac.rs/wp-content/uploads/2020/12/psychology-and-music-08_zauhar-et-al.pdf

11. Memory for Music: Research and Practice for Performers

Jane Ginsborg

Introduction

Memory is intrinsic both to appreciating and making music. We use it when we hear music, when we listen to it, and when we sing or play it. While hearing music can evoke semantic memory for factual knowledge that we have accumulated throughout our lives, it can also evoke episodic or autobiographical memory, bringing the past to life so vividly that it seems to be present for performer and listener alike. Semantic and autobiographical memory are both forms of retrospective memory, used when listening to music actively rather than hearing it passively, while prospective memory enables us to predict what is to come in the music. To perform notated music from memory, musicians must memorise it. Successful memorisation of music is typically the result of two processes. One is spontaneous and gives rise to serial cuing, while the other is deliberate, producing content-addressable memory (Chaffin et al., 2016). While many professional musicians—particularly solo singers and pianists—are expected to perform from memory nowadays, this is a relatively recent convention dating from the mid-19th century. Once it had become established, however, musicians, teachers, and psychologists began to explore both the pedagogy and the psychology of memorisation.

Aims

The main contribution of this chapter is a review of the history of the pedagogy of memorisation, an outline of the empirical research on memorisation, brief summaries of three studies conducted in the Western Balkans, summaries of three of my own studies conducted in Western Europe, and recommendations based on the research evidence. To provide a context for this contribution, I begin by giving examples of autobiographical memories evoked by music, discussing the roles of retrospective and prospective memory when listening to music, and introducing the two processes underlying successful memorisation.

Main discussion

Autobiographical memory for music

Proust referred to the experience of tasting a madeleine as stopping time. Hearing familiar music can also stop time; Davies called this the 'Darling, they're playing our tune!' effect (1978, pp. 69–70). It is because music can have this effect that radio programmes such as the BBC's *Desert Island Discs* are so popular. Celebrities tell stories about their lives, prompted by the music they have chosen, and their choices evoke listeners' memories too. Another radio programme broadcast by the BBC in 2016 provides two striking illustrations of autobiographical memory for music (Gorb, 2016). The Italian pianist and composer Francesco Lotoro interviewed the 83-year-old film director Jack Garfein, who sang a song he had first heard in a Nazi death camp 70 years earlier, composed and sung on his way to the gas chamber by a Polish boy whose name is long forgotten. Lotoro himself has amassed an archive of 8,000 scores—in some cases mere fragments notated on cheese wrappings and toilet paper—of music composed by victims of the Holocaust. One was Viktor Ullmann, whose one-act opera *The Emperor of Atlantis* was composed in Theresienstadt in 1943/44, but not performed in London until 1981. Ullmann had been working on a new monodrama for speaker and orchestra, 'The Way of Love and Death of Cornet Christoph Rilke', when he was murdered in 1944, but had orchestrated only the first movement. From detailed notes on his intended orchestration, it was possible for the composer Adam Gorb to reconstruct a fragment of the third movement, which was performed and recorded in 2015 by the BBC Philharmonic Orchestra.

The present that was experienced by both the nameless Polish boy and Viktor Ullmann was shattered violently—*dis*-membered—by the Holocaust, so that for each one the present suddenly became the past. Their music, however, was preserved and has been brought back to life; it has literally been *re*-membered and performed so that it is possible for listeners to experience the past in the present. This is one of the features of music that makes it so valuable when working with or caring for people with memory loss as the result of dementia. When the music is familiar, such as hymns sung at church or Christmas carols at home, memories can be shared without having to be articulated in words. The neurologist Oliver Sacks (2007) argues that even unfamiliar music can reach people with dementia, when talking or touching no longer seems to get through to them, because they experience music in the moment.

Retrospective and prospective memory

We rely on the contents of our long-term memory to provide a context for understanding music we are listening to for the first time, and on our short-term memory for the sequences of sounds (timbres, pitches, rhythms, harmonies) that have immediately preceded our perception of music in the moment. We use prospective memory to predict what we are about to hear, and can be delighted both by the fulfilment and the violation of our expectations (Meyer, 1956). Fulfilment and violation can be simultaneous when the expectation is veridical (i.e., for the next event in a work we know well), even though the musical event is schematically unexpected in that it breaches 'automatic, culturally generic expectations' (Bharucha, 1994, p. 216), such as the 'surprise' chord in Haydn's Symphony No. 94. More recent theories of prospective memory for music have been proposed. According to Narmour's Implication-Realization model (e.g., 1992), automatic and largely implicit bottom-up generative processes interact with top-down processes deriving from the learned knowledge of musical style. In her theory of melodic expectation, Margulis (2005) identified the roles of stability, proximity, direction, and mobility in the music for which listeners implicitly form expectations, and Huron's (2006) model encompasses imagination, tension, prediction, reaction, and appraisal (ITPRA). Neuroscientific research reviewed by Salimpoor et al. (2015) explains prospective memory for music in terms of the interaction of dopamine release with the activation of cortical regions associated with the processing of musical structures, emotion, and reward; finally, Trainor and Zatorre (2016) draw on the results of EEG and fMRI studies to support the proposed mechanisms underlying expectation and prediction.

While listeners are not necessarily performers themselves, all performers are listeners. They monitor their own performances as they unfold, often comparing them to their own or others' previous performances of the same work and, unless they are giving solo performances, listening to those of their fellow musicians. This process of monitoring, involving both retrospective and prospective memory for different kinds of information, enables performers to identify and meet each local goal as they encounter it in the music. In oral traditions, musicians rely on retrospective auditory memory to remember the sound of others' renditions and produce their own versions, if appropriate. When musicians read music from notation, imagining its sounds, they are using a skill originally known as visualisation (Gieseking & Leimer, 1932/1972) and now referred to as notational audiation (Gordon, 1976), because the sound of music can be imagined not only by readers but also improvisers and composers. In the context of score-reading, however, audiation involves translating symbols into sounds by drawing on the associations between them that the musician has learned and stored in their long-term memory.

Memorisation: Serial cuing and content-addressable memory

The skills of playing an instrument and singing, like those of reading and audiating, rely on associations stored in long-term memory. These skills are developed through practice, often involving rote repetition, and are largely procedural. They enable musicians to perform sequences of musical material such as scales, arpeggios, and chord progressions automatically, without having consciously to recall what comes next. This is known as serial cuing, since playing one passage cues the next. It is vital that musicians develop the motor, muscle, finger, or tactile (i.e., kinaesthetic) memory to acquire these skills. It is dangerous, however, for them to rely solely on serial cuing when performing from memory as sequences can so easily be disrupted, causing the musician to experience a memory lapse. Unless they also have content-addressable memory for the music, as the result of deliberate practice (Ericsson, 2013, p. 534), there is often no alternative to starting again and hoping for the best. By contrast, content-addressable memory empowers performers to retrieve the music they are to play or sing at will from their long-term memory, starting at any location in the piece. If they experience a memory lapse despite having used analytic or conceptual strategies in the course of deliberate practice, they can jump forward or back to the nearest landmark in their mental map or representation of the piece, referred to by Chaffin and his colleagues as a performance cue (PC; e.g., Chaffin et al., 2002), rather than going back to the beginning.

The history of music memorisation

It is worth remembering that only a small minority of professional musicians, mostly singers and pianists, are expected to perform Western classical music from memory, and that this has only been so since the middle of the 19th century. Before then, memorisation was deplored on the grounds that musicians could not be relied upon to play what had been written. According to Leopold Mozart (1756), 'one should not give [a beginner] [...] melodious pieces which remain easily in his memory [...] [or] he will accustom himself to play by ear and at random' (p. 35). Hummel (1828) claimed that if children played from memory, they would 'never attain to any readiness in reading the notes' (p. v). But a concert given by the cellist Bernhard Romberg (1767–1841) had already been reviewed ecstatically as follows:

> Spurning the printed music as an aide-memoire he takes his place, the magic instrument in his hands, and, without hiding himself behind a music stand, presents to the public the whole picture of a free, unrestricted ruler of the kingdom of tones. (Novellistik, 1822, pp. 25–26)

The first pianist known to have played from memory in public was Clara Wieck (later Schumann), who performed Beethoven's Sonata in

F, Op. 57, in 1837. Although she was described by Frau von Arnim as '"the most insufferable artist she had ever come across," who had the "audacity" to play the whole of her programmes by heart' (May 1912, p. 196), Liszt nevertheless played more than forty works in Vienna the following year, by composers including Beethoven, Weber, Chopin, Scarlatti, and Handel, all from memory. In 1839 Czerny explicitly recommended '[committing] to memory a good number of little, easy, but tasteful pieces; so that [...] you may be able to play by heart' (p. 41), and the first pragmatic advice to singers on memory was given by the pedagogue Maria Anfossi (1837): '[if] a phrase begins a little before the turning of the page, turn first and sing such bar or bars from memory' (p. 77). Performing from memory became popular in the second half of the 19th century, with the nine-year-old Bizet performing piano sonatas by Mozart from memory in 1847, and inspiring the parents and managers of subsequent child prodigies to demonstrate ever more impressive feats of memory as well as pianism; so it is not surprising that a pedagogy of memorisation began to develop at the very end of the 19th century.

The early pedagogy of music memorisation

Shinn (1898) was the first author to identify 'forms of memory belonging respectively to the ear, the fingers, the eye, and the intellect employed more or less continuously throughout the progress of a piece' (Mishra, 2010, p. 9), that is, what we would now call auditory, kinaesthetic, visual, and conceptual memory. Next, Theodor Leschetizky recommended the use of conceptual memory, and avoiding the inadvertent reinforcement of bad habits by establishing good habits from the start:

> Thought is indispensable in the study of pieces, as they are learned first by the brain, and from that by the fingers [...]. To memorize a piece, read it through at the keyboard only once, to get its outline without creating any faulty habits of fingering. Then take one or two measures at a time [...] analyse the harmonies, and decide upon the fingering and pedalling. (quoted in Brée, 1913/1997, p. 57)

Like Shinn, Hughes (1915) referred to memorising 'by ear, visual memory, either of the notes on the printed page or the notes on the keyboard, and by finger memory or reflex action' (p. 595), but he also introduced the idea that musicians should articulate their mental representation of the music they were memorising:

> On one or both of [ear or visual memory] are dependent the very useful and important methods of learning the harmonic and formal structure of the composition to be memorized and of being able to *say* the notes, or at least to bring up a very distinct mental picture of them. (p. 595)

At around the same time, singers were being exhorted to memorise:

> Song deals with the great human emotions expressed in words, and the singer stands face to face with his audience. Every friend of expression that has been given him he is in duty bound to make the most of. Hard work is not easy, memorizing is a work of extreme laboriousness, but when that work is done, it is in the singer's possession for ever. (Plunket Greene, 1912, p. 12)

Plunket Greene's five rules for memorising were to 'learn the song in rough; memorise it; polish it musically first; reconcile the phrasing to the text; [and] absorb the accompaniment of the song' (1912, pp. 233–37). Taylor (1914), however, recommended what we would now call automatisation: 'In studying a song, the first thing to do is memorise it, so that the mind will not be taxed with trying to recall the words and the melody' (p. 26); while Curtis (1914), like Leschetizky, recommended mental practice: 'All work of learning and memorizing music should be mental. When the mind is concentrated upon learning the melody, rhythm and construction of a composition, the voice should not be used' (p. 207).

Research on musicians' memorising strategies

These rules and recommendations were based, of course, on their authors' own experiences of teaching and performing and, although further books and articles for musicians continued (and continue) to be published, it was not until the late 1930s that music memorisation began to be a topic of interest to psychologists, inspired by the pioneering research of Rubin-Rabson (1937, 1940a,b, 1941a,b,c,d). She found that analytic pre-study improved recall, as did using mental practice and learning pieces in small sections; using a distributed rather than a massed strategy (i.e., several short practice sessions rather than one long one); and, for pianists, practising music for left and right hands separately.

The efficacy of memorising strategies based on the auditory, kinaesthetic, visual, and conceptual forms of memory identified by Shinn (1898), Leschetizky (as cited in Brée, 1913/1997)), and Hughes (1915) has been investigated empirically, with mixed results. The evidence supports the use of auditory strategies such as listening to recorded performances (Bernardi et al., 2013; Rosenthal, 1984; Rosenthal et al., 1988). Highben and Palmer (2004), for example, asked pianists to practise short, specially composed pieces of music, with and without auditory and motor feedback. Recall was best when they practised as normal and worst when they had to imagine both the feel of the keyboard and the sound of the music, although those who described themselves as being able to play by ear and did well on a test of aural abilities were least affected by not being able to hear their own playing. Bernardi et al. (2013) tested the effect of mental practice by asking pianists to practise two unfamiliar pieces by Domenico Scarlatti, one physically and the other mentally, before performing them from memory. Memorisation was most effective when the pianists were experienced in analysing the formal structure of the pieces they were learning and had used auditory imagery for pitch. Loimusalo and Huovinen (2018) also studied mental practice, and found that pianists were more likely to use imagery for pitch in tonal music and rhythm in atonal music.

Children and beginners often associate practice with repetition. This kinaesthetic strategy is vital for the development of procedural memory, which underlies serial cuing, but performers can also use it deliberately to automatise certain sequences and free them to attend to other aspects of the performance such as conveying expression. The student pianists who participated in a study by Davidson-Kelly et al. (2012) reported preferring physical strategies (e.g., practising slowly, with hands separately, varying notated rhythms) to mental strategies (e.g., analysing the music and memorising it before beginning to play). Gerling and Dos Santos (2017) found that pianists memorising Classical and Romantic works deliberately memorised kinaesthetic cues including awareness of the direction in which their hands moved at particular locations in the music, and developed their procedural knowledge of what they referred to as the topography of the keyboard and its association with the type and direction of their body movements.

While some musicians claim to make use of photographic or *eidetic* recall, others develop visual memory for the musical score in the course of learning. Nuki (1984) found that student pianists who reported deliberately using a visual strategy were quicker to memorise than those who used kinaesthetic, auditory, or combined strategies, but they were also expert in sight-reading and *solfège* and were thus likely to have had superior audiation skills. More recently, student pianists' responses to the Musical Memorization Inventory (Mishra, 2007) indicated more frequent use of analytic and auditory strategies than kinaesthetic and visual strategies.

Kinaesthetic strategies can also be used to support the development of mental (i.e., conceptual) representations. Independent analysis of video recordings of my own preparation for performance of the first Ricercar from Stravinsky's *Cantata* (Ginsborg, 2009) showed that I used different kinds of body movement as I learned and memorised. Beating a pulse provided the framework for ensuring rhythmic accuracy; conducting helped me form a metrical representation, which was crucial since the metre shifts from 4/8 to 3/8 both between and within sections. Once I had memorised the piece, gesture underpinned my communication of semantic meaning both musical and verbal.

While the deliberate memorisation of notated music involves encoding and storing visual, auditory, and kinaesthetic information in long-term memory so that it can be retrieved at will, strategies focusing on memorising one type of information over another have not been shown to be effective. To date, most efforts to link perceptual learning modalities or visual, aural, and kinaesthetic learning styles (Swassing & Barbe, 1979) with preferences for using visual, auditory, and kinaesthetic strategies when memorising music have been unsuccessful. Mishra (2007) found only very small correlations between the scores of eighty-two respondents' scores on the Learning Styles Test (LdPride, n.d.), the Visual, Aural, Read/Write, Kinesthetic (VARK) Questionnaire (Fleming, n.d.), and her own Musical Memorization Inventory. Odendaal (2013, 2016) found no evidence from several studies using a range of methods to support the applicability of perceptual learning style theory to memorisation.

Analytic or conceptual strategies are, however, vital for developing content-addressable memory, as recommended by the early pedagogues, before starting to sing (Curtis, 1914; Taylor, 1914), early in the learning process (Leschetizky, as cited in Brée, 1913/1997), and/or throughout the whole period of preparation (Shinn, 1898). These strategies are only accessible to the musician if they have semantic knowledge stored in their long-term memory of the tonal, harmonic, and compositional structures typical of the music they are learning, enabling them to divide or chunk the work to be performed into sections so that they can be learned and memorised separately before being recombined (Bernardi et al., 2013). Hughes (1915) suggested verbalising musical material; the most effective memorisers in Nuki's (1984) study were expert in sight-reading and *solfège*; and Apostolaki (2013) describes *solfège* (using either movable or fixed 'do') as a framework for verbalising. Timperman and Miksza (2019) tested the effectiveness of another way of verbalising. They asked two groups of student string players to learn a short piece of music and perform it from memory. Participants in one group were also asked to talk about the piece in detail before performing, and had better recall of it after 24 hours.

Mental practice is the strategy that has been investigated most frequently in recent years (see Mielke & Comeau, 2019). This can include formal, structural analysis, and visual, auditory, kinaesthetic, and conceptual imagery. Deliberate physical practice involves mental practice, however, so it makes sense that they should be combined (Bernardi et al., 2013).

Research on performance from memory using the longitudinal case study approach

Most of the research described above involved the participation of groups of musicians, typically students. Longitudinal case studies, by contrast, are used to investigate individual musicians' preparation for performance over extended periods of time. This method was pioneered by the cognitive scientist Roger Chaffin, who has collaborated with a number of expert musicians including the pianist Gabriela Imreh (e.g., Chaffin et al., 2002), the cellist Tânia Lisboa (e.g., Lisboa et al., 2015), and myself (e.g., Chaffin et al., 2023). In this section I will outline the methods used in longitudinal case study research before briefly summarising three studies conducted in the Western Balkans and—in more detail—three that I have conducted in Western Europe using this approach.

Methods used in the longitudinal case study approach

All longitudinal case studies use broadly similar methods. The musician audio- or video-records all their practice sessions and performances so they can subsequently be transcribed, analysed, and illustrated in practice graphs. Such graphs provide an indication of the musician's practice behaviour (e.g., the sections of the music they worked on and how often they repeated each segment). The musician annotates copies of the musical score, either at the end of each practice session or of the whole rehearsal period, to indicate their thoughts while practising. The locations of each annotation are called practice or rehearsal features. The musician annotates further copies of the score after their performance to indicate their thoughts while performing; the locations of these thoughts are called performance cues (PCs). Multiple regression analyses using PCs as predictor variables and practice behaviour as outcome variables show how musicians' mental representations of music determine their approaches to practice and performance (e.g., Ginsborg & Chaffin, 2011a), and their long-term memory for the music that has been memorised (Ginsborg & Chaffin, 2011b). Content analyses can be made of individual musicians' spoken verbal commentaries while practising (e.g., Fonte, 2020), and of the rehearsal talk of two musicians working together (e.g., Ginsborg & Bennett, 2021, 2022).

Brief summary of three longitudinal case studies (Western Balkans)

Žauhar and Bajšanski (2012) report a study, for example, of a third-year undergraduate piano student who recorded all her practice sessions as she prepared a performance from memory of Bach's Prelude and Fugue in E minor. They transcribed and analysed the recordings and were able to show from her use of structural bars as starting places that the hierarchical organization of the work informed her approach to memorization. In a subsequent study, Žauhar, Matić, Dražul, and

Bajšanski (2020) used a similar approach in a study of a second-year high school pianist's learning and memorization of a 20th-century composition, the Fourth Study by Boris Papandopulo (1956). The results of the analysis highlighted the role of the pianist's own segmentation of the piece as she practised and memorised it, rather than its formal structure, as determined by the pianist and a music theorist. To find out whether a professional pianist with more experience of analysing and performing contemporary music would make more use of the hierarchical organization of a 20th-century work while memorizing it, Žauhar, Crnjanski, and Bajšanski carried out a follow-up study in which the second author also memorized and performed Papandopulo's Fourth Study. This study is reported in detail in Chapter 10 of the present volume. While the professional pianist took a similar approach to that of the high-school student, her segmentation of the work was more closely related to the formal structure of the work, and she began to memorise it as early as the fourth practice session, suggesting that she was quicker to create a mental representation of the work on which she was able to draw when playing from memory. These studies underline the importance of including music theory, harmony, and analysis in curricula for performers to enable them to learn and memorize more efficiently and, potentially, to give more effective performances from memory.

Summary of three longitudinal case studies (Western Europe)

Study 1

My first longitudinal case study involved tracking my preparation for performance of the first Ricercar from Stravinsky's *Cantata* (see above). The performance took place in 2003, and my first reports of the research were published in 2006 (Ginsborg et al., 2006a, 2006b; Ginsborg, 2009; see also Ginsborg & Chaffin, 2011a, 2011b, and Chaffin et al., 2023). At this time a central assumption of PC theory was that PCs are a subset of practice features, suggesting that performers' thoughts while performing have been prepared in the course of their practice sessions. This was not my experience, however, nor that of other performers.

Study 2

I therefore set out to explore the role of spontaneity in a similar study of my practice and performance of Schoenberg's Two Songs Op. 14. Several months after giving the public performance, I recorded and analysed a reconstructed performance from memory, *in vivo*, with and without piano accompaniment (Ginsborg et al., 2012). While I retained some practice features as PCs in both performances (core PCs), I retained others in one performance but not the other (non-core PCs) and, crucially, some spontaneous thoughts in the first performance served as PCs in the second (functional PCs).

Study 3

Although the findings of Study 2 were promising, they were not based on repeated public performances. To show that some spontaneous thoughts (i.e., thoughts in performance that had not occurred previously in practice) could serve as PCs in a subsequent performance, I would have to give more than one performance. One of the aims of Study 3 was to ask questions arising from the findings of Studies 1 and 2; its other aim was to follow up a previous investigation of the role of familiarity and expertise in four singer-pianist duos (Ginsborg & King, 2012; King & Ginsborg, 2011).

Unlike the majority of longitudinal case studies reported by Chaffin and his colleagues, Studies 1 and 2 were carried out not by a soloist performing solo repertoire but by the members of a duo. My musical partner was my husband, the composer, conductor, and pianist George Nicholson. For Study 3, I formed a new duo with the viola player Dawn Bennett (Ginsborg & Bennett, 2021, 2022)—hitherto unknown to me other than as an academic living on the other side of the world—so that we could explore our developing familiarity with each other as well as the music: settings by Boris Tchaikovsky (1925–1996) of two poems by the English poet Rudyard Kipling, translated very loosely into Russian.

I stayed in Dawn's house in Western Australia for a week. We spent just over four hours practising independently and nearly three-and-a-half hours rehearsing together. We recorded all our individual practice sessions and joint rehearsals, and in due course the recordings were transcribed and analysed. We gave two public performances at the end of the week, and a third one when Dawn visited the UK ten months later. We each performed one of the two songs from memory, reading the other from the musical score.

After the first and second rehearsal periods, and each of the three performances, we annotated copies of our scores to indicate the locations of features and PCs in the following categories: structural (e.g., boundaries between sections, subsections, or switches, i.e., where the same passage can lead in two or more directions), basic (prepare, breath, word pronunciation, pitch, fingering, bowing), interpretive (word meaning, sound, tempo, dynamics), expressive, memory, coordinate, and shared (expressive and coordinate).

We analysed the data to answer four research questions:

1. Which practice features did we attend to, individually and together, when memorising and not memorising? Certain categories were more salient when we were memorising (e.g., for Dawn: pitch, tempo, coordination with singer; for me: preparation, and the meaning of the lyrics). By contrast, we were able to focus on other categories when we were reading from the score (e.g., sound for Dawn, subsection boundaries for me).

2. To what extent did the practice features remain salient in each of the memorised and non-memorised performances? For Dawn, memory was most salient in the first and, to a lesser extent, third performances from memory. Basic features were most salient in the second and third performances, and interpretive features and coordination with me were most salient in the third performance from memory. For me, basic features were highly and equally salient in all three performances from memory, as were shared features for both of us in the first and second performances, although less so in the third.

3. What proportions of practice features overall were retained in memorised performances as core and non-core PCs? Dawn retained 3.95% of rehearsal features as core PCs (i.e., in all three performances) but 63.2% as non-core PCs (in one or two performances), while I retained 21.2% of rehearsal features as core PCs and 24.2% as non-core PCs. Taken together, these findings indicate that attention to rehearsal features does underlie retrieval from memory, as predicted by PC theory, but that spontaneous thoughts while performing can also play an important role, as suggested by Ginsborg et al. (2012).

4. Finally, what proportions of spontaneous thoughts could be considered functional PCs? The proportions of spontaneous thoughts in the first performance that recurred in both the second and third performances were very small for both Dawn (3.2%) and myself (5.8%). By contrast, the proportions of spontaneous thoughts in the first performance that recurred in the second were comparatively high (58.1% for Dawn and 82.4% for myself). Yet while 22.7% of Dawn's spontaneous thoughts in the second performance recurred in the third, I had just one spontaneous thought in the second performance that did not recur in the third.

It is perhaps not surprising that relatively few spontaneous thoughts in the first and—to a lesser extent—the second performance functioned as retrieval cues in the third, since the two performances were separated by ten months. That the proportions of spontaneous thoughts in the first performance recurred in the second performance, however, highlights what every musician knows from experience: what happens in performance is not necessarily the same as what happens in rehearsal, and new insights can inform subsequent performances.

Conclusion: Implications for performers and their teachers

The results of the experimental and longitudinal case study research on musicians' memorising strategies and recall for music in both the Western Balkans and Western Europe, outlined above, support the following recommendations in addition to the inclusion of music theory, harmony, and analysis in conservatoire and university music department curricula. Because spontaneous memorisation is to a certain extent inevitable, performers should remember that practice makes permanent (rather than perfect) and learn as accurately as possible when first preparing for performance.

Performers should undertake deliberate practice with the aim of developing content-addressable memory for the music in order to ensure accurate and secure recall when performing. They should create a mental representation or map of the work by identifying structural boundaries that enable them to divide the music into chunks or sections, learn them separately, and then recombine them. They can of course think of these sections as chapters or episodes in a narrative or an emotional journey.

It is important to practise and memorise the links between them, as performers are more likely both to experience and to recover from a memory lapse between rather than within sections. Backward chaining can be useful, working section-by-section from the end of the piece to the beginning, and then reversing the process so as to head towards the double bar. While Gruson (1988) suggests that pianists should practise with left and right hands separately at first, evidence from my research indicates that expert singers should memorise lyrics and melodies simultaneously (Ginsborg, 2002; Ginsborg & Sloboda, 2007).

Next, performers should make the basic decisions (Chaffin et al., 2002) that vary from instrument to instrument. These may concern breathing for singers, wind, and brass players; fingering and pedalling for pianists; bowing for string players. Because such decisions are assimilated and automatised during the course of practice and rehearsal, they can be provisional at first but should be fixed as soon as possible.

Auditory, visual, and kinaesthetic memorising strategies should be used as appropriate to both the music and the individual musician. Auditory strategies include listening to recordings of the work (or the accompaniment if available) and imagining or playing along with them. All performers should develop their audiation skills so as to be able to undertake mental practice. Visual strategies include reinforcing mental representations by annotating scores in pencil or with coloured pens. Repetitive practice strengthens procedural memory and can be regarded as a kinaesthetic strategy best deployed once initial decisions shaping the conception of the work and its performance have been made. That said, these initial decisions may be rejected, and new decisions made, as performers develop their own interpretation of the work, in the course of maintenance practice or overlearning once the music has been learned and memorised, during mental practice, and when they are not thinking consciously about the music. It is worth noting these new decisions and their locations in the score, as they are potential performance cues that can prevent or enable recovery from memory lapses.

Finally, it is a convention, not a law, that music is performed from memory. Many well-known successful musicians prefer to play with the score. Audiences may prefer performances from memory (Williamon, 1999) but the effect is very small (Kopiez et al., 2017). If multiple strategies are used to memorise, then, if one fails, the others enable the performer to keep going. And if memory lapses do occur, the audience is unlikely to notice or care, provided the performer doesn't make it obvious from their own reaction (Waddell & Williamon, 2017). Ultimately, what matters most is the overall quality of the performance.

References

Anfossi, M. (1837). *Trattato teorico-pratico sull'arte del canto: A theoretical and practical treatise on the art of singing*. Published by the authoress. https://babel.hathitrust.org/cgi/pt?id=mdp.39015080971149&view=1up&seq=5&skin=2021

Apostolaki, A. (2013). The significance of familiar structures in music memorisation and performance. In E. King & H. M. Prior (eds), *Music and familiarity: Listening, musicology and performance* (pp. 283–238). Ashgate. https://doi.org/10.4324/9781315596600

Bernardi, N.F., Schories, A., Jabusch, H.-C., Colombo, B., & Altenmüller, E. (2013). Mental practice in music memorization: An ecological-empirical study. *Music Perception: An Interdisciplinary Journal, 30*(3), 275–290. https://doi.org/10.1525/mp.2012.30.3.275

Bharucha, J.J. (1994). Tonality and expectation. In R. Aiello & J.A. Sloboda (eds), *Musical perceptions* (pp. 213–239). Oxford University Press.

Brée, M. (1997). *The Leschetizky method: A guide to fine and correct piano playing*. Dover Publications. (Original work published 1913)

Chaffin, R., Demos, A.P., & Logan, T. (2016). Performing from memory. In S. Hallam, I. Cross, & M. Thaut (eds), *The Oxford handbook of music psychology* (2nd ed., pp. 559–571). Oxford University Press. https://doi.org/10.1093/oxfordhb/9780198722946.001.0001

Chaffin, R., Ginsborg, J., Dixon, J., & Demos, A. P. (2023). Recovery from memory failure when recalling a memorized performance: The role of musical structure and performance cues. *Musicae Scientiae, 27*(1), 94–116. https://doi.org/10.1177/10298649211025491

Chaffin, R., Imreh, G., & Crawford, M. (2002). *Practicing perfection: Memory and piano performance*. Lawrence Erlbaum.

Curtis, H.H. (1914). *Voice building and tone placing, showing a new method of relieving injured vocal cords by tone exercises* (3rd ed.). D. Appleton and Co. (Original work published 1896)

Czerny, C. (1839). *Letters to a young lady on the art of playing the pianoforte from the earliest rudiments to the highest state of cultivation: Written as an appendix to every school for that instrument*. R. Cocks and Company.

Davidson-Kelly, K., Moran, N., & Overy, K. (2012). Learning and memorisation amongst advanced piano students: A questionnaire study. In E. Cambouropoulos, C. Tsougras, P. Mavromatis, & K. Pastiadis (eds), *Proceedings of the 12th International Conference on Music Perception and Cognition and the 8th Triennial Conference of the European Society for the Cognitive Sciences of Music* (pp. 248–249). Thessaloniki, Greece, 23–28 July. https://www.academia.edu/67857257/Learning_and_memorisation_amongst_advanced_piano_students_a_questionnaire_survey

Davies, J.B. (1978). *The psychology of music.* Stanford University Press.

Ericsson, K. A. (2013). Training history, deliberate practice and elite sports performance: An analysis in response to Tucker and Collins review—What makes champions? *British Journal of Sports Medicine, 47*(9), 533–535. https://doi.org/10.1136/bjsports-2012-091767

Fleming, N.D. (n.d.) *VARK: A guide to learning styles.* https://vark-learn.com/

Fonte, V. (2020). *Reconsidering memorisation in the context of non-tonal piano music* [Unpublished doctoral dissertation]. Royal College of Music, London.

Gerling, C.C., & Dos Santos, R.A.T. (2017). How do undergraduate piano students memorize their repertoires? *International Journal of Music Education, 35*(1), 60–78. https://doi.org/10.1177/0255761415619427

Gieseking, W., & Leimer, K. (1972). *Piano technique.* Dover Publications. (Original work published 1932).

Ginsborg, J. (2002). Classical singers learning and memorising a new song: An observational study. *Psychology of Music, 30*(1), 58–101. https://doi.org/10.1177/0305735602301007

Ginsborg, J. (2009). Beating time: The role of kinaesthetic learning in the development of mental representations for music. In A. Mornell (ed.), *Art in motion: Musical and athletic motor learning and performance* (pp. 121–142). Peter Lang.

Ginsborg, J., & Bennett, D. (2021). Developing familiarity in a new duo. Rehearsal talk and performance cues. *Frontiers in Psychology, 12*, Article 590987. https://doi.org/10.3389/fpsyg.2021.590987

Ginsborg, J., & Bennett, D. (2022). Developing familiarity: Rehearsal talk in a newly formed duo. In R. Timmers, F. Bailes, & H. Daffern (eds), *Together in music: Coordination, expression, participation* (pp. 89–95). Oxford University Press. https://doi.org/10.1093/oso/9780198860761.001.0001

Ginsborg, J., & Chaffin, R. (2011a). Preparation and spontaneity in performance: A singer's thoughts while singing Schoenberg. *Psychomusicology: Music, Mind & Brain, 21*(1–2), 137–158. https://doi.org/10.1037/h0094009

Ginsborg, J., & Chaffin, R. (2011b). Performance cues in singing: Evidence from practice and recall. In I. Deliège & J. W. Davidson (eds), *Music and the mind: Essays in honour of John Sloboda* (pp. 339–360). Oxford University Press. https://doi.org/10.1093/acprof:osbol/9780199581566.001.0001

Ginsborg, J., Chaffin, R., & Demos, A.P. (2012). Different roles for prepared and spontaneous thoughts: A practice-based study of musical performance from memory. *Journal of Interdisciplinary Music Studies, 6*(2), 201–231. https://repository.rncm.ac.uk/111/

Ginsborg, J., Chaffin, R., & Nicholson, G. (2006a). Shared performance cues in singing and conducting: A content analysis of talk during practice. *Psychology of Music, 34*(2), 167–194. https://doi.org/10.1177/0305735606061851

Ginsborg, J., Chaffin, R., & Nicholson, G. (2006b). Shared performance cues: Predictors of expert individual practice and ensemble rehearsal. In M. Baroni, A. R. Addessi, R. Caterina, & M. Costa (eds), *Proceedings of the 9th International Conference on Music Perception and Cognition* (pp. 913–919). Bologna, Italy.

Ginsborg, J., & King, E.C. (2012). Rehearsal talk: Familiarity and expertise in singer-pianist duos. *Musicae Scientiae, 16*(2), 148–167. https://doi.org/10.1177/1029864911435733

Ginsborg, J., & Sloboda, J.A. (2007). Singers' recall for the words and melody of a new, unaccompanied song. *Psychology of Music, 35*(3), 421–440. https://doi.org/10.1177/0305735607072654

Gorb, A. (2016, January 21). *Raising the Dead* [Audio recording]. BBC Radio 4. https://www.bbc.co.uk/programmes/b06wg9gt

Gordon, E. (1976). *Tonal and rhythm patterns: An objective analysis.* SUNY Press.

Gruson, L.M. (1988). Rehearsal skill and musical competence: Does practice make perfect? In J. Sloboda (ed.), *Generative processes in music: The psychology of performance, improvisation, and composition* (pp. 91–112). Oxford University Press.

Highben, Z., & Palmer, C. (2004). Effects of auditory and motor mental practice in memorized piano performance. *Bulletin of the Council for Research in Music Education, 159,* 58–65. https://www.researchgate.net/publication/287869623_Effects_of_Auditory_and_Motor_Mental_Practice_in_Memorized_Piano_Performance

Hughes, E. (1915). Musical memory in piano playing and piano study. *Musical Quarterly, 1*(4), 592–603. https://archive.org/details/jstor-738068/page/n3/mode/2up

Hummel, J.N. (1828). *A complete theoretical and practical course of instruction on the art of playing the piano forte.* T. Boosey.

Huron, D.B. (2006). *Sweet anticipation: Music and the psychology of expectation.* MIT Press. https://doi.org/10.7551/mitpress/6575.001.0001

King, E.C., & Ginsborg, J. (2011). Gestures and glances: Interactions in ensemble performance. In A. Gritten & E.C. King (eds), *New perspectives on music and gesture* (pp. 177–201). Ashgate Publishing. https://doi.org/10.4324/9781315598048

Kopiez, R., Wolf, A., & Platz, F. (2017). Small influence of performing from memory on audience evaluation. *Empirical Musicology Review, 12*(1–2), 2–14. https://doi.org/10.18061/emr.v12i1-2.5553

LdPride. (n.d.) *Learning Styles Test*. https://www.ldpride.net/test/learning-style-test.html

Lisboa, T., Chaffin, R., & Demos, A.P. (2015). Recording thoughts while memorizing music: A case study. *Frontiers in Psychology, 5*, Article 1561. https://doi.org/10.3389/fpsyg.2014.01561

Loimusalo, N.J., & Huovinen, E. (2018). Memorizing silently to perform tonal and nontonal notated music: A mixed-methods study with pianists. *Psychomusicology: Music, Mind, and Brain, 28*(4), 222–239. https://doi.org/10.1037/pmu0000227

Margulis, E.H. (2005). A model of melodic expectation. *Music Perception: An Interdisciplinary Journal, 22*(4), 663–714. https://doi.org/10.1525/MP.2005.22.4.663

May, F. (1912). *The girlhood of Clara Schumann: Clara Wieck and her time*. Edward Arnold.

Meyer, L.B. (1956). *Emotion and meaning in music*. University of Chicago Press.

Mielke, S., & Comeau, G. (2019). Developing a literature-based glossary and taxonomy for the study of mental practice in music performance. *Musicae Scientiae, 23*(2), 196–211. https://doi.org/10.1177/1029864917715062

Mishra, J. (2007). Correlating musical memorization styles and perceptual learning modalities. *Visions of Research in Music Education, 9*, Article 4. https://opencommons.uconn.edu/vrme/vol9/iss1/4

Mishra, J. (2010). A century of memorization pedagogy. *Journal of Historical Research in Music Education, 32*(1), 3–18. https://doi.org/10.1177/153660061003200102

Mozart, L. (1756). *Versuch einer gründlichen Violinschule* [Treatise on the fundamental principles of violin-playing]. Johann Jakob Lotter.

Narmour, E. (1992). *The analysis and cognition of melodic complexity: The Implication-Realization model*. University of Chicago Press.

Novellistik (anonymous reviewer) (1822). Bernhard Romberg in Wien. *Allgemeine musikalische Zeitung mit besonderer Rücksicht auf den österreichischen Kaiserstaat, 6*(4), 25–26.

Nuki, M. (1984). Memorization of piano music. *Psychologia: An International Journal of Psychology in the Orient, 27*(3), 157–163. https://psycnet.apa.org/record/1985-27176-001

Odendaal, A. (2013). *Perceptual learning style as an influence on the practising of instrument students in higher music education* [Unpublished doctoral dissertation]. Sibelius Academy, Helsinki. https://taju.uniarts.fi/handle/10024/6532

Odendaal, A. (2016). (Mis)matching perceptual learning styles and practicing behavior in tertiary level Western Classical instrumentalists. *Psychology of Music, 44*(3), 353–368. https://doi.org/10.1177/0305735614567933

Plunket Greene, H. (1912). *Interpretation in Song*. Macmillan: Stainer and Bell.

Rosenthal, R.K. (1984). The relative effects of guided model, model only, guide only, and practice only treatments on the accuracy of advanced instrumentalists' musical performance. *Journal of Research in Music Education, 32*(4), 265–273. https://doi.org/10.2307/3344924

Rosenthal, R.K., Wilson, M., Evans, M., & Greenwalt, L. (1988). Effects of different practice conditions on advanced instrumentalists' performance accuracy. *Journal of Research in Music Education, 36*(4), 250–257. https://doi.org/10.2307/3344877

Rubin-Rabson, G. (1937). The influence of analytical pre-study in memorising piano music. *Archives of Psychology, 31*, 1–53.

Rubin-Rabson, G. (1940a). Studies in the psychology of memorizing piano music. II. A comparison of massed and distributed practice. *Journal of Educational Psychology, 31*, 270–84. https://psycnet.apa.org/record/1940-04947-001

Rubin-Rabson, G. (1940b). Studies in the psychology of memorizing piano music. III. A comparison of the whole and the part approach. *Journal of Educational Psychology, 31*, 460–76.

Rubin-Rabson, G. (1941a). Studies in the psychology of memorizing piano music. IV. The effect of incentive. *Journal of Educational Psychology, 32*(1), 45–54. https://doi.org/10.1037/h0061124

Rubin-Rabson, G. (1941b). Studies in the psychology of memorizing piano music. V: A comparison of pre-study periods of varied length. *Journal of Educational Psychology, 32*(2), 101–112. https://doi.org/10.1037/h0054496

Rubin-Rabson, G. (1941c). Studies in the psychology of memorizing piano music. VI A comparison of two forms of mental rehearsal and keyboard overlearning. *Journal of Educational Psychology, 32*(8), 593–602. https://doi.org/10.1037/H0058481

Rubin-Rabson, G. (1941d). Studies in the psychology of memorizing piano music. VII. A comparison of three degrees of overlearning. *Journal of Educational Psychology, 32*(9), 688–696. https://doi.org/10.1037/H0054174

Sacks, O. (2007). *Musicophilia: Tales of music and the brain*. Alfred A. Knopf.

Salimpoor, V.N., Zald, D.H., Zatorre, R.J., Dagher, A., & McIntosh, A.R. (2015). Predictions and the brain: How musical sounds become rewarding. *Trends in Cognitive Sciences, 19*(2), 86–91. https://doi.org/10.1016/j.tics.2014.12.001

Shinn, F.G. (1898). The memorizing of piano music for performance. *Proceedings of the Musical Association, 25*, 1–25. https://doi.org/10.1093/jrma/25.1.1

Swassing, R.H., & Barbe, W.B. (1979). *The Swassing-Barbe Modality Index: Directions for administration and scoring.* Zaner-Bloser.

Taylor, D.C. (1914). *Self-Help for singers; A manual for self-instruction in voice culture based on the old Italian method.* H. W. Gray Co.

Timperman, E., & Miksza, P. (2019). Verbalization and musical memory in string players. *Musicae Scientiae, 23*(2), 212–230. https://doi.org/10.1177/1029864917727332

Trainor, L.J., & Zatorre, R.J. (2016). The neurobiology of musical expectations from perception to emotion. In S. Hallam, I. Cross, & M. Thaut (eds), *The Oxford handbook of music psychology* (2nd ed., pp. 285–306). Oxford University Press. https://doi.org/10.1093/oxfordhb/9780198722946.001.0001

Waddell, G., & Williamon, A. (2017). Eye of the beholder: Stage entrance behavior and facial expression affect continuous quality ratings in music performance. *Frontiers in Psychology, 8*, Article 513. https://doi.org/10.3389/fpsyg.2017.00513

Williamon, A. (1999). The value of performing from memory. *Psychology of Music, 27*(1), 84–95. https://doi.org/10.1177/0305735699271008

Žauhar, V., & Bajšanski, I. (2012). Uloga formalne strukture i izvedbene zahtjevnosti glazbenoga djela kod upamćivanja notnoga teksta: studija slučaja [The role of formal structure and technical complexity of a piece of music in memorizing music score: A case study]. *Psihologijske teme, 21*(2), 225–247. https://hrcak.srce.hr/89528

Žauhar, V., Matić, A., Dražul, A., & Bajšanski, I. (2020). Memorizing the contemporary piano piece of music: The effects of the formal structure, pianist's segmentation, and technical difficulties. In B. Bogunović & S. Nikolić (eds) (2020). *Proceedings of PAM-IE Belgrade 2019.* Faculty of Music, University of Arts in Belgrade. https://www.fmu.bg.ac.rs/wp-content/uploads/2020/12/psychology-and-music-08_zauhar-et-al.pdf

PART IV

PSYCHOLOGY OF MUSICIANS—FROM MOTIVATION AND PERSONALITY TO ADDRESSING CHALLENGES AND ANXIETY

12. Motivation and Personality as Factors of Musical Accomplishments: A Developmental and Cultural Perspective

Blanka Bogunović

Introduction

Musical and cognitive capacities, motivation, and personality represent the core ingredients of long-term musical development encompassing musical, personal, and professional accomplishments. But 'after a certain point, ability plays a less important role than personality and motivational factors' (Winner, 1996, p. 283), which suggests the importance of these psychological factors for long-term musical development towards excellence. Motivation is of great interest to researchers and educators because 'understanding motivation is vital for addressing questions of how and why people take up learning a musical instrument, how they persist through the challenges of learning and practice, and how they become successful or why they quit' (Evans, 2015). Numerous studies have addressed motivation issues, mainly in music education research (e.g., O'Neill & McPherson, 2002), since its impact can be critical for pursuing proactive musical involvement or dropping out.

The extensive research into motivation contrasts with the far fewer studies investigating the relationship between personality and musical accomplishments, especially at a younger age. Many questions are still to be answered. Nevertheless, it has been confirmed that personal attributes firmly sustain musical development and motivation and that their specific profile contributes to the level of performance and educational achievements (Kemp, 1996). Research into musicians' personality mostly refers to the cutting-edge study of Kemp (1996) based on Cattell's Personality Factor Model (16 PF Model; Cattel et al., 1970). In the 1990s, the new personality research paradigm, the Five-Factor Model (FFM; Costa & McCrae, 1995), gradually took over in music-related research too (e.g., Corrigall et al., 2013; Corrigall & Schellenberg, 2015).

The international literature review shows that investigation into the degree and quality of the contributions of motivation and personality to music achievements is a challenge that needs to be responded to, since it is influenced by a multifactor matrix where internal and external settings play a role. This chapter intends to fill this gap and provide new insights into the individual and joint contributions of motivation and personality to learning and performance achievements in subsequent stages of development, which is rare in the international literature.

Aims

The chapter opens with questions about the role of motivation and personality in achieving musical excellence. At the beginning of the main discussion, I shall present a condensed review of the pertinent international research and then the series of research projects from Serbia which I either led or co-authored. Originally, they were not published in English and hence were not accessible to the broader international public. The series of studies addresses a developmental perspective of the individual and the joint impact of motivation and personality on music accomplishments from early school up to the start of a young adult professional career, rather than the final-outcome perspective. This approach will enable the following up of the specific profile of psychological attributes at each of the three stages of specialist education for the musically gifted that has existed in the Western Balkans region (WB) for around 70 years (see Chapter 1 in this volume). The intention is to make conclusions about the relevance and differential contributions of motivational features and personality traits to achievements, and to discover possible developmental changes. Attention will be given to the nexus of psychological and environmental factors where they strongly impact musical outputs at each developmental stage. The studies from the WB will be highlighted to evaluate cultural perspectives and variations.

Main discussion

Motivation as a factor of musical competence

Intrinsic motivation, as a prevailing driver of musical activities, is associated with advanced performance levels when a high level of skill and challenge are matched (Csikszentmihalyi, 1990). Extrinsic forms of motivation, sometimes enhanced by teaching in a controlling and prescriptive way or by damaging levels of competitiveness, are likely to be ineffective (Evans, 2015). In contrast, a social environment that fulfils basic psychological needs enables experiences that are closely associated with health and well-being (Evans, 2015). Thus, external motivation could be beneficial in reinforcing activities that can enhance the process of advancing competencies. Lack of, or weak motivation is one of the critical factors associated with (under)achievements and dropouts (e.g., Costa-Giomi, 2004), and can be accompanied by feelings of low competence, relatedness, and autonomy, as well (e.g., Evans et al., 2013).

Evans and McPherson (2015) carried out a 10-year longitudinal study which suggested that learners (aged 7–9) whose personal identity included a long-term perspective of themselves as musicians were better positioned to succeed and sustain their instrumental learning. The authors stated that long-term practice and self-regulation strategies were essential for forming a musical identity, as one of the precursors of higher achievements. McPherson and McCormick (2000) showed that students (children and adolescents) attributed success to effort rather than ability, although many also attributed examination results to nervousness or luck. The most important predictor of success was the student's self-efficacy.

McCormick and McPherson (2007) used an Expectancy-value cognitive approach and found that beliefs that students hold (aged 9–19) about their musical capabilities are potent predictors of their achievement in music performance examinations. Furthermore, when the achievement criteria were graded instrumental music examinations (Hallam et al., 2021), students aged 6–19, the impact of expertise level, enjoyment of performing, and self-belief in musical ability, among others, were confirmed. Those who failed were most likely to have adopted ineffective practice strategies and were less likely to enjoy performing, playing, having lessons, or practising. Personal beliefs and attitudes were examined in a qualitative study with secondary school students from different academic backgrounds in Hong Kong, with high marks and outstanding achievement in music extracurricular activities as criteria for success (Leung & McPherson, 2011). Those who pursued music rated highly aesthetic feelings, self-recognition, sense of achievement, music preference, and enjoyment. Relevant environmental factors related to pursuing music were: parental support, teacher and school influence, peer support, or being inspired by the success of others.

With Self-Determination Theory (SDT) (Ryan & Deci, 2018) as a background, based on an international sample of adult musicians, it was shown that internalised regulation correlated more strongly with music-related variables than extrinsic forms (MacIntyre et al., 2018). Intrinsic motives, developed by musicians and their teachers, help to create a desire to learn, foster the intensity of effort, and increase perceptions of competence, which contribute to a motivational cycle for music learning and performance. Recently, flow emergence was investigated in a qualitative study with selected music students at music higher education institutions (MHEIs) and with professionals (Philippe et al., 2021). It was found that intrinsic motivation, attentional focus, and self-confidence were the most important factors. There are also studies showing how beneficial flow can be in promoting personal growth and achieving excellence (see Chapter 15 in this volume).

Several cross-cultural studies have provided insight into environmental factors influencing motivation. One of these was conducted in eight countries (Brazil, China, Finland, Hong Kong, Israel, Korea, Mexico, USA) across three school grade levels (elementary to secondary school), based on the Expectancy-value theory (McPherson & O'Neill, 2010). Findings suggested that once students have experienced learning to play an instrument or singing, they become more motivated towards other school subjects. Generally, students' competence beliefs and values for music declined, except in Brazil, where they rose with age, while being lowest in Hong Kong, Israel, Mexico, and the USA. In addition, a comparison of the achievement goals of learners from individualistic and collectivistic cultures (USA and Singapore), with measures based on the 2×2 achievement goal orientation constructs (mastery approach, mastery avoid, performance approach, and performance avoid), found no significant differences in achievement goals as a function of culture (Miksza et al., 2016).

A study at a graduate music school in Mexico presented an example of the strong socio-cultural influence and educational and economic limitations on competence outcomes at MHEI (González-Moreno, 2011). It examined students' motivation—values and competence beliefs, addressing the high dropout rate. The results showed gender differences in values—female students placed a higher value on graduate school, while male students had higher expectations of success. At the same time, 95% of male participants stopped schooling because they placed less value on programme continuation. Factors affecting motivation negatively in the context of MHEI in Mexico were confirmed, including the economic impact on education, time constraints, insufficient support and communication, coupled with high expectations from advisers/ mentors and teachers. In another study, a cross-cultural comparison was conducted on undergraduate and graduate music major students from schools of music in the USA and Australia (Miksza et al., 2021). Here, no differences were found in these two cultural settings addressed to investigate competitiveness, perfectionism, and teachers' control. Results revealed that autonomous motivation orientations were stronger for those who perceived their conservatory-style environment to be more competitive and weaker for those who experienced more perfectionism and teacher control. The results have good potential for practical implications for MHEI, since students who reported greater perceptions of teacher control and expressed higher perfectionism tended to report weaker career intentions. This study is one of the few at the tertiary level of music education that systematically explored the effects of the educational style of music teachers on student motivational outcomes, and it has substantial practical implications. A new book has recently been published that argues for the power of more positive approaches to teaching (Meissner et al., 2022).

Personality as a factor of musical achievements

As stated earlier, considerably less research exists on the contribution of personality to the attainment of musical achievements and expertise. Several studies have documented personality differences typical for musicians (e.g., Bandi et al., 2023; Kemp, 1996), for diverse instrumental groups (see Chapter 14 in this volume) and genres (e.g., Benedek et al., 2014), or relatedness to musical preferences (see Chapter 6 in this volume). But lately, more studies have explored the contribution of personality traits to musical outcomes at the beginning of music tuition. Corrigall et al. (2013) aimed to examine whether personality measured by the Five-Factor Model (FFM) of personality (Extraversion, Agreeableness, Conscientiousness, Neuroticism, Openness), together with cognitive abilities, can predict the duration of musical training in a Canadian sample of students (aged 10–12). It has been revealed that high-functioning children are more likely than other children to take music lessons. The subsequent findings confirmed that personality was associated with level of musical involvement and that Openness to experience was the personality dimension with the best predictive power for pursuing music, even better than Conscientiousness (Corrigall & Schellenberg, 2015). Interestingly enough, the study also showed that parents' Openness to experience could predict children's duration of training (aged 7–9). According to the authors, Agreeableness appeared to be associated with the duration of formal music training, probably because children tend to agree with a parental decision, or they complied with the teacher's requests and therefore influence.

Diversely, the results of another study on a sample of secondary school students from Germany and the United Kingdom specified Conscientiousness and Agreeableness as the best predictors of overall performance and achievement in music development (Lin et al., 2022). This study demonstrated that personality traits contributed to the development of the self-theories related to musical engagement that affect the growth of general achievement in music. Also, Müllensiefen et al. (2015) found that self-theories of intelligence and musicality were connected to the academic achievement of secondary school students (UK) through Conscientiousness.

While using Cattell's personality model in his systematic research into musicians' personality, Kemp (1996) reported on personality traits of selected young musicians at the conservatoire, such as higher Ego strength, Conscientiousness, Adventurousness, Self-assurance, high Self-sentiment, and low Tension. Kemp stated that higher anxiety levels emerge in younger, particularly talented musicians attending specialist (boarding) music schools (Kemp, 1996). One of the few studies dealing with motivation and personality features, in a sample of adults from Sweden (Butković et al., 2015), found that music-specific flow propensity was the best predictor of time spent practising when Openness to experience, motivation, and intelligence were taken into account. In the study with adult musicians in the UK, musical sophistication was measured using self-reporting and behavioural performance tests of melodic memory and rhythm perception as achievement criteria (Greenberg et al., 2016). Openness to aesthetics was the strongest trait predictor for each of the sophistication subscales, even for performance on the musical ability tasks. In a study with professional artists, including musicians, Openness predicted creative achievement in the arts and Intellect predicted creative achievement in the sciences. Another study finds that jazz musicians score significantly higher on Openness to experience and complete a higher number of creative musical achievements (Benedek et al., 2014). Conscientiousness was also identified as a characteristic of professional musicians who had received formal music education (Rose et al., 2019). What makes comparisons possible is that many recent research studies used the Five-Factor Model as a framework for research on different age groups.

The Western Balkans regional research: Developmental perspective and comparison with international research

Relevant research studies in Croatia, North Macedonia, and Slovenia generally deal with music in mainstream education schools or music education for the gifted, focusing on motivation and personality but not on their relationship to musical achievements. Hence, in Slovenia, a few studies related to the educational setting were realised that confirmed the positive motivational impact of competition participation and its role in the short- and long-term educational and personal development goals (Rotar Pance, 2021). Another study established music as a successful tool for enhancing learning motivation among elementary school students, primarily through singing or creating music (Habe & Delin, 2010). Croatian authors established individual differences regarding instrumental groups (see Chapter 14 in this volume), as well as the reality of stereotypes that young musicians have about different instrumental groups (Butković & Modrušan, 2021), the most pronounced being Openness, Agreeableness, and propensity to alcohol consumption. In North Macedonia, some interesting results were found concerning instrumental groups (e.g., Mihajlovski, 2013). For example, piano and string players were characterised as having Originality, Anxiety, Self-discipline, Emotional instability, and higher Intelligence; string players showed Introversion; and the brass players emerged showing Extraversion, Conventionality, Emotional stability and Adjustment.

In Serbia, several research projects over two decades were carried out in a quasi-longitudinal manner, following the developmental line of the three-stage specialist music education system for gifted children (14 years of schooling) that exists mainly in Eastern Europe (Nogaj & Bogunović, 2015) and the Western Balkans countries. The system (elementary, secondary school, MHEI) enrols musically talented children who are selected by entrance examinations at each stage based on their level of musical abilities, quality of performance, and/or selected musical competencies. The system stems from the post-war idea of socialism, giving everyone educational opportunities and pledging social equality. Since the 1980s, a psychological service has been included in every bigger music school, which enabled the burst of music psychology research related primarily to the musically talented, their development and (professional) education. The two comprehensive research projects carried out in Serbia aimed to explore the psychological and environmental determinants of musical achievements at elementary and secondary specialist music schools. At the MHEI stage, there are still no results from studies with a similar research design. Therefore, individual studies will be presented concerning personality and motivational factors, while research data about teachers' roles and impact on this educational level are so far lacking. Results will be compared to the international and regional research findings.

Early years of specialist music education

The five-year longitudinal study was conducted in five elementary music schools in Serbia and resulted in several publications (e.g., Bogunović, 2010, 2021; Bogunović et al., 2006; Radoš et al., 2003). Participants were musically gifted students who were identified as such at the entrance examination, when psychological tests were applied (musical abilities, general intelligence) and interest in music and performance in hearing and rhythm tasks were examined. The sample ($N = 993$) consisted of students aged 6–12, who played different instruments; their parents[1] ($N = 512$); and their instrumental teachers ($N = 165$). The research design included psychological factors (musical and cognitive abilities, motivation, personality, psychomotor skills) and environmental factors (family support and engagement and personal, professional, and educational features of instrumental teachers) as predictors of musical achievements, sorted into two groups: academic music achievements (instrumental and *solfège* final examination marks) and performance (Public performance, four types, and Competition—six levels of competition including three award levels), which were monitored annually from the first to the fifth year. The results strongly pronounced that early intrinsic motivation, the degree and quality of family encouragement and support, and then musical abilities, were pivotal determinants of the regular music courses marks and performance achievements (canonical variance explained was 48%). The statistical significance of musical abilities here being in third place is that while they are the *conditio sine qua non* for entering into the selective music education system, for their realisation at the early beginnings of tuition, motivation and home environment play a crucial role (Radoš et al., 2003).

A closer look at the integrative pattern of salient results (Figure 12.1) gives an insight into the intertwined relations of psychological and environmental factors on performance achievements and dropouts (Bogunović, 2010). The impact of early motivational indicators on practice habits (11% variance explained) and their common contribution to overall performance achievements (16% variance explained) are

---

[1] Families were only investigated if they had two parents of different genders in order to keep the sample unified.

presented as a result of the sequence of canonical analyses. Several significant correlations were confirmed between motivational indicators and personality traits. Investigation into the degree and pattern of environmental influence on motivation showed that parental support in early childhood primarily affects motivation (16% variance explained) and then practice habits (9% variance explained). Teachers' attributes contribute to the practice habits (14%) but not motivation, which raises questions for future investigations. Further on, a discussion of each segment of results will follow.

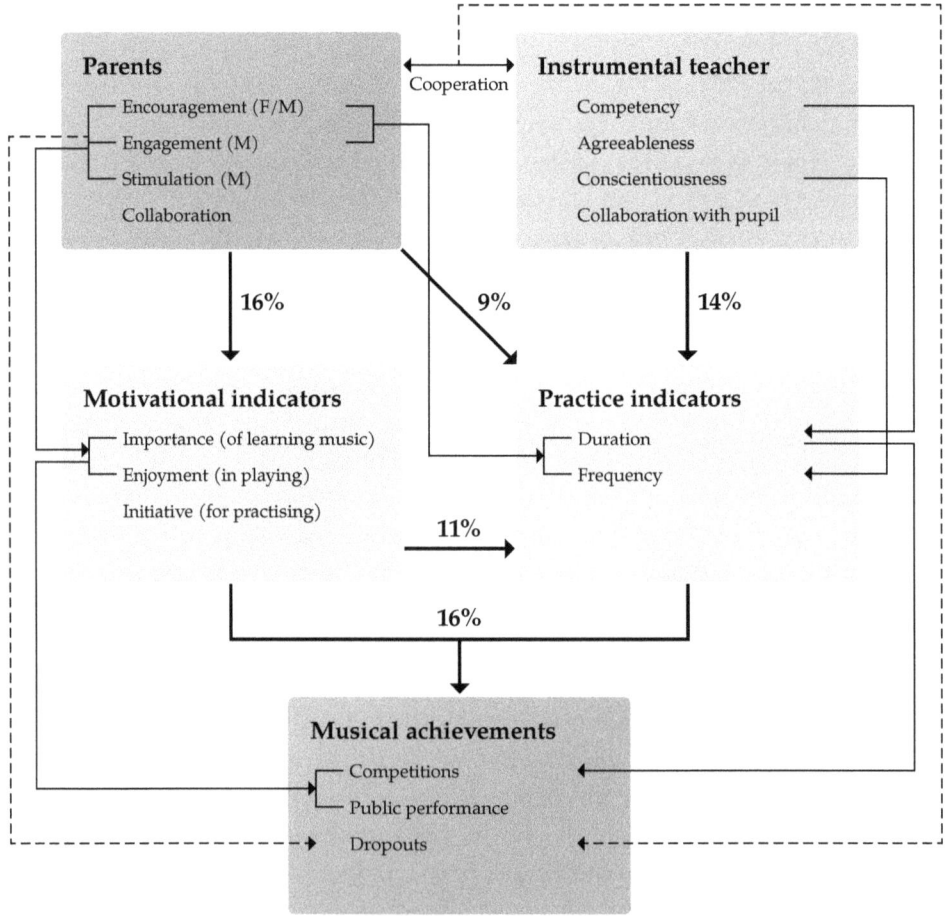

Note. Thick line: Percentage of canonical explained variance; Thin line: Significant positive correlation; Dotted line: Significant negative correlation; F: Father; M: Mother.

Fig. 12.1 Integrative pattern of music achievements factors in early specialist music education. Figure translated and adapted from Bogunović (2010, p. 290)

Initial motivational indicators (Importance, Enjoyment, Initiative) were significantly correlated with personality attributes (assessed by parents), which seem to play a role in making motivation and practice 'work' (Bogunović, 2010). Hence, these personality attributes were connected with responsible and persevering fulfilment of tasks (Disciplined, Practical, Enterprising, Efficient). The second group of attributes ensure a stable emotional basis for achieving goals (Independent, Self-assured, Emotionally stable). Moreover, the same personality traits (assessed by instrumental teachers) were significantly correlated with Public performance and Competition. We should note that other researchers also found that Conscientiousness at early school age is related to the pursuit of music learning and diligence (Corrigall & Schellenberg, 2015).

Regarding environmental factors, it was shown that a crucial role in establishing initial intrinsic motivation was played by the adequate, stimulating, encouraging, and supportive family environment before and during instrumental tuition (Bogunović et al., 2006). Instrumental teachers primarily contributed to the acquisition of practising habits (frequency and duration). More Competent teachers have students who practise for longer and have higher achievements in Competitions (Bogunović, 2010). Parents, as 'teachers at home', reinforce positive practice habits by expressing expectations that shape children's musical identities, as also pointed out by Lamont (2017). The results of the study, which investigated implicit strategies parents use to entice their children to practice, confirm these claims (Bogunović, 2021). Strategies were mainly directed towards developing a child's intrinsic strengths (65%), proactive motivational behaviour towards excellence and persistence, and personal enhancement with autonomy as the final implicit goal, namely 'mastery orientation'. It could be said that the first traces of the psychological need for autonomy were set towards introjection, as claimed by SDT theory (Evans, 2015). The other, less represented, group of strategies (33%) was based on the external 'power' supposed to 'make the child' practice. Still, further research is required into the benefits of the 'balanced approach' between internally and externally based parental strategies.

It was shown that more Competent teachers have higher scores on Agreeableness, Extraversion, and Conscientiousness (NEO-PR; Costa & McCrae, 1995), and have more successful students (Bogunović, 2010).

Dedicated, communicative, and responsible instrumental teachers, highly involved parents, and the cooperative climate they make together were prerequisites for the students' performance achievements (Figure 12.1). The specific pedagogical techniques these teachers used to acquire results will be addressed in future research since it would have great practical implications for music education. It is worth mentioning that only 6% of students reach exceptionally high (expert) results at Competitions and 17% have high efficiency in Public performances, and, indeed, the teachers influence this differentiation too.

Dropouts at the beginning of instrumental learning were related to a lack of parental support and encouragement as well as to their weak cooperation with an instrumental teacher. It indicates that relationships in a 'triad' (student-parents-teacher) may or may not create the best opportunities for music development (see also Creech, 2009). Dropouts were frequent in the early stages of music education, 25% in the first two years when the influential impact of 'important others' is prevalent and the intrinsic motivation and autonomy of the child are not yet established.

These conclusions are filling the gap in the results of international studies on the same age level, especially concerning early intrinsic motivation and the role of parents (e.g., Corrigall & Schellenberg, 2015; Leung & McPherson, 2011; McCormick & McPherson, 2007). The data about teachers' personal and professional attributes (Bogunović, 2003) that impact students' performance outcomes increase the knowledge about favourable features of successful teachers and have practical implications for the music education practice. The uncovering of typical difficulties in the collaboration between teachers and parents (Bogunović, 2010) is another contribution made by the project. The value of the project lies in its longitudinal research design, numerous predictors and systematic criteria variables, where individual and intertwined contributions to music accomplishments were involved, which have a positive effect on the validity and reliability of results.

Specialist music education at the adolescent age

The cross-sectional research project that used a similar variables pattern was carried out at the adolescent age ($N = 137$), but without the involvement of teachers' variables in the research design (Bogunović,

2010). After being selected, young musicians who have chosen musicianship as their profession enter the second developmental phase (Subotnik & Jarvin, 2005), when the task is to grow from competencies to musical expertise. Psychological attributes investigated in the study were musical abilities measured by the Wing Music Intelligence Test, standardised for the Serbian population (Radoš, 2010), intrinsic motivation, personality traits, value orientations and intelligence, and family characteristics. Students' achievements were represented by the academic music and general subjects' average achievements and the Index of musical success (joint academic and performance achievements in the previous six years, five types, frequency and awards).

The comprehensive analysis of the musical, cognitive, motivational, and personal factors related to musical achievements, as well as the family profile, showed that high musical abilities and intelligence do not guarantee a high level of musical competencies (Figure 12.2). The multiple regression analysis singled out the motive of Curiosity (12% variance explained), then Musical ability (5% variance explained) and Sensitivity (4% variance explained, at the edge of significance), as the primary factors contributing to the Index of musical success. The same pattern of motivation, musical ability, and personality has already been detected at the beginning of instrumental education (Radoš et al., 2003). Differential contributions of intrinsic motives, namely Curiosity, out of three inner motives, were the most critical factors for the overall Index of musical success. The result firmly acknowledged the inner sources of music-motivated behaviour. The Curiosity motif, which relies on cognitive processes and creativity disposed towards exploration in music, was established as a vital source for investment in musical activities at the adolescent stage.

In addition, a set of multiple regression analyses suggested the Achievement motive, Curiosity and Aspiration level were determined in the first place by Conscientiousness (13–15% of variance), Sensitivity (3–4% variance), and value orientations towards Power and Cognition (4–6% of variance) (Bogunović, 2009). Results concerning personality were in line with those reported by other authors who used FFM as a framework. They found Aesthetic sensitivity as a property of high achievers in music (Leung & McPherson, 2011; Swaminathan & Schellenberg, 2018). Next to that, Openness to aesthetics was the strongest trait predictor (Greenberg et al., 2016) for each of the music sophistication subscales, and it predicted creative achievement in the arts (Kaufman et al., 2016) and music (Benedek et al., 2014).

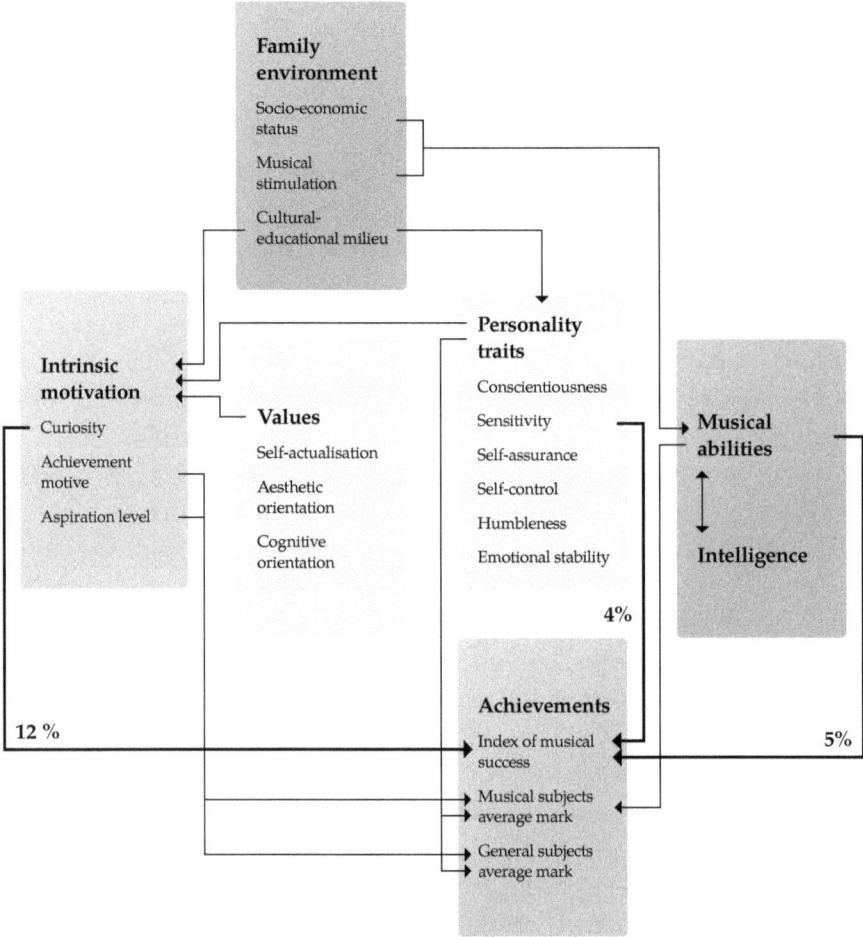

Note. Thick line: Percentage of regression analysis explained variance; Thin line: Significantly positive correlation.

Fig. 12.2 Integrative pattern of music achievements factors in the adolescent age. Figure translated and adapted from Bogunović (2010, p. 294)

The direct impact of intelligence on musical achievements was not confirmed. However, this result is not in agreement with other studies conducted in Serbian samples, in which the joint impact of intelligence and personality traits (Conscientiousness, low Neuroticism) on music performance exams was identified (Janković & Bogaerts, 2021; Pekić, 2009; Štula, 2007). There are grounds for relating these differences to the various intelligence measures applied in these studies and their relatedness to musical achievements. This aspect could be a focus for further investigations.

The results strongly supported the notion of Subotnik and Jarvin (2005) that the impact of motivation and personality traits progresses as the developmental process continues towards musical expertise. The comparison between WB studies at the two subsequent developmental stages showed the evolving profile of motivational factors responsible for high-performance achievements and their relatedness to personality traits. At the adolescent stage, Curiosity and Sensitivity grew as part of the identity profile necessary for higher artistic accomplishments. Compatible findings were established in the international study in the Canadian sample, where an Openness to experience was identified in the same age group (Corrigal & Schellenberg, 2015). Interestingly, different results in the same age group were identified in a UK and German joint sample study, in which Conscientiousness and Agreeableness were predictors of music development (Lin et al., 2022).

The indirect and pivotal effect of the environment created by adolescents' families showed its relevance for their achievements by fostering positive values and nurturing adequate personality traits, intrinsic motivation, and musical abilities (Figure 12.2). These results confirmed the claims of Subotnik et al. (2011), that opportunity and motivation are the two central variables associated with talent development. Opportunities were first provided by families who could afford extracurricular activities, which in turn enhance musical competence (e.g., Swaminathan & Schellenberg, 2018). These further foster a rich socio-cultural milieu empowering the young musician's ability to garner, respond to, and capitalise on talent-development opportunities (Gagné, 2005). The two studies from Serbia go a step further in defining the dimensions and endeavour of the rich parental milieu that directly influences pursuing music at the beginning of instrumental tuition. In later stages, it is the introjected values, personality traits, and intrinsically motivated behaviour that showed their impact on high accomplishments in music.

Young adult age at music higher education

When enrolling in MHE institution, young musicians enter the third stage of music talent development, empowering their expertise when striving for a professional career or artistry (Subotnik & Jarvin, 2005). The pilot mixed-method study was carried out at the MHE institution in Belgrade (Bogunović, 2017), where students' mindsets (Dweck, 2006) were related to self-rated psychological, musical, and professional skills and music achievements (academic, performance accomplishments, self-efficacy). Findings showed that music students express a growth mindset (open-mindedness, thriving for a challenge, enjoying learning and personal progress) (see also O'Neill, 2011). However, it does not prevail (12–25%) while a fixed mindset (avoiding challenge, perceiving personal attributes as static) was also detected (16–72%). It was shown that students with mastery orientation and higher self-efficacy have higher Self-regulation and Cognitive and emotional control. These findings are compatible with those in other countries, where intrinsic motivation and a mastery approach (MacIntyre et al., 2018), competence beliefs and values for music (McPherson & O'Neill, 2010; Miksza et al., 2016) were also confirmed in the groups of musicians at a young and/or adult age. Therefore, the findings' comparisons proved the established music motivation as a leading personal feature crucial for attaining musical achievements.

Furthermore, it was shown that MHE students' personality dimensions and facets (FFM) play a role in increasing performance skills (Bogunović, 2018). Namely, students who expressed higher Emotional stability, Agreeableness, and Conscientiousness and, more specifically, Competence, Dutifulness, Achievement striving, Discipline, and Deliberate thinking, tended to have an Analytical approach when preparing for the sight-reading tasks, while those who manifested Dutifulness and striving for Achievement endeavoured to achieve Expertness in performing. These two skills—the Analytical approach and intention to achieve Expertness in performing—represent the most favourable self-regulated strategies in performing. These findings again imply that non-cognitive factors, such as personality traits and motivational features, have an inevitable function in the self-regulated attainment of music-related cognitive and expert skills related to instrumental performance (Bogunović, 2018).

When comparing these results with international ones, it can be confirmed that Openness to experience is generally characteristic of musicians as opposed to non-musicians (e.g., Benedek et al., 2014; Greenberg et al., 2016). Next to that, musicians in formal music training at MHE institutions for classical music performance expressed Conscientiousness (Rose et al., 2019) and Emotional stability, Agreeableness and Conscientiousness (Bogunović, 2018), which are essential for the fulfilment of highly set goals and persistent long-term engagement in music. And this pattern seems to exist from the early beginnings of learning music, as also shown in previous studies (e.g., Bogunović, 2010; Corrigall & Schellenberg, 2013). These data imply that educational and professional demands are reflected in the development of certain personality traits.

Another study at an MHE institution proved the impact of socially and professionally constructed gender roles due to long-term musical education and professional engagement, which turned out to be significant for music achievements. The research study brought together students' personality dimensions (FFM), gender identity, and music performance achievements according to the previously established matrix (Public performances, Competitions, Index of musical success as a composite measure) (Bogunović & Bodroža, 2015). The findings revealed that being a biological male and having socially constructed feminine psychological traits significantly correlated with higher results in music performance (Public performance and Competitions). This finding confirmed the previous notion of Kemp (1996) about the psychological androgyny of musicians, who explained that higher levels of musicianship, interpretation, and aesthetic expression need to encompass a broad dispersion of traits that are socially conceptualised as feminine and masculine.

Furthermore, regression analysis results pointed out that female music students with higher Neuroticism, especially Vulnerability to stress, perceive themselves as less successful in music performing, probably due to a lack of self-esteem. Similar results were reported in a US sample, where it was proven that academic self-confidence is lower in gifted girls, especially in the arts (Csikszentmihalyi et al., 1997). These findings could be interpreted as an impact of cultural stereotypes about men's and women's academic and professional success.

The research results of WB studies at an MHE institution strongly confirmed a developmental process where the motivational and personality features needed for expert music accomplishments are integrated into the personality profile of young musicians and become a part of their musical identity. A mastery approach, intrinsic motivation, self-efficacy, and competence belief are anchored. The impact of social factors changes along the developmental line, starting from the immediate family environment and ending with a complex social context where musicians develop their careers.

In the WB studies, the limitations are related to the fact that the research design is not entirely consistently applied to all three educational phases in relation to achievement factors. Furthermore, the studies presented stem from the formal music education of a selection of gifted musicians in Western classical music. At the same time, international samples encompass formal and informal music education and/or engagement, as well as pop and jazz music culture. These differences call for careful comparisons to be made. The cultural comparisons were also narrowed because different research methodologies and diverse theoretical approaches were used. Future research should have a more comprehensive, systematic, developmental, and possibly cross-cultural approach to understand the pattern of psychological, educational, social, and professional preconditions of musical competence achievements, dropouts, or underachievement. To take account of practical implications, the research should include a more in-depth investigation of the strategies and techniques that teachers and parents use in order to enhance favourable motivation and personality attributes.

Conclusion

This chapter has focused on motivational features and personality traits and their joint influence on learning and performance accomplishments through a developmental perspective covering approximately 20 years. This perspective was primarily highlighted in the WB research studies exploring the three-stage educational system of the musically talented unfolding in a socio-cultural and educational context that is not broadly known about. The context of structural and systematic education for the musically talented, which still exists as a relic of socialism, demonstrates its potential value by creating opportunities for research, early talent identification, and long-term support from teachers and music psychologists. The WB research, specifically in Serbia, fills a gap in the existing research corpus by addressing the joint role of motivation and personality for musical accomplishments through a developmental perspective which is scarce within international research.

The developmental perspective of the WB studies confirmed that musical capacities are clearly *sine qua non* at the beginning of any music education, but that the joint dynamic and intertwined impact of motivation, music abilities, personality, and values are the core factors of musical accomplishments at each stage of progress. The findings suggest that motivational and personality attributes of young musicians are the subject of changes towards refinement, complexity, and intertwining along the timeline, and they empower the musical identity of the musicians to grow. The development of features favourable to musicianship is consistent with the demands and nature of the music profession, which brings new insight into the nature–nurture discussion.

The impact of the socio-cultural context on music identity development and the professional career of young, gifted musicians was identified, and it encompasses the immediate, educational, professional, and broader social environment (socio-economic and socio-cultural). In particular, the immediate family environment and educational process, especially the approach taken by instrumental teachers, foster a certain 'profile' that enables and facilitates progress towards high achievements. The balance of nature–nurture factors seems to be harmonious, though the results of the review of WB studies imply the long-term 'nurture' process being significant beyond natural capacities. These inferences suggest the confirmation of the Vygotskian socio-cultural developmental perspective, which can be advocated by the internalisation of 'intergenerational transfer' values being addressed to music experiences (Mehr, 2014). Furthermore, the three-level system functions on the 'quantity gives quality' principle of socialist societies (see Chapter 1 in this volume). The broad accessibility to free-of-charge specialist music schools enables strict selection at each educational level, giving opportunities to those who have developed and incorporated promising psychosocial features. The practical implication of the findings could be a part of the talent identification process and the nurturing of the favourable psychological attributes throughout the educational process, since they are subject to the intertwined actions of young musicians and their environment.

The comparison with relevant international research pointed out the generally corresponding, cross-culturally stable set of primarily motivational features at the early and adolescent levels, and personality traits primarily at the MHE level and adult age. The results also imply the presence of a broadly transnational pattern, probably also related to Western music culture, which is present internationally and certainly in WB, too. The general outline of psychosocial factors related to musical accomplishments is shared across different countries, dependent only on the music domain itself. But when the broader social, cultural, and economic field is involved (Csikszentmihalyi, 2004), the developmental line starts to curve, and that happens mainly at the last educational stage, at MHE (Gonzalez-Moreno, 2011), and at the beginning of the professional career (Bogunović & Mirović, 2014). Diversity in professional development and opportunities grows when the impact of modest economic conditions and the traditional social matrix is dominant (Bogunović & Bodroža, 2015; Gonzalez-Moreno, 2011), or when music represents an integral part of cultural identity and everyday practice, as in Brazil (McPherson & O'Neill, 2010). These factors can significantly affect educational and career development opportunities and music identity development. Success relies, in that case, more on the individual effort of young musicians and their families and, up to a certain point, on a major (instrumental) music teacher, that is, on the immediate social field (see Chapter 13 in this volume).

The developmental perspective of this review has implications for the educational system in WB and elsewhere, inviting an awareness of the psychological profile of maturing musicians at different ages and providing more information for parents, support for teachers, and psychological care for the musicians' well-being. During the final phases of education or at the beginning of a professional career, adequate coaching, the involvement of gate-keepers, and fair chances are needed for the healthy development of young talents and their optimal flourishing.

References

Bandi, S. A., Lukácsi, T., Kemény, V., Vida, D., Nagy, S. I., Vas, B., & Révész, G. (2023). The HEXACO personality profile of musicians. *Psychology of Music*, 51(1), 107–118. https://doi.org/10.1177/03057356221087725

Benedek, M., Borovnjak, B., Neubauer, A.C., & Kruse-Weber, S. (2014). Creativity and personality in classical, jazz and folk musicians. *Personality and Individual Differences*, 63, 117–121. https://doi.org/10.1016/j.paid.2014.01.064

Bogunović, B. (2003). How does the teacher make a difference? In R. Kopiez, A.C. Lehmann, I. Wolther, & C. Wolf (eds), *Proceedings of the 5th Triennial conference of the European Society for the Cognitive Sciences of Music (ESCOM)* (pp. 282–284). Hanover University of Music and Drama. https://www.researchgate.net/publication/312210833_HOW_DOES_THE_TEACHER_MAKE_A_DIFFERENCE_Blanka_Bogunovic

Bogunović, B. (2009). Motivation and personality traits of adolescent musicians. In D. Talevski (ed.), *First international scientific conference Gifted and talented creators of the progress (theory and practice)* (pp. 330–335), University of Sv. Kliment Ohridski.

Bogunović, B. (2010). *Muzički talenat i uspešnost* [Musical talent and successfulness] (2nd ed.). Fakultet muzičke umetnosti i Institut za pedagoška istraživanja. https://www.researchgate.net/publication/313790139_MUSICAL_TALENT_AND_SUCCESSFULNESS_-_Summary

Bogunović, B. (2017). Mentalni sklop i postignuća studenata muzike [Mindset and music students' achievements]. In M. Petrović (ed.), *Zbornik radova sa Pedagoškog foruma scenskih umetnosti–U potrazi za smislom i doživljajem u muzičkoj pedagogiji* (pp. 160–173). Fakultet muzičke umetnosti.

Bogunović, B. (2018). Sight-reading strategies and personality dimensions. In R. Parncutt & S. Sattmann (eds), *Proceedings of ICMPC15/ESCOM10* (pp. 85–90). Centre for Systematic Musicology, University of Graz. https://www.researchgate.net/publication/329702445_Sight-Reading_Strategies_and_Personality_Dimensions

Bogunović, B. (2021). Parental contribution to motivation and practice at the beginning years of instrumental tuition for the musically gifted. In S. Vidulin (ed.), *Music pedagogy in the context of present and future changes 7. Multidisciplinary crossroads: Researches in music education* (pp. 419–436). University of Juraj Dobrila.

Bogunović, B., & Bodroža, B. (2015). Gender identity and personality dimensions as correlates of music performance success. In J. Ginsborg, A. Lamont, M. Phillips, & S. Bramley (eds), *Proceedings of the ninth Triennial Conference of the European Society for the Cognitive Sciences of Music (ESCOM)* (pp. 220–225). Royal Northern College of Music. https://www.gsmd.ac.uk/sites/default/files/2022-02/ESCOM9_Manchester_2015_Abstracts_Proceedings-web.pdf

Bogunović, B., & Mirović, T. (2014). Professional competencies of musically gifted at the end of higher education in music arts. *Research in Pedagogy, 4*(1), 11–25. https://research.rs/wp-content/uploads/2015/01/02-Bogunovic-Mirovic-ENG.doc.pdf

Bogunović, B., Radoš, K., & Tošković, O. (2006). Environment, motivation, and practice as factors of instrumental performance success. In M. Baroni, A.R. Addessi, R. Caterina, & M. Costa (eds), *Proceedings of the 9th ICMPC and 6th ESCOM* (pp. 1628–1632). Alma Mater Studiorum University. https://www.researchgate.net/publication/312210685_Environment_Motivation_and_Practice_as_Factors_of_Instrumental_Performance_Success

Butković, A., & Modrušan, I. (2021). Personality differences among musicians: Real differences or stereotypes? *Psychology of Music, 49*(2), 216–226. https://doi.org/10.1177/0305735619849625

Butković, A., Ullén, F., & Mosing, M.A. (2015). Personality related traits as predictors of music practice: Underlying environmental and genetic influences. *Personality and Individual Differences, 74*, 133–138. https://doi.org/10.1016/j.paid.2014.10.006

Cattell, R.B. Eber, H.W. & Tatsuoka, M.M. (1970). *Handbook for the Sixteen Personality Factor Questionnaire*. Institute for Personality and Ability Testing.

Corrigall, K.A., & Schellenberg, E.G. (2015). Predicting who takes music lessons: Parent and child characteristics. *Frontiers in Psychology, 6*, Article 282. https://doi.org/10.3389/fpsyg.2015.00282

Corrigall, K.A., Schellenberg, E.G., & Misura, N.M. (2013). Music training, cognition, and personality. *Frontiers in Psychology, 4*, Article 222. https://doi.org/10.3389/fpsyg.2013.00222

Costa, P.T., Jr, & McCrae, R.R. (1995). Domains and facets: Hierarchical personality assessment using the revised NEO Personality Inventory. *Journal of Personality Assessment, 64*(1), 21–50. https://doi.org/10.1207/s15327752jpa6401_2

Costa-Giomi, E. (2004). 'I do not want to study piano!' Early predictors of student dropout behavior. *Bulletin of the Council for Research in Music Education, 161/162*, 57–64. https://www.researchgate.net/publication/292867665_I_do_not_want_to_study_piano_Early_predictors_of_student_dropout_behavior

Creech, A. (2009). Teacher-pupil-parent triads: A typology of interpersonal interaction in the context of learning a musical instrument. *Musicae Scientiae, 13*(2), 387–413. https://doi.org/10.1177/102986490901300208

Csikszentmihalyi, M. (1990). *Flow: The psychology of optimal experience*. Harper & Row.

Csikszentmihalyi, M. (2004). Implications of a systems perspective for the study of creativity. In R.J. Sternberg (ed.), *Handbook of creativity* (2nd ed., pp. 313–335). Cambridge University Press.

Csikszentmihalyi, M., Rathunde, K., & Whalen, S. (1997). *Talented teenagers: The roots of success and failure.* Cambridge University Press.

Dweck, C.S. (2006). *Mindset: The new psychology of success.* Ballantine Books.

Evans, P. (2015). Self-determination theory: An approach to motivation in music education. *Musicae Scientiae, 19*(1), 65–83. https://doi.org/10.1177/1029864914568044

Evans, P., & McPherson, G.E. (2015). Identity and practice: The motivational benefits of a long-term musical identity. *Psychology of Music, 43*(3), 407–422. https://doi.org/10.1177/0305735613514471

Evans, P., McPherson, G.E., & Davidson, J.W. (2013). The role of psychological needs in ceasing music and music learning activities. *Psychology of Music, 41*(5), 600–619. https://doi.org/10.1177/0305735612441736

Gagné, F. (2005). From gifts to talents: The DMGT as a developmental model. In R.J. Sternberg & J.E. Davidson (eds), *Conceptions of giftedness* (2nd ed., pp. 98–119). Cambridge University Press.

González-Moreno, P.A. (2011). Student motivation in graduate music programmes: An examination of personal and environmental factors. *Music Education Research, 14*(1), 79–102. https://doi.org/10.1080/14613808.2012.657168

Greenberg, D.M., Müllenfiesen, D., Lamb, M.E., & Rentfrow, P.J. (2016). Erratum to 'Personality predicts musical sophistication'. *Journal of Research in Personality, 60,* 63. http://dx.doi.org/10.1016/j.jrp.2015.10.003

Habe, K., & Delin, A. (2010). Uporabnost glasbe kot motivacijskega sredstva pri poucevanju v osnovni soli [Music as a motivational means in elementary school]. *Pedagoška obzorja, 25,* 35–50.

Hallam, S., Papageorgi, I., Varvarigou, M., & Creech, A. (2021). Relationships between practice, motivation, and examination outcomes. *Psychology of Music, 49*(1), 3–20. https://doi.org/10.1177/0305735618816168

Janković M., & Bogaerts, S. (2021). Predicting success in the performing arts: Ballet and music. *Psychology of Music, 49*(4), 945–957. https://doi.org/10.1177/0305735620911983

Kaufman, S.B., Quilty, L.C., Grazioplene, R.G., Hirsh, J.B., Gray, J.R., Peterson, J.B., & DeYoung, C.G. (2016). Openness to experience and intellect differentially predict creative achievement in the arts and sciences. *Journal of Personality, 84*(2), 248–258. https://doi.org/10.1111/jopy.12156

Kemp, A.E. (1996). *The musical temperament: Psychology and personality of musicians.* Oxford University Press.

Lamont, A. (2017). Musical identity, interest, and involvement. In R. MacDonald, D.J. Hargreaves, & D. Miell (eds), *Handbook of musical identities* (pp.176–196). Oxford University Press.

Leung, B.W., & McPherson, G.E. (2011). Case studies of factors affecting the motivation of musical high achievers to learn music in Hong Kong. *Music Education Research, 13*(1), 69–91. https://doi.org/10.1080/14613808.2011.553278

Lin, H.-R., Kopiez, R., Müllensiefen, D., & Hasselhorn, J. (2022). Predicting academic achievement in music in secondary schools: The role of personality and self-theories of musicality. *Psychology of Music, 50*(6), 2077–2088. https://doi.org/10.1177/03057356211073479

MacIntyre, P.D., Schnare, B., & Ross, J. (2018). Self-determination theory and motivation for music. *Psychology of Music, 46*(5), 699–715. https://doi.org/10.1177/0305735617721637

McCormick, J. & McPherson, G.E. (2007). Expectancy-value motivation in the context of a music performance examination. *Musicae Scientiae, 11*(2), 37–52. https://doi.org/10.1177/10298649070110S203

McPherson, G.E., & McCormick, J. (2000). The contribution of motivational factors to instrumental performance in a music examination. *Research Studies in Music Education, 15*(1), 31–39. https://doi.org/10.1177/1321103X0001500105

McPherson, G.E., & O'Neill, S.A. (2010). Students' motivation to study music as compared to other school subjects: A comparison of eight countries. *Research Studies in Music Education, 32*(2), 101–137. https://doi.org/10.1177/1321103X10384202

Mehr, S.A. (2014). Music in the home: New evidence for an intergenerational link. *Journal of Research in Music Education, 62*(1), 78–88. https://doi.org/10.1177/0022429413520008

Meissner, H., Timmers, R., & Pitts, S.E. (2022). *Sound teaching: A research-informed approach to inspiring confidence, skill, and enjoyment in music performance*. Routledge.

Mihajlovski, Z. (2013). Personality, intelligence and musical instrument. *Croatian Journal of Education, 15*(1), 155–172. https://doi.org/10.15516/cje.v15i0.606

Miksza, P., Evans, P., & McPherson, G.E. (2021). Motivation to pursue a career in music: The role of social constraints in university music programs. *Psychology of Music, 49*(1), 50–68. https://doi.org/10.1177/0305735619836269

Miksza, P., Tan, L., & Dye, C. (2016). Achievement motivation for band: A cross-cultural examination of the 2×2 achievement goal motivation framework. *Psychology of Music, 44*(6), 1372–1388. https://doi.org/10.1177/0305735616628659

Müllensiefen, D., Harrison, P., Caprini, F., & Fancourt, A. (2015). Investigating the importance of self-theories of intelligence and musicality for students' academic and musical achievement. *Frontiers in Psychology, 6*, Article 1702. https://doi.org/10.3389/fpsyg.2015.01702

Nogaj, A.A., & Bogunović, B. (2015). The development of giftedness within the three-level system of music education in Poland and Serbia: Outcomes at different stages. *Journal of the Institute of Educational Research, 4*(1), 153–174. https://doiserbia.nb.rs/img/doi/0579-6431/2015/0579-64311501153N.pdf

O'Neill, S.A. (2011). Developing a young musician's growth mindset: The role of motivation, self-theories, and resiliency. In I. Deliège & J.W. Davidson (eds), *Music and the mind: Essays in honour of John Sloboda* (pp. 31–46). Oxford University Press. https://academic.oup.com/book/4085/chapter-abstract/1 45785419?redirectedFrom=fulltext&login=false

O'Neill, S.A. & McPherson, G.E. (2002). Motivation. In R. Parncutt & G.E. McPherson (eds), *The science and psychology of music performance: Creative strategies for teaching and learning* (pp. 31–46). Oxford University Press.

Pekić, J. (2009). Inteligencija i osobine ličnosti kao prediktori uspešnosti muzički darovitih srednjoškolaca [Intelligence and personality traits as the predictors of success of the secondary school pupils gifted in music]. *Primenjena Psihologija, 2*(1), 75–91. https://doi.org/10.19090/pp.2009.1.75-91

Philippe, R.A., Kosirnik, C., Ortuño, E., & Biasutti, M. (2021). Flow and music performance: Professional musicians and music students' views. *Psychology of Music, 50*(4), 1023–1038. https://doi.org/10.1177/03057356211030987

Radoš, K. (2010). *Psihologija muzike* [Psychology of music] (2nd ed.). Zavod za udžbenike.

Radoš, K., Kovačević, P., Bogunović, B., Ignjatović, T., & Ačić, G. (2003). Psychological foundations of success in learning music at elementary school age. In R. Kopiez, A. Lehmann, I. Wolther, & C. Wolf (eds), *Proceedings of the 5th Triennial Conference of the European Society for the Cognitive Sciences of Music (ESCOM)* (pp. 416–419). Hanover University of Music and Drama. https://www.researchgate.net/publication/312211029_PSYCHOLOGICAL_FOUNDATIONS_OF_SUCCESS_IN_LEARNING_MUSIC_AT_ELEMENTARY_SCHOOL_AGE

Rose, D., Bartoli, A.J., & Heaton, P. (2019). Formal-informal musical learning, sex and musicians' personalities. *Personality and Individual Differences, 142*(1), 207–213. https://doi.org/10.1016/j.paid.2018.07.015

Rotar Pance, B. (2021). Motivational aspects of music competition in the context of the Music Olympiad. In S. Vidulin-Orbanić (ed.), *Proceedings of the 7th International Symposium of Music Pedagogues* (pp. 103–119). Sveučilište Juraj Dobrila: Muzička akademija.

Ryan, R.M., & Deci, E.L. (2018). *Self-determination theory: Basic psychological needs in motivation, development, and wellness.* Guilford Press.

Subotnik, R.F., & Jarvin, L. (2005). Beyond expertise: Conceptions of giftedness as great performance. In R.J. Sternberg & J.E. Davidson (eds), *Conceptions of giftedness* (2nd ed., pp. 343–357). Cambridge University Press.

Subotnik, R.F., Olszewski-Kubilius, P., & Worrell, F.C. (2011). Rethinking giftedness and gifted education: A proposed direction forward based on psychological science. *Psychological Science in the Public Interest, 12*(1), 3–54. https://doi.org/10.1177/1529100611418056

Swaminathan, S., & Schellenberg, E.G. (2018). Musical competence is predicted by music training, cognitive abilities, and personality. *Scientific Reports, 8*, Article 9223. https://doi.org/10.1038/s41598-018-27571-2

Štula, J. (2007). Struktura uspešnosti muzički darovitih srednjoškolaca [The structure of success of musically gifted secondary school students]. In M. Biro & S. Smederevac (ed.) *Psihologija i društvo* [Psychology and society] (pp. 195–207). Filozofski fakultet, Odsek za psihologiju.

Winner, E. (1996). *Gifted children: Myths and realities*. Basic Books.

13. The Lived Experience of Radical Acceleration in the Biographical Narratives of Exceptionally Gifted Adult Musicians

Olja Jovanović, Ana Altaras Dimitrijević, Dejana Mutavdžin, and Blanka Bogunović

Introduction

If giftedness manifests itself in the exceptional speed at which one acquires the skills and knowledge of a given domain (e.g., Winner, 1996), then this can be particularly salient in the realm of music. Not only is this a domain where giftedness may emerge very early on (Winner, 1996), it is also one in which those identified as gifted can progress at a pace far greater than that expected by the regular music curriculum (Gagné & McPherson, 2016). In this chapter we address the experience of radical acceleration as reflected in the narratives of four musicians who were identified as exceptionally musically gifted during childhood. To provide a context for analysing their narratives, we will first review the major points about the development of musical talent, as well as about the educational practice of acceleration.

The development of musically gifted individuals into elite musicians

The complexity of the process that may ultimately produce an elite musical performer is captured in current models of talent development (e.g., Gagné & McPherson, 2016; Subotnik & Jarvin, 2005), both in terms of the multiple stages and transitions that are deemed to constitute this process, and in the multitude of factors thought to contribute to it. Contrary to the popular image of a 'born artist', these models assume a lengthy process of honing abilities into competencies and into expertise, to eventually reach the level of eminence and artistry (Subotnik et al., 2016). Moreover, they regard the process of talent development as extending beyond formal education and encompassing the various phases of building a career as a professional musician (Gembris & Langner, 2006). As depicted in McPherson and Lehmann's (2012) model, the first three stages of musical development (sampling, specialisation, and investment) fulfil the purpose of 'getting there', yet there is also a final maintenance stage which is about 'staying there', that is, preserving the status of the successful musical performer.

At any point in this process, the level of performance is determined by numerous factors, as is the likelihood and speed of transitioning from one level to the next (Subotnik et al., 2016). According to Gagné and McPherson (2016), the achievement of expertise in music depends not only on the level and nature of the aptitudes that feed directly into the talent development process, but also on various intrapersonal and environmental catalysts, as well as factors related to the developmental process itself (see Chapter 12 in this volume). Moreover, as pointed out by Subotnik et al. (2016), it appears that different constellations of factors are relevant at different stages of talent development, and that the relative weight of these factors tends to shift over time. Thus, while success in a field almost always requires both cognitive and non-cognitive skills, and employs various types of abilities, there is a tendency for social skills, creativity, and practical intelligence to gain in importance and outweigh more analytical and technical skills as the talent development process moves towards its higher stages.

Acknowledging that each progression from one stage to the next is fraught with specific challenges, a review of the literature also suggests that two transitions stand out as being particularly difficult. The first is that of entering what McPherson and Lehmann (2012) call the 'investment stage', which means prioritising music over other endeavours and making the decision to pursue music as a profession. For highly gifted and precociously developing individuals, this 'career decision' is often made at a very young age (Gagné & McPherson, 2016; Jung & Evans, 2016), in fact before the child has had a chance to seriously consider alternative life paths, so that 'it's only later in adolescence that prodigies can begin to doubt themselves and their commitment to music performance' (Subotnik et al., 2016, p. 287). The second great challenge is the individual's professional integration once they have completed their musical education (Gaunt et al., 2012), that is, the transition from studying music to entering the job market and the music industry (Gembris & Langner, 2006; Jung & Evans, 2016); again, in the case of musically precocious students, this may happen as early as adolescence. The above-mentioned shift in the weight of factors that lead to success is especially obvious at this point in talent development, because it is with this transition that an array of 'non-musical' competencies come into play (Gaunt et al., 2012; Gembris & Langner, 2006; Jarvin & Subotnik, 2010), and personality factors tend to outweigh other variables.

In sum, while the speed of progress through the various stages of musical talent development may largely depend on the person's level of musical abilities (Gagné & McPherson, 2016), the desired outcome of becoming a professional musician is also contingent upon other characteristics and competencies, such as personal charisma, determination, and social and practical skills. Even for those with an exceptional gift in music, the talent development process may assume various individual trajectories and lead to outcomes other than world-class eminence.

Playing fast forward: Accelerated talent development

One way to ensure a positive outcome of the talent development process is, of course, the provision of adequate educational interventions, and a major intervention in accommodating gifted learners is acceleration. Basically, acceleration consists in adjusting the pace of formal learning to meet the precocious development and abilities of gifted learners. Although considered essential in gifted education (Mayer, 2005; Rogers, 2007; Winner, 1996), it is also surrounded by some controversy, especially when it comes to its grade-based forms (e.g., early entrance to school/college, grade skipping), wherein the student is placed within an older age cohort. Nevertheless, in the field of academic giftedness, acceleration—including radical grade-based acceleration of 2+ years—is a well-researched intervention (Dare et al., 2019; Neihart, 2007), with findings of quantitative studies usually testifying to its beneficial effects, both short-term and long-term, on students' academic achievement, motivation, and productivity (e.g., Rinn & Bishop, 2015; Sayler & Brookshire, 1993). Available findings also suggest that acceleration does not entail any significant socio-emotional risks, yet we must agree with Gronostaj et al. (2016) that little is known about these effects, and that a large-scale quantitative approach cannot depict the complexity of the experience of grade skipping from an individual perspective. Several qualitative studies have sought to address this issue, revealing that while the experience of grade skipping is generally a positive one, accelerands may also experience some difficulties in social adjustment (Jett & Rinn, 2019) and dealing with the high expectations put on them (Mun & Hertzog, 2019).

Addressing acceleration in musical education presents us with a paradox: radical acceleration is more common, but far less explored in this field than others, and the literature seems to provide more questions than answers about how acceleration shapes the development of musical talent (Gagné & McPherson, 2016). To further complicate things, radical acceleration in musical schooling may require corresponding adjustments to regular education: thus, for a musically precocious teenager to enter the conservatory, their general schooling must also often be accelerated, although the student may not be academically brilliant. Also, while for academically gifted students the choice is whether to skip grades or not (without having to leave regular school), musical accelerands have to deal with the decision of committing themselves to music rather than anything else. Thus, acceleration can add further challenges and complexities to the process of talent development in music.

Aims

Given that radical acceleration is often part and parcel of musical talent development, yet little is known about how it shapes and affects this process, our study focused on the lived experience of acceleration from the perspective of adult musicians—those who have reached the final stages of the talent development process. We were specifically interested in how they experienced the two critical developmental transitions mentioned above—deciding to study music at university level and starting a career as a professional musician (i.e., entering the investment and the maintenance stage; McPherson & Lehmann, 2012)—since they made these transitions at a rather young age.

We were further interested in whether the experience of radical acceleration and the process of talent development would bear any specific features related to the socio-cultural background of the accelerands—more precisely, to their origins in the Western Balkans, specifically Serbia. We raised this issue on the assumption that the experience of acceleration may greatly depend on the structure and organisation of music education (cf. Gagné & McPherson, 2016), which is different in Serbia from other investigated countries (see Nogaj & Bogunović, 2015). We also had in mind that musicians from Serbia who are now in their young adulthood were born and/or raised in politically and socially turbulent times which were characterised by a devaluation of culture—a fact that might have left a specific mark on their experience of developing a talent in classical music. Finally, given that Serbia is a relatively small country, and success in classical music usually means moving abroad, we reasoned that the talent development process might include yet further challenges for musical accelerands from this country.

Method

To uncover the meanings that gifted musicians ascribe to their experiences of radical acceleration, we chose a narrative approach—a method which entails an exploration of the narrator's motivation, values, and meaning-making systems along a temporal dimension (Spector-Mersel, 2011), and ultimately allows for an in-depth understanding, while also ensuring methodological and scientific rigour (Leung, 2010). The Ethics Commission of the Faculty of Music, University of Arts in Belgrade approved the research.

Participants

The study included a purposive sample[1] of four participants, aged 32–45 years, who were identified early in their lives as exceptionally musically gifted, and who, in terms of talent development, are now amidst the artistic, concert-career developmental phase (Manturzewska, 1990). Each participant had the experience of radical acceleration in their music education. Further information about the participants' characteristics is provided in Table 13.1.

---

1   Participants were nominated for the study by one of the authors, who holds a teaching position at the Faculty of Music in Belgrade.

Table 13.1 Characteristics of participants

Name[a]	Gender	Instrument	Starting MHE Age	Starting MHE Country	Starting MHE Age	MHE[c], country		Currently stationed, country	Age[b]
						Graduate studies	Postgraduate studies		
Marija	Female	Piano	6	Serbia	15	Serbia, France	Serbia, France	France	45
Ana	Female	Violin	4	Serbia	15	Serbia	Serbia, USA	Serbia	43
Marko	Male	Violin	6	Serbia	14	Serbia	Serbia, Germany	Germany, Denmark	37
Filip	Male	Cello	5	Serbia	15	Serbia	Serbia, Austria, Italy	Serbia	32

[a] Names were changed to preserve the anonymity of participants.

[b] Age of participants at the time of data collection.

[c] Abbreviation for "music higher education".

A horizontal version of this table may be viewed online at https://hdl.handle.net/20.500.12434/0e1f026f

Data collection

Data were derived from semi-structured narrative interviews focusing on the experience of acceleration in the context of the participant's overall life story. The interviews started with the instruction: 'Please tell me the story of your life. You may start with the year 19** (year of birth) and then describe, as detailed as possible, those aspects of your life that you consider important.' The interviews were facilitated by a biographical timeline previously prepared by the researchers (see the Appendix to this chapter). The questions following the storytelling aimed at prompting participants to reappraise their experiences, reconnect their past with the present, reveal the interaction between experience and context, and put 'meaning' into the foreground for conscious examination (Leung, 2010). At the end of the interview, participants were asked to think about the life stories they had told, to identify important 'chapters' in them, and to give titles to those chapters (cf. Thomsen & Berntsen, 2008).

Data collection took place in 2021, during the COVID-19 pandemic, via the web-based video-conferencing tool Zoom. The content was audio recorded with the participants' consent. Reflexive memos kept by the researcher facilitated the process of analysis and reduced the potential for bias (Birks et al., 2008). The interviews lasted 70–100 minutes and resulted in 87 pages of interview transcripts.

Data analysis

We approached the data inductively, following the four-stage process of Interpretative Phenomenological Analysis (for details, see Smith & Osborn, 2004). Analysis began with a close interpretative reading of the first case where initial codes were annotated in the comments. These initial codes were translated into emergent themes at a higher level of abstraction. This process was repeated for each case. Patterns were documented cross-case and transformed into a narrative account, supported by verbatim extracts from each participant. The analysis of the timelines provided a contextual understanding of the individual participants' experience of acceleration. At this point, a researcher who had not participated in the data analysis independently judged the coherence between the findings and the transcripts, ensuring the trustworthiness of the study.

Although participants' narratives covered the period from early childhood to the present, and yielded six recognisable 'life chapters', in line with the above-stated focus of our study we will here only present the results concerning two of these: entering music education at university level and starting professional life as a musician (Table 13.2).

Table 13.2 Overview of the two life chapters and themes

Life chapters	Themes
Maturing as a musician	- Entering HME at a young age
	- Juggling studies and career
	- Identity foreclosure
	- Seeking refuge in music
Starting to live the life	- Entering the profession at a young age
	- Experiencing the gap between education and profession
	- Experiencing new professional horizons
	- Experiencing diversification of private roles

Results

The findings portray how our exceptionally gifted participants perceive and reflect on the part of their lives from the time they entered music higher education institutions (MHEI), up to their first steps as independent professionals in the music industry, and they encompass information on selected events, people, and the overall socio-historical-cultural context. These portrayals are organised around the key themes identified in the participants' narratives.

Maturing as a musician

Entering university at a young age

The transition to university is a challenging period that involves navigating a number of important new tasks: making friends, establishing independence, and developing a different approach to learning (e.g., Brooks & DuBois, 1995). While all four participants entered university early, at 14–15 years of age, their experiences of this transition differ. Like

Jet and Rinn's (2019) participants, both Marko and Filip reflected on some of the negative impacts on their social development and romantic relationships, and on missing out on certain experiences that are common for adolescents. Ana, however, talks about being cared for by her fellow students, since she was amongst the youngest in the group. From the perspective of academic tasks, all participants emphasise that they had difficulties mastering certain (non-musical) subjects at university level:

> I have to admit that, in my opinion, acceleration has very negative consequences, especially in some social aspects, since my fellow students were much older than me... My voice, for example, has been changing [...] when I took *solfège* during the entrance exam, [...] my voice cracked non-stop, the others laughed. It was very difficult for me to bear it then. Not to mention I started smoking at the age of 14, since I was surrounded by people who smoked, I thought it was something extremely cool. [...] In essence, there are some things that a person should experience before entering university, developing that certain level of awareness. (Marko)

> I remember we had Psychology and Pedagogy in the second year, Sociology in the third year. That was hell for me because, I mean, at 14–15 I didn't understand anything. No... That terminology. It was terrible for me. (Ana)

During this period, learning from a 'master teacher' is seen as a privilege and presumes a close relationship, loyalty, and trust. Our interviews were rich with data about recognising excellent music teachers and moving to their institutions, even if they were in a different country or continent.

> I was ranked first in the entrance exam and graduated in three years. Since Professor M. was about to retire, and I wanted to graduate in his class, I had to merge my third and fourth year at the university—which I did. [...] so at the age of 17 I enrolled in master studies and at 19 I obtained my master's degree. (Marko)

Juggling studies and career

Since our participants were already accomplished young musicians by this stage, they had a variety of professional engagements which required that teachers adjust the schedule for them, but they still had to juggle their studies with their professional activities. Looking back on this intensive period, all participants observed that it was only later in life that they 'had discovered the beauty of procrastination', as Filip described it. During that period, our participants sought to expand their presence in the field of music and establish themselves in the professional community:

> So, I travelled a lot. And there was always some, some pressure. I mean, it was physically demanding, since you had to get up [early], and do your duties, and studies, and travel to those countless masterclasses and seminars, and find money for that... (Filip)

Identity foreclosure

Although the transition between childhood and adulthood usually provides an opportunity to explore one's past, current, and potential selves and take ownership of one's life (Erikson, 1956), our participants do not remember questioning their choice of a music career during adolescence. In Marko's words, they 'didn't have the luxury of questioning' it, because by that age they had already invested long hours into music practice. Also, due to their outstanding accomplishments in music, their identities as (future) musicians were positive and stable, albeit foreclosed:

> I mean, it was kind of natural. You don't think about it at all. (Ana)

> I didn't question myself. Well, how could I have questioned myself—I had been in music education for 15 years at that time, I was playing the cello and I really wasn't interested in anything else. (Filip)

> In my mind, I have never wondered if I should be something else. But it's not like passion guided me. No! It was just like that. I did it. I was good at it, obviously. And you get into a machine where there are no such questions anymore. That's it. That's my life. But after a while, you start asking yourself: 'Could I do something else now?' (Marija)

The participants' narratives revealed a strong tendency to be perfect as musicians, illustrating Dews and Williams's (1989, p. 46) statement: 'Music, perhaps more than any other artistic pursuit, demands a high level of perfection from those hopeful of being successful in it.' This perfectionism is rooted in familial and cultural expectations (cf. Flett et al., 2002). For example, Ana described how coming from a well-known musical family set high standards for her, while Filip mentioned that being aware of his parents' material and non-material investments into his career raised the bar for him. Sometimes, high standards are perceived or explicated as a feature of the music profession or certain positions, as in Marko's case.

> Because classical musicians must always be top-notch. Everything has to be perfect, always; you always strive for an ideal and perfection. So, you always demand the maximum from yourself—the best. That is why we are so insecure. In the end, never satisfied. [...] A mistake is not an option. It cannot happen. And that burdened me a lot. [...] It can happen to anyone, but it cannot happen to me, since I was a concertmaster, since I'm his daughter...[2] (Ana)

> This is an act that I still can't understand— They [his parents] sold the apartment we lived in to obtain the money for buying me an instrument. [...] It was a burden for me: that someone is selling an apartment, automatically means asking a lot from me. However, in 2003 it happened that I went to a competition in the Czech Republic and did not pass to the second round [*laughs*]. They had just bought a new instrument for me, so it should have been great. Right? However, I did not live up to those expectations and that's it. [...] I may have been too young to really understand the burden of it all. (Filip)

> Of course, [*giggles*] the reason for such a contract is that I am expected not to make any mistakes. Never. Which is a lot of pressure, of course. And, since it is still a radio orchestra, from the moment I take my seat in the orchestra, everything is recorded. [...] ...nerves of steel [*laughter*]... (Marko)

Seeking refuge in music

Some participants' university studies partly took place during the specific circumstances of the bombing of Serbia in March–June 1999. These participants reported that music and intensive practice had a protective role, shielding them from the disturbing political and social reality:

> I think it's good because we were really dedicated to art, to music. In the circumstances in which we grew up that saved us mentally. (Ana)

---

2   Ana's father was an accomplished and well-known musician in the national context.

For Marija, music was literally a way out: she had earned a scholarship abroad where she continued her studies. However, she recognises that she was not prepared for this sudden transition, having to leave her friends and family and adapt to a new life and environment. Moreover, being in constant transition created an everlasting sense of longing, with music as the only constant:

> So, all these, all these accelerations, in fact, have created in me some... a kind of lack... I call it [lacking of] a home. I mean, of one's country, and city, and Mom and Dad, and... Which has become a very, very important place for me, psychologically. My problem or my... a fact that I have to... that I deal with, more or less well, depending on the moment... Like when you go home, and you sense some familiar smell, and it feels right. Well, that's what I'm looking for. I mean, that's my whole life. And the only place that offers me that, in fact, is the piano. (Marija)

Starting to live the life

Entering the profession at a young age

Radical acceleration also meant gaining an early entrance into the profession and highly prestigious professional roles from a young age. This transition was experienced differently depending on the type of position. Those who held stable positions that required working with other people (e.g., as a concertmaster) had to master non-musical and particularly social skills relevant for their new role; those who became independent musicians had to learn how to be more visible and how to attract an audience. Generally, participants reported feeling they lacked non-musical skills (e.g., foreign languages, communication, leadership):

> At the age of 19, I started working—permanent employment—and in fact, I haven't spent a single day without being permanently employed since then [...] In fact, I can freely say that I have been working since I was 14. (Marko)

> I was already known in professional circles at the time of my studies, so the director of the Belgrade Philharmonic had heard me [play], knew that I was from a musical family. And they called, suggesting that I audition for the position of the concertmaster, I was 19 at the time. And it was, like: 'Well, why not.' [...] But, since being a concertmaster is not just about playing well... You practically have to manage 100 people. [...]

Then I learned communication [skills] along the way: how to manage people; they look upon me as an authority. 100 people! You have to be, I mean... [*laughter*] It's very strange. Challenging, at the same time, at 20 years of age. No, it wasn't easy. (Ana)

Experiencing the gap between education and profession

In line with the notion that 'Only those who can reinvent themselves will make the leap between childhood giftedness and adult creativity' (Winner & Martino, 2000, p. 107), participants reflected on how, at this stage, they were expected to make a shift from technical proficiency to innovation and creativity, to give their playing a new meaning. For some of the participants it was a transition from the role of performer to that of a meaning maker, and their musical education had not prepared them for this. As Bennett (2013) explains, music education traditionally focuses on virtuosic performance, and is unlikely to encourage broader views of what it means to be a successful musician:

And that's the problem that you're... totally unprepared for... You come, in fact... as if you were heading into space. You have to speed up, like [*makes 'vroom' sound*] when a rocket is launched. Because you had a drill for 20 years. Literally. And then, they drop you into some airless space and you are so, aaaaah... (Marija)

Experiencing new professional horizons

After university, life begins. The completion of studies and the expertise gained were experienced as an expansion of their professional horizons that gave them opportunities to explore different musical genres and activities (cf. Palmer & Baker, 2021). At the same time, this also meant taking responsibility for oneself, freedom in decision-making, and financial independence (cf. Subotnik et al., 2016), which are the hallmarks of adulthood (Arnett, 2000):

And then, there was a period when I started making a living, making a living from what I was educated for [*laughs*]. Um, then it became my life (How should I put it?), professionally. I was no longer dependent on anyone, not only financially, but I also found my own path... (Marija)

Reminiscent of Bennett's (2007) findings, our participants describe themselves as being engaged in different professional activities and in different fields of music, whether they were independent musicians or employed full-time as performers. They ascribe their professional progression to a combination of social capital, high quality performance, and positive chance:

> I needed to get a new instrument. This one wasn't satisfactory anymore... That was a student's instrument and I needed a better one for my career. Well, I was lucky ... In 2012, I met a lady in Italy who was a financial adviser there, at that school. She heard me play among other students, that is, cellists. And she showed great affection for me and approached me saying that my instrument is awful, but that I play wonderfully and that she will organise something for me. And she really did, a few months later, an event in Milan where she invited me. [...] She invited the elite from that city who were ready to support a young musician... one from Serbia — a third-world country [*laughter*], or fifth-world [*through laughter*]. And then, they raised funds... And then I got a new instrument. (Filip)

At this stage, Marija and Marko are living and working abroad. Both of them described how while they have easily become recognised for their music skills, they feel at the same time that they will always be foreigners:

> You are simply not one of them. Never. I have a passport here [France], but still, I am not a product of their school. And you have that strange name, hard to pronounce. I have never experienced any political..., like: 'You are Serbs'. However, 'You are the Foreigner' is present. No matter who you are, it is always there, ...you will always be the Foreigner. (Marija)

Experiencing diversification of private roles

The gendered dynamics that came into play while participants were talking about their past and current selves and their plans for the future, resonate with the findings of previous studies (Cook, 2018; Teague & Smith, 2015), including those focused on adults who are gifted in other domains (Ferriman et al., 2009). For the female participants, the central focus of their career-related plans was to accommodate for childbearing and parenting: they tended to look for professional positions that provide more stability (e.g., a position at a university) and/or more time for family roles (e.g., teaching). On the other hand, this interaction between career-related plans and other aspects of life was not salient in the accounts of the male participants.

> It has speeded up a lot, in fact. And, also, when the children are born, and responsibilities to them, and the husband, and the household, and… So, it's just a lot of roles that you perform… A lot of roles. And in each of them, at least that's how we were brought up, I think militarily: 'Work (uh), wash the ashtrays, but do the best you can.' Like that. So, even now, with that kind of responsibility in me, with 15 roles that I perform during the day; I have to be perfect in each one. That is, in fact, a bit too much for an ordinary person. (Ana)

Discussion

The 'gauntlet was thrown down' by McPherson (2016), who called for more research about prodigies in socio-cultural milieus other than English-speaking ones. This study deals with exceptional musical talents coming from the Western Balkans whose education was radically accelerated, and who told us their life stories while looking back at their musical development. This chapter focused on two important transitions of musical prodigies: firstly, when they make conclusive career decisions (Jung & Evans, 2016) about their music education, and, secondly, later on, when they take on the role of professionals.

Radical acceleration from an individual perspective

Like other qualitative research on acceleration (Jett & Rinn, 2019; Mun & Hertzog, 2019), this study revealed the experience of radical accelerands to be quite complex. On the one hand, early identification and promotion of talent may instil a feeling of security in young accelerands, with the domain of music acting as a 'secure base' or 'place of comfort', which one can always resort to. On the other hand, it may bring potential health risks, such as early substance abuse due to the pressure to 'act older', as well as the risk of identity foreclosure, that is, of automatically extending the identity of a 'child prodigy' into that of an 'exceptional performer' (Evans & McPherson, 2017) without acknowledging the fragile nature of the prodigy or the fact that there is more to life than 'talent development'. Moreover, while opening up great possibilities for musical development (Martin, 2016), radical acceleration can also reduce the opportunities the prodigy has to acquire knowledge and skills in other areas, and thus can limit their chances of a career change—which is a considerable drawback given the uncertainties and demands of a musical career, even for those who are exceptionally talented. Finally, while radical acclerands consistently 'win' in social comparisons of ability (being younger, but progressing faster in the field of music than most other students), and thus may construct positive identities as musicians (Davidson, 2017), they also experience a 'loss' when it comes to their sense of belonging to a peer group (rather than just having 'fellow students').

Radical acceleration from a contextual perspective

Given that context is viewed as critically important for both understanding and developing talent (Plucker & Barab, 2005), the question is how (and how much) it affects the experience of radical acceleration? Firstly, our participants' narratives reveal how the nature of music education in Serbia has affected their musical and personal development. The strong emphasis on developing musical skills and performing publicly, in a highly structured educational environment, is recognised by our participants as both an advantage and a disadvantage. On the one hand, this educational approach has helped them to become easily recognised as outstanding music performers in different contexts, transcending national, ethnic, and cultural backgrounds in music practices (Folkestad, 2017); on the other hand, it has failed to build the psychosocial skills (e.g., communication, leadership, self-regulation) that are necessary for long-term success in a music career (Jung & Evans, 2016). Secondly, living in a country where state funding for the development of musical talents is scarce has made it necessary for the individual to be proactive to ensure the resources for practising and performing; to look for enrichment activities abroad; and, consequently, to also master foreign languages, as a tool for becoming a member in relevant professional and social communities. Thirdly, the strong dedication to music, to the development of musical skills, and to meeting the expectations in this particular field also provided some protection against the adverse political and social events of the immediate environment. Music was an 'escape hatch' from the grey reality of serious political upheavals. Yet, at the same time, the exclusive commitment to music entailed a specific kind of vulnerability: the continual need to confirm one's worth and identity as the 'perfect musician'. Finally, a special challenge for our prodigies was moving to another country and adjusting to the language, culture, and customs of a new place, while at the same time 'mastering the field' (Subotnik & Jarvin, 2005): making networks, arranging concerts, and finding funds. Although, in the participants' narratives, migration seemed to open up different experiences of the world and music for them, it also meant changing their relationship to their homeland and settling into a new environment, which sometimes persisted in reminding them that they were 'foreigners'. Still, music was there to provide some comfort and to evoke the feeling of being at home, of having a solid identity and place in the world.

Limitations and future directions

This study is based on participants' retrospective accounts, which provided an opportunity to situate the experience of acceleration within the broader framework of their life stories; to explore what they perceive as critical events and how they interpret causal connections between events; and how they create links between the events and aspects of themselves (McLean, 2005). Nevertheless, focusing on past experiences in a specific context calls for caution when drawing implications for the here and now. Additionally, we aimed to describe the experience of radical acceleration for musically gifted individuals of a particular cultural context. In order to gain a fuller understanding of both the musical and general development of accelerands, cross-cultural research is needed (Ziegler et al., 2018). We thus hope that future research on the radical acceleration of musically gifted individuals will allow us to collect their stories as they are emerging, across lifespans and diverse socio-cultural milieus.

Conclusion

Four adult musical prodigies reflected on their experiences of radical acceleration against the backdrop of their lives, navigating the complex socio-political context of Serbia, in addition to the complexity of early professional engagements, and an accelerated educational journey. Rather than just being an 'educational intervention', acceleration shapes numerous aspects of life, not limited to professional careers and artistry, but affecting social, emotional and identity development. We have found multiple examples of evidence for the notion that 'context matters', which further highlights the need for more research on the development of musical talents in different parts of the world and to explore different ways in which acceleration can happen (McPherson, 2016). Although certain similarities were found among the four individuals in the centrality of music for identity, refuge, and motivation, our findings also highlight the idiosyncrasy and complexity of the talent development process, indicating the need to provide individualised support to the maturing musical prodigy.

Acknowledgement

It was a worthwhile research endeavour to learn how adult musical prodigies reflect on their experiences of radical acceleration against the backdrop of their lives. We are grateful to Istra Pečvari and Zlata Maleš for their assistance in recruiting the participants, as well as to our participants for sharing their life stories with us.

References

Arnett, J.J. (2000). Emerging adulthood: A theory of development from the late teens through the twenties. *American Psychologist, 55*(5), 469–480. https://doi.org/10.1037/0003-066X.55.5.469

Bennett, D. (2007). Utopia for music performance graduates. Is it achievable, and how should it be defined? *British Journal of Music Education, 24*(2), 179–189. https://doi.org/10.1017/S0265051707007383

Bennett, D. (2013). The role of career creatives in developing identity and becoming expert selves. In P. Burnard (ed.), *Developing creativities in higher music education: International perspectives and practices* (pp. 234–244). Routledge. https://doi.org/10.4324/9781315885223

Birks, M., Chapman, Y., & Francis, K. (2008). Memoing in qualitative research: Probing data and processes. *Journal of Research in Nursing, 13*(1), 68–75. https://doi.org/10.1177/1744987107081254

Brooks, J.H., & DuBois, D.L. (1995). Individual and environmental predictors of adjustment during the first year of college. *Journal of College Student Development, 36*(4), 347–360. https://www.researchgate.net/publication/232514967_Individual_and_Environmental_Predictors_of_Adjustment_During_the_First_Year_of_College

Cook, J.A. (2018). Gendered expectations of the biographical and social future: Young adults' approaches to short and long-term thinking. *Journal of Youth Studies, 21*(10), 1376–1391. https://doi.org/10.1080/13676261.2018.1468875

Dare, L., Nowicki, E.A., & Smith, S. (2019). On deciding to accelerate: High-ability students identify key considerations. *Gifted Child Quarterly, 63*(3), 159–171. https://doi.org/10.1177/0016986219828073

Davidson, J.W. (2017). Performance identity. In R. MacDonald, D.J. Hargreaves, & D. Miell (eds), *Handbook of musical identities* (pp. 364–382). Oxford University Press. https://doi.org/10.1093/acprof:oso/9780199679485.003.0020

Dews, C.L.B., & Williams, M.S. (1989). Student musicians' personality styles, stresses, and coping patterns. *Psychology of Music, 17*(1), 37–47. https://doi.org/10.1177/0305735689171004

Erikson, E.H. (1956). The problem of ego identity. *Journal of the American Psychoanalytic Association, 4*(1), 56–121. https://doi.org/10.1177/000306515600400104

Evans, P., & McPherson, G.E. (2017). Processes of musical identity consolidation during adolescence. In R. MacDonald, D. J. Hargreaves, & D. Miell (eds), *Handbook of musical identities* (pp. 213–231). Oxford University Press. https://doi.org/10.1093/acprof:oso/9780199679485.003.0012

Ferriman, K., Lubinski, D., & Benbow, C. P. (2009). Work preferences, life values, and personal views of top math/science graduate students and the profoundly gifted: Developmental changes and gender differences during emerging adulthood and parenthood. *Journal of Personality and Social Psychology, 97*(3), 517–532. https://doi.org/10.1037/a0016030

Flett, G. L., Hewitt, P. L., Oliver, J. M., & Macdonald, S. (2002). Perfectionism in children and their parents: A developmental analysis. In G. L. Flett & P. L. Hewitt (eds), *Perfectionism: Theory, research, and treatment* (pp. 89–132). American Psychological Association. https://doi.org/10.1037/10458-004

Folkestad, G. (2017). Post-national identities in music: Acting in a global intertextual musical arena. In R. Macdonald, D.J. Hargreaves, & Miell, D. (eds), *Handbook of musical identities* (pp. 122–136). Oxford University Press. https://doi.org/10.1093/acprof:oso/9780199679485.003.0007

Gagné, F., & McPherson, G.E. (2016). Analyzing musical prodigiousness using Gagné's Integrative Model of Talent Development. In G.E. McPherson (ed.), *Musical prodigies: Interpretations from psychology, education, musicology, and ethnomusicology* (pp. 3–114). Oxford University Press. https://doi.org/10.1093/acprof:oso/9780199685851.003.0001

Gaunt, H., Creech, A., Long, M., & Hallam, S. (2012). Supporting conservatoire students towards professional integration: One-to-one tuition and the potential of mentoring. *Music Education Research, 14*(1), 25–43. https://doi.org/10.1080/14613808.2012.657166

Gembris, H., & Langner, D. (2006). What are instrumentalists doing after graduating from the music academy? In H. Gembris (ed.), *Musical development from a lifespan perspective* (pp. 141–162). Peter Lang. https://www.peterlang.com/document/1101004

Gronostaj, A., Werner, E., Bochow, E., & Vock, M. (2016). How to learn things at school you don't already know: Experiences of gifted grade-skippers in Germany. *Gifted Child Quarterly, 60*(1), 31–46. https://doi.org/10.1177/0016986215609999

Jarvin, L., & Subotnik, R.F. (2010). Wisdom from conservatory faculty: Insights on success in classical music performance. *Roeper Review, 32*(2), 78–87. https://doi.org/10.1080/02783191003587868

Jett, N., & Rinn, A.N. (2019). Radically early college entrants on radically early college entrance: A heuristic inquiry. *Journal for the Education of the Gifted, 42*(4), 303–335. https://doi.org/10.1177/0162353219874430

Jung, J.Y., & Evans, P. (2016). The career decisions of child musical prodigies. In G.E. McPherson (ed.), *Musical prodigies: Interpretations from psychology, music education, musicology and ethnomusicology* (pp. 409–423). Oxford University Press. https://doi.org/10.1093/acprof:oso/9780199685851.003.0018

Leung, P.P.Y. (2010). Autobiographical timeline: A narrative and life story approach in understanding meaning-making in cancer patients. *Illness, Crisis & Loss, 18*(2), 111–127. https://doi.org/10.2190/IL.18.2.c

Manturzewska, M. (1990). A biographical study of the life-span development of professional musicians. *Psychology of Music, 18*(2), 112–139. https://doi.org/10.1177/0305735690182002

Martin, A.J. (2016). Musical prodigies and motivation. In G.E. McPherson (ed.), *Musical prodigies: Interpretations from psychology, education, musicology, and ethnomusicology* (pp. 320–337). Oxford University Press. https://doi.org/10.1093/acprof:oso/9780199685851.003.0013

Mayer, R.E. (2005). The scientific study of giftedness. In R.J. Sternberg & J.E. Davidson (eds), *Conceptions of giftedness* (2nd ed., pp. 437–447). Cambridge University Press. https://doi.org/10.1017/CBO9780511610455.025

McLean, K.C. (2005). Late adolescent identity development: Narrative meaning making and memory telling. *Developmental Psychology, 41*(4), 683–691. https://doi.org/10.1037/0012-1649.41.4.683

McPherson, G.E. (ed.). (2016). *Musical prodigies: Interpretations from psychology, education, musicology, and ethnomusicology*. Oxford University Press. https://global.oup.com/academic/product/musical-prodigies-9780199685851?cc=rs&lang=en&#

McPherson, G.E., & Lehmann, A.C. (2012). Exceptional musical abilities: Musical prodigies. In G.E. McPherson & G.F. Welch (eds), *The Oxford handbook of music education: Vol. 2* (pp. 31–50). Oxford University Press. https://doi.org/10.1093/oxfordhb/9780199928019.013.0003_update_001

Mun, R.U., & Hertzog, N.B. (2019). The influence of parental and self-expectations on Asian American women who entered college early. *Gifted Child Quarterly, 63*(2), 120–140. https://doi.org/10.1177/0016986218823559

Neihart, M. (2007). The socioaffective impact of acceleration and ability grouping: Recommendations for best practice. *Gifted Child Quarterly, 51*(4), 330–341. https://doi.org/10.1177/0016986207306319

Nogaj, A.A., & Bogunović, B. (2015). The development of giftedness within the three-level system of music education in Poland and Serbia: Outcomes at different stages. *Journal of the Institute for Educational Research, 47*(1), 153–174. https://doiserbia.nb.rs/img/doi/0579-6431/2015/0579-64311501153N.pdf

Palmer, T., & Baker, D. (2021). Classical soloists' life histories and the music conservatoire. *International Journal of Music Education, 39*(2), 167–186. https://doi.org/10.1177/0255761421991154

Plucker, J.A., & Barab, S.A. (2005). The importance of contexts in theories of giftedness: Learning to embrace the messy joys of subjectivity. In R.J. Sternberg & J.E. Davidson (eds), *Conceptions of giftedness* (pp. 201–216). Cambridge University Press. https://doi.org/10.1017/CBO9780511610455.013

Rinn, A.N., & Bishop, J. (2015). Gifted adults: A systematic review and analysis of the literature. *Gifted Child Quarterly, 59*(4), 213–235. https://doi.org/10.1177/0016986215600795

Rogers, K.B. (2007). Lessons learned about educating the gifted and talented: A synthesis of the research on educational practice. *Gifted Child Quarterly, 51*(4), 382–396. https://doi.org/10.1177/0016986207306324

Sayler, M.F., & Brookshire, W.K. (1993). Social, emotional, and behavioral adjustment of accelerated students, students in gifted classes, and regular students in eighth grade. *Gifted Child Quarterly, 37*(4), 150–154. https://doi.org/10.1177/001698629303700403

Smith, J.A., & Osborn, M. (2004). Interpretative phenomenological analysis. In G. M. Breakwell (ed.), *Doing social psychology research* (pp. 229–254). Blackwell Publishing; British Psychological Society.

Spector-Mersel, G. (2011). Mechanisms of selection in claiming narrative identities: A model for interpreting narratives. *Qualitative Inquiry, 17*(2), 172–185. https://doi.org/10.1177/1077800410393885

Subotnik, R.F., & Jarvin, L. (2005). Beyond expertise: Conceptions of giftedness as great performance. In R.J. Sternberg & J.E. Davidson (eds), *Conceptions of giftedness* (2nd ed., pp. 343–357). Cambridge University Press. https://doi.org/10.1017/CBO9780511610455.020

Subotnik, R.F., Jarvin, L., Thomas, A., & Maie Lee, G. (2016). Transitioning musical abilities into expertise and beyond: The role of psychosocial skills in developing prodigious talent. In G.E. McPherson (ed.), *Musical prodigies: Interpretations from psychology, education, musicology, and ethnomusicology* (pp. 279–293). Oxford University Press. https://doi.org/10.1093/acprof:oso/9780199685851.003.0011

Teague, A., & Smith, G.D. (2015). Portfolio careers and work-life balance among musicians: An initial study into implications for higher music education. *British Journal of Music Education, 32*(2), 177–193. https://doi.org/10.1017/S0265051715000121

Thomsen, D.K., & Berntsen, D. (2008). The cultural life script and life story chapters contribute to the reminiscence bump. *Memory, 16*(4), 420–435. https://doi.org/10.1080/09658210802010497

Winner, E. (1996). *Gifted children: Myths and realities*. Basic Books.

Winner, E., & Martino, G. (2000). Giftedness in non-academic domains: The case of the visual arts and music. In K.A. Heller, F.J. Mönks, R.J. Sternberg, & R.F. Subotnik (eds), *International handbook of giftedness and talent* (2nd ed., pp. 95–110). Elsevier. https://shop.elsevier.com/books/international-handbook-of-giftedness-and-talent/heller/978-0-08-043796-5

Ziegler, A., Balestrini, D.P., & Stöger, H. (2018). An international view on gifted education: Incorporating the macro-systemic perspective. In S. Pfeiffer (ed.), *Handbook of giftedness in children* (pp. 15–28). Springer, Cham. https://doi.org/10.1007/978-3-319-77004-8_2

Appendix

Fig. 13.1 Filip's life path

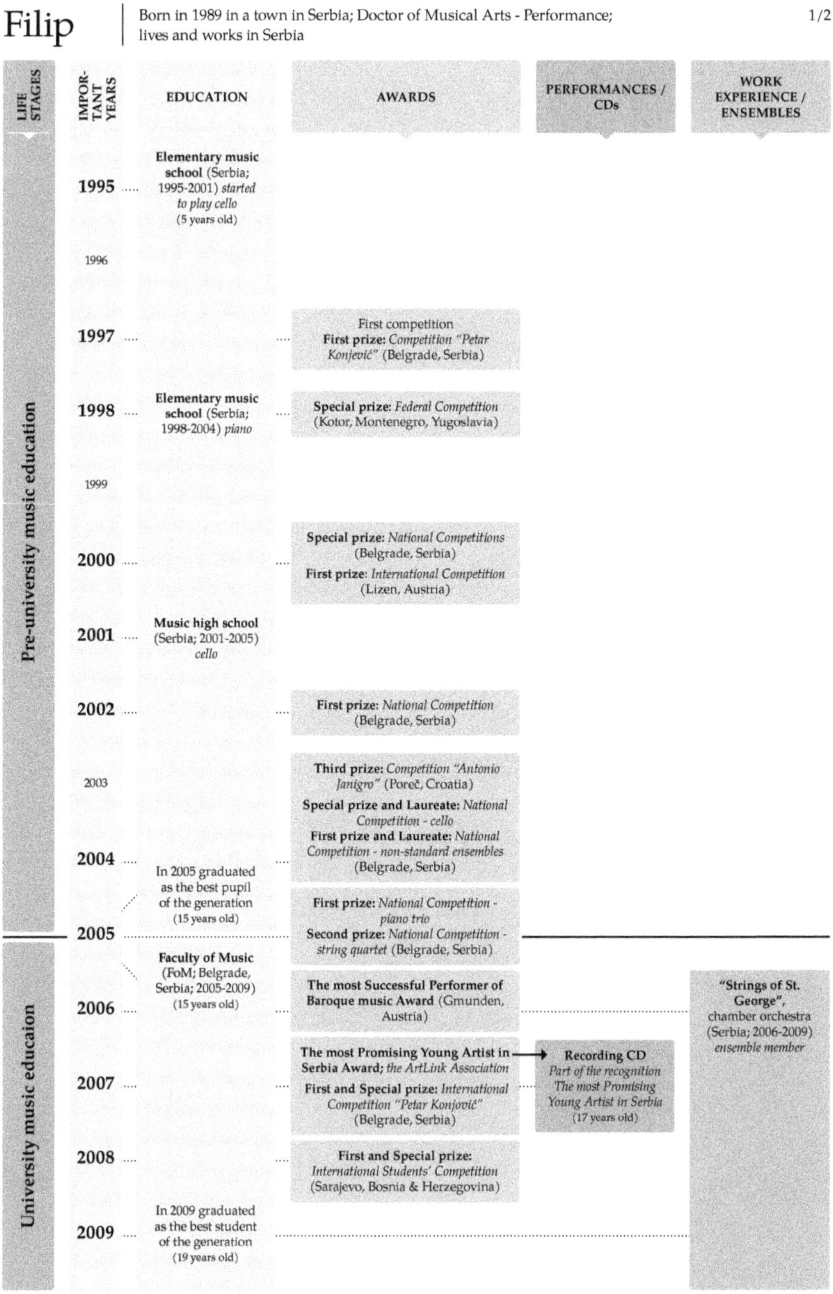

Filip — Born in 1989 in a town in Serbia; Doctor of Musical Arts - Performance; lives and works in Serbia

LIFE STAGES	IMPORTANT YEARS	EDUCATION	AWARDS	PERFORMANCES / CDs	WORK EXPERIENCE / ENSEMBLES
Pre-university music education	1995	Elementary music school (Serbia; 1995-2001) *started to play cello* (5 years old)			
	1996				
	1997		First competition **First prize:** *Competition "Petar Konjević"* (Belgrade, Serbia)		
	1998	Elementary music school (Serbia; 1998-2004) *piano*	**Special prize:** *Federal Competition* (Kotor, Montenegro, Yugoslavia)		
	1999				
	2000		**Special prize:** *National Competitions* (Belgrade, Serbia) **First prize:** *International Competition* (Lizen, Austria)		
	2001	Music high school (Serbia; 2001-2005) *cello*			
	2002		**First prize:** *National Competition* (Belgrade, Serbia)		
	2003		**Third prize:** *Competition "Antonio Janigro"* (Poreč, Croatia) **Special prize and Laureate:** *National Competition - cello* **First prize and Laureate:** *National Competition - non-standard ensembles* (Belgrade, Serbia)		
	2004	In 2005 graduated as the best pupil of the generation (15 years old)	**First prize:** *National Competition - piano trio* **Second prize:** *National Competition - string quartet* (Belgrade, Serbia)		
University music education	2005	Faculty of Music (FoM; Belgrade, Serbia; 2005-2009) (15 years old)			
	2006		**The most Successful Performer of Baroque music Award** (Gmunden, Austria)		"Strings of St. George", chamber orchestra (Serbia; 2006-2009) *ensemble member*
	2007		**The most Promising Young Artist in Serbia Award**; *the ArtLink Association* **First and Special prize:** *International Competition "Petar Konjević"* (Belgrade, Serbia)	→ **Recording CD** *Part of the recognition The most Promising Young Artist in Serbia* (17 years old)	
	2008		**First and Special prize:** *International Students' Competition* (Sarajevo, Bosnia & Herzegovina)		
	2009	In 2009 graduated as the best student of the generation (19 years old)			

Filip

Born in 1989 in a town in Serbia; Doctor of Musical Arts - Performance; lives and works in Serbia

LIFE STAGES	IMPORTANT YEARS	EDUCATION	AWARDS	PERFORMANCES / CDs	WORK EXPERIENCE / ENSEMBLES
	2009	**FoM** (Belgrade, Serbia; 2009-2015) *music doctoral studies* (19 years old)			**FoM** (Belgrade, Serbia; 2009-2012) *teaching assistance, String department*
	2010	**Mozarteum University** (Salzburg, Austria; 2009-2010) *specialization*	First Audience prize, diploma of the Ilija M. Kolarac endowment, recognition of the "Friends of Mica Pavlović" fund: *Jeunesses Musicales International Competition* (Belgrade, Serbia)	Participation in Concerts for Life and Peace (Italy and Israel/Palestine)	
	2011	**Scuola di Musica di Fiesole** (Florence, Italy; 2009-2012) *specialization*	Final round: *International Johannes Brahms Competition* (Pörtschach, Austria)		**Belgrade Philharmonic Orchestra** (Serbia; 2011-2019) *principal cellist* (21 years old)
	2012	**MUK Privatuniverstät Wien** (Austria; 2010-2013) *master studies*	First prize: *International Cello Competition* (Liezen, Austria) Finale: *Fidelio Spezial Wettbewerb* (Wien, Austria)		
Professional life after graduation	2013	Master degree in cello performance cum laude **MUK Privatuniverstät Wien** (Wien, Austria)			
	2014				
	2015	The youngest Serbian Doctor of Musical Arts - Performance; **FoM** (Belgrade, Serbia) (25 years old)			
	2016				**"Strings of St. George"**, chamber orchestra (Serbia; 2016-2018) *ensemble member*
	2017				**Faculty of Arts in Niš** (Serbia; 2017-2018) *asst. professor of cello; teacher of Methodics of teaching string instruments*
	2018		The Young Artist of the 2017 Award; *"Muzika klasika"* magazine Acknowledgement for outstanding merits and contribution to the faculty *FoM*		**Piano trio "X"** member (2017-2020) **FoM** (Belgrade, Serbia; 2018 - present) *asst. professor of chamber music*
	2019		With Trio "X" received the **"Brivio Sforza" Award for Ensemble of the Year**; The Art Association "Le Dimore del Quartetto" (Milan, Italy)	CD "X" new compositions for cello by Serbian authors	
	2020			Named as one of the 5 best albums in 2020 Violoncello Foundation (NY, USA)	
	2021		City of Belgrade Award for the "extraordinary interpretation of compositions" on the album "X" CD "X" nominated for the Listeners' Choice Award: *Violoncello Foundation* (NY, USA)	Several concerts in Milan (Italy) Evening concert promotion of album "X", Kolarac (Belgrade, Serbia)	**Belgrade Chamber Orchestra** (Belgrade, Serbia; 2021 - present) *principal cellist*

14. The Personality of Music Students with Diverse Vocal and Instrumental Skills

Ana Butković

Introduction

Individual differences in personality are widely investigated, and since the development of the Big Five model (Goldberg, 1990) and the Five-Factor Model (Costa & McCrae, 1992), a framework with five broad personality factors (Extraversion, Agreeableness, Conscientiousness Neuroticism, Openness) has become dominant in personality psychology. Meta-analyses have indicated that those five personality traits are associated with diverse outcomes, such as job performance (Barrick & Mount, 1991), academic performance (Poropat, 2009), job satisfaction (Judge et al., 2002), relationship satisfaction (Malouff et al., 2010), subjective well-being (DeNeve & Cooper, 1998), and resilience (Oshio et al., 2018). A recent study investigated whether these associations between personality traits and different life outcomes were replicable. Soto (2019) conducted preregistered, high-powered replications of 78 previously published trait-outcome associations and found that 87% of the replication attempts were statistically significant in the expected direction. In addition, a subsequent study showed that most trait-outcome associations were generalised across gender, age, and ethnicity (Soto, 2021).

Individual differences in five personality factors have also been related to occupational choices. Two meta-analyses (Barrick et al., 2003; Hurtado Rúa et al., 2019) have examined the association between the Five-Factor Model of personality and Holland's (1997) occupational types, and found the highest association between Openness and the artistic type. However, the results have also indicated that the measurement scale was a significant moderator of this association, suggesting that the obtained correlations might differ depending on the measures applied to assess personality traits. Using longitudinal data from Germany, John and Thomsen (2014) found that personality scores are linked with the probability of working in a specific occupational group. Similarly, Wells et al. (2016) found that personality significantly influenced the probability of an individual choice or of an individual being chosen for a particular occupation using a longitudinal data set from Australia.

Another interesting research question is whether personality differences in specialty selection in a specific occupation exist. Recently, Woods et al. (2016, p. 265) have given two possible propositions about the correlation between personality traits and occupational specialty. One proposal is that personality traits that lead to a gravitation towards specific occupations are not associated with job specialisation within those occupations. This is because people choosing a specific occupation are similar in their personality traits, and professional environments for different careers within the same occupation are similar as well. The other proposal is that personality traits are associated with specialty choice when traits are conceptually related to job activity variation across different job specialisations. If there are within-occupation career choices that vary in their appeal to people who are high or low on a specific trait (e.g., Agreeableness), then that trait (i.e., Agreeableness) will be associated with a particular choice of specialty. This issue was mainly investigated in the medical profession (e.g., Borges & Savickas, 2002; Mullola et al., 2018; Woods et al., 2016). In the UK, Woods et al. (2016) found that Agreeableness and Neuroticism were associated with selected specialties of doctors, while in Finland, Openness was associated with physicians' career choices (Mullola et al., 2018). These two competing hypotheses about the correlation between personality traits and occupational specialty are also examined in this study.

In music psychology, both the personality of musicians and their differences from people in other occupations or the general population, and personality differences related to specialty selection have been investigated. Studies have indicated differences in the personality of musicians compared to the personalities of those in other occupations and the general population. Vaag et al. (2018) compared Norwegian musicians to the general workforce. They found that musicians displayed higher degrees of Neuroticism and Openness to experience, and lower degrees of Conscientiousness. Similarly, Swedish musicians, both professional and amateur, were compared with non-musicians from a sample from the Swedish Twin Registry (Kuckelkorn et al., 2021). Significant group differences were found in Openness, with professionals scoring higher than amateurs, who in turn scored higher than non-musicians, and with professionals showing higher Neuroticism, lower Agreeableness, and lower Conscientiousness than amateurs. Butković and Rančić Dopuđ (2017) compared Croatian male musicians who self-identified as classical or heavy-metal musicians to the general population norms and found the former had higher scores on Extraversion, Agreeableness, and, especially, Intellect. A comparison of vocalists, instrumentalists, and non-musicians across the US indicated that vocalists had higher scores on Extraversion and Openness/Intellect than non-musicians (Torrance, 2017). Mihajlovski (2016) compared musicians and a control sample of non-musicians from Macedonia. Significant differences were found in Neuroticism, Openness, and Conscientiousness, with musicians scoring higher. Sandgren (2019) compared vocalist and instrumentalist music students to a control group of psychology students and found no personality differences between them, while vocalists had higher scores than the control group on Extraversion, Agreeableness, and Openness. Gjermunds et al. (2020) compared samples of self-identified musicians and non-musicians recruited on the Internet and found that the musicians had significantly higher scores on Openness and lower scores on Conscientiousness. In sum, the review of the literature has indicated that the results were consistent only for musicians having a higher level of Openness, in line with two meta-analyses findings that Openness is the most essential personality trait for the artistic type (Barrick et al., 2003; Hurtado Rúa et al., 2019).

Next, findings about the association between personality traits and occupational specialty in musicians are reviewed with special reference to the personality scale applied in the study, since the measurement scale was found to be a moderator of the personality-occupational type association (Hurtado Rúa et al., 2019), and the generalisability of trait-outcome associations across personality measures has not yet been examined (Soto, 2021). The first group of studies applied personality measures of the Five-Factor Model (Costa & McCrae, 1992). Langendörfer (2008) examined the personality of professional orchestra members in Germany using NEO Five-Factor Inventory (NEO-FFI) and found that string players had higher Conscientiousness than the other musicians. Bogunović (2012) compared pianists, string players, and wind instrument players together with solo singers and music theorists using NEO Personality Inventory Revised (NEO-PI-R) in a combined sample of pupils, students, and professional musicians, and found differences in Extraversion, Openness, and Agreeableness. Mihajlovski (2013) compared piano, strings, woodwind, and brass instrumentalists, using NEO-PI-R in a combined sample of Macedonian pupils, students, and professional musicians. The largest difference was found for Openness, with brass players having lower scores than the other groups.

The second group of studies applied personality scales based on the International Personality Item Pool (IPIP). Torrance (2017) compared personality traits in music students of different ensemble instrumental section groups using IPIP-50. Significant MANOVA results were found for Agreeableness and Neuroticism. Personality differences were not found using the same scale between classical and heavy-metal male musicians (Butković & Rančić Dopuđ, 2017). Torrance and Bugos (2017) examined personality differences using the Big Five IPIP scale amongst music students divided into vocalist and instrumentalist groups, and found that vocalists had higher Extraversion than instrumentalists. Similar differences were found in a study investigating popular music genre musicians, namely bassists, drummers, guitarists, and vocalists, and using Mini-IPIP to measure personality (Cameron et al., 2015). Singers showed higher Extraversion than bassists and drummers and had higher scores on the Intellect/Imagination dimension than drummers.

The third group of studies applied versions of the Big Five Inventory (BFI) measure, also used in this study. Vaag et al. (2018) examined differences in a sample of professional musicians. They found with BFI-20-N that vocalists scored higher on Openness to experience, while string players scored higher on Neuroticism (both bowed and plucked) and Introversion (only bowed). Two studies on music students examining differences between instrumental groups found no personality differences between musicians (Butković & Modrušan, 2021; Sandgren, 2019). Butković and Modrušan (2021) applied a short BFI-10 measure, which measures each of the five factors with only two items, to pianists, singers, string, woodwind, brass, and music pedagogy students; while Sandgren (2019) applied a longer BFI measure with 44 items to only vocalists and instrumentalists. Kuckelkorn et al. (2021) found with BFI-44 that singers were higher on Extraversion than instrumentalists amongst both professional and amateur groups of musicians. They also found personality differences between instrumental players, but the patterns were inconsistent. Since most studies reviewed here indicated that Openness and Extraversion are personality traits which show personality differences among different musicians' specialisations, personality differences in this study are expected for those two traits.

In sum, findings on the relations between personality traits and occupational specialty in musicians are mixed. Studies have applied various personality measures, examined distinct instrumental groups, had different sample sizes and design, and obtained inconsistent results. Significant differences between instrumental groups concerning personality traits (Extraversion, Openness, Agreeableness, Conscientiousness) have mainly been found with measures of the Five-Factor Model. However, these findings were from studies using personality measures with the highest number of items, e.g., NEO-PI-R. Studies using IPIP measures indicated personality differences between vocalists and instrumentalists, especially in Extraversion. As for BFI, the largest studies, with Norwegian (Vaag et al., 2018) and Swedish (Kuckelkorn et al., 2021) musicians, found significant personality differences, while smaller studies (Butković & Modrušan, 2021; Sandgren, 2019) have not found them. Therefore, based on these previous findings, a measure of the Five-Factor Model with a larger number of items compared to the one previously used on the Croatian sample was used in this study. In addition, some studies included only professional musicians, some only music students, and some had combined samples that covered a wide age range, from music pupils to professional musicians. The age and gender composition of the sample might have influenced the results (e.g., Soto et al., 2011). Therefore, a gender-balanced sample of music students who were more homogeneous in age and professional experience was used in this study to examine personality differences.

Aims

This study aimed to examine personality differences in a sample of music students with diverse vocal and instrumental skills using a longer 44-item BFI measure. Music students as a group are relatively homogeneous in age, and in Croatia, they have already been through 10 years of music education before starting their studies, which pertains to the finding that 10 years or more are needed to become an expert in a field (Richman et al., 1996). Two competing hypotheses are stated, based on Woods et al.'s (2016) propositions and prior results. The first is that personality traits are not associated with an occupational specialty in music, so there will be no personality differences among instrumental groups. The opposite hypothesis is that personality traits are conceptually related to job activity variation across instrumental groups, which means that personality differences between instrumental groups will be found. Job activation variation among musicians can stem from different technical demands of the instruments (how they are played, a physical difficulty for a player, practice time) or job positions (solo, chamber, orchestra). Based on the results from previous studies, personality differences are primarily expected in Openness and Extraversion, with vocalists having higher scores than instrumentalists.

Methods

Participants and procedure

Students of the Academy of Music in Zagreb participated in the study ($N = 370$, 58% female). They filled in the questionnaire during their psychology classes. They were asked about their study group. Students who did not specify their study programme ($n = 7$) and who only mentioned the department they were studying at ($n = 8$) were excluded from the sample, since they could not be allocated to any instrumental group/study programme. The remaining 355 students belonged to the following groups: theory and conducting ($n = 18$), musicology ($n = 28$), music pedagogy ($n = 63$), voice ($n = 25$), keyboard ($n = 66$), string ($n = 90$) and wind ($n = 65$) instruments.

Since the study aimed to examine personality differences among music students with diverse vocal and instrumental skills, only voice, keyboard, and string and wind instrument students ($N = 246$, 55% female) were included in further analysis. The participants were mainly (93%) in their first year of studies ($M = 19.31$, $SD = 1.98$, range 15–35 years). Additional analyses were run with a string group divided into bowed ($n = 44$) and plucked ($n = 12$) strings, and a wind group divided into woodwind ($n = 29$) and brass ($n = 15$) players. This was done since previous studies have indicated that personality differences are obtained for specific instrumentalist groups such as brass players (e.g., Mihajlovski, 2013) or bowed strings (e.g., Vaag et al., 2018). The number of participants is smaller compared to the number included in the main analysis because students who did not specify their instrument were not included in this level of analysis.

The study was approved by the Department of Psychology's Ethics Committee.

Materials

All participants in the study filled in the Big Five Inventory (BFI; John et al., 1991, 2008) which has 44 items: eight measuring Extraversion and Neuroticism, nine measuring Agreeableness and Conscientiousness, and 10 measuring Openness. Participants indicated on a scale from 1 (disagree strongly) to 5 (agree strongly) the extent to which they agreed or disagreed with each item. Cronbach's alpha reliabilities for each dimension in this study are presented in Table 14.1.

Data analysis

For descriptive analyses means, standard deviations and reliability were calculated. To test for mean differences between the groups, ANOVA was run, followed by post-hoc analyses conducted using Tukey's HSD test. The eta squared (η^2) was calculated as an effect size measure. The data were analysed using IBM SPSS Statistics (Version 26) software.

Results

Descriptive statistics for personality traits in four instrumental groups and ANOVA results are presented in Table 14.1. Obtained mean values for personality traits were in line with previous findings in a student sample in Croatia (e.g., Tödtling, 2013). Bonferroni correction was calculated to adjust for multiple comparisons, and obtained value was $p < .008$. Applying this correction, no significant differences in personality between music student groups were found for Neuroticism, Extraversion, Agreeableness, or Conscientiousness. The ANOVA did show significant differences in Openness with medium large effect size, $F(3,242) = 8.73$, $p < .001$, $\eta^2 = .10$. A post-hoc Tukey procedure indicated that wind instrumentalists ($M = 3.81$, $SD = .59$) had lower Openness scores than keyboard instrumentalists ($M = 4.18$, $SD = .45$) and vocalists ($M = 4.29$, $SD = .47$).

Table 14.1 Descriptive statistics for four instrumental groups and results of ANOVA

Measure		Voice $n = 25$		Keyboard $n = 66$		String $n = 90$		Wind $n = 65$		ANOVA		
	α	M	SD	M	SD	M	SD	M	SD	$F(3,242)$	p	η^2
N	.82	2.37	.57	2.66	.73	2.74	.66	2.74	.90	1.81	.147	.02
E	.79	3.94	.49	3.49	.70	3.48	.63	3.62	.61	3.78	.011	.04
O	.79	4.29[1]	.47	4.18[1]	.45	4.03	.44	3.81[2]	.59	8.73	<.001***	.10
A	.64	3.89	.44	3.54	.45	3.59	.56	3.62	.62	2.62	.051	.03
C	.76	3.64	.54	3.51	.64	3.38	.57	3.54	.58	1.82	.145	.02

Note. α = Cronbach's alpha reliability; n = number of participants; M = mean; SD = standard deviation; F = F – ratio; p = p value; η^2 = eta squared; N = Neuroticism; E = Extraversion; O = Openness; A = Agreeableness; C = Conscientiousness. Means with different superscripts differ at the $p < .001$ level with Tukey's HSD test. Different superscripts indicate between which groups post-hoc Tukey indicated statistically significant differences (1 differs from 2).

*$p < .05$; **$p < .01$; ***$p < .001$

A horizontal version of this table may be viewed online at https://hdl.handle.net/20.500.12434/23b8a5a1

14. The Personality of Music Students

Table 14.2 Descriptive statistics for six instrumental groups and results of ANOVA

Measure	Voice n = 25		Keyboard n = 66		Bow string n = 44		Pluck string n = 12		Woodwind n = 29		Brass n = 15		ANOVA		
	M	SD	M	SD	M	SD	M	SD	M	SD	M	SD	F(5,185)	p	η^2
N	2.37	.57	2.66	.73	2.66	.69	2.79	.78	2.77	.93	2.84	1.10	1.05	.389	.03
E	3.94	.49	3.49	.70	3.54	.67	3.42	.47	3.50	.56	3.60	.83	1.98	.084	.05
O	4.29[1]	.47	4.18[1]	.45	4.08	.45	3.98	.42	3.89	.61	3.56[2]	.51	5.90	<.001***	.14
A	3.89	.44	3.54	.45	3.70	.53	3.34	.61	3.65	.63	3.50	.72	2.55	.029	.06
C	3.64	.54	3.51	.64	3.34	.60	3.32	.61	3.54	.61	3.45	.51	1.08	.375	.03

Note. n = number of participants; M = mean; SD = standard deviation; F = F – ratio; p = p value; η^2 = eta squared; N = Neuroticism; E = Extraversion; O = Openness; A = Agreeableness; C = Conscientiousness. Means with different superscripts differ at the p < .001 level with Tukey's HSD test. Different superscripts indicate between which groups post-hoc Tukey indicated statistically significant differences (1 differs from 2).

*p < .05; **p < .01; ***p < .001

A horizontal version of this table may be viewed online at https://hdl.handle.net/20.500.12434/fac078d9

Analyses were repeated on subgroups to examine if additional personality differences would be revealed, and the results are presented in Table 14.2. Again, Bonferroni correction was calculated to adjust for multiple comparisons ($p < .003$). ANOVA showed significant differences in Openness with large effect size, $F(5,185) = 5.90$, $p < .001$, $\eta^2 = .14$. A post-hoc Tukey procedure indicated that brass players had lower Openness scores ($M = 3.56$, $SD = .51$) than keyboard instrumentalists ($M = 4.15$, $SD = .45$) and vocalists ($M = 4.28$, $SD = .50$).

Discussion

The aim of this study was to examine personality differences in a sample of music students with varying vocal and instrumental skills using a longer 44-item BFI measure. Music students in Croatia have already had 10 years of systematic music education which means they have a high level of expertise, and are studying to become professional musicians. In addition, they are more homogeneous in age than, for example, professional musicians working in orchestras, which can influence the personality differences. Results were not in line with the hypothesis that personality traits are not conceptually related to job activity variation across instrumental groups, since we found some personality differences. However, personality differences were not found in all personality traits or between all groups of musicians, which is partially in line with the hypothesis that there are personality differences between different job specialisations amongst musicians. In the primary analysis, significant differences between instrumental groups were found in Openness. In line with the hypothesis and previous studies (Bogunović, 2012; Cameron et al., 2015; Kuckelkorn et al., 2021; Mihajlovski, 2013; Vaag et al., 2018), significant differences in Openness were found between wind and keyboard instrumentalists, and between wind instrumentalists and vocalists. Contrary to expectations and some previous findings, differences were not found for other personality traits or between the other groups of musicians that were included. Analyses of subgroups confirmed the earlier results regarding Openness (Mihajlovski, 2013), with significant differences shown between brass players and keyboard instrumentalists, and brass players and vocalists.

Results of this study indicate that personality differences in Openness are important for distinguishing between musicians and other professions, and between different job specialisations in the musical profession. Several studies, including this one, found that vocalists had the highest Openness score (Cameron et al., 2015; Kuckelkorn et al., 2021; Vaag et al., 2018), while Mihajlovski (2013) found, as in this study, that brass players had the lowest Openness score. These findings could mean that people higher in Openness are attracted to the musical profession, and that amongst people who decide to enter the musical profession those who are highest in Openness are attracted to being vocalists, while those with lower Openness scores are more attracted to wind instruments, especially brass. Of course, it is difficult to know without longitudinal data if going to the music school also contributes to the development of Openness, and not just *vice versa*.

The literature review has indicated that instrumental group samples and applied personality measures influence the personality differences of musicians playing different instruments. Personality measures with more items seem to be needed to detect variations in the Openness dimension between instrumental groups, since Butković and Modrušan (2021) found no personality differences when Openness was measured with only two items. Concerning the type of samples used in diverse studies, it is clear that they cover a variety of instrumentalists and vocal performers. This could mean that different findings in studies might be due to comparing different groups of musicians. Therefore, it might be worthwhile examining the specific demands of each music job specialisation to figure out between which groups the differences in Openness could be expected, and which groups of musicians should be included in the study.

Furthermore, a better understanding of personality differences between musicians could be obtained by examining the personality facets as well. So far, the study that applied NEO-PI-R with facet results indicated that brass players had the lowest scores on the Fantasy facet, followed by the Aesthetics facet (Mihajlovski, 2013). To the best of my knowledge, no study has so far examined facets of Openness in vocalists, so it is not known on which Openness facets vocalists score the highest. People scoring high on the Fantasy facet have an active fantasy life and are easily absorbed in different experiences. Panero et al. (2016) found that drama students score higher on Fantasy than music and non-arts students, while music students score higher than non-arts students on the Absorption scale. These authors concluded that actors are more able to focus their attention so that they can become absorbed in their character, and that musicians and non-artists do not practise this skill. I believe that singers are more similar in this respect to actors than musicians, which may lead to their higher Openness scores. A study using Cattell's 16 Personality Factor (16PF) measure compared singers, keyboard, strings, woodwind, and brass players, and found that brass players scored lowest on imaginativeness while singers scored the highest (Buttsworth & Smith, 1995). It could be that the demands of the vocal profession, which include singers being able to immerse themselves in different characters and roles, attract people who are better in using their imagination and becoming absorbed, and these demands could also further influence the development of particular personality traits.

One of the tested hypotheses was that there would be personality differences in Extraversion. The finding that vocalists have higher Extraversion than other instrumental groups has been established in both classical music (Torrance & Bugos, 2017) and popular genre (Cameron et al., 2015) musicians. After Bonferroni correction was applied, ANOVA results for Extraversion, $F(3,242) = 3.78, p = 0.011$, were not significant and this hypothesis was not confirmed. However, there are some job activity variations related to singers' professions, which may lead to differences in Extraversion. Vocalists are musicians and actors; they have to interact with the audience during their performances and to enjoy being in the spotlight. Studies have shown that professional actors have higher Extraversion than the general population (Nettle, 2006). This should not come as a surprise, since it has been shown that a central feature of Extraversion is social attention, or a tendency to behave in certain ways to attract social attention (Ashton et al., 2002). Standing on the stage and singing seem to be good ways to attract social attention. Recently, there have been attempts to develop a general reward-processing theory of extraverted personality, which suggests that individual differences in Extraversion may be associated with differential processing of rewards (Smillie et al., 2019). This would suggest that extraverts are motivated to obtain rewarding stimuli, and therefore choose an occupation where their work can be rewarded, for example with applause, flowers, and celebrity status. Future studies should examine whether vocalists score higher only on some Extraversion facets, such as Assertiveness.

Personality differences of expert musicians with diverse instrumental skills have been examined in America with two studies in the US (Torrance,

2017; Torrance & Bugos, 2017) and one in Canada (Cameron et al., 2015); in Western Europe with two studies in Sweden (Kuckelkorn et al., 2021; Sandgren, 2019), one in Norway (Vaag et al., 2018), and one in Germany (Langendörfer, 2008); and in the Western Balkans with two studies in Croatia (Butković & Modrušan, 2021; Butković & Rančić Dopuđ, 2017), one in Serbia (Bogunović, 2012), and one in Macedonia (Mihajlovski, 2013). No specificities in the research on this topic have been observed related to the region. Kuckelkorn et al. (2021) suggested that personality differences were not primarily related to instrument choice *per se*, but that they are moderated by other factors such as musical genre and the social context of music-making. Therefore, only a more systematic approach that considered possible factors such as training characteristics in particular instrumental groups or typical job characteristics would provide more insight.

One of the limitations of this study was the relatively small number of participants in some subgroups (e.g., plucked strings and brass) and differences in the sizes of compared groups. These differences reflect the number of music students enrolled in specific study programmes, with the highest enrollment quotas being for keyboard and bowed string instrumentalists. BFI is not a short personality measure, which means that it has more items per personality factor, but it only gives information on the factor level, not the facet level. Future studies should examine personality differences in personality facets and personality aspects, the level of personality hierarchy suggested by DeYoung et al. (2007). It could be expected that differences between musicians would be found in the Openness aspect, but not in the Intellect aspect. Furthermore, all studies examining personality differences of instrumental groups, including this one, used self-reporting to gather personality data. Although self-perceptions are helpful and contain some truth about a person, they can also significantly deviate from a person's true personality (Vazire & Carlson, 2010). Future studies could examine whether similar personality differences are found using peer reports. Finally, longitudinal studies are needed to examine how these personality differences develop and what practical educational implications these findings could have.

Conclusion

This study confirmed the finding that there are differences in Openness between distinct groups of musicians, with vocalists having the highest Openness scores among musicians, and brass players having the lowest. The finding corresponds with the suggestion that specialties in music have specific job demand characteristics, which make them appealing to people with different Openness scores. It seems that longer personality measures are needed to capture these differences. In future studies, the measurement of personality aspects and facets could contribute to a better understanding of these personality differences, as well as the use of longitudinal designs.

References

Ashton, M.C., Lee, K., & Paunonen, S.V. (2002). What is the central feature of extraversion? Social attention versus reward sensitivity. *Journal of Personality and Social Psychology, 83*(1), 245–252. http://dx.doi.org/10.1037/0022-3514.83.1.245

Barrick, M.R., & Mount, M.K. (1991). The big five personality dimensions and job performance: A meta-analysis. *Personnel Psychology, 44*(1), 1–26. https://doi.org/10.1111/j.1744-6570.1991.tb00688.x

Barrick, M.R., Mount, M.K., & Gupta, R. (2003). Meta-analysis of the relationship between the five-factor model of personality and Holland's occupational types. *Personnel Psychology, 56*(1), 45–74. https://doi.org/10.1111/j.1744-6570.2003.tb00143.x

Bogunović, B. (2012). Personality of musicians: Age, gender, and instrumental group differences. In E. Cambouropoulos, C. Tsougras, P. Mavromatis, & K. Pastiadis (eds), *Proceedings of the 12th International Conference on Music Perception and Cognition and the 8th Triennial Conference of the European Society for the Cognitive Sciences of Music* (pp. 120–121). http://icmpc-escom2012.web.auth.gr/files/papers/120_Proc.pdf

Borges, N.J., & Savickas, M.L. (2002). Personality and medical specialty choice: A literature review and integration. *Journal of Career Assessment, 10*(3), 362–380. https://doi.org/10.1177/10672702010003006

Butković, A., & Modrušan, I. (2021). Personality differences among musicians: Real differences or stereotypes? *Psychology of Music, 49*(2), 216–226. https://doi.org/10.1177/0305735619849625

Butković, A., & Rančić Dopuđ, D. (2017). Personality traits and alcohol consumption of classical and heavy metal musicians. *Psychology of Music, 45*(2), 246–256. https://doi.org/10.1177/0305735616659128

Buttsworth, L. M., & Smith, G.A. (1995). Personality of Australian performing musicians by gender and by instrument. *Personality and Individual Differences, 18*(5), 595–603. https://doi.org/10.1016/0191-8869(94)00201-3

Cameron, J. E., Duffy, M., & Glenwright, B. (2015). Singers take center stage! Personality traits and stereotypes of popular musicians. *Psychology of Music, 43*(6), 818–830. https://doi.org/10.1177/0305735614543217

Costa, P.T., Jr., & McCrae, R.R. (1992). Four ways five factors are basic. *Personality and Individual Differences, 13*(6), 653–665. https://doi.org/10.1016/0191-8869(92)90236-I

DeNeve, K.M., & Cooper, H. (1998). The happy personality: A meta-analysis of 137 personality traits and subjective well-being. *Psychological Bulletin, 124*(2), 197–229. https://psycnet.apa.org/doi/10.1037/0033-2909.124.2.197

DeYoung, C.G., Quilty, L.C., & Peterson, J.B. (2007). Between facets and domains: 10 aspects of the Big Five. *Journal of Personality and Social Psychology, 93*(5), 880–896. https://doi.org/10.1037/0022-3514.93.5.880

Gjermunds, N., Brechan, I., Johnsen, S.Å.K., & Watten, R.G. (2020). Personality traits in musicians. *Current Issues in Personality Psychology, 8*(2), 100–107. https://doi.org/10.5114/cipp.2020.97314

Goldberg, L.R. (1990). An alternative 'description of personality': The Big-Five factor structure. *Journal of Personality and Social Psychology, 59*(6), 1216–1229. https://doi.org/10.1037/0022-3514.59.6.1216

Holland, J.L. (1997). *Making vocational choices: A theory of vocational personalities and work environments* (3rd ed.). Psychological Assessment Resources.

Hurtado Rúa, S.M., Stead, G.B., & Poklar, A.E. (2019). Five-factor personality traits and RIASEC interest types: A multivariate meta-analysis. *Journal of Career Assessment, 27*(3), 527–543. https://doi.org/10.1177/1069072718780447

John, K., & Thomsen, S.L. (2014). Heterogeneous returns to personality: The role of occupational choice. *Empirical Economics, 47*(2), 553–592. https://doi.org/10.1007/s00181-013-0756-8

John, O.P., Donahue, E.M., & Kentle, R.L. (1991). *The Big Five Inventory—Versions 4a and 54*. University of California, Berkeley, Institute of Personality and Social Research. https://www.ocf.berkeley.edu/~johnlab/bfi.htm

John, O.P., Naumann, L.P., & Soto, C.J. (2008). Paradigm shift to the integrative Big-Five trait taxonomy: History, measurement, and conceptual issues. In O.P. John, R.W. Robins, & L.A. Pervin (eds), *Handbook of personality: Theory and research* (3rd ed., pp. 114–158). Guilford Press. https://www.researchgate.net/publication/289963274_Paradigm_shift_to_the_integrative_big_five_trait_taxonomy_History_measurement_and_conceptual_issues

Judge, T.A., Heller, D., & Mount, M.K. (2002). Five-factor model of personality and job satisfaction: A meta-analysis. *Journal of Applied Psychology, 87*(3), 530–541. https://doi.org/10.1037/0021-9010.87.3.530

Kuckelkorn, K.L., de Manzano, Ö., & Ullén, F. (2021). Musical expertise and personality—Differences related to occupational choice and instrument categories. *Personality and Individual Differences, 173*, Article 110573. https://doi.org/10.1016/j.paid.2020.110573

Langendörfer, F. (2008). Personality differences among orchestra instrumental groups: Just a stereotype? *Personality and Individual Differences, 44*(3), 610–620. https://doi.org/10.1016/j.paid.2007.09.027

Malouff, J.M., Thorsteinsson, E.B., Schutte, N.S., Bhullar, N., & Rooke, S.E. (2010). The Five-Factor Model of personality and relationship satisfaction of intimate partners: A meta-analysis. *Journal of Research in Personality, 44*(1), 124–127. https://doi.org/10.1016/j.jrp.2009.09.004

Mihajlovski, Z. (2013). Personality, intelligence and music instrument. *Croatian Journal of Education, 15*, 155–172. https://cje2.ufzg.hr/ojs/index.php/CJOE/article/view/606

Mihajlovski, Z. (2016). Musician as a distinctive personality structure—Yes or no? *Croatian Journal of Education, 18*, 125–143. https://doi.org/10.15516/cje.v18i0.2113

Mullola, S., Hakulinen, C., Presseau, J., de Porras, D.G.R., Jokela, M., Hintsa, T., & Elovainio, M. (2018). Personality traits and career choices among physicians in Finland: Employment sector, clinical patient contact, specialty and change of specialty. *BMC Medical Education, 18*(1), Article 52. https://doi.org/10.1186/s12909-018-1155-9

Nettle, D. (2006). Psychological profiles of professional actors. *Personality and Individual Differences, 40*(2), 375–383. https://psycnet.apa.org/doi/10.1016/j.paid.2005.07.008

Oshio, A., Taku, K., Hirano, M., & Saeed, G. (2018). Resilience and Big Five personality traits: A meta-analysis. *Personality and Individual Differences, 127*, 54–60. https://psycnet.apa.org/doi/10.1016/j.paid.2018.01.048

Panero, M.E., Goldstein, T.R., Rosenberg, R., Hughes, H., & Winner, E. (2016). Do actors possess traits associated with high hypnotizability? *Psychology of Aesthetics, Creativity, and the Arts, 10*(2), 233–239. https://psycnet.apa.org/doi/10.1037/aca0000044

Poropat, A.E. (2009). A meta-analysis of the five-factor model of personality and academic performance. *Psychological Bulletin, 135*(2), 322–338. https://psycnet.apa.org/doi/10.1037/a0014996

Richman, H.B., Gobet, F., Staszewski, J.J., & Simon, H.A. (1996). Perceptual and memory processes in the acquisition of expert performance: The EPAM model. In K.A. Ericsson (ed.), *The road to excellence: The acquisition of expert performance in the arts and sciences, sports, and games* (pp. 167–187). Lawrence Erlbaum. https://doi.org/10.4324/9781315805948

Sandgren, M. (2019). Exploring personality and musical self-perceptions among vocalists and instrumentalists at music colleges. *Psychology of Music, 47*(4), 465–482. https://doi.org/10.1177/0305735618761572

Smillie, L.D., Jach, H.K., Hughes, D.M., Wacker, J., Cooper, A.J., & Pickering, A.D. (2019). Extraversion and reward-processing: Consolidating evidence from an electroencephalographic index of reward-prediction-error. *Biological Psychology, 146*, Article 107735. https://doi.org/10.1016/j.biopsycho.2019.107735

Soto, C.J. (2019). How replicable are links between personality traits and consequential life outcomes? The Life Outcomes of Personality Replication Project. *Psychological Science, 30*(5), 711–727. https://doi.org/10.1177/0956797619831612

Soto, C.J. (2021). Do links between personality and life outcomes generalize? Testing the robustness of trait-outcome associations across gender, age, ethnicity, and analytic approaches. *Social Psychological and Personality Science, 12*(1), 118–130. https://doi.org/10.1177/1948550619900572

Soto, C.J., John, O.P., Gosling, S.D., & Potter, J. (2011). Age differences in personality traits from 10 to 65: Big Five domains and facets in a large cross-sectional sample. *Journal of Personality and Social Psychology, 100*(2), 330–348. https://doi.org/10.1037/a0021717

Tödtling, M. (2013). *Personality and basic psychological needs satisfaction as predictors of self-esteem* [Unpublished doctoral dissertation]. University of Zagreb, Croatia.

Torrance, T.A. (2017). *Music ensemble participation: Personality traits and music experience* [Unpublished doctoral dissertation]. University of South Florida, Tampa.

Torrance, T.A., & Bugos, J.A. (2017). Music ensemble participation: Personality traits and music experience. *Update: Applications of Research in Music Education, 36*(1), 28–36. https://doi.org/10.1177/8755123316675481

Vaag, J., Sund, E.R., & Bjerkeset, O. (2018). Five-factor personality profiles among Norwegian musicians compared to the general workforce. *Musicae Scientiae, 22*(3), 434–445. https://doi.org/10.1177/1029864917709519

Vazire, S., & Carlson, E.N. (2010). Self-knowledge of personality: Do people know themselves? *Social and Personality Psychology Compass, 4*(8), 605–620. https://psycnet.apa.org/doi/10.1111/j.1751-9004.2010.00280.x

Wells, R., Ham, R., & Junankar, P.N. (2016). An examination of personality in occupational outcomes: Antagonistic managers, careless workers and extraverted salespeople. *Applied Economics, 48*(7), 636–651. https://doi.org/10.1080/00036846.2015.1085636

Woods, S.A., Patterson, F.C., Wille, B., & Koczwara, A. (2016). Personality and occupational specialty: An examination of medical specialties using Holland's RIASEC model. *Career Development International, 21*(3), 262–278. https://psycnet.apa.org/doi/10.1108/CDI-10-2015-0130

15. Theoretical and Practical Challenges in Dealing with Music Performance Anxiety

Katarina Habe and Michele Biasutti

Introduction

Being a professional musician is both a blessing and a curse. Ironically, although professional musicians routinely score above average in psychological well-being (Ascenso et al., 2018) and report the highest levels of job satisfaction, at the same time they face numerous occupational stressors that induce medical problems in the physical, social, and psychological domains (Kenny & Ackermann, 2015; Matei & Ginsborg, 2017). Through constant performing challenges, musicianship can also become a source of serious distress and can negatively affect the well-being of a musician. In particular, coping with music performance anxiety (MPA) is a major psychological issue among professional musicians. The reported prevalence of MPA among musicians ranges from 16.5% to as high as 60% (Fernholz et al., 2019).

Both genetic factors and learning environments are relevant factors in shaping MPA (De Figueiredo Rocha, 2020). Certain personality traits are significant predictors of MPA, and research reports evidence that MPA is significantly positively connected to trait anxiety (Antonini Philippe et al., 2023; Cox & Kenardy, 1993; Kokotsaki & Davidson, 2003; Osborne & Kenny, 2005; Wiedemann et al., 2021) and neuroticism (Miranda, 2020). Kemp (1996) claims that anxiety manifests itself in emotional instability and in a form of frustrated tension and low self-sentiment. Furthermore, negatively charged emotions predict more than half of the differences in MPA between individuals (Sadler & Miller, 2010), whilst the correlation between MPA and perfectionism is positive and significant and increases with age (Patston & Osborne, 2016).

One of the issues in addressing MPA is the differentiation between maladaptive and adaptive forms of MPA. The adaptive forms should be evaluated for their productive capacity in enhancing coping strategies and resilience. The discussion as to whether MPA can be both beneficial and detrimental for musicians has not yet been clarified (Kenny, 2011). In formal music education, the labelling of pre-performance tension as negative reinforces the belief that MPA induces fear in pupils, building up negative or even catastrophic expectations. In addition, instead of accepting pre-performance tension as a normal pre-performance phenomenon with adaptive features that can be regulated with the use of preventive strategies (MacAfee & Comeau, 2020), teachers and pupils tend to perceive pre-performance tension as an experience that causes anxiety instead of music performance flow.

Aims

This chapter examines the terminological challenge of defining MPA as reflected in differences in relevant contemporary models of MPA. We complement existing reviews by highlighting the research studies regarding MPA in the Western Balkans (Croatia, Montenegro, Serbia and Slovenia). Finally, we address some of the preventive and interventionist approaches in dealing with MPA, with an emphasis on the idea of reconsidering MPA as pre-performance excitement (Brooks, 2014) that has the capacity for contributing to optimal states of flow (Csikszentmihalyi, 1990).

Main discussion

Challenges to delineating music performance anxiety

Performance anxiety, also known as 'stage fright', is a situational form of anxiety triggered by social exposure while performing. However, Kenny (2011) outlines that MPA should be distinguished from stage fright and social anxiety. Even though these phenomena share some commonalities, there are several important differences between them.

In contrast to individuals with social anxiety, individuals with MPA have high expectations of themselves and a greater fear of their own performance evaluation. Their feared task is cognitively and physically demanding. For those with MPA, the audience is likely to be real, rather than imaginary, as is the case in many examples of social anxiety. People with MPA are more likely to be concerned about their ability to perform competently. They are also more likely to remain in the threatening performance situation than people with social anxiety, who will typically escape or avoid the feared situation.

Kenny (2011) defines MPA as a distressing and persistent anxious apprehension related to music performance. She outlines the importance of accurately naming the phenomenon and emphasises that there is significant inconsistency in how it is described. Kenny suggests a tripartite typology of MPA that differentiates between (1) severe MPA as a focal disorder in an otherwise healthy musician; (2) severe MPA as an expression of social anxiety; and (3) severe MPA as a more complex psychopathology in which the individual may suffer from an extreme combination of emotional, cognitive, and somatic anxiety, along with severe problems with a sense of self and self-esteem.

(Music) performance anxiety models

The relationship between MPA and performance outcomes can be explained using different psychological models, and a few in particular have been frequently used. The Yerkes–Dodson law (1908) explains that optimal performance is associated with a moderate level of arousal. That means optimal performance requires a specific amount of pressure to enhance attention and concentration, memory recall, and emotional expressivity. Some positive aspects could be associated with a moderate level of excitement. Steptoe (1989, 2001) has reported evidence to support the inverted U-model of the relationship between physiological arousal and performance. Several other models explain the relationship between MPA and performance outcomes, such as the multidimensional anxiety theory (Martens et al., 1990), the catastrophe model of anxiety and performance (Hardy & Parfitt, 1991), Kerr's (1987) reversal theory (Gould & Krane, 1992), and the Individual Zone of Optimal Functioning (IZOF) model (Hanin, 2000).

Lang (1971) proposed a three-dimensional model of fear, consisting of behavioural, physiological, and verbal components that are related yet independent. Two dimensions of relatedness were identified between them: concordance–discordance and synchrony–desynchrony. The amount of response equivalence between the three components is expressed as degree of synchrony, while the rate of change of the three components is referred to as concordance. Craske and Craig (1984) confirmed Lang's three-systems model based on musicians. Martens et al. (1990) identified two components of performance anxiety in sport: cognitive anxiety and somatic anxiety. Their model predicts that cognitive anxiety will remain high prior to the performing situation; however, somatic anxiety will be low immediately before the event. The relevance of cognitive symptoms was emphasised in the catastrophe model of anxiety (Hardy & Parfitt, 1991), which states that the cognitive component determines whether the effects of the somatic component are small or large. The catastrophe theory claims that physiological arousal results in a performance catastrophe only when cognitive anxiety is high. Later, Hardy et al. (2007) added a third factor to their model, i.e., the effort required to perform the task. They proposed that there might be two different catastrophe models of performance: the original one and the one that includes effort as a moderating variable. In the later model, high cognitive anxiety and high effort predict performance catastrophe. Some of the models propose that self-efficacy, self-esteem and self-confidence mediate the relationship between somatic/cognitive anxiety and performance (González et al., 2018; Kayani et al., 2021; Miller & Chesky, 2004; Zarza-Alzugararay et al., 2020).

The mediating role of personality in the relationship between MPA and performance success was outlined in the reversal theory (Apter, 1982), which examines the positive and negative aspects of the stress-moderating effects of personality characteristics (see Chapter 12 in this volume). The name 'reversal theory' originates from the fact that meta-motivational states, which constitute the level of arousal (telic/paratelic) and hedonic quality (pleasantness/unpleasantness), interact in ways that either improve or impair music performance. Wilson and Roland (2002) redefined the relationship between MPA and performance by proposing a three-dimensional extension in line with three major sources of stress: trait anxiety (a personal characteristic), situational stress (environmental pressures like public performance and auditions), and task mastery. As to cognitive symptoms, an inversely linear relation to performance success is present (Blascovich & Mendes, 2010), meaning that negative cognitions are more detrimental to performance than increasing physiological arousal.

The Barlow anxiety model (2000) seems most commonly used amongst MPA researchers. Barlow's model proposes an integrated set of triple vulnerabilities that can account for the development of anxiety: a generalised biological vulnerability (genetics [trait anxiety], endocrine, etc.); a generalised psychological vulnerability (affection, cognition and its processing, attention, and personality traits), based on early experiences in developing a sense of control over salient events; and a specific psychological vulnerability, whereby anxiety comes to be associated with certain environmental stimuli through learning processes. Young performers with high trait anxiety (genetic vulnerability), who come from social environments with high music expectations, yet who do not get enough social support (generalised psychological vulnerability) and are exposed to frequent social evaluations of their performance in competitive environments (specific psychological vulnerability), might be triggered by physiological, cognitive, and behavioural responses of MPA. According to the Individual Zone of Optimal Functioning (IZOF) model, performance is successful when pre-competition anxiety is within or near the individual's optimal zone (Hanin, 2000). As such, IZOF mitigates the effects of MPA. Unfortunately, only a few studies applied IZOF when coping with MPA (McGinnis & Milling, 2005).

In sum, the level of arousal that might affect the success of a music performance depends upon the interaction of (1) the performer's susceptibility to experiencing anxiety (gender, age, trait anxiety, self-esteem, self-concept, and self-efficacy); (2) the performer's task efficacy (process of preparation, learning approach, motivation to learn, task difficulty/value, and anxiety coping strategies); and (3) the characteristics of the performance environment (audience presence, perceived degree of exposure, and venue characteristics). These factors are shaped by developmental experiences and cognitive appraisal of self and environment.

Research studies of MPA in the Western Balkans

The MPA studies conducted in the Western Balkans report that music students and professionals experience MPA regularly and emphasise the importance of dealing with maladaptive anxiety. The studies in the Western Balkan countries (see Table 15.1) cover a span of students from elementary specialist music school up to adult, mainly classical musicians. They are mainly empirical, except for the theoretical work of Kontić and Zatkalik (2020), which employs a psychoanalytic approach. There, the importance of developing a cohesive self and ego strength, which have the potential to master anxiety, is outlined as a guideline for the music-educational process.

Most empirical studies focus on the experiences of music students (Bačlija Sušić, 2018; Mirović & Bogunović, 2013a,b), with a few investigating professional musicians (Butković et al., 2022; Damjanović & Rosandić, 2019; Leva Bukovnik, 2018; Mazzon et al., 2023). A Slovene study on elementary school musicians (Habe & Kržič, 2017) showed that MPA is experienced less by pupils who started performing early in childhood; those with positive initial performing experiences; and those who enjoy being on stage. A Croatian study on younger musicians explored the role of the Functional Music Pedagogy approach, with music improvisation as its basic methodological tool for coping with MPA (Bačlija Sušić, 2018).

With one exception, all studies explored MPA with classical musicians. Comparing across genres, Leva Bukovnik (2018) established that classical singers experience significantly higher levels of MPA compared to jazz and pop singers. Many findings confirm earlier research with other populations in Western countries. For example, MPA was found to be more prevalent in female than male musicians (Butković et al., 2022; Habe & Kržič, 2017), in line with reports of higher levels of MPA in female musicians across developmental periods (Brugués, 2011; Yondem, 2007).

Table 15.1 Summary of the studies on MPA conducted in the Western Balkan region

Author(s)	Country	Study Type	Participants	Measurements	Research Findings
Bačlija Sušić, 2018	Croatia	Quantitative	Classical musicians: pupils from 4th to 6th grade of Music School N = 232	The Music Performance Anxiety Inventory for Adolescents (MPAI-A) (Osborne & Kenny, 2005).	Functional Music Pedagogy (FMP) approach, which regularly uses improvisation in its teaching practice. Does not have a significant effect on music performance anxiety in children.
Butković et al., 2022	Croatia	Quantitative	Classical musicians: music students and professional orchestral musicians N = 239	Kenny Music Performance Anxiety Inventory–Revised (K-MPAI-R) (Kenny, 2016); Almost Perfect Scale–Revised (APS-R) (Slaney et al., 2001).	In the regression analysis with gender, age, and dimensions of adaptive and maladaptive perfectionism as predictors, 46% of the MPA variance was explained with gender, age, and discrepancy as significant predictors. Higher MPA was predicted by being female, a younger musician, and having a higher maladaptive perfectionism.
Damjanović & Rosandić, 2020	Montenegro	Quantitative	Classical musicians: professional musicians N = 60	Kenny Music Performance Anxiety Inventory (Kenny et al., 2004); NEO Five Factor Inventory (NEO-FFI) (Costa & McCrae, 1995); Multidimensional Perfectionism Scale (MPS-F) (Flett & Hewitt, 2002).	The existence of certain personality aspects amongst professional musicians was confirmed, as well as the expression of a moderate but clinically relevant degree of anxiety and perfectionism, and showed their intercorrelations.

Author(s)	Country	Study Type	Participants	Measurements	Research Findings
Habe, 1998	Slovenia	Quantitative	Classical musicians: conservatory music students N = 104	Social Anxiety Scale for Adolescents (LSAA) (Puklek, 1997); The State-Trait Anxiety Inventory (STAI X-2) (Spielberger et al., 1983); Performance Anxiety Questionnaire (PAQ) (Cox & Kenardy, 1993).	Statistically important interaction between MPA and trait anxiety and social anxiety. MPA is more prevalent in female than in male music students. MPA differs regarding different performing settings and is highest at solo performance.
Habe & Križič, 2017	Slovenia	Quantitative	Classical musicians: 10–15-year-old music pupils N = 261	The Scale of Performance Anxiety (Habe, 2002).	No differences in MPA between younger (aged 10–12) and older (aged 13–15) music students were detected. It was found that MPA is more prevalent in girls than in boys. Less MPA is experienced by students who started performing early in childhood, those with positive first-performing experiences, and in those who enjoy being on stage. There were no differences in MPA regarding instrumental groups, although singers evidently reported the highest rates of MPA compared to other groups. There was a low negative correlation between MPA and final grades in instrumental/theoretical practice.

Author(s)	Country	Study Type	Participants	Measurements	Research Findings
Kontić & Zatkalik, 2020	Serbia	Phenomenological study (psychoanalytic approach)	Classical musicians	Phenomenological analyses	Two major challenges in performing were confirmed: (1) balancing between regression (primary processes) and high control of memory and motor activity (secondary processes), which reflects in a split of the ego, with freely floating anxiety that is difficult to master; (2) musicians are presenting to the audience their most vulnerable preverbal self. Implications for the development of cohesive self and ego strength that are able to master anxiety are presented. It is outlined that music education should not be one-sided, focused solely on musical performance, but ought to engage with the development of the personality as a whole.
Leva Bukovnik, 2018	Slovenia	Quantitative	Classical, jazz, pop, ethno singers: music students and professional musicians $N = 282$	The Scale of Performance Anxiety (Habe, 2002); Reflection/Rumination Questionnaire (RRQ) (Trapnell & Campbell, 1999); Frost Multidimensional Perfectionism Scale (FMPS) (Frost et al., 1990).	The low negative link between MPA and personal standards was showed, while there is a medium positive link between MPA and doubts about actions, parental expectations, and parental criticism. There is a medium positive link between MPA and rumination and a low positive with reflection. Regarding the musical genre, classical singers experience the highest levels of MPA, followed by jazz, pop, and ethno singers.

Author(s)	Country	Study Type	Participants	Measurements	Research Findings
Mirović & Bogunović, 2013a	Serbia	Quantitative	Classical musicians: music students and students from other faculties $N = 176$	The Music Performance Anxiety Inventory for Adolescents (MPAI-A); (Osborne & Kenny, 2005) Frost Multidimensional Perfectionism Scale (FMPS) (Frost et al., 1990); Young Schema Questionnaire (Young & Brown, 1998).	Music students experience a high degree of trait anxiety, which is correlated with all three aspects of MPA. Somatic and cognitive MPA are correlated with concern over mistakes, doubts about actions, parental criticism, low frustration tolerance, and social isolation. Performance evaluation anxiety is correlated with concern over mistakes, doubts about actions, low frustration tolerance, and social isolation. Performance context anxiety is correlated only with low frustration tolerance
Mirović & Bogunović, 2013b	Serbia	Quantitative	Classical musicians: music students $N = 100$	Spielberger's Test Anxiety Inventory – Trait (STAI-T) (Spielberger et al., 1983); Beck Depression Inventory (BDI) (Beck et al., 1961); Young Schema Questionnaire (Young & Brown, 1998).	Music students differ from non-music students, having more prominent anxiety and depressive symptoms, as well as more prominent maladaptive schemas. The obtained differences, i.e., higher vulnerability in musicians, are discussed in the context of the teaching process and the professional demands imposed upon them.

15. Challenges of dealing with music performance anxiety

Author(s)	Country	Study Type	Participants	Measurements	Research Findings
Mirović, 2013	Serbia	Mixed methods	Classical musicians: music students $N = 65$ $N = 92$	Performance Anxiety Inventory for Musicians (PerfAIM) (Barbeau, 2011).	Music students struggle with dysfunctional MPA on both, cognitive and emotional level, with irrational beliefs and a number of behavioural and physical symptoms. Based on the reported observation, the course for developing psychological skills for optimal performance was carried out with the aim to (1) improve their performance and overall functioning, and (2) help them to decrease MPA and stress. The course has proven to be effective according to the individual comments of the participants; however, its effectiveness was not yet confirmed empirically.

A horizontal version of this table may be viewed online at https://hdl.handle.net/20.500.12434/94331893

Lately, a series of studies in the Western Balkans region explored the relationship between MPA and perfectionism. The relationship was confirmed in Croatian, Montenegrin, and Serbian musicians (Butković et al., 2022; Damjanović & Rosandić, 2019; Mirović & Bogunović, 2013a). Leva Bukovnik (2018) investigated MPA and perfectionism amongst Slovene musicians. Results indicated a small negative correlation between MPA and personal standards and a medium positive correlation between doubt about an action, parental expectations, and parental criticism, suggesting a difference in relationship depending on control.

Studies confirmed a significant connection between trait anxiety and MPA (Habe, 1998; Mirović & Bogunović, 2013a,b), and a significant correlation between the dimensions of neuroticism and anxiety in professional musicians (Damjanović & Rosandić, 2019). Mirović (2016) investigated MPA from the most practical perspective. She presented the results of music performance coaching, conducted during a course at the Faculty of Music in Belgrade. The course consisted of cognitive-behavioural coaching, performance coaching, body techniques, and communication coaching.

If we summarise all of the studies from the Western Balkans region, we can conclude that the prevailing studies include a quantitative transversal approach. There is a lack of qualitative studies to gain an in-depth insight into the problems of MPA. Even more significantly, there are no experimental or longitudinal studies that could increase the scientific value of these research studies. It would be advisable to broaden the age span of the participants, especially to a younger age, when, with the use of the right systematic psychological approach, MPA could be prevented. In addition, the inclusion of musicians from different music genres would be beneficial and provide a more complex picture of MPA. Last, but not least, it would be highly recommended if the diagnostic approach when exploring the experience of MPA in relation to different psychological phenomena could be redirected towards examining the efficiency of different intervention approaches— we require more experimental and qualitative studies on the efficiency of different psycho-educational interventions conducted by instrumental and singing teachers.

Prevention and intervention of music performance anxiety

In our opinion, a devoted focus on developing preventive strategies for dealing with MPA should begin from the early years of music education. In that period, music teachers play a significant role in preventing MPA through their acceptance of and psychological support for pupils. The instilling of MPA in its positive form early on, and the fact that there are several approaches for dealing with it, are two of the most fundamental conditions for a successful performance career. It is equally critical that students at a higher music education level receive health education concerning prevention strategies (Kenny, 2005; Matei et al., 2018; see Chapter 16 in this volume). A holistic approach is required that considers psycho-physiological symptoms, the actions of teachers, along with the educational process and psychological and therapeutic interventions, where required. Considerations about flow are important, as is the reframing of negative aspects of MPA into positive ones.

Physiological symptoms reduction

Breathing and relaxation techniques are the most generally reported MPA coping measures, regardless of an individual's age (Studer et al., 2011). Strategies that have been shown to be effective and widely used for preventing or treating MPA include the Alexander Technique, the Feldenkrais Method, body mapping, visualisation, breathing exercises, meditation, autogenic training, and progressive muscular relaxation (Braden et al., 2015; Klein et al., 2014).

Teachers' actions

Several authors argue that the educational process itself can function as an MPA coping strategy. Common strategies employed in teaching are developing techniques for studying, memorising and solving problems, crafting techniques for gradual pre-performance training, and preparing students emotionally (e.g., Maciente, 2016). The music teacher can use several preventive MPA strategies during lessons, including (1) stretching and relaxing before playing (Khalsa et al., 2009); (2) providing positive feedback; (3) setting performance goals with music students; (4) using guided questions to get the student to think about the piece; (5) practising centred breathing with the student; (6) selecting a musical piece that accords with a student's skills; and (7) using positive imagery to support pupils.

Preventive strategies can be behavioural, emotional, or cognitive. In younger music students, performing in groups, role playing, non-formal performance, increasing performing opportunities, and balancing performing skills and challenges, have all been demonstrated to be effective behavioural prevention measures (Habe, 2001). Therefore, music teachers should enable their students to (1) practise entering and exiting the stage; (2) include breathing relaxation during performance rehearsal; (3) simulate the lighting, acoustics, and ambiance of real-time performance; (4) practise performing in front of classmates; (5) practise performing with distractions (phone ringing, coughing, talking); and (6) focus on pleasant imagery during rehearsal (McKinney, 2008). In every case, psychological skills training should be part of the music curriculum in instrumental practice from the very beginning of music education in terms of cognitive and emotional preventive methods, and the effectiveness of those methods should be tested.

From a didactic point of view, improvisation might be considered a useful and effective developmental tool for coping with MPA (Hill, 2017). The use of music itself to reduce anxiety began to develop in the 1990s, based on free improvisation methods (Oshinsky, 2008). Free improvisation emphasises the creative process, and puts decisions concerning the musical content at the performer's discretion, reducing or eliminating predetermined expectations, and thus lowering levels of performance anxiety. Biasutti (2017) outlines the educational importance of music improvisation, which implies playfulness, authenticity, flexibility, originality, and counteracts the fear of making mistakes. Studies show that free improvisation can significantly decrease MPA in young musicians (Ladano, 2016). Such practices should be integrated into education, as improvisation is a separate skill that takes time to learn and may be found nerve-wracking itself without proper embedding.

One group of researchers recently proposed that music teachers should be exposed to basic training in performance coaching by psychologists and psychotherapists, to help them guide their students successfully. The authors suggest using an evidence-based coaching model focused on acceptance and commitment coaching that enables psychological flexibility (Shaw et al., 2020).

Psychological interventions

Despite a teacher's proactive actions, at times psychological interventions may also be required. Sinico and Winter (2013) argue that the choice of strategies is closely related to the symptoms experienced by a given musician. They classify these strategies into cognitive (altering negative or distorted thinking patterns related to performance), behavioural (altering behaviours utilising systematic desensitisation), and cognitive-behavioural (changing problematic thoughts and behaviour patterns). Of these, meta-analytical studies comparing strategies for coping with MPA (e.g., Burin & Osório, 2017; Goren, 2014) found that the most effective strategies incorporate cognitive restructuring and exposure therapy as parts of cognitive behavioural therapy (CBT). In addition, multimodal interventions have proven effective, including (1) a combination of behavioural exposure with group discussion, expert feedback, and cognitive strategies (Spahn et al., 2016); (2) a combination of mindfulness training and CBT interventions (Steyn et al., 2016); and (3) exposure to performance in virtual reality (Bissonnette et al., 2015).

The limitation of much of the research is a gap in longitudinal approaches that offer a more developmental and educational perspective on coping with MPA. There is a need to explore the effectiveness of different preventive psychological strategies for coping with diverse pre-performance sensations (bodily, cognitive, emotional) of music pupils from the early years on. The other limitation we recognise is the predominant use of questionnaires to test the effectiveness of coping approaches. A mixed-method approach is required that combines psychological and physiological measures with qualitative observations of behaviour and performance. Importantly, if we want to change attitudes towards MPA and work towards its prevention, we should focus on young musicians who are at their music-educational beginnings, including measures that are appropriate for them.

From performance anxiety to flow in music performance

Even though Kenny conceptualised MPA most thoroughly, the question remains whether addressing pre-performance pressure as anxiety is really the most accurate approach for coping with it. The majority of musicians experience only moderate pre-performance strain

(Kaleńska-Rodzaj, 2020). The fact is that musicians from an early age experience pre-performance arousal, which can be perceived as an expected accompanying phenomenon with many beneficial effects. Conversely, terms such as 'PA', 'stage fright', 'tremor', and 'performance phobia', can all trigger negative associations and produce negative emotions. Because the pre-performance arousal phenomenon at its core has many beneficial adaptive aspects, it is crucial that these positive elements are not excluded from whatever nomenclature is used. Brooks (2014) proposed the term 'pre-performance excitement', arguing that this term changes the performer's point of view from a 'threat mindset' to an 'opportunity mindset' and thus improves the subsequent performance. She claims that reappraising one high-arousal emotion (anxiety) as another high-arousal emotion (excitement) is easier and more effective than trying to shift from high arousal (anxiety) to low arousal (calmness). Therefore, it would be advisable to reconsider MPA and reframe it as 'music pre-performance excitement' because of its more positive connotations, and to use the term MPA only for severe pre-performance tension.

Furthermore, when positive attitudes toward pre-performance arousal are developed and performing skills and performing challenges are balanced, musicians can access psychological flow—an optimal state of functioning during performance situations. Flow is attained when people are deeply absorbed in an activity, internally motivated, and filled with positive emotions (Bakker, 2005). Some scholars refer to this optimal performing state as being 'in the zone' (Stamatelopoulou et al., 2018; Swann et al., 2017) or gaining 'peak experience' (Biasutti, 2017). In the music profession, flow is considered an important factor in achieving well-being in musicians (Chirico et al., 2015; Fritz & Avsec, 2007; Habe et al., 2019). Interpreting PA according to the 'flow model' (Csikszentmihalyi, 1997), PA occurs when challenges are high and skills are low (Biasutti, & Habe, 2023). Meanwhile, flow occurs when skills and challenges are both high (Antonini Philippe et al., 2022). Skills in this context are not only technical and interpretative skills, but also psychological skills like emotion regulation, concentration, memory recall, and mental resilience.

Flow and MPA are negatively correlated and facilitating flow can provide a powerful tool to reduce MPA (Li, 2019; Cohen & Bodner,

2019). Furthermore, Li (2019) shows that the four dimensions of flow (clear goals, unambiguous feedback, autotelic experience, and loss of self-consciousness) are significantly negatively correlated with MPA, and that strategies related to these four dimensions may help reduce MPA. However, she also points out that MPA and flow can exist simultaneously. The author sums up her research findings by explaining that both flow and MPA are related to motivation, emotions, attention, well-being, and musical emotion contagion, with flow having positive and MPA having negative correlations with the referred factors.

Fullagar et al. (2013) report an inverse relationship between flow and MPA and propose a three-factor facilitator model, consisting of subject preparation, teachers' qualifications to deal with this focus, and building flow experience. These three axes are intertwined and require access to particular valences, such as learning and preparation, which involve well-being, creativity, motivation, and the mobilisation of musical skills.

Conclusion

Although MPA is one of the most common performing issues in musicianship, we believe that a comprehensive strategy would approach it holistically by including its positive and negative forms. A strategic plan for effectively coping with MPA requires a developmental, educational and individualised approach. It must enable young musicians to enjoy performing and (with adult support) to courageously challenge themselves with increasing performing demands, while helping them develop a positive self-image and self-efficacy (Osborne, 2016).

The importance of psychological factors in musical instrument training and performance has to be highlighted in education from the early years onwards. This includes music teachers promoting the use of adaptive coping strategies during musical activity amongst their pupils (Biasutti & Concina, 2014), and music curricula offering opportunities (e.g., lectures, workshops) for students to learn about coping with MPA. More effort should be invested in supporting children to develop preventive strategies. This includes the adoption of a process-oriented rather than an achievement-focused approach (Zarza-Alzugaray et al., 2020), and gradual adaptation to the performance situation (Habe & Kržič, 2017).

The first step towards effectively coping with MPA, in our opinion, would be to reappraise pre-performance anxiety as excitement in music performance. If integrated in music education, young musicians can adopt an opportunity mindset (as opposed to a threat mindset) (Adams, 2019; Tan et al., 2021) to recognize pre-performance arousal as an inherent aspect of music performance, with various benefits. The second step is the regular use of preventive strategies, developing psychological and musical skills. Preventive strategies in music education may strengthen performance self-efficacy, which is significantly correlated to MPA (Gonzales et al., 2018). The use of acceptance and commitment coaching performed by instrumental or singing teachers during individual classes may be a third effective step in coping with MPA (Shaw et al., 2020).

Finally, MPA has to be addressed openly by teachers of individual instrumental or vocal practice from the early years onwards. There is a reluctance to speak about MPA amongst musicians, inhibiting an education system that promotes knowledge of and pro-active coping with MPA (Biasutti & Concina, 2014). Teachers should be equipped with basic psychological understanding and coaching techniques (Clarke et al., 2020; Juncos et al., 2017), so music students should learn these during their academic education. Research embedded in music education is an important way to deepen understanding and improve local practice.

We hope our review of the research on MPA contributes to build a bridge between theory and practice in psychological preparation for music performance from the beginnings of music education onwards. Our chapter highlights the relevance of communication between research and practice and outlines the importance of a continuous process in building psychological skills for optimal music performance as a regular aspect of music education, and as part of the development of a healthy, integrated, musical self-conception. We should start at the root of the problem, approaching pre-performance sensations more from the well-being perspective and from the perspective of holistic music education, which enables the development of not just an academic, but also a non-academic positive musical self-conception (Spychiger, 2017).

References

Adams, K. (2019). Developing growth mindset in the ensemble rehearsal. *Music Educators Journal, 105*(4), 21–27. https://doi.org/10.1177/0027432119849473

Antonini Philippe, R., Kosirnik, C., Ortuño, E., & Biasutti, M.(2022). Flow and music performance: Professional musicians and music students' views. *Psychology of Music, 50*(4), 1023–1038. https://doi.org/10.1177/03057356211030987

Antonini Philippe, R., Cruder, C., Biasutti, M., Crettaz von Roten, F. (2023). The Kenny Music Performance Anxiety Inventory - Revised (K-MPAI-R): Validation of the Italian version, *Psychology of Music, 51*(2), 565–578, https://doi.org/10.1177/03057356221101430

Apter, M.J. (1982). *The experience of motivation: The theory of psychological reversals.* Academic Press.

Ascenso, S., Perkins, R., & Williamon, A. (2018). Resounding meaning: A PERMA wellbeing profile of classical musicians. *Frontiers in Psychology, 9*, Article 1895. https://doi.org/10.3389/fpsyg.2018.01895

Bačlija Sušić, B. (2018). The relation between pedagogical approaches in music education and students' performance anxiety. *Journal of Elementary Education, 11*(2), 143–157. https://doi.org/10.18690/rei.11.2.143-157.2018

Bakker, A.B. (2005). Flow among music teachers and their students: The crossover of peak experiences. *Journal of Vocational Behavior, 66*(1), 26–44. https://doi.org/10.1016/j.jvb.2003.11.001

Barbeau A.K. (2011). Performance Anxiety Inventory for Musicians (PerfAIM): A new questionnaire to assess music performance anxiety in popular musicians [Unpublished master's thesis]. University of McGill.

Barlow, D.H. (2000). Unraveling the mysteries of anxiety and its disorders from the perspective of emotion theory. *American Psychologist, 55*(11), 1247–1263. https://doi.org/10.1037//0003-066x.55.11.1247

Biasutti, M. (2017). Flow and optimal experience. In J.P. Stein (ed.), *Reference module in neuroscience and biobehavioral psychology* (pp. 522–528). Elsevier. https://doi.org/10.1016/B978-0-12-809324-5.06191-5

Biasutti, M., & Concina, E. (2014). The role of coping strategy and experience in predicting music performance anxiety. *Musicae Scientiae, 18*(2), 189–202. https://doi.org/10.1177/1029864914523282

Biasutti, M., & Habe, K. (2023). Teachers' perspectives on dance improvisation and flow. *Research in Dance Education, 24*(3), 242–261. https://doi.org/10.1080/14647893.2021.1940915

Bissonnette, J., Dubé, F., Provencher, M., & Moreno Sala, M.T. (2015). Virtual reality exposure training for musicians: Its effect on performance anxiety and quality. *Medical Problems of Performing Artists, 30*(3), 169–177. https://doi.org/10.21091/mppa.2015.3032

Blascovich, J., & Mendes, W.B. (2010). Social psychophysiology and embodiment. In S.T. Fiske, D.T. Gilbert, & G. Lindzey (eds), *Handbook of social psychology* (pp. 194–227). John Wiley & Sons, Inc. https://doi.org/10.1002/9780470561119.socpsy001006

Braden, A.M., Osborne, M.S., & Wilson, S.J. (2015). Psychological intervention reduces self-reported performance anxiety in high school music students. *Frontiers in Psychology, 6*, Article 195. https://doi.org/10.3389/fpsyg.2015.00195

Brooks, A.W. (2014). Get excited: Reappraising pre-performance anxiety as excitement. *Journal of Experimental Psychology: General, 143*(3), 1144–1158. https://doi.org/10.1037/a0035325

Brugués, A. (2011). Music performance anxiety—part 1: A review of its epidemiology. *Medical Problems of Performing Artists, 26*(2), 102–105. https://doi.org/10.21091/mppa.2011.2015

Burin, A.B., & Osório, F.L. (2017). Music performance anxiety: A critical review of etiological aspects, perceived causes, coping strategies and treatment. *Archives of Clinical Psychiatry, 44*(5), 127–133. https://doi.org/10.1590/0101-60830000000136

Butković, A., Vukojević, N., & Carević, S. (2022). Music performance anxiety and perfectionism in Croatian musicians. *Psychology of Music, 50*(1), 100–110. https://doi.org/10.1177/0305735620978692

Chirico, A., Serino, S., Cipresso, P., Gaggioli, A., & Riva, G. (2015). When music 'flows': State and trait in musical performance, composition and listening: A systematic review. *Frontiers in Psychology, 6*, Article 906. https://doi.org/10.3389/fpsyg.2015.00906

Clarke, L.K., Osborne, M.S., & Baranoff, J.A. (2020). Examining a group acceptance and commitment therapy intervention for music performance anxiety in student vocalists. *Frontiers in Psychology, 11*, Article 1127. https://doi.org/10.3389/fpsyg.2020.01127

Cohen, S., & Bodner, E. (2019). The relationship between flow and music performance anxiety amongst professional classical orchestral musicians. *Psychology of Music, 47*(3), 420–435. https://doi.org/10.1177/0305735618754689

Costa, P.T. and McCrae, R.R. (1995) Domains and facets: Hierarchical personality assessment using the Revised NEO Personality Inventory. *Journal of Personality Assessment, 64*, 21–50. https://doi.org/10.1207/s15327752jpa6401_2

Cox, W.J., & Kenardy, J. (1993). Performance anxiety, social phobia, and setting effects in instrumental music students. *Journal of Anxiety Disorders, 7*(1), 49–60. https://doi.org/10.1016/0887-6185(93)90020-L

Craske, M.G., & Craig, K.D. (1984). Musical-performance anxiety: The three-systems model and self-efficacy theory. *Behaviour Research and Therapy, 22*(3), 267–280. https://doi.org/10.1016/0005-7967(84)90007-x

Csikszentmihalyi, M. (1990). *Flow: The psychology of optimal performance.* Harper & Row.

Csikszentmihalyi, M. (1997). *Finding flow: The psychology of engagement with everyday life.* Basic Books.

Damjanović, B., & Rosandić, H. (2019, October 26–29). Personality structure, anxiety and perfectionism among professional musicians. In B. Bogunović & S. Nikolić (eds), *First International Conference Psychology and Music—Interdisciplinary Encounters. Abstract Booklet* (pp. 84–86). Faculty of Music, University of Arts in Belgrade. https://psychologyandmusicconference.files.wordpress.com/2021/08/ab_pam-ie-2019.pdf

De Figueiredo Rocha, S. (2020). Musical performance anxiety (MPA). In V.V. Kalinin, C. Hocaoglu, & S. Mohamed (eds), *Anxiety disorders: The new achievements.* IntechOpen. https://doi.org/10.5772/intechopen.91646

Fernholz, I., Mumm, J.L.M., Plag, J., Noeres, K., Rotter, G., Willich, S.N., Ströhle, A., Berghöfer, A., & Schmidt, A. (2019). Performance anxiety in professional musicians: A systematic review on prevalence, risk factors and clinical treatment effects. *Psychological Medicine, 49*(14), 2287–2306. https://doi.org/10.1017/S0033291719001910

Flett, G.L. & Hewitt, P. L. (2002). *Perfectionism: Theory, research, and treatment.* American Psychological Association.

Fritz, B.S., & Avsec, A. (2007). The experience of flow and subjective well-being of music students. *Psihološka Obzorja/Horizons of Psychology, 16*(2), 5–17. https://psycnet.apa.org/record/2007-15271-001

Frost, R.O., Marten, P.A. Perfectionism and evaluative threat. *Cognitive Therapy and Research, 14,* 559–572 (1990). https://doi.org/10.1007/BF01173364

Fullagar, C.J., Knight, P.A. &, Sovern, H.S. (2013). Challenge/skill balance, flow, and performance anxiety. *Applied Psychology: An International Review, 62*(2), 236–259. https://doi.org/10.1111/j.1464-0597.2012.00494.x

González, A., Blanco-Piñeiro, P., & Díaz-Pereira, M.P. (2018). Music performance anxiety: Exploring structural relations with self-efficacy, boost, and self-rated performance. *Psychology of Music, 46*(6), 831–847. https://doi.org/10.1177/0305735617727822

Goren, L. (2014). *A meta-analysis of non-pharmacological psychotherapies for music performance anxiety* [Unpublished doctoral dissertation]. California Institute of Integral Studies, San Francisco.

Gould, D., & Krane, V. (1992). The arousal–athletic performance relationship: Current status and future directions. In T.S. Horn (ed.), *Advances in sport psychology* (pp. 119–142). Human Kinetics Publishers. https://psycnet.apa.org/record/1993-98520-006

Habe, K. (1998). Izvajalska anksioznost pri glasbenikih [Performance anxiety in musicians]. Psihološka obzorja, 7(3), 5–28. https://www.dlib.si/details/URN:NBN:SI:DOC-LY6XKTAM

Habe, K. (2001). Različni načini obvladovanja treme [Different ways of coping with performance anxiety]. *Glasba v šoli: revija za glasbeni pouk v osnovnih in srednjih šolah, za glasbene šole in zborovstvo, 6*(3/4), 18–28.

Habe, K. (2002). Vpliv izvajalske anksioznosti na uspešnost glasbenega nastopanja [Influence of performance anxiety on music performance achievements]. *Psihološka obzorja / Horizons of Psychology, 9*, 2, 103–120. http://psiholoska-obzorja.si/arhiv_clanki/2000_2/habe.pdf

Habe, K., Biasutti, M., & Kajtna, T. (2019). Flow and satisfaction with life in elite musicians and top athletes. *Frontiers in Psychology, 10*, Article 698. https://doi.org/10.3389/fpsyg.2019.00698

Habe, K., & Kržič, V. (2017). Doživljanje izvajalske anksioznosti učencev glasbene šole v zgodnjem mladostništvu [Experiencing performance anxiety among music students in early adolescence]. *Glasbenopedagoški zbornik Akademije za glasbo v Ljubljani, 26*, 33–48. https://zalozba.upr.si/ISSN/2712-3987/26-2017/2712-3987.13(26)33-48.pdf

Hanin, Y.L. (2000). Individual Zones of Optimal Functioning (IZOF) model: Emotion-performance relationship in sport. In Y.L. Hanin (ed.), *Emotions in sport* (pp. 65–89). Human Kinetics.

Hardy, L., Beattie, S., & Woodman, T. (2007). Anxiety-induced performance catastrophes: Investigating effort required as an asymmetry factor. *British Journal of Psychology, 98*(1), 15–31. https://doi.org/10.1348/000712606x103428

Hardy, L., & Parfitt, G. (1991). A catastrophe model of anxiety and performance. *British Journal of Psychology, 82*(2), 163–178. https://doi.org/10.1111/j.2044-8295.1991.tb02391.x

Hill, J. (2017). Incorporating improvisation into classical music performance. In J. Rink, H. Gaunt, & A. Williamon (eds), *Musicians in the making: Pathways to creative performance* (pp. 222–240). Oxford University Press. https://doi.org/10.1093/acprof:oso/9780199346677.003.0015

Juncos, D.G., Heinrichs, G.A., Towle, P., Duffy, K., Grand, S.M., Morgan, M.C., Smith, J.D., & Kalkus, E. (2017). Acceptance and commitment therapy for the treatment of music performance anxiety: A pilot study with student vocalists. *Frontiers in Psychology, 8*, Article 986. https://doi.org/10.3389/fpsyg.2017.00986

Kaleńska-Rodzaj, J. (2020). Pre-performance emotions and music performance anxiety beliefs in young musicians. *Research Studies in Music Education, 42*(1), 77–93. https://doi.org/10.1177/1321103X19830098

Kayani, S., Kiyani, T., Kayani, S., Morris, T., Biasutti, M., & Wang, J. (2021). Physical activity and anxiety of Chinese university students: Mediation of self-system. *International Journal of Environmental Research and Public Health, 18*, 4468. https://doi.org/10.3390/ijerph18094468

Kemp, A.E. (1996). *The musical temperament: Psychology and personality of musicians.* Oxford University Press. https://doi.org/10.1093/acprof:oso/9780198523628.001.0001

Kenny, D.T. (2005). A systematic review of treatments for music performance anxiety. *Anxiety, Stress & Coping, 18*(3), 183–208. https://doi.org/10.1080/10615800500167258

Kenny, D.T. (2011). *The psychology of music performance anxiety.* Oxford University Press. https://doi.org/10.1093/acprof:oso/9780199586141.001.0001

Kenny, D.T., & Ackermann, B. (2015). Performance-related musculoskeletal pain, depression and music performance anxiety in professional orchestral musicians: A population study. *Psychology of Music, 43*(1), 43–60. https://doi.org/10.1177/0305735613493953

Kenny, D.T., Davis, P., & Oates, J. (2004). Music performance anxiety and occupational stress amongst opera chorus artists and their relationship with state and trait anxiety and perfectionism. *Journal of Anxiety Disorders, 18*(6), 757–777. https://doi.org/10.1016/j.janxdis.2003.09.004

Kerr, J.H. (1987). Cognitive intervention with elite performers: Reversal theory. *British Journal of Sports Medicine, 21*(2), 29–33. http://doi.org/10.1136/bjsm.21.2.29

Khalsa, S.B.S., Shorter, S.M., Cope, S., Wyshak, G., & Sklar, E. (2009). Yoga ameliorates performance anxiety and mood disturbance in young professional musicians. *Applied Psychophysiology Biofeedback, 34*(4), 279–289. https://doi.org/10.1007/s10484-009-9103-4

Klein, S.D., Bayard, C., & Wolf, U. (2014). The Alexander Technique and musicians: A systematic review of controlled trials. *BMC Complementary and Alternative Medicine, 14*, Article 414. https://doi.org/10.1186/1472-6882-14-414

Kokotsaki, D., & Davidson, J.W. (2003). Investigating musical performance anxiety among music college singing students: A quantitative analysis. *Music Education Research, 5*(1), 45–59. https://doi.org/10.1080/14613800307103

Kontić, A., & Zatkalik, M. (2020). Some remarks on the performance anxiety among musicians: A psychoanalytic perspective. In B. Bogunović, & S. Nikolić (eds), *Proceedings of PAM-IE Belgrade 2019* (pp. 61–69). Faculty of Music, University of Arts in Belgrade. https://www.fmu.bg.ac.rs/wp-content/uploads/2020/12/psychology-and-music-07_kontic-zatkalik.pdf

Ladano, K. (2016). Free improvisation and performance anxiety in musicians. In A. Heble, & M. Laver (eds), *Improvisation and music education* (pp. 45–59). Routledge. https://doi.org/10.4324/9781315737393

Lang, P.J. (1971). The application of psychophysiological methods to the study of psychotherapy and behavior modification. In A.E. Bergin, & S.L. Garfield (eds), *Handbook of psychotherapy and behavior change* (pp. 75–125). Wiley.

Leva Bukovnik, S. (2018). *Doživljanje izvajalske anksioznosti v povezavi s perfekcionizmom in refleksijo/ruminacijo pri solističnih pevcih različnih glasbenih žanrov* [The experience of performance anxiety in conjunction with perfectionism and reflection/rumination of solo singers in different music genres] [Unpublished master's thesis]. Filozofska fakulteta, Oddelek za psihologijo, Maribor. https://dk.um.si/IzpisGradiva.php?id=71491&lang=eng&prip=dkum:10865668:r3

Li, L. (2019). *An investigation of relationship between Flow Theory and music performance anxiety* [Unpublished doctoral dissertation]. University of Missouri–Columbia. https://mospace.umsystem.edu/xmlui/handle/10355/69961

MacAfee, E., & Comeau, G. (2020). Exploring music performance anxiety, self-efficacy, performance quality, and behavioural anxiety within a self-modelling intervention for young musicians. *Music Education Research, 22*(4), 457–477. https://doi.org/10.1080/14613808.2020.1781074

Maciente, M.N. (2016). *Estratégias de enfrentamento para a ansiedade de performance musical (APM): Um olhar sobre musicos profissionais de orquestras paulistas* [Coping strategies for Music Performance Anxiety (MPA): A look at professional musicians from São Paulo orchestras] [Unpublished doctoral dissertation]. Escola de Comunicaçaões e Artes, Sao Paulo [SP]. https://doi.org/10.11606/T.27.2016.tde-08092016-153009

Martens, R., Burton, D., Vealey, R.S., Bump, L.A., & Smith, D.E. (1990). Development and validation of the Competitive State Anxiety Inventory-2. In R. Martens, R.S. Vealey, & D. Burton (eds), *Competitive anxiety in sport* (pp. 117–190). Human Kinetics.

Matei, R., Broad, S., Goldbart, J., & Ginsborg, J. (2018). Health education for musicians. *Frontiers in Psychology, 9*, Article 1137. https://doi.org/10.3389/fpsyg.2018.01137

Matei, R., & Ginsborg, J. (2017). Music performance anxiety in classical musicians – what we know about what works. *British Journal of Psychology International, 14*(2), 33–35. https://doi.org/10.1192/S2056474000001744

Mazzon, L., Passarotto, E., Altenmüller, E., & Vercelli, G. (2023). Music performance anxiety and the Italian sport psychology S.F.E.R.A. model: An explorative study on 77 professional musicians. *Psychology of Music, 0*(0). https://doi.org/10.1177/03057356231198239

McGinnis, A.M., & Milling, L.S. (2005). Psychological treatment of musical performance anxiety: Current status and future directions. *Psychotherapy: Theory, Research, Practice, Training, 42*(3), 357–373. https://doi.org/10.1037/0033-3204.42.3.357

McKinney, D.L. (2008). Mental strategies to improve playing. *American Music Teacher, 57*(6), 26–28.

Miller, S.R., & Chesky, K. (2004). The multidimensional anxiety theory: An assessment of and relationships between intensity and direction of cognitive anxiety, somatic anxiety, and self-confidence over multiple performance requirements among college music majors. *Medical Problems of Performing Artists, 19*(1), 12–22. https://doi.org/10.21091/mppa.2004.1003

Miranda, D. (2020). The emotional bond between neuroticism and music. *Psychomusicology: Music, Mind, and Brain, 30*(2), 53–63. https://doi.org/10.1037/pmu0000250

Mirović, T. (2016). Performance coaching for music students. In *Proceedings from the 2nd International Congress in Cognitive Behavioral Coaching* (pp. 23–28). Medimond Publishing Company. http://www.edlearning.it/ebook/T616.pdf

Mirović, T., & Bogunović, B. (2013a). Music education and mental health of music students. *Zbornik Instituta za pedagoška istraživanja, 45*(2), 445–463. https://doiserbia.nb.rs/img/doi/0579-6431/2013/0579-64311302445M.pdf

Mirović, T., & Bogunović, B. (2013b). Kognitivno-emocionalni aspekti izvođačke treme studenata muzike [Cognitive-emotional aspects of performance anxiety in music students]. In M. Petrović (ed.), *Igraj, igraj, igraj: tematski zbornik* (pp. 117–128). Fakultet muzičke umetnosti, Univerzitet umetnosti u Beogradu. https://www.researchgate.net/publication/313773532_Kognitivno-emocionalni_aspekti_izvodacke_treme_studenata_muzike

Osborne, M.S. (2016). Building performance confidence. In G.E. McPherson (ed.), *The child as musician: A handbook of musical development* (pp. 422–440). Oxford University Press. https://doi.org/10.1093/acprof:oso/9780198744443.003.0023

Osborne, M. S., & Kenny, D. T. (2005). Development and validation of a music performance anxiety inventory for gifted adolescent musicians. *Journal of Anxiety Disorders, 19*(7), 725–751. https://doi.org/10.1016/j.janxdis.2004.09.002

Oshinsky, J. (2008). *Return to child: Music for People's guide to improvising music and authentic group leadership: Philosophy, games, and techniques.* Primed E-launch LLC.

Patston, T., & Osborne, M.S. (2016). The developmental features of music performance anxiety and perfectionism in school age music students. *Performance Enhancement and Health, 4*(1–2), 42–49. https://doi.org/10.1016/j.peh.2015.09.003

Puklek, M. (1997). *Sociocognitive aspects of social anxiety and its developmental trend in adolescence* [Unpublished master's thesis]. University of Ljubljana.

Sadler, M.E., & Miller, C.J. (2010). Performance anxiety: A longitudinal study of the roles of personality and experience in musicians. *Social Psychological and Personality Science, 1*(3), 280–287. https://doi.org/10.1177/1948550610370492

Shaw, T.A., Juncos, D.G., & Winter, D. (2020). Piloting a new model for treating music performance anxiety: Training a singing teacher to use acceptance and commitment coaching with a student. *Frontiers in Psychology, 11*, Article 882. https://doi.org/10.3389/fpsyg.2020.00882

Sinico, A., & Winter, L. (2013). Music performance anxiety: Use of coping strategies by tertiary flute players. In G. Luck & O. Brabant (eds), *Proceedings of the 3rd International Conference on Music & Emotion (ICME3)* (pp. 407–416). University of Jyväskylä, Department of Music. https://vbn.aau.dk/ws/portalfiles/portal/196968348/ICME3_PAP_COMPLETE_2014.02.12.pdf

Slaney R. B., Rice K. G., Mobley M., Trippi J., & Ashby J. S. (2001). The Revised Almost Perfect Scale. *Measurement and Evaluation in Counseling and Development, 34*, 130–145. https://doi.org/10.1080/07481756.2002.12069030

Spahn, C., Walther, J.-C., & Nusseck, M. (2016). The effectiveness of a multimodal concept of audition training for music students in coping with music performance anxiety. *Psychology of Music, 44*(4), 893–909. https://doi.org/10.1177%2F0305735615597484

Spielberger, C.D., Gorsuch, R.L., Lushene, R., Vagg, P.R., & Jacobs, G.A. (1983). *Manual for the State-Trait Anxiety Inventory*. Consulting Psychologists Press, Palo Alto.

Spychiger, M.B. (2017). From musical experience to musical identity: Musical self-concept as a mediating psychological structure. In R. MacDonald, D.J. Hargreaves, & D. Miell (eds), *Handbook of musical identities* (pp. 267–287). Oxford University Press. https://doi.org/10.1093/acprof:oso/9780199679485.003.0015

Stamatelopoulou, F., Pezirkianidis, C., Karakasidou, E., Lakioti, A., & Stalikas, A. (2018). 'Being in the zone': A systematic review on the relationship of psychological correlates and the occurrence of flow experiences in sports' performance. *Psychology, 9*(8), 2011–2030. https://doi.org/10.4236/psych.2018.98115

Steptoe, A. (1989). Stress, coping and stage fright in professional musicians. *Psychology of Music, 17*(1), 3–11. https://doi.org/10.1177/0305735689171001

Steptoe, A. (2001). Negative emotions in music making: The problem of performance anxiety. In P.N. Juslin & J.A. Sloboda (eds), *Music and emotion: Theory and research* (pp. 291–307). Oxford University Press.

Steyn, B. J. M., Steyn, M. H., Maree, D. J. F., & Panebianco-Warrens, C. (2016). Psychological skills and mindfulness training effects on the psychological wellbeing of undergraduate music students: An exploratory study. *Journal of Psychology in Africa, 26*(2), 167–171. http://doi.org/10.1080/14330237.2016.1163906

Studer, R., Gomez, P., Hildebrandt, H., Arial, M., & Danuser, B. (2011). Stage fright: Its experience as a problem and coping with it. *International Archives of Occupational and Environmental Health, 84*(7), 761–771. https://doi.org/10.1007/s00420-010-0608-1

Swann, C., Crust, L., Jackman, P., Vella, S.A., Allen, M.S, & Keegan, R. (2017). Psychological states underlying excellent performance in sport: Toward an integrated model of flow and clutch states. *Journal of Applied Sport Psychology, 29*(4), 375–401. https://doi.org/10.1080/10413200.2016.1272650

Tan, J., Yap, K., & Bhattacharya, J. (2021). What does it take to flow? Investigating links between grit, growth mind-set, and flow in musicians. *Music & Science, 4*. Advance online publication. http://dx.doi.org/10.1177/2059204321989529

Trapnell, P. D., & Campbell, J. D. (1999). Rumination-Reflection Questionnaire [Database record]. APA PsycTests. https://doi.org/10.1037/t07094-000

Wiedemann, A., Vogel, D., Voss, C., & Hoyer, J. (2021). How does music performance anxiety relate to other anxiety disorders? *Psychology of Music, 50*(1). https://doi.org/10.1177/0305735620988600

Wilson, G.D., & Roland, D. (2002). Performance anxiety. In R. Parncutt, & G.E. McPherson (eds), *The science and psychology of music performance: Creative strategies for teaching and learning* (pp. 47–61). Oxford University Press. https://doi.org/10.1093/acprof:oso/9780195138108.003.0004

Yerkes, R.M., & Dodson, J.D. (1908). The relation of strength of stimulus to rapidity of habit-formation. *Journal of Comparative Neurology and Psychology, 18*(5), 459–482. https://doi.org/10.1002/cne.920180503

Yondem, Z.D. (2007). Performance anxiety, dysfunctional attitudes and gender in university music students. *Social Behavior and Personality: An International Journal, 35*(10), 1415–1426. https://doi.org/10.2224/sbp.2007.35.10.1415

Young, J. E., & Brown, G. (1998). *Young Schema Questionnaire Short Form.* Cognitive Therapy Center.

Zarza-Alzugaray, F.J., Casanova, O., McPherson, G.E., & Orejudo, S. (2020). Music self-efficacy for performance: An explanatory model based on social support. *Frontiers in Psychology, 11*, Article 1249. https://doi.org/10.3389/fpsyg.2020.01249

16. How do European and Western Balkans Conservatoires Help Music Students with their Health and Well-being?

Raluca Matei and Jane Ginsborg

Introduction

A large proportion of musicians, from students to professionals, experience problems with their psychological well-being and physical health. These include music performance anxiety (MPA) (see Chapter 15 in this volume), performance-related musculoskeletal disorders (PRMDs), noise-induced hearing loss (NIHL), and issues related to musicians' lifestyles. Problems such as these have been documented, investigated, discussed, and reported widely (e.g., Burin & Osório, 2016; Matei & Ginsborg, 2017, 2020; Rotter et al., 2020). The purpose of the present chapter is to consider the ways in which music higher education (MHE) institutions in Europe and the Western Balkans (WB) have begun to address musicians' health problems during their training so that they are able to prevent or at least mitigate them throughout their professional careers.

Like other schools, MHE institutions have the potential to be healthy settings, as defined by Dooris et al. (2010) and the World Health Organization (Wilkinson & Marmot, 2003). These settings (WHO, 2021) facilitate the implementation of policies and measures that respect social and cultural differences, and strive to improve the health of students, members of staff, families, and the community more widely. Furthermore, they provide health education and enhance health literacy, which enables individuals to obtain, interpret, and understand health information and services, and develop the decision-making skills to make use of health information so as to improve or maintain their health (WHO, 2012).

By the middle of the first decade of the 21st century, health education programmes had begun to be introduced into MHE institutions (Manchester, 2007a,b,c). According to evaluations published in the peer-reviewed literature, such programmes have now been delivered to music students in Germany (Zander et al., 2010), Iceland (Árnason et al., 2018), the Netherlands (Baadjou et al., 2018), Spain (López & Martínez, 2013), the United Kingdom (Clark & Williamon, 2011; Matei et al., 2018; Matei & Ginsborg, 2022), Taiwan (Su et al., 2012), Canada (Barton & Feinberg, 2008), and the United States (Laursen & Chesky, 2014).

While courses varied in length, delivery, and the expertise of tutors involved, their content was generally broad, including information about the musculoskeletal system, risk factors and preventative strategies for PRMDs, healthy lifestyles, managing stress and anxiety, national guidelines, and reliable sources of health-related information. Somatic movement, the Alexander Technique, and the Feldenkrais Method were also taught. Preventing hearing loss was rarely addressed.

Aims

Given that it is likely that many other such courses are delivered without having been developed systematically, evaluated, or reported in peer-reviewed journals, we aimed to find out about these other courses in Europe and the WB and to compare them. We did so by administering two cross-sectional surveys consisting of an *ad hoc* questionnaire. We report the methods and results of the study and discuss its findings in the light of relevant published literature.

Method

Participants

Initially, the survey was administered to representatives of MHE institutions in 11 European countries. They were asked to respond with reference to health education-related initiatives that had been completed or were scheduled to take place in the academic year 2016–17. At the suggestion of the editors of this book, the survey was subsequently shared with representatives of MHE institutions in the WB, who were asked to respond with reference to similar initiatives completed or scheduled to take place in 2019–20. Representatives of MHE institutions included school administrators, course leaders, and other relevant personnel who reported having played a key role in designing, implementing, or evaluating a health education course.

Procedure

The original survey was created using Online Surveys (n.d.) and designed for distribution to the European Association of Conservatoires (AEC). Its members comprise 300 institutions in 57 countries (AEC, n.d.). The first author contacted 240 institutions in 38 countries within Europe via the AEC newsletter, individual emails sent to MHE institutions named on the AEC website between August and December 2017, and her own personal contacts. Ethical approval was granted by the Conservatoires UK Research Ethics Committee. The follow-up survey was administered in the form of a Word document. Respondents were recruited with the help of a researcher and music psychologist based in Serbia, who facilitated contact with 18 individuals at five institutions in Croatia, Serbia, and Slovenia. Ethical approval was granted by the Birkbeck Ethics Committee, University of London, UK.

Materials

The survey consisted of a preamble and 38 questions. It was designed to take 15–20 minutes to complete. It was explained in the preamble that health, in the context of the present study, referred to both mental and physical health. Health education was defined as comprising 'consciously constructed opportunities for learning involving some form of communication designed to improve health literacy, including improving knowledge, and developing life skills which are conducive to individual and community health' (WHO, 1998, p. 4), and communicating information concerning the underlying social, economic, and environmental conditions impacting on health, as well as individual risk factors and behaviours, and use of the healthcare system.

In the survey itself, respondents were asked to provide demographic information; the name of the course; its aims and objectives; when it began and if it was continuing; whether and, if so, why it had been modified; if it was embedded in the curriculum; and whether it was compulsory. They were asked to nominate the stakeholders involved in the design of the course; list the theoretical assumptions on which it was based; identify its target audience; provide its duration and the frequency and size of classes. They were asked to describe the nature of the sessions; who delivered them and the topics covered; and to say how the course was assessed; whether it incorporated lectures and seminars; face-to-face and/or online; and the sources of information used in sessions. They were asked to report whether the course had been or was to be evaluated, and if so how and when; also, whether students' awareness, knowledge, perceived competency, and responsibility for health issues had been or was to be assessed. They were asked how qualitative and quantitative data were to be analysed and by whom; and how and to whom findings were to be disseminated. Response options included yes/no and multiple-choice answers, Likert-type scales and free text.

Respondents were asked to submit separate responses for each stand-alone or modified existing course, seminar, guest lecture, or other activity that was designed for educating music students and/or teachers about health and well-being as a primary strategy for promoting health, completed in or planned for 2016–17 (Europe) or 2019–20 (WB). The content of the data was analysed descriptively.

Results

Institutions

Twenty-one replies were received in response to the original survey (2016–17) from 17 European MHE institutions in 11 countries. Unless otherwise specified, one response was received from each of the following institutions: Austria: University of Music and Performing Arts Vienna; Belgium: Royal Conservatoire of Brussels; Royal Conservatoire, Antwerp; Finland: Turku Arts Academy; France: Pôle d'Enseignement Supérieur de la Musique et de la Danse Bordeaux, Aquitaine; École Supérieure Musique et Danse Nord de France, Lille; Germany: University of Music and Performing Arts Munich (two responses); University of Music, Drama, and Media, Hanover; University of Music Würzburg; Institute of Musicians' Medicine, University of Music Carl Maria von Weber, Dresden; Iceland: Iceland University of Arts, Reykjavik (two responses); Italy: Padua Conservatory of Music; Poland: The Grażyna and Kiejstut Bacewicz Academy of Music, Łódź; Sweden: Stockholms Musikpedagogiska Institut (two responses); Malmö Academy of Music; Switzerland: Zurich University of the Arts; Basel Academy of Music; and the Netherlands: Codarts, Rotterdam. Respondents at the Athens Conservatoire in Greece and Saint Louis College of Music in Rome, Italy, indicated that they did not offer any relevant programmes. Other respondents represented MHE institutions offering more than 20 programmes; they said it would be too time-consuming for an individual survey to be completed for each one, but did not reply when the first author offered a phone conversation instead.

Nine replies were received in response to the second survey (2019–20) from five institutions in three WB countries: Croatia: Academy of Music, University of Zagreb; Academy of Music, Juraj Dobrila University, Pula (three responses); Serbia: Faculty of Music, University of Arts in Belgrade (three responses); Academy of Arts, University of Novi Sad; and Slovenia: Academy of Music, University of Ljubljana. Of the 18 individuals contacted by the first author, six did not respond and four indicated that they did not have anything relevant to report. One response from Sarajevo was removed as it referred only to a course that had been delivered in 2018–19.

Course design

Their aims and objectives varied, but in both Europe (Survey 1) and the WB (Survey 2) courses aimed to raise awareness, help prevention, improve knowledge, prepare students for public performing, provide adequate training, and improve students' resilience. In Europe, courses had first been implemented between 1979 and 2017 (one in 1979, four between 1994 and 1998, and 14 between 2008 and 2017). Nineteen were ongoing and one had ended. In the WB, they had first been implemented between 2010 and 2019 (one each in 2010, 2015, 2016, and 2018, and three in 2019). Seven were ongoing and one was no longer being delivered.

In Europe, 17 courses had been modified while only the two implemented in 2014 and 2016 had not (two respondents did not know). Seven modifications involved providing opportunities for students to give feedback and evaluation; four involved introducing additional expertise from guest lecturers and course leaders; and three modifications concerned the use of current research. Two respondents also mentioned 'increased curriculum', and further modifications listed by individual respondents consisted of a new partnership between the conservatoire and the college of physiotherapy, the introduction of a stress-management course, a greater focus on prevention, 'increased emphasis on strength training', and [increased] 'resources available'. In the WB, three of the nine courses had been modified, in two cases to accommodate new research, and, according to three further individual respondents, to reflect students' needs, having to reduce the course, and the expertise of changing course leaders.

Seventeen of the 21 courses in Europe and eight of the nine courses in the WB were embedded in the school curriculum. Fourteen of the courses in Europe were compulsory, while the other seven were optional; two of the courses in the WB were compulsory, four were optional, and the remaining three were compulsory for some and optional for other groups of students. The first was compulsory only for students in the department of music pedagogy, the second was compulsory for students of music theory but not performance, and the third was compulsory for students of music theory, musicology, and music pedagogy but optional for students of vocal and instrumental performance, conducting, and composition.

In both Europe and the WB, representatives of three or four stakeholder groups contributed to the course design. In Europe, these included health professionals (17 responses); music teachers (16 responses); music students (12 responses); managerial staff (10 responses); researchers (eight responses); administrative staff (five responses); and a dance teacher (one response). One course had been designed exclusively by music teachers and another had been designed exclusively by music students. In the WB, stakeholders included health professionals (three responses); music teachers (two responses); music students (three responses); researchers (seven responses); and psychologists (three responses), but no members of the school's managerial or administrative staff.

Seventeen of the 21 respondents from MHE institutions in Europe and eight of the nine respondents in the WB agreed that the course was informed by explicit theoretical assumptions or a model. In Europe, two disagreed and two did not know, while in the WB only one disagreed. The numbers of responses to each category of assumptions and models listed are shown in Table 16.1. In Europe, individual respondents referred to the biopsychosocial model; the general salutogenesis approach combined with adaptations of models from the literature; current models of musicians' performance anxiety with reference to Kenny (2011) and literature on pain perception; and the Music in Health Settings model initiated by the European Research, Development and Innovation (ERDI) cooperation, 2011–13. Other sources of information (according to individual responses unless otherwise specified) included experience and knowledge from previous years (two responses); the course director or leader's expertise (two responses); the recommendations of the German Association for Music Physiology and Musicians' Medicine (DGfMM; two responses); team teaching; and the incorporation of sports medicine into the course on the assumption that musicians are comparable to athletes. In the WB, courses were designed according to the principles of Rational Emotive Behaviour Therapy (REBT) and Eric Berne's Transactional Analysis. Other sources of information included models of mental training for musicians (two responses); the professional experience of psychologists or course leaders working in specialist music schools (two responses); and research data.

Table 16.1 Theoretical assumptions and models informing course design

Theoretical assumptions	Europe $n = 17$	The WB $n = 9$
Somatic education models such as Alexander Technique, the Feldenkrais Method, or Body Mapping	10	2
Any set of assumptions based on published scientific articles on musicians' health and well-being	10	7
Any set of assumptions based on internal institutional data (e.g., surveys)	7	3
A known psychological model such as the Health Belief Model (or other similar models)	5	3
Recommendations made by the Health Promotion in Music Schools (HPMS)	4	0
Any set of assumptions based on opinions (of experts or not)	4	3
Any set of assumptions based on anecdotal evidence (i.e., evidence collected in an informal manner, based on personal testimony)	3	3
Other sources of information	9	2

Course delivery

In Europe, eight courses were offered to both undergraduate and postgraduate students, 18 only to undergraduate students, and 10 only to postgraduate students. Eighteen were offered to students of instrumental and vocal performance, and 17 to music education students. The longest courses took more than two years or lasted for one year (four responses each), although the majority lasted a term (five responses). Three single-day courses were reported, and one that took only an hour. Again, the majority of courses were delivered on a weekly basis (seven responses), every other week, once a month, or irregularly (two responses each), or once or twice a year. In the WB, four courses were offered to both undergraduate and postgraduate students, six only to undergraduate students, and five only to postgraduate students. Six were offered to all instrumentalists and nine to music education students. Although one course lasted a year, the majority took a term (six responses) and the other two consisted of a month-long course and a single event offered once during the year, respectively. The remaining seven courses were delivered weekly.

Six courses in Europe were delivered to small groups of up to 14 students, while five were delivered to larger groups, four to a combination of small and large groups, and three, in addition to a combination of different-sized groups, to individual students. Twenty were delivered face-to-face while the other course included some online teaching as well. Delivery methods included lectures (six responses), seminars (two responses) and both (12 responses), together with other methods described as tutorials, demonstrations, and workshops. In 11 cases, courses were reported as including both theoretical and practical sessions. Eight were more practical than theoretical and four were purely practical. Of the nine courses in the WB, five were delivered to small and four to large groups; methods were described as lectures (four responses), seminars (one response), and both (four responses). Four courses were delivered face-to-face and five both face-to-face and online. Five were both theoretical and practical, two were more theoretical than practical, and two were purely theoretical.

In both Europe and the WB, courses were largely delivered by combinations of lecturers in different disciplines. In Europe, lecturers were described as musicians and/or music teachers (19 responses); physiotherapists (13 responses); health professionals (medical doctors, nurses, psychiatrists) (12 responses; other types of health professional listed in addition comprised an ear specialist, a medical doctor, a dietician, a speech and vocal therapist, a nursing lecturer, and a sports researcher); specialists in occupational and/or public health (10 responses; other specialists comprised a teacher of Dalcroze eurhythmics who specialised in ergonomics, a mental coach, a hearing specialist, a performance/presentation coach, a movement teacher/researcher, and teachers of Alexander Technique, Feldenkrais, breathing techniques, yoga, and Pilates/fitness conditioning); psychologists (seven responses); and researchers (six responses). One course was delivered only by music teachers and another by the Dalcroze teacher. In the WB, lecturers were described as musicians and/or music teachers (seven responses); psychologists (six responses); specialists in occupational and/or public health (four responses; others were described as a specialist in vibroacoustic therapy and a transactional analyst); health professionals (two responses; besides doctors, nurses, and psychiatrists, a music therapist, and trainer in Neuro-Linguistic Programming); and a physiotherapist. One course was delivered exclusively by music teachers and another exclusively by psychologists.

Course content

In both Europe and the WB courses covered a wide range of topics (see Table 16.2). The majority of courses in Europe covered anatomy and/or physiology, ergonomics, PRMDs, pre-performance routines, physical activity/exercise, mental skills, stress/stress management, performance anxiety and dealing with it, practice strategies and planning, and information on relevant health services within the institution, or within close geographical proximity. Most of the courses in the WB, however, only covered pre-performance routines, mental skills, stress/stress management, managing performance anxiety, practice strategies and planning, and mental health.

In Europe, course content relied primarily on staff knowledge and expertise (19 responses); textbooks or books, journal articles, and links to websites (13 responses each); and in one case, a compendium written by the teacher. In five cases, course content was derived exclusively from staff knowledge and expertise. In the WB, it was derived primarily from books (eight responses); journal articles (seven responses); staff knowledge and expertise, and links to websites (six responses each).

Table 16.2 Course topics

Course topics	Europe n	The WB n
Anatomy and/or physiology	17	2
Ergonomics	17	1
Performance-related musculoskeletal disorders (PRMDs) (including physical injury and the prevention and/or treatment of PRMDs)	15	4
Pre-performance routines	15	5
Physical activity/exercise	15	4
Mental skills	14	6
Stress and stress management	14	6
Performance anxiety and effective solutions for dealing with performance anxiety	13	7
Practice strategies and/or practice planning	12	7
Information on relevant health services within the institution, or within close geographical proximity	11	1
Mental health	10	5
Noise-induced hearing loss (NIHL) and use of hearing protection	10	1
Sleep	10	4
Nutrition	8	3
Memorisation techniques	8	4
Time management techniques	8	2
Alcohol abuse	7	4
Substance use	6	4
Smoking	5	4
Other	2	1

Course evaluation

The achievements of students on courses in Europe were assessed by written essays (seven responses); oral exams (five responses); both (three responses); and a range of other methods described in nine further responses: attendance, performance, multiple-choice tests, written health projects or examinations, questionnaires, and discussions with students. Student achievement in the WB was assessed by written essays (six responses); oral exams (five responses); both (four responses); and, in addition, a self-reflective diary and two book reviews ('very practical, [...] but not marked').

In Europe, 19 of the 21 respondents reported having collected or intending to collect student feedback via surveys and interviews to evaluate course effectiveness. Four reported administering questionnaires on behaviour change and health outcomes. Behaviour-change questionnaires, administered exclusively by two respondents, included the short-form 36-item (SF-36) health survey (Ware & Sherbourne, 1992) or were designed specifically for the course and/or as part of larger research projects. Health outcome questionnaires included the Pain Vigilance and Awareness Questionnaire (McCracken, 1997); Pain Catastrophizing Scale (Sullivan et al., 1995); Beck Depression Inventory (Beck et al., 1988); and an *ad hoc* questionnaire. In the WB, four respondents reported having collected or intending to collect student feedback via surveys (four responses) and interviews (two responses); none mentioned evaluating course effectiveness via questionnaires.

Table 16.3 displays the number of respondents in Europe and the WB that reported assessing students' perceived competency with respect to health risks associated with professional singing/playing an instrument; perceived responsibility for avoiding health risks associated with professional singing/playing an instrument; perceived awareness; and perceived/actual knowledge.

Table 16.3 Respondents' assessment of students' perception of various aspects of health risks behaviour

Students' perception — course outcome	EU n	How?	WB n	How?
Competency with respect to professional health risks	12	Via quality assurance, interviews and questionnaires, concerts and performances, seminar papers and personal feedback, and actual or planned research studies by the respondents or relevant staff.	1	Via exams, practical assignments, and seminars.
Responsibility for avoiding health risks	10	Via self-evaluations, interviews, feedback from instrumental teachers, reflective tasks, questionnaires, and scientific studies.	2	Via practical assignments and class discussions.
Risk awareness	10	Via students' resumés, observations and self-evaluations, questionnaires, reflective tasks, feedback from the students' council, and a research study on the effectiveness of the course.	4	Via the official university survey, discussions, and performance diaries.
Actual knowledge	9	Via quality assurance, questionnaires and seminar papers, observations, self-evaluations, seminar papers, and written tests.	6	Via examinations both oral and written, interviews, discussions on the practical application of techniques, and videos describing the individual music therapy sessions conducted.

Eleven of the 21 courses in Europe were (to be) evaluated when they finished; one course evaluation was in the process of being prepared for publication. The remainder were evaluated at different points in time, including before the course started and after it finished. Quantitative and qualitative data were analysed by members of the administrative staff in six cases, and by researchers in five; others involved in data analysis included the faculty dean, vice-rector for didactic affairs, quality assurance officer, psychologists, teachers, and PhD students. Eighteen respondents reported that findings would be used to improve future courses, 13 that they would be disseminated to relevant stakeholders, and nine that they would be published. In the WB, five of the nine of the courses were evaluated when they finished, one throughout the course, and another through students' reflective diaries. Data were analysed in most cases by researchers and psychologists, but also by members of the administrative staff and PhD students. Again, seven respondents reported that findings would be used to improve future courses.

Discussion

While the 21 courses in Europe and nine in the WB had similar aims and objectives, focusing on raising awareness of health and prevention and improving knowledge, training, and resilience, they took various forms and were implemented with different degrees of rigour. It is notable that in the WB, courses on musical development, music therapy, and music pedagogy also included elements of health education.

Having been implemented earlier, courses in Europe were more likely to have been modified, but similar reasons for modification—new research, students' needs and feedback, and changes in course leaders and lecturers—were given in both regions. The vast majority of courses were embedded in the school curriculum. In Europe the majority were compulsory, but in the WB they tended to be optional. In both regions they were designed by several groups of stakeholders, but only in Europe did these include management and administrative staff. It may be particularly useful, when developing evidence-based initiatives for health education and promotion designed specifically for musicians, to take a multilevel approach involving an interdisciplinary team.

The design and content of most of the courses in both regions were based on psychological models, the findings of published research data, and in some cases internal institutional data. Somatic education models were reported by more respondents in Europe than in the WB, perhaps because practices such as the Alexander Technique, Feldenkrais Method and Body Mapping are more popular in Europe. In both regions, courses were designed largely for undergraduate students of music performance and education, and delivered weekly over the course of a single term to different-sized classes, although some courses in Europe lasted one, two, or more years, perhaps because health promotion has been established there for longer than in the WB. While most courses in both regions were both theoretical and practical, there was an emphasis on the latter in several European, but not WB, courses. Particularly when initiatives are developed by non-musicians, it may be easier to rely on the published literature than to develop procedures for in-practice implementation of the research findings. In both regions, courses were delivered by a range of health professionals, occupational and public health specialists, psychologists, researchers, and musicians. More physiotherapists were involved in course delivery in Europe, while more psychologists were involved in course delivery in the WB. Perhaps as a result, course topics in Europe were more likely to include anatomy, physiology, ergonomics, NIHL and the use of hearing protection, while those in the WB focused on performance anxiety, stress management, mental skills, and strategies for practising and memorising. Local and institutional health services were also more likely to be mentioned in European courses, possibly because health education was introduced in the WB only relatively recently and some aspects of the wider infrastructure for health promotion (e.g., policies, services, and regulations) may be less well developed. In both regions, course content derived from books, journal articles, and website links, and was supported by staff knowledge and expertise.

Students' written essays and oral examinations were assessed, although they were also assessed on their attendance, contributions to discussion, and performances. Course effectiveness was largely evaluated using student surveys and interviews; only in Europe were questionnaires on behaviour change and health outcomes administered. Perceived or actual knowledge of health education outcomes was assessed at the end of most courses in the WB and in half of those in Europe; similarly, half of the European courses also evaluated students' perceived competency, responsibility, and awareness. Course evaluations were more likely to take place over time in Europe than in the WB. In both regions their findings were used to inform future improvements, but it was notable that they were more likely to be disseminated to relevant stakeholders, and also to be submitted for publication, in Europe.

Some limitations of the study should be acknowledged. The wide diversity of initiatives revealed by the survey data may be attributable to the invitation to respondents to refer to stand-alone or modified existing courses, seminars, guest lectures, or other relevant activities. Certain response options could have been specified more clearly; for instance, it could have been emphasised that 'links to websites' meant reliable sources of information only. Firm conclusions cannot be drawn as the response rate was low and there was a disparity between the numbers of respondents in the two regions. It will be interesting and useful to learn more about the MHE institution curricula more generally, for comparison with approaches to health education.

A division can nevertheless be observed, from the survey findings and respondents' informal comments, between the MHE institutions where health education programmes are well integrated into institutional approaches to music education and the curriculum, and those where they emerge from the intuitions of particular teachers. It would seem more responsible to develop 'best practice' on the basis of the available evidence, while recognising that this is often inconclusive or lacking.

Performing to the highest standards is essential for musicians' well-being, as well as that of their audiences; accordingly, musicians should be taught pre-performance routines, body awareness, relaxation techniques, and mental/psychological skills. It is also important to raise their awareness of NIHL and use of hearing protection, as well as health-related behaviour change techniques they can implement in their daily lives (Matei et al., 2018; Matei & Ginsborg, 2020). They should have opportunities to learn from role models and to discuss health-related topics. Music teachers should be trained in musicians' health and MHE institutions should be able to refer students to relevant health services such as counselling.

Given the complex nature of health education, the most effective strategies for designing programmes and curricula are likely to involve multidisciplinary networks discussing potential solutions and recommendations (Matei & Phillips, 2023a,b). Local resources are invaluable in the development and implementation of individual health education initiatives, but they should also make use of guidelines specifically designed for music MHE institutions that are sufficiently flexible for new ideas to be incorporated and experiments undertaken so as to encourage health promotion in MHE institutions more broadly. One set of broad guidelines has already been developed; this is a list of consensus-based recommendations emerging from the Health Promotion in Schools of Music (HPSM) project in the US, which aimed to incorporate health promotion within the professional training of musicians. The recommendations included adopting a health promotion framework; developing and offering an undergraduate occupational health course for music majors; educating students about hearing loss as part of ensemble-based instruction; and assisting students to engage actively with health care resources (Chesky et al., 2006). More recently, Healthy Conservatoires in the UK has adopted the healthy settings approach (WHO, n.d.), aiming to adapt available best practice to the domain of the performing arts in the context of higher education (Healthy Conservatoires, n.d).

Conclusion

As in Europe, health education is increasingly being provided in music MHE institutions in the WB. This is encouraging. The enhanced development of a curriculum for health and well-being requires a multidisciplinary, multilevel approach, embedded in musicians' access to a network of services, healthcare professionals, and forms of prevention, mitigation, and treatment, where theory is combined with practical implementation and continued development. Such guidance will need to be multilingual, culturally sensitive, and offer long-term development.

References

Árnason, K., Briem, K., & Árnason, Á. (2018). Effects of an education and prevention course for university music students on their body awareness and attitude toward health and prevention. *Medical Problems of Performing Artists, 33*(2), 131–136. https://doi.org/10.21091/mppa.2018.2021

Association Européenne des Conservatoires, Académies de Musique et Musikhochschulen (AEC). (n.d.). *Our members.* https://aec-music.eu/members/our-members/

Baadjou, V.A.E., Verbunt, J.A.M.C.F., van Eijsden-Besseling, M.D.F., de Bie, R.A., Girard, O., Twisk, J.W.R., & Smeets, R.J.E.M. (2018). Preventing musculoskeletal complaints in music students: A randomized controlled trial. *Occupational Medicine, 68*(7), 469–477. https://doi.org/10.1093/occmed/kqy105

Barton, R., & Feinberg, J.R. (2008). Effectiveness of an educational program in health promotion and injury prevention for freshman music majors. *Medical Problems of Performing Artists, 23*(2), 47–53. https://doi.org/10.21091/mppa.2008.2010

Beck, A.T., Steer, R.A., & Garbin, M.G. (1988). Psychometric properties of the Beck Depression Inventory: Twenty-five years of evaluation. *Clinical Psychology Review, 8*(1), 77–100. https://doi.org/10.1016/0272-7358(88)90050-5

Burin, A.B., & Osório, F.L. (2016). Interventions for music performance anxiety: Results from a systematic literature review. *Archives of Clinical Psychiatry, 43*(5), 116–131. http://dx.doi.org/10.1590/0101-60830000000097

Chesky, K.S., Dawson, W.J., & Manchester, R. (2006). Health promotion in schools of music: Initial recommendations for schools of music. *Medical Problems of Performing Artists, 21*(3), 142–144. https://doi.org/10.21091/mppa.2006.3027

Clark, T., & Williamon, A. (2011). Evaluation of a mental skills training program for musicians. *Journal of Applied Sport Psychology, 23*(3), 342–359. https://doi.org/10.1080/10413200.2011.574676

Dooris, M., Cawood, J., Doherty, S., & Powell, S. (2010). *Healthy Universities: Concept, model and framework for applying the health settings approach within higher education in England. Final project report.* Healthy Universities. http://www.healthyuniversities.ac.uk/wp-content/uploads/2016/10/HU-Final_Report-FINAL_v21.pdf

Healthy Conservatoires. (n.d.). *Wellbeing framework.* https://healthyconservatoires.org/framework/

Kenny, D.T. (2011). *The psychology of music performance anxiety.* Oxford University Press. https://doi.org/10.1093/acprof:oso/9780199586141.001.0001

Laursen, A., & Chesky, K. (2014). Addressing the NASM health and safety standard through curricular changes in a brass methods course: An outcome study. *Medical Problems of Performing Artists, 29*(3), 136–143. https://doi.org/10.21091/mppa.2014.3029

López, T.M., & Martínez, J.F. (2013). Strategies to promote health and prevent musculoskeletal injuries in students from the High Conservatory of Music of Salamanca, Spain. *Medical Problems of Performing Artists, 28*(2), 100–106. https://doi.org/10.21091/mppa.2013.2018

Manchester, R.A. (2007a). Health promotion courses for music students: Part 1. *Medical Problems of Performing Artists, 22*(1), 26–29. https://doi.org/10.21091/mppa.2007.1006

Manchester, R.A. (2007b). Health promotion courses for music students: Part 2. *Medical Problems of Performing Artists, 22*(2), 80–81. https://doi.org/10.21091/mppa.2007.2017

Manchester, R.A. (2007c). Health promotion courses for music students: Part 3. *Medical Problems of Performing Artists, 22*(3), 116–119. https://doi.org/10.21091/mppa.2007.3025

Matei, R., Broad, S., Goldbart, J., & Ginsborg, J. (2018). Health education for musicians. *Frontiers in Psychology, 9*, Article 1137. https://doi.org/10.3389/fpsyg.2018.01137

Matei, R., & Ginsborg, J. (2017). Music performance anxiety in classical musicians—what we know about what works. *British Journal of Psychiatry International, 14*(2), 33–35. https://doi.org/10.1192/s2056474000001744

Matei, R., & Ginsborg, J. (2020). Physical activity, sedentary behavior, anxiety, and pain among musicians in the United Kingdom. *Frontiers in Psychology, 11*, Article 560026. https://doi.org/10.3389/fpsyg.2020.560026

Matei, R., & Ginsborg, J. (2022). Health education for musicians in the UK: A qualitative evaluation. *Health Promotion International, 37*(2), daab146. https://doi.org/10.1093/heapro/daab146

Matei, R., & Phillips, K. (2023a). Critical thinking in musicians' health education. Findings from four workshops with experts (Part I). *Health Promotion International, 38*(2), daac187. https://doi.org/10.1093/heapro/daac187

Matei, R., & Phillips, K. (2023b). Health education in conservatoires: what should it consist of? Findings from workshops with experts (Part II). *Health Promotion International, 38*(1), daac179. https://doi.org/10.1093/heapro/daac179

McCracken, L.M. (1997). 'Attention' to pain in persons with chronic pain: A behavioral approach. *Behavior Therapy, 28*(2), 271–284. https://doi.org/10.1016/S0005-7894(97)80047-0

Online Surveys. (n.d.). https://www.onlinesurveys.ac.uk/

Rotter, G., Noeres, K., Fernholz, I., Willich, S.N., Schmidt, A., & Berghöfer, A. (2020). Musculoskeletal disorders and complaints in professional musicians: A systematic review of prevalence, risk factors, and clinical treatment effects.

International Archives of Occupational and Environmental Health, 93, 149–187. https://doi.org/10.1007/s00420-019-01467-8

Su, Y.-H., Lin, Y.-J., Tang, H.-Y., Su, M.-J. & Chen, H.-S. (2012). Effectiveness of an e-learning curriculum on occupational health for music performers. *Telemedicine and e-Health, 18*(7), 538–543. https://doi.org/10.1089/tmj.2011.0215

Sullivan, M.J.L., Bishop, S.C., & Pivik, J. (1995). The Pain Catastrophizing Scale: Development and validation. *Psychological Assessment, 7*(4), 524–532. https://doi.org/10.1037/1040-3590.7.4.524

Ware, J.E.Jr., & Sherbourne, C.D. (1992). The MOS 36-item short-form health survey (SF-36): I. Conceptual framework and item selection. *Medical Care, 30*(6), 473–483. https://doi.org/10.1097/00005650-199206000-00002

Wilkinson, R., & Marmot, M. (eds). (2003). *Social determinants of health: The solid facts* (2nd ed.). World Health Organization. https://iris.who.int/bitstream/handle/10665/326568/9789289013710-eng.pdf?sequence=1&isAllowed=y

World Health Organization (WHO). (n.d.). *Healthy settings.* https://www.who.int/teams/health-promotion/enhanced-wellbeing/healthy-settings

World Health Organization (WHO). (1998). *Health promotion glossary.* https://www.who.int/publications/i/item/WHO-HPR-HEP-98.1

World Health Organization (WHO). (2021). *Health promotion glossary of terms 2021.* https://www.who.int/publications/i/item/9789240038349

Zander, M.F., Voltmer, E., & Spahn, C. (2010). Health promotion and prevention in higher music education: Results of a longitudinal study. *Medical Problems of Performing Artists, 25*(2), 54–65. https://doi.org/10.21091/mppa.2010.2012

17. Conclusion: Progressing the State of the Art of Music Psychology

Renee Timmers, Blanka Bogunović, and Sanela Nikolić

Introduction

This book contributes to the state of the art of music psychology in at least three ways: firstly, each chapter of the book offers fresh insight and understanding to its particular research area, with findings also having further implications for the broader field of psychology and music in general, and the psychology of music, specifically. Secondly, the book is significant in promoting research from the Western Balkans, a region where research in the psychology of music has developed consistently over more than four decades (see Chapter 1, by Blanka Bogunović, Renee Timmers, and Sanela Nikolić for an overview), and with proactive encouragement it should feature more prominently on the international stage. Thirdly, the book is an example of an initiative to address the urgent issue of rebalancing the unevenness in scholarly dissemination that is influenced by socio-political and linguistic barriers and inequality in scholarly practices. This concluding chapter discusses research findings, overlaps and distinctions in the psychology of music in the Western Balkans and Western Europe, as evidenced in this book.

Current state of the discipline: Research findings

Firstly, taking the contributions of the chapters in this volume together, we reflect on the insights developed in this book irrespective of regional origin. Part 1 investigated the psychology of aesthetic experiences and emotions—emphasising underlying dimensionality (Chapter 2, by Dragan Janković and Maja Mađarev), practice-based perspectives of musical experts on aesthetics (Chapter 3, by Sanela Nikolić and Ivana Miladinović Prica), and understanding aesthetic emotions cross-culturally as functional and embodied (Chapter 4, by Renee Timmers, Scott Bannister, and Thomas M. Lennie). The three chapters share an emphasis on interactions between cognitive evaluation related to meanings attributed to music and situated, embodied experiences with music. As an affective experience, situated aesthetic experiences may be characterised by variations in arousal and valence plus a cognitive evaluative dimension (Chapter 2); these cognitive evaluations and affective experiences become specialised with musical knowledge and expertise (Chapter 3), and are contextualised in function depending on the cultural and listening situation (Chapter 4).

The theoretical conception raised in Chapter 2 is based on experimental studies from which the Valence, Arousal, and Cognitive evaluation (VACe) model of the aesthetic experience of music is formulated. This model parallels approaches in the visual arts that highlight the role played by meanings evoked by artworks in the formation of aesthetic experiences.

A nuanced example was offered in Chapter 3 of the idiosyncratic aesthetic approach of three music experts involved in creating a musical piece through composition, public performance and critical reception. Qualitative analysis found themes related to metacognitive layers of aesthetic experiences, considering 'music completeness,' imagery and metaphors, and specialised musical knowledge. The highlight of this chapter is the participation of two cutting-edge expert musicians who have had an impact on Serbian neo-avant-garde music since the 1970s. Our understanding of the specialist musical knowledge of the performer is further developed in the chapters on memorisation strategies (Chapter 10 by Valnea Žauhar, Dunja Crnjanski, and Igor Bajšanski and Chapter 11 by Jane Ginsborg), whilst receptive approaches to bringing contemporary music to a broad audience are explored in Chapter 7 (by John Sloboda).

Closing Part 1, Chapter 4 situates research on aesthetic emotions in the context of understandings of music cognition as dynamic, embodied and functionally embedded. It argues that a functional perspective focused on contextual aesthetic affordances of music will facilitate the investigation and understanding of aesthetic emotion across diverse cultural contexts. Such aesthetic affordances engage closely with structural aspects of music, with bodily and physiological associations, and with relational meanings and values attributed to music. This chapter provides further detail about the affective and conceptual dimensions presented in Chapter 2, whilst offering a bridge to 4E cognition of music as discussed in Chapter 9 (by Andrea Schiavio and Dylan van der Schyff).

The chapters in Part 2 examined music listening experiences at a young age (Chapter 5, by Mirsada Zećo, Marina Videnović, and Lejla Silajdžić), in adolescence (Chapter 6, by Ivana Stepanović Ilić, Marina Videnović, Zora Krnjaić, and Ksenija Krstić), and for adults in concert settings (Chapter 7, by John Sloboda). All three chapters connect with the theme of active sense-making, using a range of research methodologies (action research, empirical large sample-based, practice-led research). For young children, sound exploration and guidance to create a fantasy story help to support focal attention to the musical sounds and creative engagement with musical structures, as well as enhancing the imagination, aural skills, and cognitive development (Chapter 5). The didactic approach explored in the chapter gives children rich opportunities to be creative regardless of musical abilities and previous knowledge, offering a promising avenue for inclusive music education. Whilst acknowledging the challenges to incorporate this practice into the relatively traditional forms of music education in general schools in the Western Balkans, the authors advocate for the use of unconventional sound instruments in music workshops that can add novelty, flexibility and inclusion into existing practice anywhere.

Later in life, adolescents choose and prefer music that supports values and attitudes they identify with, which involves a certain level of geopolitical specificity (Chapter 6). The presented research shows parallels between models of musical preferences developed and tested in Western, often English-speaking countries, and musical preferences in Serbian adolescents, as well as rediscovering previously established relationships between musical tastes and the values adolescents hold. Some differences were found too, concerning preferences for specific genres related to the Serbian socio-historical context, and relationships between preferences for rebellious music and antagonistic values. This raises questions related to the role of music preferences and values for the development of adolescents' musical tastes and their interaction with their socio-cultural context.

Meaningful engagement with music, including unfamiliar music, may be supported by experimenting with how music is presented in concert settings, allowing more active involvement by audiences, and presenting music in contexts that balance predictability and novelty (Chapter 7). The author points out the role of music higher education institutions (MHEIs) as important bearers of novelty, originality and freedom for experimentation that are 'natural homes for researchers' (p. 158), as 'opposed to commercial or municipal arts organisation settings, where the research-informed innovation is a greater challenge, but one which may have more profound effects on the industry, if achieved' (p. 158). The chapter illustrates the power of practice-based research to bridge innovations in academia and industry, and concludes with an invitation to conduct more comparative research into experiences of, and motivations for, concert attendance in different countries, which could tailor artistic and organisational responses more closely to socio-cultural realities in different countries.

Cross-inspiration between the chapters of Part 2 may also highlight the relevance of values for adult music listeners, and the role of early exposure and creative development as a primer for long-term musical enjoyment, as advocated in Chapter 5. These chapters complement the growing body of research on engagement with music across the life-span and the rewards associated with contextual music listening, including research into audience motivations and barriers (e.g., Burland & Pitts, 2016; Pitts, 2017; Pitts & Price, 2020; Rickard & McFerran, 2012).

Chapters in Part 3 developed insight into the intrinsically social aspects of music performance and the ways performers relate to others, whether those others are physically present or imagined (Chapter 8, by Andrea Schiavio, Henrique Meissner, and Renee Timmers). It outlined the understanding of music cognition as embodied, embedded, extended, and enactive (Chapter 9, by Andrea Schiavio and Dylan van der Schyff) and gave both an overview and detailed case studies of strategies of expert memorisation of complex music by performers (Chapters 10, by Valnea Žauhar, Dunja Crnjanski, and Igor Bajšanski and 11, by Jane Ginsborg). Findings concerning performers' thoughts and attitudes about others in Chapter 8 are relevant for the understanding of emotions during practice and performance, including potential triggers for negative emotions or supporting factors for positive emotions, complementing insights on performance anxiety discussed in Chapter 15. Chapter 8 illustrates differences between the experiences of practice and performance, which may influence how musicians may need to prepare for a performance in terms of felt emotions and performance strategies, with implications for motivation, memorisation and skill development. Chapter 9 highlights the relevance of bodily factors including how they drive musical creativity and discovery and the embedding of skill development in 'musically relevant brain-body-world synergies' (p. 205). These perspectives chime with the action research of Chapter 5 that encouraged children to improvise sounds using resonant instruments, with the extended reality explained by musicians in Chapter 8, with shifts in our understanding of aesthetic appreciation and aesthetic emotions argued in Chapter 4, and the notion of experiential knowledge outlined in Chapter 3. Such experiential knowledge accompanied by theoretical knowledge is also key to the memorisation strategies discussed in Chapters 10 and 11. These latter chapters outline how musicians memorise through deliberate practice: repeating shorter or longer sections, anchoring actions through identifying structural moments and groupings, and creating a mental map that consists of goal-directed actions, where the goals are the production of particular musical sounds or events and gestures (Schiavio et al., 2017). These are close body-mind-instrument-sound interactions shaped over years of cultural experience (Loaiza, 2016; Reybrouck, 2020).

The final part of the book considers the psychological aspects of becoming a musician: factors contributing to musical accomplishments (Chapter 12, by Blanka Bogunović), confrontations brought about by accelerated musical development when one is identified as musically talented early in life (Chapter 13, by Olja Jovanović, Ana Altaras

Dimitrijević, Dejana Mutavdžin, and Blanka Bogunović), attributes associated with different professional orientations in music (Chapter 14, by Ana Butković), and the challenges involved in the public performance of music (Chapter 15, by Katarina Habe and Michele Biasutti). All these factors combine in the provision of supportive and high-quality music education, including education promoting musicians' health and well-being as discussed in the final chapter, Chapter 16, by Raluca Matei and Jane Ginsborg. Chapter 14 reminds us that different music professions have their own challenges and appeals, including for different instrument groups, and, as also identified in Chapter 8, for solo vs. group performance. These findings correspond with the suggestion that specialties in music have specific job characteristics, which make them appealing to people with different personality dimensions. Few specificities have been observed so far in research on personality differences between expert musicians with diverse instrumental skills when comparing between regions or contexts. As such, little is known about the details of variations in the psychology of different musicians, including going beyond performance of western classical music, limiting tailored preparation for the profession.

Chapter 12 models the complexity of the interaction between psychological and environmental factors that contribute to musical accomplishment, and how these develop with age. The reported findings address a gap in the existing research corpus by investigating the joint role of motivation and personality dimensions for musical accomplishments through a developmental perspective. The role of personality may be related to the sensitivity to and aesthetic enjoyment of music, but also to other characteristics closely associated with musical skill development, such as conscientiousness and self-assurance. Such personality factors emerge as influential later in development, showing more strongly in adolescents and young adulthood than in childhood. The cultural perspective provided by the comparisons with the research done internationally showed similarities as well as some differences. Interpretation of these differences is complicated by the many co-occurring differences in music education systems, theoretical backgrounds, and musicians' profiles that were presented in the studies.

Chapter 13 further highlights the relevance of motivation, personal commitments, interests and values, and their interactions with an educational and musical environment, through an examination of the reflections of adult musicians on their past experiences as students experiencing radical accelerated specialist music education. This chapter showcases the positive and some negative sides of this motivation for music. On the one hand, acceleration as an educational approach has helped them to become internationally recognised, outstanding music performers, transcending national, ethnic, and cultural backgrounds through music. On the other hand, acceleration risks failing to build the psychosocial skills that are necessary for long-term resilience and success in a music career. Choosing migration to countries with culturally richer milieus to ensure an adequate environment for professional development opened different experiences of the world and music, but it also affected their relationship to their homeland and brought the challenges of settling into a new environment.

The final two chapters address ways in which musicians can be supported to be better able to cope with the demands of being a musician, including the mental pressures of public performance, physical challenges of long hours of performance, and hearing protection. Chapter 15 complements existing music performance anxiety (MPA) models by highlighting the research studies regarding MPA in the Western Balkans, which are mostly oriented toward personality attributes closely connected to MPA. It addresses some of the preventive and intervention approaches in dealing with MPA, with an emphasis on the idea of reconsidering MPA as pre-performance excitement that has the capacity to contribute to optimal states of flow. In Chapter 16, the cross-sectional survey gives information about the ways in which MHE institutions in Europe and the Western Balkans have begun to improve support for musicians' health and well-being during their training. While most courses in both regions were theoretical and practical, there was an emphasis on the latter in several European, but not Western Balkans, courses. Courses in Europe were more involved with physical health and hearing protection, while more psychologists were involved in course delivery in the Western Balkans, focused on performance anxiety, stress management, mental skills, and strategies for practising and memorising. Since health education was introduced in the Western Balkans only relatively recently, some aspects of the wider infrastructure for health promotion (e.g., policies, services, and regulations) may be less well developed. Music teachers and health services such as counselling are seen as relevant for students' health and well-being at the MHE institutions. Both chapters illustrate increases in supportive considerations of musicians' psychology and health, informing improvements in higher education practices and enhancing the training of the next generation of performers and teachers.

This connection with the real-world applications of research findings must continue to be developed and strengthened in different directions, pushing researchers to define concrete methods to support musicians and robust ways to model complex interacting factors. The aim is to enhance our understanding of the development of a diversity of musicians, the risks and opportunities of the profession and its strands, the interests and needs of diverse audiences, and the interaction and communication between musicians and audiences—both as interests in themselves, and as a way to improve and expand practice. Despite the strong representation and institutionalisation of the music humanities disciplines within the frame of the Western Balkans MHE institutions, psychology of music as a social science has often been pushed forward by the individual efforts of enthusiastic experts, who become representatives of the discipline. Increasingly such enthusiasts and representatives include professionals in musical practice—music educators, composers and performers. Knowledge and applications of this knowledge are developed in research communities but also among musicians who acknowledge the importance of psychological approaches to musical phenomena for the empowerment of their skills and practices.

Setting targets for future research: Equality, diversity, and inclusion in research practices

Whilst it is common to publish books after conferences, and indeed there is a legacy of book publications after ESCOM conferences (e.g., Deliège & Sloboda, 1996, 2004; Deliège & Wiggins, 2006), it is fairly uncommon for such books to explicitly promote research in specific geographical regions. Indeed, the setup of this book is unusual in selecting and therefore prioritising authors from specific locations rather than including authors primarily based on topic area, relevance of expertise and research track record. This decision was made purposefully. We argue that it was important to do so and will be important for future books to address power imbalances that influence the realisation, publication, citation, visibility, and impact of research (Davies et al., 2021; Palser et al., 2022). Such power imbalances are economic in terms of funding and resource availability for research and discipline development, as well as linguistics, given the prevalence of English as the major language for academic publication. They are also political, socio-cultural and educational, with differences in resources for higher education, international exchange, and the promotion of open research agendas. For example, in the context of the Western Balkans, some differences are becoming visible between those countries who are part of the European Union (EU) such as Croatia and Slovenia and those who are not, with greater opportunities for exchange afforded to countries within the EU.

Systemic inequalities in research are strong and multifaceted. In the past decade, awareness has been increasing, and the demand to decolonise research and improve equality, diversity, and inclusion (EDI) of research practices is being more strongly heard (Wolbring & Nguyen, 2023). This concerns practices embedded in universities but also practices of publication, peer review, collaboration, and citation. We are offering only a very small adjustment in this ocean of unequal power dynamics. However, we do hope it can set off a ripple that will contribute to a greater visibility and flourishing of the psychology of music in the Western Balkans, and, in conjunction, a greater acknowledgement, acceptance and visibility of research in other regional areas.

Looking back on the chapters in this volume, we observe complementarity, overlaps and some differences in knowledge and research practices in music psychology in the Western Balkans from those that are known in Western Europe, such as the UK (our main reference). Overall, those commonalities are most strongly observed which concern, for example, the strong interdisciplinarity of the research field: researchers with a background in psychology teach in music departments and collaborate with musicians, and vice versa, music educators, musicians and music theorists adopt psychological research methods, or collaborate with psychologists, linguists, and/or therapists to inform and develop research and understanding. All chapters of the book showcase such synergies between music, sciences and humanities, enabling the adoption of systematic empirical research methods, whilst also facilitating the embedding of research in ecologically valid contexts and addressing research questions relevant to musical practices, and building on existing musical knowledge and expertise.

Similarly, many chapters showcase collaborations between junior and senior researchers, researchers who bring different types of expertise, and researchers with different nationalities and genders, among others. This collaborative approach as a core characteristic means in principle, respect for otherness and plurality of thinking as an important quality of the research field. From this, the general determinants of an interdisciplinary research approach are distinguished as *complementarity*—as learning from others and adopting oneself; *sharing*—as dealing with the same subjects, themes, questions, and problems within different research communities, and *over complementarity*—as overcoming differences in the approaches of social sciences and sciences on the one hand, and the humanities on the other through standing for a holistic and pragmatic approach. This comprehensive strategy is an important precursor for supporting EDI as a general research principle open to different research communities.

Despite prevailing commonalities, specific complementarity between research in the two regions can be seen in subtle differences in research focuses and traditions. As outlined in the introductory chapter of this book, several countries of the Western Balkans have a long tradition of specialist music education equipped to educate and train musicians who excel in a range of musical skills such as composition, music performance, *solfège* (music-analytical hearing), and musical improvisation. In a highly competitive context, music education is specialised to educate musical talent and prodigies from an early age on, whilst also needing to excel at the level of tertiary education, and professional practice. Questions of motivation and skill development are key, combined with questions of the affordances of music and a profession in music, and the (changing) nature of aesthetic experiences—both for musicians and for audiences. This musical context of highly specialised music education is noticeable in the advances made to understand motivational, personality and environmental factors contributing to musical achievements (Chapter 12), to musical career paths (Chapter 13), and choices (Chapter 14), and interactions between long-term specialised engagement with music and aesthetic experiences of music (Chapter 3). Sustained research efforts in this area have enabled the definition of models of interacting factors shaping the ability for musical achievement and how these differ for musical learners at a younger age or during adolescence and young adult age (Chapter 12). These specialisms are reflective of specific contexts where the psychology of music has been able to flourish due to direct interdisciplinary encounters between psychologists working as psychological consultants in the applied field of specialist music education for the gifted. Consequently, the themes are often related to psychological processes and attributes, and issues related to the education of future musicians and their profession. With greater recognition of psychology of music as an independent and flourishing research field in the Western Balkans, the scope of research is likely to broaden over the years to come.

Several chapters identify and discuss ways in which research questions and findings are situated in particular contexts and, as such, require care when generalisations are made. For example, Sloboda (Chapter 7) acknowledges that their experiments in concert presentation of live performed music have been targeted towards classical music and conducted with audiences in the UK with particular demographic characteristics. Whilst the dimensions identified may be useful to capture variability in audience preferences in other contexts too, they may be less valid where other genres of music and audiences are concerned. Comparing findings from a Serbian population sample and studies conducted elsewhere, Stepanović Ilić and colleagues (Chapter 6) identify parallels between relationships between musical preferences and values held by adolescents. However, they also note deviations related to perspectives on, and the status of, folk music in Serbia, which was combined with preferences for music categorised as rebellious. We may expect further variations in the role that music may play among adolescents, depending on the connotations of the music, as well as variations in values held by adolescents, depending on circumstances—local history is only one of these.

This is not to diminish the validity of the research, but rather to caution against over-generalisations and claims of universality. Over-generalisation receives strong criticism as a colonial tendency:

the assumption that WEIRD[1] perspectives (Henrich et al., 2010) are representative (Jacoby et al., 2020). Such tensions between finding generalisable results and acknowledging situatedness and contextual dependencies affect the core of psychological research, where the lack of generalisability is often interpreted as a limitation. A stronger voice for the humanities in the psychology of music should help to overcome this reluctance in acknowledging diversity and limitations of generalisation. In the meantime, there is pressure for psychological research in marginalised countries to show generalisable results, as without this, it may be harder to overcome marginalisation. A general need for a shift in approach and understanding seems therefore to be necessary. This shift involves the acknowledgement of diversity and its relevance for the understanding of music psychology and cognition, including variations in education, as well as socio-cultural and individual factors shaping the affordances of music. These questions have started to be addressed in this volume and other work and are likely to shape future research directions more strongly.

The Western Balkans is not alone in possessing an active music psychology research scene. Pockets of research and discovery can be found across many European regions, and indeed in many countries across the world. This is exemplified by the successful conferences on music psychology promoting regional networks and international links (ESCOM, n.d.). At the fully virtual ICMPC in 2021, organised by the University of Sheffield, co-organisers came from Australia, Azerbaijan, Lithuania, Poland, India, Mexico, Colombia, and South Africa. Whilst the largest representation was from the UK, Germany and United States, presenters came from a total of 43 countries, highlighting the great geographical spread of this growing area of research. Including and referencing authors from underrepresented countries is only one aspect of the larger decolonisation and EDI agenda. Relevant initiatives include book translations supported by the Irène Deliège translation fund from non-English languages to English, but also the publications of special issues related to conferences and symposia, such as the 2023 special issue in memory of the Polish researcher Maria Manturzewska in *Musicae Scientiae* (Chełkowska-Zacharewicz et al., 2023). A further step

---

1 WEIRD stands for people from Western Educated Industrialised Rich Democratic countries.

is to co-design and co-write a full volume collaboratively, something that our University of Sheffield colleague Dr Cayenna Ponchione-Bailey (2022) is embarking on with musician-colleagues from Afghanistan living in exile. These steps should be readily adopted, and are important given the various inequalities that affect research dissemination and flourishing in regions with lower economic prosperity and higher socio-political and/or linguistic barriers. The rise of co-produced and participatory approaches to research is a promising step in an important direction, to diminish preconceptions of research paradigms and earlier findings in order to shape research questions and methodologies and instead enable a more inclusive approach, leading to greater diversity in perspectives (e.g., see guidance by UK Research and Innovation [n.d.], and dedicated chapters of Leavy, 2022).

Conclusion

In conclusion, we are proud of the contributions offered in this volume and grateful to all authors for their participation in this project and their patience in realising the full volume. The book is rich in insight and research findings, which are significant in functioning as a guide, and in informing and shaping future research. They offer examples of successful research approaches in contexts of limited funding and resources. Several studies have included a large number of participants (Chapter 6) or have been developed and conducted over a large number of years (Chapter 12). Many initiate new research directions (e.g., Chapters 3, 5, 6 and 13). We hope to have set an example that will have its followers, and that we can look forward to future volumes that will support the dissemination of research that is lesser known to an international readership, and, consequently, will promote regions of interest that international audiences should take note of. We also hope to inspire the further flourishing of psychology of music in the Western Balkans and other regions that have been on the relative margins of attention in music psychology, and encourage new generations of researchers to take up an interest in this area. The promise of research in the psychology of music is its development of knowledge and understanding, combined with the potential for real-world application. Applications of the research presented in this book relate to music education across different ages, health and well-being development, the fostering of creativity and imagination, promoting rewarding audience experiences and adding to the vibrancy of the concert scene. Technology and collaborations with music providers, community musicians and therapists will further broaden the potential for application. We believe that locality has a role to play in sharpening the specificity and applicability of research. However, locality alone is not sufficient: research flourishes with international exchange and dialogue, where novel paradigms and shifts in understanding are scrutinised, shared, and developed. Inclusive research practices will be most beneficial to ensure critical exchange, collaboration and a critical mass to continue to enhance research outcomes, and build on what has been already examined, modelled and found, including in the Western Balkans and Western Europe.

This is not to overlook the considerable challenges that remain for the psychology of music to flourish worldwide, in contexts of economic limitations, political unrest and institutional inertia. As an example, internal and external factors are at stake in facilitating the flourishing of the discipline in the Western Balkans. A first requirement would be to overcome the overreliance on passionate individuals by increasing momentum, recognition and continuity of the discipline at MHEIs, through integration in the curriculum and inclusion as a postgraduate specialisation. Music is, as a research domain, multi-disciplinary, empirical and practice based. Psychological methods and theories align well with its empirical and practical orientation. Analogously, there is room for the psychology of music to be emancipated in psychology departments by acknowledging the key insights that musical behaviour and cognition offer to the understanding of human psychology. A second step is to further promote internationalisation, professional development and quality enhancement. Following the LOTUS review (2022) of leadership and organisation at European Universities, Prchal (2022) argues that such requirements for learning and development relate to individuals and institutions. This is also where internal and external factors come together: internationalisation and professional development can come from strengthened engagement with the international research community, meaning exchange at conferences, research visits, collaborations, and exploration of the potential for regional specialisations and international research networks.

References

Burland, K., & Pitts, S. (eds). (2016). *Coughing and clapping: Investigating audience experience.* Routledge. https://doi.org/10.4324/9781315574455

Chełkowska-Zacharewicz, M., Kaleńska-Rodzaj, J., & Nogaj, A. (2023). Guest Editorial. *Musicae Scientiae, 27*(4), 823–826. https://doi.org/10.1177/10298649231192395

Davies, S.W., Putnam, H.M., Ainsworth, T., Baum, J.K., Bove, C.B., Crosby, S.C., ... & Bates, A.E. (2021). Promoting inclusive metrics of success and impact to dismantle a discriminatory reward system in science. *PLoS Biology, 19*(6), Article e3001282. https://doi.org/10.1371/journal.pbio.3001282

Deliège, I., & Sloboda, J.A. (eds). (1996). *Musical beginnings: Origins and development of musical competence.* Oxford University Press. https://doi.org/10.1093/acprof:oso/9780198523321.001.0001

Deliège, I., & Sloboda, J.A. (eds). (2004). *Perception and cognition of music* (2nd ed.). Psychology Press.

Deliège, I., & Wiggins, G.A. (eds). (2006). *Musical creativity: Multidisciplinary research in theory and practice.* Psychology Press. https://doi.org/10.4324/9780203088111

European Society for the Cognitive Sciences of Music (ESCOM). (n.d.). *ESCOM Regional Representatives.* https://www.escomsociety.org/regional

Henrich, J., Heine, S.J., & Norenzayan, A. (2010). Most people are not WEIRD. *Nature, 466*(7302), 29–29. https://doi.org/10.1038/466029a

Jacoby, N., Margulis, E.H., Clayton, M., Hannon, E., Honing, H., Iversen, J., ... & Wald-Fuhrmann, M. (2020). Cross-cultural work in music cognition: Challenges, insights, and recommendations. *Music Perception, 37*(3), 185–195. https://doi.org/10.1525/mp.2020.37.3.185

Leavy, P. (2022). *Research design: Quantitative, qualitative, mixed methods, arts-based, and community-based participatory research approaches.* Guilford Publications.

Loaiza, J.M. (2016). Musicking, embodiment and participatory enaction of music: Outline and key points. *Connection Science, 28*(4), 410–422. https://doi.org/10.1080/09540091.2016.1236366

LOTUS (2022). Leadership and Organisation for Teaching and Learning at European Universities. Final report from the LOTUS project. Brussels, European University Association. https://eua.eu/downloads/publications/final%20lotus%20report_december%202022_fin.pdf

Palser, E.R., Lazerwitz, M., & Fotopoulou, A. (2022). Gender and geographical disparity in editorial boards of journals in psychology and neuroscience. *Nature Neuroscience, 25*(3), 272–279. https://doi.org/10.1038/s41593-022-01012-w

Pitts, S.E. (2017). What is music education for? Understanding and fostering routes into lifelong musical engagement. *Music Education Research, 19*(2), 160–168. https://doi.org/10.1080/14613808.2016.1166196

Pitts, S.E., & Price, S.M. (2020). *Understanding audience engagement in the contemporary arts*. Routledge. https://doi.org/10.4324/9780429342455

Ponchione-Bailey, C. (2022). The orchestras and orchestral music of Afghanistan. Promoting the flourishing of Afghanistan's orchestral music internationally. https://www.orchestralmusicofafghanistan.org/

Prchal, M. (2022). The never-ending pursuit as learning institutions: An example in the field of higher music education. *Expert Voices*. https://eua.eu/resources/expert-voices/292:the-never-ending-pursuit-as-learning-institutions-an-example-in-the-field-of-higher-music-education.html

Reybrouck, M. (2020). *Musical sense-making: Enaction, experience, and computation*. Routledge. https://doi.org/10.4324/9780429274015

Rickard, N.S., & McFerran, K. (2012). *Lifelong engagement with music: Benefits for mental health and well-being*. Nova Science Publishers.

Schiavio, A., van der Schyff, D., Kruse-Weber, S., & Timmers, R. (2017). When the sound becomes the goal. 4E cognition and teleomusicality in early infancy. *Frontiers in Psychology*, Article 1585. https://doi.org/10.3389/fpsyg.2017.01585

UK Research and Innovation (UKRI). (n.d.). *Co-production in research*. https://www.ukri.org/manage-your-award/good-research-resource-hub/research-co-production/

Wolbring, G., & Nguyen, A. (2023). Equity/equality, diversity and inclusion, and other EDI phrases and EDI policy frameworks: A scoping review. *Trends in Higher Education, 2*(1), 168–237. https://doi.org/10.3390/higheredu2010011

Index

4E cognition 15, 121, 191, 208–209, 373, 386

ability. *See* musical ability 100–101, 104, 107, 112, 115, 154, 183, 189, 195–196, 198–199, 226, 255, 257, 269, 276, 296, 299, 301, 325, 381

acceleration 16, 281, 283–285, 287, 289, 292, 295–298, 301, 377

accomplishment. *See also* achievement 15, 255–256, 266, 269–270, 272–274, 290, 375–376

achievement 15, 122, 257–261, 268, 272, 277–278, 282–283, 339, 362, 381

action research 116, 373, 375

activities. *See* musical activities 1, 8–9, 19, 100, 104, 107–110, 113–116, 120, 123, 140, 196, 205, 210, 257–258, 269, 277, 289, 293–294, 296, 366

adolescence. *See also* adolescents 16, 123–124, 126–127, 136–140, 282–283, 290, 299, 344, 347, 373, 381

adolescents. *See also* adolescence 14, 93, 121, 123–131, 133–138, 140–141, 257, 269, 289, 373–374, 376, 381

aesthetic experience. *See also* aesthetic
 aesthetic experience 13, 27–35, 37–43, 45–52, 54–58, 60, 63–68, 70, 74–75, 85, 87, 94, 372, 380–381
 of contemporary music 13, 47, 50, 52, 67
 ratings 35, 38

aesthetic. *See also* aesthetic experience
 aesthetic 1, 11, 13–14, 25, 27–52, 54–58, 60–71, 73–87, 89, 91–94, 114, 120, 158, 202, 258, 267, 271, 372–373, 375–376, 380–381

appreciation 1, 13, 45, 69, 82, 85, 375
 emotional response 79–80
 emotions 13–14, 28, 32, 48–49, 64–66, 73–80, 83–84, 86–87, 91–92, 94, 372–373, 375
 enjoyment 83–84, 376
 evaluation 32, 35–36, 41–42, 63, 75
 preference 34–35, 37–38, 44

affective
 dimensions 27
 experience 30–44, 46, 372

agency 154, 156–157, 165, 171, 173, 181, 209

agreeableness 260, 262, 265, 269–271, 305–309, 311

Altaras Dimitrijević, Ana 16

Antović, Mihailo 11, 17

arousal 13, 29–43, 46, 48, 51, 75, 77, 83, 85, 93, 124, 325–327, 338, 340, 343, 372

audience experience 147, 151, 157, 159, 385

audiences 14, 52, 76, 143–148, 152–154, 159–160, 182–183, 366, 374, 378, 380–381, 383

Augustin, Dorothee M. 45, 69

Baadjou, Vera 352, 368
Bačlija Sušić, Blaženka 7, 17
Bajšanski, Igor 15, 23
Balkwill, Laura-Lee 73, 82–83, 88
Baltzis, Alexandros 125–127, 134–139
Bannister, Scott 13
Barton, Rebecca 352, 368
Biasutti, Michele 16, 19–20, 199–200, 206, 279, 323, 336, 338–341, 344–345, 376
Bodroža, Bojana 271, 274–275

Bogunović, Blanka 1, 3, 6, 10–11, 15–16, 18, 20–23, 46, 49–50, 67, 70, 208, 230, 252, 255, 262–268, 270–271, 274–276, 279, 281, 285, 301, 308, 314, 317–318, 328, 334, 343, 345, 347, 371, 375–376
Borgo, David 197, 206
Bratina, Tomaž 106, 120
Brattico, Elvira 31, 38, 43–44, 47–48, 67–70, 74, 88
Burnard, Philip 103, 117, 185, 299
Butković, Ana 7–8, 16, 18, 261–262, 276, 305, 307–309, 315, 317–318, 328, 334, 342, 376

career
  path 380
  professional 256, 270, 273–274
case study 15, 67, 147, 228–230, 240–242, 245, 250, 252
Chaffin, Roger 211–214, 223–231, 235, 240–243, 246–250
Chemero, Anthony 192–193, 206
Chesky, Kris 326, 347, 352, 367–368
child 15, 101–105, 110–111, 113–116, 119–122, 153, 236, 265–266, 276, 282, 295, 299–302, 347
  development 5
children. *See* child 9, 14, 17, 21, 99–117, 119–122, 124, 155, 161, 235, 238, 257, 260, 262, 265, 280, 295, 300, 302, 339, 373, 375
Clarke, Eric 50, 68, 110, 165–166, 184
classical
  concerts 144–146, 157
  music 13, 15, 23, 30, 33, 46–48, 50, 52, 64–67, 70, 106, 134, 143–146, 157, 159–160, 184, 235, 271–272, 285, 300, 316, 344, 376, 381
  musician 152, 160, 291, 328, 341, 346, 369
  music performance 159, 271, 300, 344
cognition
  embodied. *See also* 4E cognition 192–193, 206, 209
cognitive
  evaluation 13, 30–43, 75–76, 372

collaboration 2, 6–8, 105, 147, 158, 184–185, 198, 227, 266, 379, 384
collaborative
  aspect 198
  exchange 10
  learning 159, 198, 207, 210
  process 159
  work 8
competence 19, 173, 181, 249, 257–259, 269–270, 272, 280, 385
composer 13, 15, 18, 49, 51–55, 58, 60, 63–66, 71, 144, 153, 161, 165, 202, 213, 229, 232–233, 243
comprehensive approach 30
Conscientiousness 260–261, 265, 267, 269–271, 305, 307, 309, 311
contemporary music 13, 15, 47–48, 51–53, 59, 67–70, 75, 89, 103, 127, 134, 159, 213, 227, 242, 373
context 4, 8, 12–14, 16, 18, 28, 41, 49, 73–76, 78–84, 86–87, 97, 102, 123, 127, 129, 133–134, 137, 139, 146–147, 151, 158–159, 165–167, 175, 178, 181–182, 192, 194, 197, 199–202, 204–205, 207, 229, 232–234, 248, 259, 272–273, 275–276, 278–279, 281, 287–288, 291, 296–298, 301, 317, 338, 353, 367, 373–374, 376, 379–381, 383–384
coping strategies 324, 327, 339, 342, 348
course
  design 356–358
  evaluation 362–363
COVID-19 14, 20, 143, 147, 154, 156–157, 197, 199, 205–206, 209, 215, 287
creative potential. *See also* creativity 99, 115, 200
creativity. *See also* creative potentional 8, 14, 17, 19–20, 43, 45–46, 51, 68, 88–89, 99, 102, 104, 114, 117–122, 159, 166, 175, 177, 180, 182, 184–185, 194, 205–206, 267, 275–276, 282, 293, 320, 339, 375, 384–385
Crnjanski, Dunja 15, 211, 214, 242, 372, 375

cross-cultural 2, 13, 15, 20, 73, 75, 82–83, 85–88, 91–95, 123, 258–259, 272, 278, 297, 385
Csikszentmihalyi, Mihaly 257, 271, 274, 276–277, 324, 338, 343

Davies, Sarah, W. 379, 385
decolonisation 382
Deliège, Irene 4, 19, 49, 68, 248, 279, 378, 382, 385
Demos, Alexander P. 228–229, 247, 249–250
development
  professional 274, 377, 384
developmental
  perspective 9, 20, 256, 261, 272–274, 376
  psychology 139, 301
diversity 2, 16, 47, 92, 274, 366, 378–379, 382–383, 386
Dobrota, Snježana 7–8, 19–20, 124, 127, 133, 140
Dobson, Melissa 144–145, 147, 154, 159
Dolan, David 3, 147, 149–150, 159
Duffy, Bernadette 99, 103, 115, 118
Dukić, Helena 7, 19
dynamics 79, 149, 175, 192–194, 197, 199–200, 204–205, 208, 244, 294, 379

EDI. See Equality, Diversity and Inclusion 379–380, 382, 386
education 5–11, 14, 16–23, 36, 43, 49, 60, 66, 71, 92, 99–104, 112, 114–122, 139, 142, 158–160, 167, 183–184, 197, 205–210, 229–230, 248–251, 255–256, 258–259, 261–264, 266–267, 270–280, 282–285, 288, 290, 293, 295–296, 299–302, 309, 314, 320–321, 324, 335–336, 339–341, 344–347, 351–354, 358, 364–370, 373–374, 376–382, 384, 386
educational
  process xix, 273–274, 328, 335
  psychology 6, 251
Eerola, Tuomas 31, 40, 44, 77–78, 81, 87–89, 91–93, 142

electronic 33, 52–54, 61, 79, 94, 124–125, 127–129, 135
emotion
  basic 29, 31, 44, 73–74, 82, 89–90
  musical 48, 69, 74, 82, 86, 89, 91–92, 95, 209, 339
  music-evoked 48, 84, 91
emotional
  experiences 25, 30, 64, 76–78, 83, 85
  responses 27, 45, 51, 54–55, 69, 73–74, 76–77, 81, 83, 85, 89, 92–94
empirical research methods 380
enjoyment 70, 81, 83–84, 89–90, 148, 151–152, 185, 257–258, 278, 374, 376
Ensemble for Different New Music 53, 68–69
environment 10, 42, 100–101, 107, 112, 115, 158, 160, 175, 179, 190–193, 196–205, 210, 257, 259, 263, 265, 269, 272–274, 292, 296–297, 327, 377
environmental influence 264
Equality, Diversity and Inclusion. See EDI 386
erformance-related musculoskeletal disorder 352, 360–361
Ericsson, Anders, K. 212, 226, 228–230, 235, 248, 320
ESCOM. See European Society for the Cognitive Sciences of Music 3–4, 11, 19, 21–22, 275–276, 279, 378, 382, 385
Ethnomusicology 53, 300–302
Europe 1–4, 12–13, 16–17, 123, 138, 158, 223, 232, 241–242, 245, 262, 317, 351–354, 356–365, 367, 371, 377, 379, 384
European Society for the Cognitive Sciences of Music. See ESCOM 3, 19, 142, 248, 275, 279, 318, 385
Evans, Paul 255, 257, 265, 277–278, 282–283, 295–296, 299–300
expectancy. See also expectation 64–65, 69, 79, 92, 257–258, 278
expectation. See also expectancy 11, 51, 59–60, 63–67, 69, 79, 86, 90, 116, 132, 208, 233–234, 247, 249–250, 252, 259,

265, 284, 290–291, 296, 299, 301, 314, 324–325, 327, 334, 336
experience
  lived 16, 55, 66, 281, 284
  of radical acceleration 281, 284–285, 296–297
expert
  memorisation 212, 228, 375
  musicians 195, 211–212, 214, 224, 226–227, 240, 316, 372, 376
expertise 3, 35, 42, 48, 50, 52, 56, 60, 64–67, 105, 185, 189, 200, 204, 224–225, 230, 243, 249, 257, 260, 267, 269–270, 279, 282, 293, 302, 314, 320, 352, 356–357, 360, 365, 372, 378, 380
Extraversion 260, 262, 265, 305, 307–311, 316, 318, 321

factor analysis 30, 128–129, 141
Fechner, Gustav Theodor 31, 40, 44–45
FFM. *See* Five-Factor Model 256, 260, 267, 270–271
Five-Factor Model. *See* FFM 256, 260–261, 305, 307, 309, 320
flow 16, 19–21, 65, 176, 201, 258, 261, 276, 279, 324, 335, 337–339, 341–344, 346, 348–349, 377
Ford, Biranda 144, 146–147, 161
formal structure 23, 212–214, 219, 221–226, 230, 237–238, 242, 252

Gabrielsson, Alf 73, 77, 90
Gagné, Francoys 269, 277, 281–284, 300
Gallagher, Shaun 185, 208
Gardikiotis, Antonis 125–127, 134–136, 138
Gembris, Heiner 3, 282–283, 300
genres 7, 33, 36, 76, 84, 101, 124–128, 130–131, 133–136, 167, 260, 293, 328, 334, 346, 374, 381
gifted adults 301
giftedness 277, 279–281, 283, 293, 301–302
Ginsborg, Jane 3–4, 15–16, 22, 71, 212–213, 217, 223–225, 227–229, 231, 239, 241–244, 246–249, 275, 323, 346, 351–352, 366, 369, 372, 375–376

Gligo, Nikša 6
Gosling, Samuel D. 124–125, 128–130, 133–134, 136, 140, 321

Habe, Katarina 7, 11–12, 16, 19–20, 117, 262, 277, 323, 328, 334, 336, 338–339, 341, 344, 376
Hallam, Susan 88, 91, 223, 227–229, 247, 252, 257, 277, 300, 400
Hargreaves, David J. 102, 115–116, 118–119, 124, 126–127, 136–137, 139–140, 166, 184, 277, 299–300, 348
health
  literacy 351, 354
  promotion 358, 365, 367–370, 377
health education
  for musicians 346, 369
Henrich, Joseph 382, 385
Hess, Peter 100, 106, 119
Høffding, Simon 166, 181, 185

identity 54, 116, 119, 123–124, 126, 138–139, 161, 257, 269, 271–275, 277, 288, 290, 295, 297–299, 301, 348
imagination 14, 99, 102–105, 109–116, 118–122, 150, 173–174, 177, 180, 182, 184, 186–187, 234, 308, 316, 373, 384
improvisation 20, 61, 80, 102–103, 105, 108, 110–112, 114–119, 122, 149–150, 152, 156, 177, 184, 197, 201, 208, 210, 249, 328, 336, 341, 344–345, 380
inclusion 6, 144, 146, 245, 334, 373, 378–379, 384, 386
individual differences 18, 90, 107, 138, 262, 275–276, 279, 305, 316, 319–320
Individual Zone of Optimal Functioning. *See* IZOF 325, 327
inequality. *See also* marginalisation 16, 371
instrument 20, 33, 89, 99, 103, 106, 109, 112, 115, 140, 165, 168, 176, 189, 200–202, 208–209, 234–235, 246–247, 250, 255, 258, 276, 278, 291, 294, 308, 310–311, 317, 319–320, 339, 362, 375–376
instrumental groups 7, 9, 16, 260, 262, 308–317, 320

interdisciplinarity 3, 17, 379
Interpretative Phenomenological Analysis. *See* IPA 13, 52, 287
intersubjectivity 166–167, 173–174, 180, 183–185
interventions 154, 283, 334–335, 337, 368
Introversion 262, 308
IPA. *See* Interpretative Phenomenological Analysis 52, 55–56, 62
IZOF. *See* Individual Zone of Optimal Functioning 325, 327, 344

Jacoby, Nori 73, 83, 91–92, 382, 385
Janković, Dragan 13, 27, 29–32, 34, 40–42, 44, 46, 75–76, 269, 277, 372
Jaušovec, Norbert 11, 20
Jovanović, Olja 16, 61, 281, 375
Juslin, Patrik N. 28, 45, 47–48, 50, 59, 69, 73–74, 77, 79–80, 83–85, 91, 348

Kemp, Anthony 255–256, 260–261, 271, 277, 323, 345
keyboard instrument 311, 314
King, Elaine C. 243, 247, 249
Kolundžija, Nada 52–53, 67, 69–70
Konečni, Vladimir 28, 45, 48, 69, 74, 77, 91
Koutsoupidou, Theano 102–103, 115, 119
Kraus, Nina 101, 119, 122
Krnjaić, Zora 14, 121–123, 126, 137, 139, 141–142, 373
Krstić, Ksenija 14, 117, 121, 123, 136–139, 141, 373
Kuckelkorn, Karen 307–309, 314–315, 317, 320

Lamont, Alexandra 3, 83, 90, 116, 119, 265, 275, 277
Langendörfer, Franziska 307, 317, 320
Laursen, Amy 352, 368
learning
  periods 215–216, 219–222, 224–225
Leder, Helmut 31, 38, 40, 45, 48–50, 67, 69
Lefevre, Michelle 108, 119
Lennie, Thomas M. 13, 73, 78, 87, 92, 372

lesson 107, 119–121, 179, 199, 206, 258, 260, 276, 302, 335
Leva Bukovnik, Sintija 328, 334, 346
life chapters 288
linguistic barriers 371, 383
listening to music 14, 22–23, 32–33, 42, 57, 63–64, 66, 73, 85, 88–89, 124, 231–232
lived experience 16
live performance 143, 149
live-streaming 155
lockdown 147, 155, 157, 160, 206
longitudinal case study 15, 211, 241–242, 245

Mađarev, Maja 13, 27, 44, 75–76, 372
Manchester, Ralph 352, 368–369
marginalisation. *See also* inequality 382
Margulis, Elizabeth H. 91, 148, 160, 233, 250, 385
Marković, Slobodan 10, 20, 23, 28, 44–46
Martinović Bogojević, Jelena 8, 20, 22
Matei, Raluca 16, 323, 335, 346, 351–352, 366, 369, 376
material 33, 35, 49–50, 53–54, 57, 59, 61, 63–64, 78, 86, 106, 110, 128, 153, 168, 189–190, 192, 194, 201, 208, 212, 217, 221, 223–224, 227, 234, 240, 291, 311, 353
McPherson, Gary E. 121–122, 139, 210, 255, 257–258, 266–267, 270, 274, 277–279, 281–284, 295, 298–302, 347, 349
meaning 11, 13, 17, 22, 31–33, 35, 37, 39–45, 54–55, 70, 78, 81–83, 85, 90, 100, 102, 120, 161, 166, 186, 193, 196–197, 199, 202, 204, 208, 239, 244, 250, 285, 287, 293, 300–301, 327, 341, 372–373, 384
medical problems
  of performing artists 342, 347, 368–370
Meissner, Henrique 14, 165, 183, 185, 259, 278, 374
memorisation. *See also* memorising strategies 212, 226–227, 372, 375
memorising. *See also* memorisation 8, 15, 23, 211–212, 214–216, 223, 225,

229–230, 236–239, 244–246, 248, 251, 335, 365, 377
memory
  autobiographical 231–232
  content-addressable 231, 234–235, 240, 245
  declarative 211
  lapses 246–247
  prospective 231–234
  recall 325, 338
  retrospective 231
Menninghaus, Winfried 74–76, 87, 92, 94–95
meta-analysis 43, 92, 159, 319–320, 343
Meyer, Leonard B. 51, 59, 64–65, 70, 88, 129, 233, 250
MHEI. *See* music higher education institutions 5, 258–259, 262, 288, 374, 384
Mihajlovski, Zoran 9, 20, 262, 278, 307–308, 310, 314–315, 317, 320
Miksza, Peter 226, 230, 240, 252, 259, 270, 278
Miladinović Prica, Ivana 13, 47, 52–53, 70, 75, 372
Milanković, Vera 10, 20–21
Milojković, Milan 53, 67, 70
mind 28, 31–33, 35–36, 40–43, 71, 86, 91, 107–108, 115, 118, 124, 126, 136–137, 149, 159–161, 166, 169, 175, 185, 193, 197, 204–210, 229, 237, 248–250, 279, 285, 290, 347, 349, 375
Miranda, Dave 124–126, 133, 139, 323, 347
Mirović, Tijana 10, 21, 274, 276, 328, 334, 347
Mishra, Jennifer 236, 239, 250
motivation
  intrinsic 257–258, 263, 265–267, 269–270, 272
MPA. *See* music performance anxiety 16, 323–329, 334–340, 343, 346, 351, 377
multiple memory systems 211
music 1–23, 25, 27–30, 32–71, 73–95, 97, 99–107, 112–151, 153–161, 163, 165–168, 171–177, 181, 183–186,

189–190, 192–199, 201–215, 217, 219, 221–243, 245–252, 255–285, 288–302, 305–311, 314–321, 323–328, 334–349, 351–359, 363–386, 400
musical ability. *See* ability 22, 257, 261, 267
musical activities. *See* activities 100–102, 105, 109, 165, 189, 195, 198, 203, 257, 267
musicality 84, 103, 190, 202, 204, 207, 260, 278
music higher education instutions. *See* MHEI 5, 16, 258, 288, 351, 374
musician
  adult 16, 258, 261, 281, 284, 377
  chamber 214
  experienced 213, 223, 225–226
  expert 195, 211–212, 214, 224, 226–227, 240, 316, 372, 376
  young 5, 16, 53, 261–262, 267, 269–270, 272–274, 279, 289, 336–337, 339–340, 344, 346
musicianship 267, 271, 273, 323, 339
musicking 161, 172–173, 175, 177–178, 180–183, 186, 198, 204–206, 209, 385
music-making 102–103, 115, 165, 167, 171, 177, 181, 185, 192, 195, 317
musicologist 13, 47, 51–53, 55, 58, 60, 63–66
musicology 6, 11, 53, 247, 250, 275, 300–302, 310, 356
music performance anxiety. *See* MPA 16, 18, 166, 185, 323–324, 335, 341–349, 351, 368–369, 377
Mutavdžin, Dejana 10, 16, 18, 21, 199, 208, 281, 376

narrative approach 285
Nešić, Vladimir 11, 21
neuroaesthetics 43, 68, 78, 88
Neuroticism 260, 269, 271, 305–308, 311, 323, 334, 347
new music 36, 53, 68–69, 148, 153, 159
Nikolić, Sanela 1, 3, 11, 13, 18, 22–23, 47, 50, 70, 75, 230, 252, 343, 345, 371–372

non-musicians 9, 49, 51, 195, 271, 307, 365

occupation 306, 316
O'Neill, Susan 147, 160, 255, 258, 270, 274, 278–279
openness 114, 127, 135–136, 174, 260–262, 267, 269, 271, 277, 305–311, 314–318

PAM-IE 3, 8, 11, 18, 21–23, 70, 230, 252, 345. *See* Psychology and Music: Interdisciplinary Encounters
Parncutt, Richard 3–4, 21, 275, 279, 349
participants 13–14, 30, 33–36, 38–39, 41–42, 49, 51–52, 54–57, 59–60, 62, 64–67, 73, 77–78, 84, 105–106, 115, 128, 136, 148, 151, 153, 167–168, 172, 174, 176–177, 179–182, 198–199, 202, 224, 227, 240, 259, 263, 285–298, 310–311, 317, 334, 353, 383
participation 3, 10, 33, 105, 143–144, 146, 153–154, 157, 159–160, 171, 185–186, 197, 240, 248, 261, 321, 372, 383
PCs. *See* performance cues 211–212, 219, 221–222, 224, 241–245
pedagogy 5–6, 9–10, 18–19, 21, 114–115, 183–184, 206, 231–232, 236, 250, 275–276, 289, 308, 310, 328, 356, 364
perception 1, 7, 15, 19, 27, 41, 45, 48, 51, 63, 67–68, 82, 88–95, 115, 118, 121, 140, 142, 161, 184, 189–191, 194–197, 202–204, 206–209, 228, 233, 247–250, 252, 258–259, 261, 317–318, 321, 357, 363, 385
Perdomo-Guevara, Elsa 166, 185
perfectionism 18, 259, 290, 300, 324, 334, 342–343, 345–347
erformance-related musculoskeletal disorder 351
performance. *See also* performing
  anxiety. *See also* music performance anxiety 12, 16, 18, 166, 178, 182, 185, 323–326, 335–337, 340–349, 351, 357, 360–361, 365, 368–369, 375, 377
  cues. *See* PCs 211, 228–229, 241, 246–249

  live 143, 149
  optimal 325, 343
  related musculoskeletal disorder. *See* PRMD 351, 361
  skills 8, 12, 270
performer 6–8, 13, 47, 51–52, 54, 57–59, 61, 63, 66, 144–145, 149–150, 152–156, 166, 181, 185, 197, 200–202, 214, 225, 227, 231, 234–235, 238, 242, 245–247, 281–282, 293–296, 315, 327, 336, 338, 345, 370, 372, 374–375, 377–378
performing. *See also* performance
  artists 342, 347, 368–370
  music 71, 172, 175, 186, 201, 211
Perry, Frank 106, 120
personality
  attributes 9, 265, 272–273, 377
  differences 9, 16, 260, 276, 306–310, 314–318, 320, 376
  dimensions 270–271, 275, 318, 376
  measures 307, 309, 315, 318
  traits 7, 16, 18–19, 139, 256, 260, 264–265, 267, 269–272, 274–275, 279, 305–311, 314, 316, 318–321, 323, 327
Pesek, Albinca 11, 21, 106, 120
Petrović, Milena 10, 20–21, 275, 347
physiological measures 83, 337
pianist
  professional 213–214, 222–227, 242
piano
  performance 214, 228, 247, 249
  student 213–214, 223–224, 227, 241, 248
piece of music 23, 37, 41, 49, 52, 58, 65, 211, 213, 226–227, 230, 240, 252
Pitts, Stephanie E. 47, 70, 159, 185, 278, 374, 385–386
practice
  amount of 15, 214, 219, 221, 227
  deliberate 229, 235, 245, 248, 375
  diary 215, 221–222
  features 242–244
  instrumental 336
  mental 237–238, 240, 246–247, 249–250
  process 214, 216, 225

sessions 215–217, 221, 227, 237, 241–243
strategies 257, 360–361
practising music 174, 186, 238
preferences 7, 14, 18–20, 60, 78, 84–85, 93, 121, 123–140, 142, 208, 239, 260, 299, 373–374, 381
pre-performance
  excitement 16, 324, 338, 377
  routines 360–361, 366
prevention 19, 335–337, 356, 361, 364, 367–368, 370
prodigies 16, 236, 282, 295, 297–298, 300–302, 380
profession 118, 143, 267, 273, 282, 288, 291–293, 306, 315–316, 338, 376, 378, 380–381
psychological 3, 6, 8–12, 14–17, 19, 21–22, 27, 43–44, 46–47, 67, 71, 73, 88–94, 120, 124, 138, 189, 200, 228–229, 255–257, 262–263, 265, 267, 270–272, 274, 277, 279–280, 300, 319–321, 323, 325, 327, 334–343, 346, 348–349, 351, 358, 364, 366, 370, 375–376, 378–379, 381–382, 384
psychologist 5–6, 8–10, 12, 14, 69, 128, 227, 231, 237, 273, 299, 336, 341, 353, 357, 359, 364–365, 377, 379, 381
psychology
  and music 1, 5, 7, 9, 371
  developmental 139, 301
  music 3–8, 10–12, 15, 21, 32, 88, 91, 95, 228, 247, 252, 262, 306, 371, 379, 382–383
  of music 1–12, 17–18, 22, 28, 44, 59, 68–71, 88, 90, 93–95, 117–119, 121, 138–141, 159, 184, 210, 229–230, 248–249, 251–252, 275–279, 299, 301, 318–319, 321, 341–343, 345–346, 348–349, 368, 371, 378–379, 381–384
  of musicians 15, 253
Psychology and Music - Interdisciplinary Encounters. See PAM-IE 21–22

qualitative
  research 14, 16, 68, 71, 117, 295, 299

studies 284, 334

Rabinowitch, Tal-Chen 166, 185
Radoš, Ksenija 5, 9–11, 22, 263, 267, 276, 279
Regional Development Initiative 3
Regional Network Psychology and Music. See RNPaM 3, 11, 22
regions 1–2, 12–13, 128, 196, 234, 364–366, 376–378, 380, 382–383
rehearsal 151–153, 176, 181, 185, 229, 241, 243–246, 248–249, 251, 336, 341
Reić Ercegovac, Ina 7, 19–20, 124–125, 127, 133, 136, 140
relaxation 29–30, 48, 51, 79, 99–100, 102, 119, 335–336, 366
Rentfrow, Peter J. 95, 124–125, 128–130, 133–134, 136, 140, 277
repetition 148, 213–215, 217, 219, 222, 225, 234, 238
research
  practices 378–379, 384
  psychological 47, 88, 379, 382
  studies 12, 16, 261, 272, 278, 324, 328, 334, 344, 363, 377
resilience 305, 320, 324, 338, 356, 364, 377
responses 3, 13, 27, 30, 36–39, 41, 44–45, 50–51, 54–55, 59, 64–67, 69, 71, 73–83, 85–86, 88–89, 92–94, 103–104, 107, 110–111, 122, 144, 148–151, 154–155, 158, 168–169, 175–176, 180–181, 183, 194, 239, 248, 326–327, 354–355, 357–360, 362, 366, 374
responsibility 175–177, 181–182, 293, 295, 354, 362–363, 365
risk taking 150, 152, 177
RNPaM. See Regional Network Psychology and Music 3–4, 11, 22
Rojko, Pavel 6, 8, 22
Rosandić, Helena 328, 334, 343
Rotar Pance, Branka 8, 20, 261, 279
Rubin-Rabson, Grace 237, 251

Saarikallio, Suvi 84, 93, 124, 140, 142
sample of music students 16, 309, 314
Sandgren, Maria 307–309, 317, 321

Satne, Glenda 166, 185
Savić, Miroslav Miša 52–54, 58, 61–63, 67, 69–70
Schellenberg, Glenn 100, 120–121, 256, 260, 265–267, 269, 271, 276, 280
Scherer, Klaus 28, 31, 41, 44, 46, 48, 71, 76, 89, 94–95
Schiavio, Andrea 3, 14–15, 100–101, 121, 165–166, 181, 185, 189, 194, 198, 201, 203, 206, 209, 373–375, 386
Schilbach, Leonhard 166, 173, 186
Schwartz, Shalom H. 14, 123, 126, 128, 130, 132, 135, 137, 141
segmentation 23, 49, 213–214, 219, 221–222, 224, 226, 230, 242, 252
self 11, 21–22, 42, 66, 74, 76–78, 81, 84, 95, 122, 132, 138–139, 145, 165, 170–174, 177–183, 185, 193, 199, 203, 207–208, 210, 229–230, 252, 257–258, 260–261, 270–272, 278–279, 296, 301, 307, 317, 321, 323, 325–328, 339–340, 342–343, 345–349, 362–363, 376
Serbian Psychological Society 3, 9–10
serial cuing. *See also* performance cues 231, 234–235, 238
Short Test of Musical Preferences. *See* STOMP 124
Silajdžić, Lejla 14, 99, 373
skills 1, 8, 10, 12, 15, 17, 20, 66, 100–103, 116, 122, 184, 196, 198, 200, 209, 234–235, 239, 246, 263, 270, 281–283, 292–294, 296, 302, 305, 309–310, 314, 316, 336, 338–340, 348, 352, 354, 360–361, 365–366, 368, 373, 376–378, 380
Sloboda, John 3–5, 14, 19, 22, 28, 45, 49, 71, 79, 94, 143–144, 146–147, 149–150, 152, 154, 159–161, 246–247, 249, 279, 348, 373, 378, 381, 385
Small, Christopher 146, 161, 167, 186
social context 14, 86, 165, 175, 272, 317
social psychology 11, 45–46, 138, 140–141, 300, 318–319, 321, 342
socio-cultural context 16, 127, 273, 374
sound
  experience 99–100, 108, 112
  qualities 62, 101, 105, 114–115

specialist music education 262–264, 266, 377, 380–381
stage fright. *See also* music performance anxiety 324, 338, 348–349
Stefanija, Leon 12, 22, 84, 94
Stepanović Ilić, Ivana 14, 100, 117, 121–123, 126, 134, 137, 140–142, 373, 381
stimuli 28, 30, 33–34, 36, 41–42, 44, 51, 189, 316, 327
STOMP. *See* Short Test of Musical Preferences 124, 128, 140
structure 15–17, 20, 22–23, 29–30, 42–43, 46, 48–51, 60–61, 63–69, 94, 101, 123–125, 127, 129, 131, 140–141, 153, 191–192, 194, 201, 211–214, 219, 221–226, 228, 230, 234, 237–238, 240, 242, 247, 252, 280, 284, 319–320, 343, 348, 373
students 3, 10, 12, 16, 20–21, 33, 35, 52, 102–105, 112, 115, 120, 128, 139–141, 148, 150, 165, 167–168, 183, 187, 196–200, 210, 213, 224–227, 230, 240, 248, 250, 257–260, 262–263, 265–267, 270–271, 275, 278–280, 283–284, 289, 294, 296, 299–300, 302, 305, 307–311, 314–315, 317, 328, 335–336, 339–345, 347–349, 351–352, 354, 356–359, 362–369, 377–378, 399
Subotnik, Rena F. 267, 269–270, 279–283, 293, 297, 300, 302
success 53, 257–259, 267, 271, 274–277, 279–280, 282–283, 285, 296, 300, 326–327, 377, 385

talent
  development 269–270, 281–285, 296, 298, 300
  development process 282–285, 298
taste 57, 123, 125–127, 130, 133–137, 139, 161, 200, 208, 374
teacher 5, 7–8, 105, 109, 113–114, 116–117, 121, 167, 173, 183, 187, 196–200, 205–207, 209–210, 227, 231, 245, 258–260, 262–266, 272–276, 289, 324, 334–337, 339–341, 347–348, 354, 357, 359–360, 363–364, 366, 378

teaching 20, 33, 101, 103, 114, 117, 119–120, 185, 199, 205–206, 225, 227, 229, 237, 257, 259, 278–279, 285, 295, 335, 349, 357, 359, 385
Tekman, Hasan G. 125–127, 133–136, 142
thematic analyses 110
theorists 6, 8, 41, 194, 308, 379
therapy 6–7, 18–19, 81, 116, 118–119, 122, 337, 342–344, 349, 357, 359, 363–364, 369
Thompson, Evan 119, 122, 193, 210
Thompson, William Forde 73, 81–83, 88, 91, 93, 95, 140–141
Timmers, Renee 1, 3–4, 13–14, 21, 68, 73, 78–80, 88, 90, 95, 119, 121, 165, 184–185, 189, 208–209, 248, 278, 371–372, 374, 386
Toelle, Jutta 147, 152, 161
Torrance, Tracy A. 307–308, 316–317, 321
trait anxiety 323, 326–327, 334, 345, 348

University of Arts in Belgrade 3, 6, 9–10, 18, 21–23, 68, 70, 199, 230, 252, 285, 343, 345, 355

Vaag, Jonas 306, 308–310, 314–315, 317, 321
VACe model. *See* Valence, Arousal and Cognitive evaluation model 41, 43
valence 13, 29–44, 75, 83, 372
Valence, Arousal and Cognitive evaluation model. *See also* VACe model 40, 43, 372
values 14, 29, 35, 38, 64, 81–82, 87, 121, 123, 126–128, 130–132, 134–142, 258–259, 269–270, 273, 285, 299, 311, 373–374, 376, 381

van der Schyff, Dylan 15, 121, 185, 189, 194, 201, 209–210, 373, 375, 386
verbal responses 36–39, 107
vibrational instruments 100–103, 105–107, 112
Videnović, Marina 14, 99–102, 104, 115, 117, 120–123, 134, 136–137, 141–142, 373
Vidulin, Sabina 8, 18, 20, 22–23, 275, 279
Vilč, Brigita 7, 23

WB. *See* Western Balkans 5, 256, 269, 272–274, 351–365, 367
Western Balkans. *See* WB 1–5, 11–17, 223, 232, 241, 245, 256, 261–262, 284, 295, 317, 324, 328, 334, 351, 371, 373, 377–384
Western Europe 1–2, 12–13, 16–17, 123, 223, 232, 241–242, 245, 317, 371, 379, 384
Williamon, Aaron 54–56, 71, 181, 184, 209, 213, 224–225, 228, 230, 246–247, 252, 341, 344, 352, 368
Winner, Ellen 255, 280–281, 283, 293, 302, 320
workshops 105–116, 153, 339, 359, 369, 373

Zander, Mark 352, 370
Žauhar, Valnea 8, 15, 18, 22–23, 211, 213–214, 219, 223–225, 230, 241–242, 252, 372, 375
Zećo, Mirsada 14, 99, 101, 106, 122, 373
Zentner, Marcel 28, 46, 48, 71, 74, 76, 95

About the Team

Alessandra Tosi was the managing editor for this book.

Lucy Barnes proofread this manuscript.

Anja Pritchard created the index and Alt-text.

Jeevanjot Kaur Nagpal designed the cover. The cover was produced in InDesign using the Fontin font.

Cameron Craig typeset the book in InDesign and produced the paperback and hardback editions. The main text font is Tex Gyre Pagella. The heading font is Californian FB.

Cameron also produced the PDF and HTML editions. The conversion was performed with open-source software and other tools freely available on our GitHub page at https://github.com/OpenBookPublishers.

Jeremy Bowman created the EPUB.

This book need not end here...

Share

All our books — including the one you have just read — are free to access online so that students, researchers and members of the public who can't afford a printed edition will have access to the same ideas. This title will be accessed online by hundreds of readers each month across the globe: why not share the link so that someone you know is one of them?

This book and additional content is available at:
https://doi.org/10.11647/OBP.0389

Donate

Open Book Publishers is an award-winning, scholar-led, not-for-profit press making knowledge freely available one book at a time. We don't charge authors to publish with us: instead, our work is supported by our library members and by donations from people who believe that research shouldn't be locked behind paywalls.

Why not join them in freeing knowledge by supporting us:
https://www.openbookpublishers.com/support-us

Follow @OpenBookPublish

Read more at the Open Book Publishers BLOG

You may also be interested in:

The Power of Music
An Exploration of the Evidence
Susan Hallam and Evangelos Himonides

https://doi.org/10.11647/obp.0292

Music in Evolution and Evolution in Music
Steven Jan

https://doi.org/10.11647/obp.0301

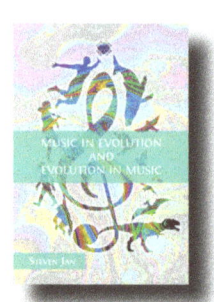

Classical Music Futures
Practices of Innovation
Neil Thomas Smith, Peter Peters and Karoly Molina (eds)

https://doi.org/10.11647/obp.0353

www.ingramcontent.com/pod-product-compliance
Lightning Source LLC
Chambersburg PA
CBHW040746020526
44116CB00036B/2962